Praise for *The Blackwell I*

"The stated goal of this welcome ... e
shortcomings of L. R. Palmer's ... ...nguage,
unrevised since its publication in ... worthy, and the
execution is in many ways a succes.

Bryn Mawr Classical Review

"Clackson and Horrocks have produced a wide-ranging, theoretically sophisticated, and still thoroughly manageable book that will not easily be superseded."

New England Classical Journal

"James Clackson and Geoffrey Horrocks have succeeded admirably in their aim, presenting a mass of data within persuasive narrative."

Times Literary Supplement

"The hefty Blackwell *History of the Latin Language* [focuses] on the evolution of the sounds, vocabulary, word and sentence structure over the centuries."

Chicago Tribune

"[The authors] set the tone with an honesty that is appreciated . . . Marvelous treatment of understudied languages . . . Carefully, admirably, proofread . . . Recommended."

Choice

"This book is the best single volume work on the Latin language. A comprehensive survey of the major topics in Latin linguistics, it is valuable not only to specialists in that field but also to Latin literary scholars, and to students of Indo-European and Romance historical linguistics generally."

Philip Burton, University of Birmingham

The Blackwell History of the Latin Language

James Clackson and Geoffrey Horrocks

A John Wiley & Sons, Ltd., Publication

This paperback edition first published 2011
© 2011 James Clackson and Geoffrey Horrocks

Edition history: Blackwell Publishing Ltd (hardback, 2007)

Blackwell Publishing was acquired by John Wiley & Sons in February 2007.
Blackwell's publishing program has been merged with Wiley's global Scientific,
Technical, and Medical business to form Wiley-Blackwell.

Registered Office
John Wiley & Sons Ltd, The Atrium, Southern Gate, Chichester, West Sussex,
PO19 8SQ, United Kingdom

Editorial Offices
350 Main Street, Malden, MA 02148-5020, USA
9600 Garsington Road, Oxford, OX4 2DQ, UK
The Atrium, Southern Gate, Chichester, West Sussex, PO19 8SQ, UK

For details of our global editorial offices, for customer services, and for
information about how to apply for permission to reuse the copyright material in
this book please see our website at www.wiley.com/wiley-blackwell.

The right of James Clackson and Geoffrey Horrocks to be identified as the
author of this work has been asserted in accordance with the UK Copyright,
Designs and Patents Act 1988.

Library of Congress Cataloging-in-Publication Data

Clackson, James.
   The Blackwell history of the Latin language / James Clackson and
Geoffrey Horrocks.
      p. cm.
   Includes bibliographical references and index.
   ISBN 978-1-4051-6209-8 (hardcover : alk. paper)
   ISBN 978-1-4443-3920-8 (paperback : alk. paper)   1. Latin language–History.
I. Horrocks, Geoffrey C.   II. Title.

   PA2057.C58 2007
   470.9–dc22

                                                              2007018802

A catalogue record for this book is available from the British Library.

Set in 10/12pt Galliard by Graphicraft Limited, Hong Kong

Contents

Preface

The impetus to write this book came after teaching various joint courses on Latin historical linguistics to undergraduates reading Classics at Cambridge over the past ten years. Although we consistently recommended L. R. Palmer's *The Latin Language* to students as a readable account of the history of the language, we became increasingly aware of some of the shortcomings that have become apparent in the 50 years since Palmer's book was written. In particular, there have been considerable advances in linguistic theory and method, as well as important discoveries of texts in Latin (and in the other languages spoken in pre-Roman Italy), and a better understanding of the Indo-European background to the language. Furthermore, Palmer has comparatively little to say about the processes by which Latin became standardized, nor did he have the advantage of modern sociolinguistic theory to help explain the interactions between the spoken language and the Classical standard. Accordingly, we set out to write a new history of Latin that overcame some of the shortcomings we saw in Palmer. We decided to model the structure of the work on Geoff Horrocks's book *Greek: A History of the Language and its Speakers*, including detailed discussion of a number of texts from all periods with glossing for each word. In this way we hope that the book will be accessible to those who have little or no Latin, but are interested in linguistics or language history, as well as to classics undergraduates, graduates and professional Latinists. In order to appeal to this large and diverse constituency we have included expositions of some topics which may be familiar to some readers, such as the comparative method in historical linguistics, but we hope that all readers will find something new. We have included a glossary of some linguistic terms for Latinists who are new to the subject; these readers may also find an introductory volume to historical linguistics helpful, such as Herbert Schendl *Historical Linguistics* (Oxford, 2001) or Mark Hale *Historical Linguistics: Theory and Method* (Oxford, 2007).

There are other changes of emphasis from Palmer's work. On the whole our focus has been on Latin as a language, and its relationship to the history of Rome and Roman imperialism. We have in consequence concentrated more on linguistic than stylistic issues, and we have been less concerned to describe the particular idioms and vocabulary choices of Roman literary figures, except in so far as they have proved important for the subsequent development of Latin. Accordingly, the reader should not expect to find here very much in the way of appreciations of the music of Vergilian verse or descriptions of the metrical patterns found at the end of periodic sentences (*clausulae*) in Classical prose, though the latter are very briefly considered in chapter VI. We have not presented a systematic overview of the phonology, morphology, and syntax of the language, concentrating instead on specifics where these are relevant to the history of linguistic innovations and replacements. The necessary basic information can be easily found in standard grammars and handbooks. Finally, we devote proportionately much less space to the development of the Latin vocabulary than Palmer, who was writing before the publication of the *Oxford Latin Dictionary* and when the ongoing *Thesaurus Linguae Latinae* was still in its infancy. These works now allow the reader to trace word histories in a much more systematic way than was possible when *The Latin Language* came out, and we have preferred to restrict the space given to lexical discussions in order to allow a corresponding increase in the exposition of syntactic changes.

We hope that readers will benefit from being able to appreciate the history of Latin in its entirety, from the pre-historic origins to the end of its existence as a language with native speakers. But we are aware that people have many different needs from a book such as this, and some may prefer to read a chapter at a time. In view of this, we have decided to present specific bibliographies for each chapter. We have also appended a further bibliography of standard and useful reference works at the end of the volume.

Of the eight chapters of this book, we each took individual responsibility for four: James Clackson wrote the outer chapters, I, II, VII and VIII and Geoff Horrocks wrote the inner core: chapters III, IV, V and VI. All translations of Latin texts cited are our own. We each read, commented on and discussed the other's work in draft. We have also benefited from the input of successive groups of students taking the 'E3' course at the Classics Faculty who were unwitting guinea pigs as readers of many of the Latin texts that appear in this book. We are particularly grateful to Jim Adams, for allowing us to use material from his forthcoming book *Regional Diversity in Latin*, and to Michael Crawford, for giving us access to his new reading of CIL I^2 5. An anonymous and well-informed reader for Blackwell's saved us from innumerable errors and made many welcome and constructive suggestions for improvement. The usual disclaimers apply, of course. And finally we wish to thank Anna Oxbury for copyediting our manuscript so expertly and professionally, and for devising a range of excellent solutions to rather complex problems of layout and presentation.

We dedicate our book to Gill Horrocks and Véronique Mottier.

Note on marking of Latin Long Vowels:

It has been our general practice only to mark in long vowels in Latin orthography when they are directly relevant to the discussion at hand. Hence we normally write, for example, occido 'I kill', except when explaining the changes to Latin diphthongs in non-initial syllables, when we write occīdō.

Chapter I

Latin and Indo-European

1.1   Introduction

Latin is an Indo-European language. This means that Latin is genetically related to most of the modern (and the ancient) languages of Europe, as well as many languages of India, Iran and Central Asia. The genetic relationship accounts for the large numbers of similarities, both in vocabulary and in grammar, between Latin and Greek, Sanskrit, Gothic, Old Irish and many other ancient languages which no alternative hypothesis (such as chance similarity, linguistic borrowing or convergence) can explain. Over the last 200 years linguists have undertaken a systematic comparison of the similarities between the Indo-European (henceforth IE) languages to build up a picture of what the non-attested parent ('Proto-Indo-European', henceforth PIE) must have looked like. The reconstruction of PIE is, in places, highly abstract and highly complex, and for many individual features there is still considerable debate amongst experts in the field as to which reconstruction is the most plausible. Even so, it is possible to arrive at a picture of the parent language which is widely accepted, and use that to set the background to the development of Latin. The reader will have to take much of what is said about PIE on trust in this chapter, since this is not a book about PIE, but about Latin.

Why should the historian of Latin be interested in PIE? Apart from the intrinsic interest of knowing the relationships between Latin and other languages, we can suggest a number of reasons. Firstly, in order to understand the development of Latin, it is necessary to see what it started out as. Thus the development of the Latin verbal system, or Latin word order, has its roots already in PIE structures. Secondly, a knowledge of the background to Latin can help assess the question of its relationship to neighbouring languages – as we shall see in the next chapter. Thirdly, a knowledge of PIE may actually help us to understand some features of Latin vocabulary or grammar. To take a single example, one of the earliest Latin inscriptions known is a sixth century graffito scratched around a pottery vessel, known as the 'Duenos vase' (CIL I² 4, see 1.4.5 below). The final 15 letters of the inscription read *nemedmalostatod*, and this was long recognized as *ne med malos (s)tatod* an earlier form of *ne me malus stato* not me-ACC bad-NOM set.3sg.IMPER 'let no bad man set me', although the use of the verb *sto* 'I stand, set' in this context was unexplained. Comparative Indo-European linguistics, however, offered a solution to this problem (first proposed by Rix 1985). Other IE languages, such as Irish and Hittite, share a verbal root which can be reconstructed as *tā-* (*teh₂-) and which means 'steal'. If we assume that this verbal root also survived into an early stage of Latin, then we can interpret the sequence as *ne me malus *tato* not me-ACC bad-NOM steal.3sg.IMPER 'let no bad man steal me', a commonplace formula on inscriptions on moveable objects in the ancient world. This attestation remains the only appearance of this verbal root in the whole Latin corpus, and its meaning is only recoverable through IE comparison.

1.2   The IE Language Family

The IE language family comprises over 80 different languages and varieties. All of the living languages, and most of the varieties which are no longer spoken can be assigned to one of the subgroups of the family. Some ancient languages have left such scanty remains that their position in the family, and in some cases, even their membership of the family, remains in doubt. As we shall see in the next chapter, some of these scantily attested languages are relevant to the early history of Latin, and we shall discuss them in more detail there. Here we shall confine ourselves to giving an overview of the different branches of the IE language family.

1   *Anatolian.* The Anatolian branch is the earliest attested branch of Indo-European. The best attested language in the Anatolian family is Hittite, which is written in the cuneiform script, adopted from Semitic languages of the ancient Near East and for which the earliest texts date from the sixteenth century BC. A number of other languages are now also recognized to belong to the Anatolian family. Two others are recorded from the period before 1000 BC, both

in cuneiform (Palaic and Luwian – Luwian is also attested in a hiero-glyphic script which is not used for any other language), and from a later period other languages are recorded in alphabetic scripts, including Lydian, Lycian and Carian.

2   *Greek.* The Greek branch of Indo-European is the second earliest attested, with texts written in the Linear B syllabary surviving from the fourteenth century BC and later. Greek is extensively attested in alphabetic script from the eighth century BC onwards.

3   *Indo-Iranian.* The two large language families termed Indic and Iranian share a number of common innovations which guarantee that they both derive from the same branch of Indo-European. The first evidence for Indo-Iranian is also in the second millennium BC, and consists in the inclusion of some terms and phrases relating to riding and horsemanship in cuneiform sources. The major early textual remains of the Indic branch are the hymns of the Rg-Veda (written in an archaic form of Sanskrit, often termed Vedic), and of the Iranian branch the Gathas, the hymns attributed to Zarathrustra in the Avesta (their language is known as Avestan or Gathic Avestan). Both of these texts were orally transmitted for centuries before being written down, but internal evidence suggests that they are both of great antiquity, and scholars generally assign a date to around 1000 BC for the composition of the Gathas and a couple of centuries earlier for the oldest Vedic hymns. Indo-Iranian, Greek and Anatolian are the three most important branches for the reconstruction of PIE.

4   *Latin and the languages of Italy.* As we shall see in the next chapter, it is a moot point how closely the IE languages of Italy are related to each other. Several subgroups are recognizable: Latino-Faliscan, comprising Latin and the neighbouring language Faliscan which are attested from the seventh–sixth century BC, although the early inscriptions are short and difficult to interpret in both languages; the Sabellian group, known principally through Oscan and Umbrian and attested first in the South Picene inscriptions which date from the sixth century BC; Venetic, attested in short inscriptions from the sixth century BC is also IE. The Messapic language, attested from inscriptions from the same date in the area at the extreme south-east of Italy shows greater divergence from the other languages of Italy.

5   *Celtic.* The only surviving languages of the Celtic branch are Irish, Scots Gaelic, Welsh and Breton, but the family once extended over a much wider section of Western Europe. The earliest attestations of Celtic are inscriptions from France, Italy and Spain in the centuries immediately before and after the beginning of the Christian era. Extensive textual evidence for Celtic is much later, with the first Old Irish glosses recorded in the seventh century AD. The interrelationship

of the Celtic languages is still debatable, but the following subgroups are recognized:

(a) Goidelic: the branch which comprises Irish, Scots Gaelic and Manx.
(b) Brythonic: the branch which comprises Welsh, Cornish and Breton.
(c) Celtiberian, known from inscriptions in Spain.
(d) Gaulish, known from inscriptions mainly in France.
(e) Lepontic, known from inscriptions in northern Italy.

Owing to an imperfect knowledge of branches (c), (d) and (e), it is difficult to be sure whether a 'continental Celtic' sub-group, comprising all the Celtic languages from outside the British Isles with the exception of Breton, actually reflects any linguistic reality.

6 *Germanic.* The Germanic language group is first known from sources in the first millennium AD; the first extensive text is the Gothic Bible translation made in the fourth century. Old English is attested from the eighth century, and Old High German, Old Saxon and Old Norse from the following century.

7 *Armenian.* The Armenian branch comprises just one language, known in its classical form from the Bible translation and theological and historical works written in the fifth century AD.

8 *Slavic.* The first texts to record a Slavic language are the Bible version and translations of Greek texts made by Cyril and Methodius in the late ninth century.

9 *Baltic.* The Baltic subgroup comprises Lithuanian, Latvian and the now extinct Old Prussian. The first texts were written in the fourteenth–sixteenth centuries.

10 *Albanian.* Albanian has only a relatively shallow time depth, being first attested in texts written by missionaries and others from the late Middle Ages to the early modern period.

11 *Other poorly attested languages.* There are also a number of languages which are only known from short inscriptional texts or glosses recorded by Classical authors which are reckoned to be IE, but whose relationship to other languages remains in doubt. These include Phrygian, Thracian, Illyrian, Sicel and Lusitanian.

1.3 Reconstructed PIE

The reconstruction of PIE entails the assumption that a single language was spoken at some point in time from which all the different IE varieties have evolved. However, the reconstructed picture can never reach the stage of giving an adequate description of PIE. This is due to the nature of reconstruction through the **comparative method** (CM). The CM operates through identification of sets of correspondences in languages which are known to be related, and forming of hypotheses to explain the correspondence. We may, for example construct a correspondence set of word forms with identical meaning and similarity of form, as follows:

Latin	Greek	Sanskrit	English
pater	*patēr*	*pitar-*	*father*
pes	*poús*	*pad-*	*foot*
plenus	*plērēs*	*pūrṇá-*	*full*
pro	*pró*	*prá*	*for*
pellis	*pélas*		Old English *fell* 'hide'
pecu		*paśú*	Old English *feoh* 'livestock'
piscis			*fish*

In all these words (and several others) we see a correspondence between initial *p-* in Latin, Greek and Sanskrit, and initial *f-* in English. The words are not limited to one particular lexical field and they represent core items in the lexicon. We can reconstruct a single PIE phoneme as the forebear of these sounds in the daughter language, traditionally denoted **p*. The same process is used to reconstruct the whole phonemic system for PIE. When we come to morphology, however, we find reconstruction is not so straightforward. To take a notorious example, we can compare the genitive singular of the *o*-stem declension (the Latin 2nd declension; in this table we have added further IE languages to those given above):

Latin	(Homeric) Greek	Sanskrit	Old English	Hittite	Lithuanian
-ī	*-oio*	*-asya*	*-es*	*-as*	*-o*

These forms are not reconcilable to a single prototype, and in order to make sense of the differences one must hypothesize motivations for replacement of an earlier form in one language branch or another. The Hittite ending *-as* is identical with the nominative singular ending *-as* (both can be derived from **-os*), and this is usually seen as an especially archaic form, and one which would be liable to be replaced in order to disambiguate the two categories. The Greek and Sanskrit forms can both be derived from an extended form **-osyo*, which is found in other branches of IE, suggesting that the replacement of **-os* already took place within the parent language. It is clear that in order to explain these different genitive singular endings, we must reconstruct a proto-language with diachronic, or dialectal, variation. It can thus be difficult to reconcile the reconstructed morphology to the reconstructed phonology – are we to assume that the different chronological or dialectal variants of the proto-language shared the same phonemic system? This seems unlikely from what we know of attested languages, but there is no way to restrict the reconstruction of phonemes to one particular morphological reconstruction.

The CM gives the impression that reconstructed PIE is a single point from which the daughter languages all derive separately. In actual fact, it is unlikely that the reconstructed data that linguists operate with were concentrated together in an actual speech-community at one time and place. It is more likely that the reconstructed items are diffusely arrayed in time and space and across the speaker population. The comparative linguist must therefore draw up a framework in order to fit the reconstructed data into plausible temporal and spatial slots. For example, in order to explain the reconstruction of both a genitive singular marker *-os* and *-osyo*, one model would propose that the language ancestral to Hittite and the rest of the Anatolian branch split off from PIE at an earlier date than other languages. The only check on whether this model is correct is its own explanatory power and internal consistency, and it may be possible to construct two, or more, separate models which both give adequate explanations of the reconstructed data. In dealing with hypotheses about the Indo-European language family, it will be necessary to bear these methodological points in mind.

1.4   Latin and IE

A presentation of reconstructed PIE is beyond the scope of this work. In this section, we shall present some of the salient features of PIE for the history of Latin, in order to give an idea of what Latin has inherited from PIE and where it has diverged.

1.4.1   Phonology

The reconstruction of PIE is most secure in the domain of phonology. This is because the phoneme system contains a small, finite and ordered set of elements. Phonological change is, on the whole, regular, well studied and well documented. This means that it is usually possible to compare two cognate sounds, such as Latin *p* and English *f* in the example given above, and identify the sound which is most likely to be ancestral to them. In the case of *p* and *f*, for example, we know of many secure examples of the change *p* > *f* in the world's languages, but far fewer of *f* > *p*, so we can reconstruct the ancestral sound as **p* (written with an asterisk since it is a hypothetical, unattested form). However, we must be aware of the limits of our reconstruction; we may be able to reconstruct the phonemic system without complete certainty about the phonetic realization of those phonemes. We have no way of knowing, for example, whether a reconstructed *d was a true dental or an alveolar or some other linguo-dental consonant, although we can be sure that it was opposed to two other consonants with the same place of articulation, *t and *d^h, and other consonants with the same manner of articulation, but a different place of articulation, such as *g. Nor do we know for certain that the reconstructed phonemes *d and *g were distinctively voiced, and some models of PIE claim that they had a different manner of articulation. In reconstructed PIE, it is the oppositions between the phonemes that are important, rather than the distinctive features *per se* that articulate these oppositions. The standardly reconstructed phoneme system of PIE is as follows:

Consonants
Stops:

Labial	Dental	Palatal	Velar	Labio-velar
*p	*t	*k′	*k	*k^w
(*b)	*d	*g′	*g	*g^w
*b^h	*d^h	*g′^h	*g^h	*g^wh

Fricatives: *s
'Laryngeals': *h₁, *h₂, *h₃
Nasals: *m, *n
Continuants: *r, *l, *y, *w

Vowels

　　　　*e, *o, *a (*ē, *ō, *ā)
　　　　*m̥, *n̥, *r̥, *l̥, *i, *u (*ī, *ū)

Some explanatory points should be made about the above tables:

1   'Labio-velars' is the term given to a series of consonants which have reflexes in Eastern IE languages (Indo-Aryan, Iranian, Slavic, Baltic, Armenian) as velars or palatalized velars, but which in the earliest stages of Western IE languages (Greek, Germanic, Celtic, Latin) appear as velars with concomitant lip-rounding, or sometimes as labials. Typical cognate sets are the following:

* k^wo-/k^wi- 'who?': Sanskrit *ká-*, Greek *tís*, Germanic (English) *who*, Latin *quis*
* g^wem- 'come': Sanskrit *gam-*, Greek *baínō*, Germanic (English) *come*, Latin *uenio*
* g^wow- 'cow': Sanskrit *gav-*, Greek *boûs*, Germanic (English) *cow*, Latin *bos*

(Note that in some of the Greek and English cognates, the labio-velars have been further obscured by specific sound-changes: *tís* shows a characteristic Greek development to a dental before a front vowel, and in English *cow* and *come* the labial element has been lost before a back vowel.)

It can be seen from the above examples that Latin *qu-* derives from PIE *k^w, but *g^w develops differently. In most words it is continued by Latin *u* [w] but there are also cases, as *bos*, where it appears as a labial stop. The words which show this development (and also forms which have *p* in place of PIE *k^w) are normally explained as borrowings from other IE varieties spoken in Italy which regularly develop labial stops from original labio-velars. These will be discussed more fully in the next chapter. Alongside labio-velars, there are also 'velar' and 'palatal' series, which have different outcomes in some IE languages, but merge as velar consonants in prehistoric Latin. Schrijver (1991: 425–36) has suggested that the two series had different effects on a following *e*: *ke-* giving Latin *ca-* (as *carpo* 'I pluck' < *skerp-*), and *$k'e$-* giving Latin *ce-* (as *cedo* 'give!' < *$k'e$-*). Unfortunately, there are only six etymologies to support Schrijver's claim, and a few counterexamples, so Schrijver's theory remains unproven at present (see Meiser 1998: 82f.).

2 'Voiced aspirates' is the traditional term for a series of consonants which are reconstructed from the comparison of voiceless aspirates *p^h*, *t^h*, *k^h* in Greek, voiced aspirates *b^h*, *d^h*, *g^h* in Sanskrit, and voiced consonants in Germanic (English *b*, *d*, *g*), Iranian, Armenian, Baltic and Slavonic. Note the following examples of cognate sets for PIE *b^h* and *d^h*:

* *b^her-* 'carry': Greek *p^hérō*, Sanskrit *b^hárāmi*, Germanic (English) *bear*, Armenian *berem*
* *neb^h-* 'cloud': Greek *$nép^h$os*, Sanskrit *$náb^h$as-*, Germanic (German) *Nebel* 'fog', Old Church Slavonic *nebo* 'heaven'
* *$d^h uh_2 mo$-* 'vapour, smoke': Greek *$t^h ūmós$*, Sanskrit *$d^h ūmá$-*, Old Church Slavonic *dymŭ*
* *$rud^h ro$-* 'red': Greek *$erut^h rós$*, Sanskrit *$rud^h irá$-*, Germanic (English) *red*, Slavonic (Russian) *rudyj* 'red-haired'.

It can be seen from the table that these consonants are not opposed to a voiceless aspirate series (as the voiced aspirates of Sanskrit are), and it may be better to envisage them as originally 'breathy-voiced' in PIE, although we shall retain the traditional terminology of 'voiced aspirate'. The reconstruction of voiced aspirates without voiceless aspirates has been held to violate a linguistic universal, and has led to attempts to refashion the PIE consonant stem entirely. One such attempt, independently proposed by the American Paul Hopper and the Georgian Thomas Gamkrelidze (see Szemerényi 1996: 152), involves re-casting the reconstructed voiced stops as ejectives (or 'glottalics'), and then interprets the opposition between the other two series as only reliant on the feature [voice], with aspiration not a distinctive feature. The question of the reconstruction of the PIE stops is still under debate, but the 'glottalic' model does not seem to have any extra explanatory power when it comes to the derivation of the Latin consonant system from PIE, since PIE *p, *t, *k, etc. are continued as voiceless stops in Latin and *b, *d, *g, etc. as voiced stops, whereas the voiced aspirate series develop either to Latin fricatives in word-initial position or to voiced stops word-medially. Thus the Latin cognates to *$b^h er$-, *neb^h-, *$d^h uh_2 mo$- and *$rud^h ro$- are *fero*, *nebula*, *fumus* and *ruber*. We shall return to investigate these Latin developments more fully in the following chapter, but for our present purposes we need only state that the Latin reflexes are most economically derived from original 'voiced aspirates': the word-initial development to fricatives can be accounted for by the original feature [aspiration] (cross-linguistically the move from aspirates to fricatives is widely attested), whereas in word-internal position the feature [voice] is preserved.

3   'Laryngeals' is the traditional term used to refer to three consonants which are hypothesized to have existed from their effect on neighbouring vowels, and whose presence can be detected by systematic vowel alternations in different morphological environments. Laryngeals have no direct reflexes as consonants in any IE language outside the Anatolian branch, where they are sometimes continued by velar or pharyngal fricatives (and even there *h_1 may leave no trace). Despite their widespread loss, laryngeals appear to have had different outcomes in different language branches, and they must be reconstructed for early, prehistoric stages of Latin in order to explain certain developments. The treatment of laryngeals in Latin is generally similar to that found in neighbouring IE languages, although aspects of their behaviour are complex, and there are still areas of disagreement (Schrijver (1991) gives a detailed treatment of laryngeal developments in Latin, in a book of over 500 pages). The basic effect of laryngeals on neighbouring vowels is as follows: we have omitted the details of the development in Anatolian languages, citing Hittite or Luwian forms only where the laryngeal has a consonantal outcome (note that H = any of *h_1 *h_2 *h_3):

(a)   following vowels laryngeals are lost with lengthening of a preceding short vowel; the three laryngeals have differing effects on the vowel *e:

*iH > Latin $\bar{\imath}$, Greek $\bar{\imath}$, Sanskrit $\bar{\imath}$
  *$g^w ih_3 wo$- 'alive' > Latin *uīuus*, Sanskrit *jīvá-*
*uH > Latin $\bar{u}$, Greek $\bar{u}$, Sanskrit $\bar{u}$
  *$d^h uh_2 mo$- 'vapour, smoke' > Latin *fūmos* Greek *t^{h}ūmós*, Sanskrit *d^{h}ūmá-*, Hittite *tuhhai-*

$*oH$ > Latin $\bar{o}$, Greek $\bar{o}$, Sanskrit $\bar{a}$

$*d^h oh_1$- 'put, place' in Latin *sacer-dōs* 'priest'

$*eh_1$ > Latin $\bar{e}$, Greek $\bar{e}$, Sanskrit $\bar{a}$

$*d^h eh_1$- 'put, place' > Latin *fēci*, Greek *títʰēmi*, Sanskrit *dádʰāmi*

$*eh_2$ > Latin $\bar{a}$, Greek $\bar{a}$ (in Doric and other dialects), $\bar{e}$ (in Attic and Ionic), Sanskrit $\bar{a}$

$*peh_2$- 'pasture' > Latin *pāsco*, Hittite *pahs*-

$*eh_3$ > Latin $\bar{o}$, Greek $\bar{o}$, Sanskrit $\bar{a}$

$*deh_3$- 'give' > Latin *dōs*, Greek *dídōmi*, Sanskrit *dádāmi*

(b)   before vowels laryngeals are generally lost, but, again, the three laryngeals have differing effects on the vowel $*e$:

$*Hi$ > Latin *i*, Greek *i* (but $*h_2 i$ may go to *ai*), Sanskrit *i*

$*h_2 im$- 'copy' > Latin *imitor* 'I copy', Hittite *himna*- 'substitute'

$*Hu$ > Latin *u*, Greek *u* (or possibly *eu, au, ou*), Sanskrit *u*

$*h_1 us$-*to*- 'burnt' > Latin *ustus*, Sanskrit *uṣṭá*-

$*Ho$ > Latin *o*, Greek *o*, Sanskrit *a*

$*h_2 owi$- 'sheep' > Latin *ouis*, Greek *ówis*, Sanskrit *ávi*-, Luwian *hawis*

$*h_1 e$ > Latin *e*, Greek *e*, Sanskrit *a*

$*h_1 esti$ 'is' > Latin *est*, Greek *estí*, Sanskrit *asti*

$*h_2 e$ > Latin *a*, Greek *a*, Sanskrit *a*

$*h_2 ent$- 'front' > Latin *ante*, Greek *antí*, Hittite *hant*-

$*h_3 e$ > Latin *o*, Greek *o*, Sanskrit *a*

$*h_3 ek^w$- 'eye' > Latin *oculus*, Greek *ómma* (< $*óp$-*m*-), Sanskrit *ákṣi*

(c)   when laryngeals stand between other consonants, they develop to vowels:

$*Ch_1 C$ > Latin *a*, Greek *e*, Sanskrit *i*, other IE language branches *a* or lost

$*d^h h_1(k)tó$- 'put' > Latin *factus*, Greek *tʰetós*, Sanskrit *hitá*-

$*Ch_2 C$ > Latin *a*, Greek *a*, Sanskrit *i*, other IE language branches *a* or lost

$*sth_2 tó$- 'standing, stood' > Latin *status*, Greek *statós*, Sanskrit *sthitá*-

$*Ch_3 C$ > Latin *a*, Greek *o*, Sanskrit *i*, other IE language branches *a* or lost

$*dh_3 tó$- 'given' > Latin *datus*, Greek *dotós*

4   The reconstruction of the PIE vowel $*a$ and the long vowels. As the above tables relating to laryngeals show, the reconstruction of these vowels is closely related to the reconstruction of laryngeals. If Latin *a* can go back to PIE $*h_2 e$ or a laryngeal between two consonants, then is there any need to reconstruct a separate PIE phoneme $*a$? If Latin long $\bar{e}$ can be derived from a sequence $*eh_1$, can we then dispense with the reconstructed vowel $*\bar{e}$ in the PIE phoneme inventory? We have followed

a model of PIE which holds that both *a and the long vowels should be reconstructed, although the reasons for this are dependent upon phenomena in the Indo-Iranian and Anatolian languages. For the history of Latin, however, the difference between original *h_2e and *a, or between original *$\bar{e}$ and *eh_1, is irrelevant, since the laryngeal consonants were lost at such an early stage in prehistory that they make no difference to the language.

5   The short vowels *$m̥$, *$n̥$, *$r̥$, *$l̥$, *i, *u have a special status in PIE, since they act as allophones of the consonants *m, *n, *r, *l, *y, *w respectively, depending on their position in the word. For example, consonantal *r occurs adjacent to a vowel sound: as *$ph_2term̥$ 'father-ACC' (Greek *patéra*, Sanskrit *pitáram*), and the vocalic *$r̥$ between two consonants: *$ph_2tr̥su$ 'father-LOC.PL' (Greek *patrási*, Sanskrit *pitr̥su*). As the example of *$ph_2tr̥su$ shows, Sanskrit has retained the vocalic allophone of *$r̥$ but in Greek it regularly developed to *ra* or *ar*. Latin *u* and *i* still retain some vestiges of this alternation between consonant and vowel: for example, in the paradigm of the verb *uoluo*, *uoluit* 'he rolls' (with *u* = [w]), but *uolutus* 'rolled'. However, in Latin vocalic *u* and consonantal *u* are now separate phonemes (note the minimal pair *uoluit* [wolwit] 'he rolls' and *uoluit* [woluit] 'he wanted'). In Latin the PIE short vowels *$m̥$, *$n̥$, *$r̥$, *$l̥$ have developed to combinations of vowel and consonant, *em, *en, *or and *ol respectively, as shown by the following etymologies:

*$k̑m̥tom$ 'hundred' > Latin *centum*, Greek *hekatón*, English *hundred*
*$tn̥to$- 'stretched' > Latin *in-tentus*, Greek *tatós*, Sanskrit *tatá*-
*$k̑r̥d$- 'heart' > Latin *cord*-, Greek *kardía*
*$ml̥d$- 'soft, weak' > Latin *mollis*, Greek *bladús*, Sanskrit *mr̥dú*-

1.4.2 Latin morphosyntactic developments from PIE

The term 'ablaut' (also known as 'vowel gradation') describes a systematic alternation of vowels within a morphological paradigm. For PIE the following types of ablaut can be reconstructed.

1   Shift of word-accent within a paradigm with a concomitant loss of the unaccented vowel (quantitative ablaut). For example, the reconstructed paradigm for the noun 'god':

*$dyéw$ 'god' vocative	Greek *Zeú*, Sanskrit *dyàus*
*$diw-és$ 'god' genitive	Greek *Di(w)-ós*, Sanskrit *div-ás*

(note that *y/*i are allophones of a single phoneme, as are *w/*u). Or the reconstructed present tense paradigm of the verb 'go':

*$éy-mi$ 'I go'	Greek *eî-mi*, Sanskrit *émi*
	In Sanskrit, *e* derives from *ei
*$i-mé$ 'we go'	Greek *í-me-n*, Sanskrit *i-má-si*

2 Change in vowel quality within the same syllable (qualitative ablaut).
   For example the vowel of the suffix in the word meaning 'family' or
   'stock' (the suffix is usually represented as *-e/os-).

*g'énh₁-os 'family, stock' nominative Greek *gén-os*, Latin *gen-us*
*g'énh₁-es-os 'family, stock' genitive   Greek *gén-e-os*, Latin *gen-er-is*

The processes of quantitative and qualitative ablaut mean that every morpheme in PIE has (at least) three alternative morphs, one with the vowel
*e, one with the vowel *o and one with no vowel. There are also recon-
structed ablaut forms with a long vowel, *ē or *ō (for example, the nominative singular of the word for 'god' is sometimes reconstructed *dyēws).
However, these forms are more restricted in distribution, and the motivation for them is disputed.

   In many roots, the effects of 'laryngeals' or other sound changes have
disguised the original pattern and obscured the relationship between different ablaut forms. Latin *datus* 'given' < *dh₃-to- and *dōs* 'gift' < *deh₃-t-,
for example, are respectively reconstructed with the root in an ablaut form
without a vowel, and one with the vowel *e, although the vowels in Latin
are *a* and long *o*. Compare also the attested Latin form with the reconstructed ablaut variants in the following:

factus 'made' < *dʰh₁k-to-
fēcī 'I made' < *dʰeh₁k-
imitor 'copy' < *h₂im-
aemulus 'rival' < *h₂eim-

The reconstruction of laryngeals thus enables many different vowel alternations to be reconciled to either an *e/*o or an *e/zero alternation.

   In order to illustrate the operation of ablaut and its fate in Latin we
can take the suffix which is used to form comparatives of adjectives. In
PIE this could take the form *-yos- (cf. Latin *melius* 'better' which continues an earlier *mel-yos), *-is- (continued in Latin *mag-is* 'more'), and
*-yes- (probably continued in Latin *mulier* 'woman' < *ml̥-yes-, perhaps
originally part of the paradigm of *melior*, but with a later shift in meaning (from 'the better woman' to 'the best woman in the house', hence
'wife, woman', see Klingenschmitt 1992: 130). There was also a form with
lengthened vowel *-iōs* which was restricted to the nominative singular. The
Latin paradigm of the comparative, outside of the neuter nominative/
accusative singular, alternates between *-ior* in the masculine and feminine
nominative singular (as *melior*) and *-iōr-*, with lengthened vowel, in the
rest of the paradigm. This pattern is a completely new development, and
shows the spread of the lengthened form of the suffix throughout the

paradigm, with subsequent phonological changes. It is worth sketching out the hypothetical development of the paradigm in Latin prehistory, since this shows not only the analogical developments which led to the loss of ablaut as a regular process, but also the interchange between sound change and analogy in the creation of Latin paradigms.

Stage I *-yōs nominative singular masculine
*-is nominative/accusative singular neuter
*-yos-ṃ accusative singular masculine
etc.

The first change to affect this paradigm in Latin prehistory is the spread of the ablaut form *-yos from the masculine forms to the neuter; Latin *melius* thus represents a very early replacement of *melis*. The old form of the neuter in *-is survives only in *magis* 'more', which early became isolated from its paradigm owing to its widespread use as an adverb.

Stage II *-yōs nominative singular masculine
*-yos nominative/accusative singular neuter
*-yos-ṃ accusative singular masculine
etc.

The next change to affect the paradigm was the spread of the long ō from the nominative to the rest of the paradigm, with the exclusion of the neuter singular, which did not enter into any of the subsequent paradigmatic changes (hence Classical Latin -ius).

Stage III *-yōs nominative singular masculine
*-yōs-eṃ accusative singular masculine

Stage III must have been reached at the beginning of the historical period, since we have a few forms cited in later Latin authors, such as *meliosem* and *maiosibus*. However, in the course of the fourth century BC intervocalic *-s- developed to -r- in Latin. This change reintroduced irregularity into the paradigm, since it led to a paradigm of the following type (a separate change also led to *y realized as Latin i by this date):

Stage IV *-iōs nominative singular masculine
-iōr-em accusative singular masculine

In order to avoid this irregularity, the form of the suffix was extended to the nominative masculine from the oblique cases, (although the neuter singular nominative was again left untouched by this change).

Stage V   *-iōr*   nominative singular masculine
            -iōr-em   accusative singular masculine

This stage is attested in Plautus, where the vowel of the final syllable of the nominative singular of a comparative can still be scanned as long, as *stultiōr*. But a change which took place at the beginning of the second century BC led to long vowels being shortened before final *-r*, *-l* and *-t*, and led to the paradigm as we know it from Classical Latin.

This rather lengthy exposition shows that ablaut had ceased to be a productive morphological process before the Early Latin period. While we can find traces of ablaut throughout Latin, not every morphological alternation of vowel quantity or quality can be attributed to it, and there may be an explanation within the history of the language. In some cases there may be two competing accounts of the same phenomenon. For example, there is a curious alternation between the nominative stem *iecur* 'liver' and the oblique forms such as genitive *iocineris* which exist alongside genitive *iecineris* and *iecoris* (see Rix 1965 for attestations). This word preserves a very archaic declension type, with a nominative/accusative marked in *-r* and a stem formed with *-n-* in the other cases, which is also found in Hittite, Sanskrit and Greek, but lost in other IE languages. Given the archaic nature of the paradigm, it has been thought that the alternation between the root form *iec-* and *ioc-* reflects an archaic ablaut pattern (Schindler 1994: 398). However, Latin nouns have generally obliterated all traces of paradigmatic ablaut in the root – so Latin has a genitive *Iouis* from **dyew-es* beside *Iū-piter*, from the vocative **dyew* (with added *-piter* 'father'), in place of **diwés* which lies behind the Greek and Sanskrit forms (see above); and another possible account for *iocineris* has been given by Klingenschmitt (1992: 118) who takes *iocineris* to be metathesized from an earlier genitive *iecinoris* (with *-or-* from the nominative **iecor > iecur*).

1.4.3   Nominal declensions

PIE nouns were inflected for case and number. The case system comprised all the paradigmatic cases found in Latin (including the locative), and one further case, the instrumental which had the grammatical sense of *instrument* or *means* and could also be used locally to denote *path* or *association*. The locative case survived into Latin long enough to be retained in place names (such as *Romae* 'at Rome') and a handful of nouns in Classical Latin (such as *ruri* from *rus* 'countryside' and *humi* from *humus* 'ground'); in Early Latin there is a greater number of locatives, including forms such as *militiae* 'in the army' in Ennius. In contrast, the instrumental was lost early in the prehistory of Latin, and its functions were merged with those of the ablative. The merger of instrumental and ablative probably arose through overlap between the function ORIGIN of the ablative and PATH of the instrumental – compare the analogous overlaps in English between 'he was hit by/with a stone', 'he came from the next room/he came through the door.' Formally, the merged case was usually denoted by the old ablative marker. This is demonstrably the case for the second (*o*-stem) declension, where the ablative marker *-ōd* is directly continued in Early Latin -*od*, Classical Latin -*ō*. The other stem classes did not have a separate marker for the ablative in PIE, but in a prehistoric Latin innovation, shared also by other languages of Italy, the pattern of ablative marked by long vowel + *d* was extended. This is the origin of the 1st declension ablative -*a* (Early Latin -*ad*), 4th declension -*u* (Early Latin -*ud*), and 5th declension -*e* (Early Latin -*ed*). The 3rd declension ending of Classical Latin, -*e* may instead continue the inherited locative ending *-i*, reflecting the late syncretism of the locative to the ablative-instrumental (all three cases being widely used after prepositions). In Early Latin there is inscriptional evidence for endings -*ed* and especially -*id* in the 3rd declension (see Meiser 1992: 210–2 on the Early Latin forms).

Latin has also reduced the dimensions of the category of *number* from PIE, which had a dual, used to denote pairs of objects and formally surviving only in the Latin forms *duo* and *ambo*, and possibly also a separate 'collective' used to denote several inanimate objects conceived of as constituting a group. The reconstruction of the category 'collective' is disputed. In form, the collective is thought to have taken the ending of the neuter plural, and originally it construed with singular verbs, as neuter plurals still are in some of the earlier IE languages. Vestiges of the collective might exist in Latin heteroclite plurals such as *loca* alongside *loci* from *locus* 'place', although there is little or no discernible difference in meaning here, and in the curious agreement rule of Classical Latin whereby an adjective in concord with two conjoined inanimate nouns of differing gender is inflected as neuter, as in the Livian formula *porta et murus tacta sunt* gate-FEM and wall-MASC touched-NEUT.pl be-3pl 'the gate and wall were struck [by lightning].'

The actual *forms* of the different case inflections in Latin sometimes continue PIE forms directly, as is the case with the accusative singular ending -*m* which derives from a PIE marker *-m*; in the consonant declension the ending -*em* shows the normal Latin reflex of a vocalic *-m̥*. Other endings differ from PIE nominal inflections, but can be derived from earlier *pronominal* endings. The analogical extension of case endings from pronouns to nouns is a process that continued from within PIE itself, where the special *o*-stem ablative ending, *-ōd*, most likely originates from a pronominal declension, all the way through to Classical Latin, in which endings such as genitive -*ius* are extended to some nominals (hence

Table 1.1 Early Latin case endings and their origins

	PIE noun endings	PIE pronoun endings	I (*a*-stems)	II (*o*-stems)	IIIa (C-stems)	IIIb (*i*-stems)	IV (*u*-stems)
Nom.sg. masculine/feminine	*-s (except *a*-stems)	*-ø	-a	-os	-s	-is, -s	-us
Nom.Acc.sg.neut.	*-m/ø	*-d	(no neuters)	-om	ø	*i > -e	-u/-ū
Acc.sg.	*-m	*-m	-am	-om	-em (< *-m)	-im/-em	-um
Gen.sg.	*-es/*-os	*-osyo	-ās / -āī	-ī / -osio > -oeo	-es > -is / -os > -us	*-eis	-ous/-uos
Dat.sg.	*-ei		-ai/-ā	-oi/-ō	-ei	-ei	-uei/-ū
Loc.sg.	*-i		-ai	-ei	*-i > -e	*-ēi	*-ēu
Abl.sg.	*-ōd/ø	*-d	-ād	-ōd	-e/-ēd	-īd	-ūd
Nom.pl.	*-es	*-oi	-ai	*-oi > -ei	-ēs	-eis > -īs	-ūs
Neut.pl.	*-a		(no neuters)	-a	-a	-ia	-ua
Acc.pl.	*-ms		-ās	-ōs	-ēs	-īs	-ūs
Gen.pl.	*-om	(*-āsom)	*-āsom > -ārum	-om / -ōrom	-om	-iom	-uom
Dat./Abl.pl.	*-bʰos/*-ōis (*o*-stems) *-oisu (*o*-stem loc. pl.)		*-ais > -eis *-ābos > -ābus	-ois > -eis	-ibos	-ibos	-ibos -ubos

genitive *totius* from *totus* 'all'). Pronominal endings are usually extended first to the *o*- or *a*-stem declensions, reflecting the formal similarities between some pronominal stems and these declensions – compare, for example, the demonstrative/anaphoric pronoun with stem **to-/tā-* (**teh₂-*) (accusative **tom* and **tām* (**teh₂m*)) – and arising from the frequent collocation of demonstratives and nouns. Endings taken from the pronouns are usually restricted to these two declensions, as is the case with the nominative plural endings *-ai* (CL *-ae*) and *-oi* (CL *-i*), although as we have seen, the type of the ablative singular of the *o*-stems eventually spreads to all the declensions.

Table 1.1 gives a synopsis of the nominal declensions as they look in the earliest Latin texts, before the later monophthongizations. Note that not all of the forms given below are directly attested as such; many of them can only be assumed on the basis of their later shape in Latin. Where this is the case, unattested forms are shown with an asterisk. The table also includes the reconstructed PIE nominal, and where relevant to Latin, pronominal endings. Note the variety of different exponents for the same case often in the same declension; sometimes the difference reflects Indo-European alternants (*-ous/-uos* for genitive singular of *u*-stems), sometimes it appears to be peculiarly Latino-Faliscan (genitive singular *-ī*) versus the rare *-osio* (on the Lapis Satricanus, *c*.490 BC, and in the name *Mettoeo Fufetioeo* in Ennius *Ann*. 120 (Skutsch)); we shall consider this ending in more detail later in this chapter). Sometimes, as in the dative singular feminine *-ai* or *-a*, the difference results from sound changes which may have been dialectal.

Table 1.1 gives separate paradigms for consonant stem and *i*-stem nouns (denoted IIIa and IIIb) respectively. In Classical Latin there is still a distinction between the two paradigms in the genitive plural, where original consonant stem nouns mostly have the ending *-um*, original *i*-stem nouns the ending *-ium*. This explains some well-known 'irregularities' of the grammars, such as *canum*, genitive plural of *canis* 'dog', and *iuuenum*, gentive plural of *iuuenis* 'young man', both of which are originally consonant stems despite the nominative singulars in *-is*, and *mentium*, *gentium* etc. genitive plurals of *mens* 'mind', *gens* 'family' and suchlike, which were originally *i*-stems with nominative singulars **mentis*, **gentis* in which the *i* was lost by syncope. However, even in the genitive plural there is confusion between the two endings: *mensis* 'month' has genitive plurals *mensum* and *mensium* attested, *parens* 'parent' has *parentum* and *parentium*, and the consonant stem *nox* regularly takes the *i*-stem form *noctium*. In other cases in Classical Latin the picture is yet more muddled. The ablative singular in *-ī* is preferred for adjectives (even consonant-stem (C-stem) adjectives) and some nouns with a nominative singular in *-is*, but is not used for nouns such as *mens* and *gens*. The accusative singular ending *-im* is restricted to a small set of nouns, and not used with adjectives. The Classical Latin situation is the endpoint of centuries of interaction between the two paradigms, which may have had its starting point in the early syncope of short *i* in nouns such as **mentis* (Classical *mens*) which led to their identification as a consonant stem. At all stages of attested Latin there is borrowing of endings between the two paradigms. In the case of the dative and ablative plural consonant stem nouns show a reflex of the *i*-stem ending *-ibos* from our earliest texts, and *i*-stem forms such as ablative singular *-id* are found more widely used with consonant stem nouns in early inscriptions than the scantily attested form *-ed*.

The sharp-eyed reader will have noticed that the table given for Latin nominal declensions does not include a column for the 5th declension. The 5th declension has no correspondence in any other IE language, and seems to have arisen through an association of various different nouns which had, or were interpreted as having, a stem in **-ē*, such as *rēs* 'possession' < **rehₗy-* and *diēs* 'day', abstracted from an original accusative **diēm*. Joining this group is a number of nouns in *-iēs* which seem to bear a relationship with 1st-declension nouns in *-ia* (note doublets such as *materiēs* and *materia*), although no completely satisfactory explanation for the origin of the suffix *-iēs*, has yet been found. The parallelism between the 5th and 1st declensions, which both contain predominantly feminine nouns, is further seen in the adaptation of the endings to the model of the *a*-stems. Thus the genitive singular *-ēī* replaces earlier genitive *-ēs*, just as in the 1st declension *-ās* was replaced by *-āī* in the third century BC. The *-ī* ending is taken from the 2nd declension, and the genitive plural *-ērum* is modelled after genitive plural *-ārum*.

1.4.4 The verbal system

Whereas the Latin nominal system largely continues the categories inherited from PIE (with the loss of some categories, such as dual, collective and instrumental), the Latin verbal system is radically different from the reconstructed PIE system. Indeed, the divergences between the verbal systems of the daughter languages are such that there is uncertainty over which reconstruction for PIE best explains the divergent developments in the daughter languages. The principal difficulty arises from trying to integrate the verbal system of the Anatolian languages with that which can be reconstructed for the other early branches of PIE. Traditionally, the picture of the PIE verb has been constructed from comparison of the Greek and Sanskrit verbal systems, with some assistance from Latin and Germanic. However, many of the verbal categories which exist in Greek and Sanskrit, such as the perfect, the aorist, and the optative and subjunctive moods, are absent from Anatolian, but various formal considerations make it unlikely that these categories have just been lost. Instead, it is possible to draw up a different model of the PIE verb which promotes the Anatolian evidence, and sees the Greek and Sanskrit agreements as later innovations. The current debate over the reconstruction of the verbal system centres on the issue of the chronology of these changes (see Clackson 2007 ch. 5 for discussion). Is it possible that the Anatolian model just represents an earlier stage of PIE, and that the Greek-Sanskrit model can be retained in order to explain the Latin verb? Or should we view the Greek-Sanskrit model as viable only for Greek and Sanskrit, and inadequate for Latin? Current thinking in PIE is moving towards acceptance of the notion that the Anatolian languages did split off from the other PIE languages at an early stage, and consequently that the Greek-Sanskrit model may be valid for all the IE branches other than Anatolian, and we shall accordingly rely on this model of our presentation of the verb. However, as we shall see in the discussion of the endings of the Latin passive, in some cases it is possible that the Latin data is not best explained by this model.

The model of the IE verb arrived at by comparison of Greek and Sanskrit bears some similarity to the verb as known from Classical Latin. The Latin verbal paradigm opposes two basic stems, the *infectum* and *perfectum*, from which different tense and mood paradigms are formed – the present, future and imperfect indicatives, present and imperfect subjunctives, present and future imperatives derive from the infectum stem, and the perfect, future perfect and pluperfect indicatives, perfect and pluperfect subjunctives from the perfectum stem. In the same way the reconstructed PIE verb opposes three different stems, from which derive a number of paradigms encoding tense and mood, as exemplified in Table 1.2. In PIE, as in Latin, there is the further dimension of *voice*, which we shall discuss below. Several aspects of the system given above require immediate explanation. First, the difference between the stems. The present and aorist stem shared the same morphology: the endings of the imperfect

Table 1.2   Tense and mood in the reconstructed PIE verb

	Present stem	Aorist stem	Perfect stem
Indicative	Present	Aorist	Perfect
	Imperfect		?Pluperfect
Subjunctive	Present subjunctive	Aorist subjunctive	?
Optative	Present optative	Aorist optative	?
Imperative	Present imperative	Aorist imperative	?
Participle	Present participle	Aorist participle	Perfect participle

indicative are identical to those of the aorist indicative; the present subjunctive, optative, imperative and participle were formed in the same way as their aorist counterparts. The similarity of morphology mirrors a similarity of function. Both stems were used to refer to events, actions and processes, and differed only in the category of aspect. The exact nature of the aspectual difference is probably not recoverable, but broadly speaking the present stem corresponded to imperfective aspect and the aorist stem to perfective aspect. The PIE perfect stem (which is not to be confused with the Latin perfect) stands apart from the other two stems, both in morphology – the endings of the perfect were completely different from those used for the other two stems – and in function. Perfects appear originally to have referred to states, and, in Greek at any rate, the productive meaning of the perfect is a state which results from a past action. Originally, perfects could be used parallel to the present tense to refer to states in the present. Relics of this situation exist in the few Latin verbs where morphological perfects have present-referring meaning, such as *odi* 'I hate' or *memini* 'I remember'.

Latin has reduced the inherited system of three stems to two. The reduction reflects two separate processes, the replacement of a system fundamentally based on aspect with one centred on tense, and the re-interpretation of the PIE perfect to denote an action in the past rather than the state resulting from that action – re-interpretations of this sort are familiar from the history of the 'have' perfects of many Western European languages. These two developments meant that at a prehistoric stage Latin had two past-referring stems co-existing side by side, the old aorist and the old perfect. The two categories were merged together before our earliest extensive Latin records, although it is clear from the number of duplicate forms in Early Latin that the merger must have taken place relatively recently. Thus Classical Latin *facio* has a paradigm with perfect *feci*, which must reflect an original aorist stem, but in Early Latin the reduplicated perfect stem is also attested as *vhevhaked* (CIL I² 3, from Praeneste, *vh* = *f*); *parco* 'I spare' has a perfect *peperci* in Classical Latin (from an old perfect) but in Early Latin it also shows a perfect *parsi* from an earlier aorist and the new formation *parcui*; *pango* 'I fix' has perfect *pepigi*, but also *panxi* from an old aorist in Ennius. Note that the merged 'perfectum' formation in Latin can encode both of the earlier functions of a perfect: present-referring *feci* 'I have made' (used with 'primary sequence') and *feci* 'I made' (used with 'historic sequence').

The injunctive and Latin primary/secondary endings

In Table 1.2, the present stem of the PIE verb is reconstructed with two different indicative formations, the present and the imperfect. The morphology of these two tenses as they appear in Sanskrit is on the whole the same, except that each tense bears an extra marker, as can be seen clearly in the 3rd person singular:

present indicative	*bharat-i* 'he carries'	< PIE *$b^h eret$-**i**
imperfect indicative	*a-bharat* 'he was carrying'	< PIE ***e**-$b^h eret$

the present indicative is marked with a final *-i*, and the imperfect has a prefix *a-* < PIE *e-(called the *augment* in traditional grammar). The past-referring aorist indicative is also marked by the augment in Sanskrit; there is no indicative marked with final *-i* from the aorist stem, since such a tense with present reference would be incompatible with the perfective aspect. The unmarked counterparts to these forms, both in the present and aorist system, are found in Vedic Sanskrit, where they are named the *injunctive*. The present injunctive has the following form:

injunctive	*bharat* 'he carries'	< PIE $b^h eret$

The injunctive of Vedic Sanskrit is a relic category with three different principal uses, which may all be inherited from PIE:

1 with the particle *mā* it forms prohibitions;
2 it may also serve as a replacement for a verb form marked for tense or mood in a string of verbs;
3 it appears in narrative contexts referring to actions by gods or heroes in myth.

These 'unmarked' verb forms were therefore liable to confusion with either modal forms (functions 1 and 2) or indicative forms (functions 2 and 3). In Latin, the corresponding unmarked forms made from the original present stem of the verb had a different fate from those made from the aorist stem. Those from the present stem were largely lost, as were the present stem forms marked with the augment for past time, the PIE imperfect paradigm. The only survival of the original unmarked forms are some imperative forms, for example, the passive/deponent imperatives in *-re*. In the *aorist* system on the other hand, the old injunctive replaces the aorist indicative tense as the standard marker of past time. We can see this development as an extension of function 2 given above. The unmarked stem of the verb would be most frequently used in long narratives of past events, with an initial verb form marked for past tense followed by a number of subsequent unmarked forms. The prevalence of the unmarked form may have led to the ousting of the less frequent marked form. Note also that the loss of the original imperfect can be linked to the loss of the category of aspect. In Latin the imperfect is not typically used as a narrative tense, unlike in languages which preserve an overall aspectual distinction such as Greek.

There is no trace of the *augment* as a means of marking past tense in Latin. But the earliest Latin inscriptions do retain the distinction between a set of endings associated with present tense and another set with non-present or non-indicative verb forms. The forms with present reference are collectively termed *primary* endings and are opposed to *secondary* endings. Ultimately the primary endings derive from a set with 3rd person singular *-ti*, and the secondary endings continue the injunctive endings with 3rd person singular *-t*. The effects of sound change mean that the original distinction between the two sets of endings has changed by the time of Early Latin:

	Primary	Secondary
PIE	*-ti*	*-t*
Early Latin	*-t*	*-d*.

It should be noted that the form reconstructed as PIE *-t* may have been realized as /-*d*/ word finally (see Ringe 2000), and so the only change which need be posited for Latin is the loss of final -*i* (a change it has undergone in common with the Sabellian languages, see Chapter II). The Early Latin distinction between primary and secondary endings did not affect all persons: there was no distinction between primary and secondary in the 2nd person singular, nor, as far as we can tell, in the 1st and 2nd person plural. This overlap between the different categories eventually led to their levelling, and in Classical Latin the only vestige of their survival is in the 1st person singular. In this person the primary ending -*ō* (besides secondary -*m*) was used in place of expected *-mi*, and this morph remains restricted to primary contexts.

Thematic and athematic endings

PIE verbal morphology showed two separate sets of personal endings for the present and aorist paradigms, which did not encode any functional difference, but were associated with different morphological classes. These two conjugations are termed *thematic* and *athematic*. Examples of reconstructed forms of the two conjugations in the present indicative (active) are given below, with their continuations in Latin:

	Thematic	Athematic
3rd person singular	*h_2eg'-e-ti* (*agit*)	*h_1es-ti* (*est*)
1st person plural	*h_2eg'-o-me* (*agimus*)	*h_1s-me* (*sumus*)

As can be seen from the examples, in the thematic endings a vowel is inserted between the stem and the ending. This vowel, termed the *thematic* vowel, may have a surface form **e* or **o*. Athematic endings are distinguished by having no link vowel before the ending, which is attached directly to the stem. Thematic verbs do not show the vowel alternation in the root syllable that was characteristic of the athematic class (note the variation between the root form **h₁es-* and **h₁s-* in the verb 'to be', which survives in Latin *es-t/s-umus*). Different personal endings were associated with the athematic and thematic conjugations in some parts of the paradigm. For Latin, the only survival of this is the 1st person singular, where the primary ending was **-ō* for the thematics, but **-mi* for athematics. Already in PIE the athematic class was losing ground to the thematics, and all of the athematic verbs inherited into Latin show some degree of influence from the thematic paradigm. Thus the athematic 1st person singular ending **-mi* only survives in the Latin verb form *sum* 'I am'. Other irregular verbs in Latin derive in part from athematic forms, note *eo* 'I go' (athematic forms include first plural *imus*) and *uolo* 'I want' (athematic 3rd person singular *uult*).

Modal forms

Two modal forms other than the imperative are reconstructed for PIE, the subjunctive and the optative. These are continued in Greek and Vedic Sanskrit, although it is not easy to give a simple summary of their different functions. The subjunctive is often characterized as a mood of volition: it is used in commands, prohibitions and exhortations, and speakers may use subjunctives to refer to events that they expect will take place. The optative is used in wishes, but it may be better seen as the mood of the counterfactual, or at least the mood which is further removed from the here and now than the subjunctive – note that the optative is used in counterfactual conditionals in Greek (in part) and in Sanskrit. Latin does not continue both moods as modal forms, but the same morphological formations survive. The old PIE subjunctive becomes the Latin future, the old PIE optative becomes the Latin subjunctive. This pattern can be seen in Table 1.3, which sets a series of PIE subjunctive and optative formations beside their Latin outcomes. Line 1 presents the clearest case, the verb 'to be', where the Latin future directly continues the old subjunctive and the Latin subjunctive continues the original optative formation. In Early Latin the subjunctive has the form *siem, sies, sied* in the singular, and *sīmus, sītis, sient* in the plural; this vestige of the earlier vowel alternation pattern is ironed out by the time of Classical Latin, to give a stem *si-/sī-* (*sim, sīs, sit, sint*). Line 2 shows how the originally athematic verb *uolo* 'I want' also retains the original optative as a

Table 1.3 The outcomes of the PIE moods in Latin

	PIE subjunctive → Latin future		PIE optative → Latin subjunctive	
1.	*$h_1$es-et(i)	erit	*h_1s-ieh$_1$-t	sied
2.			*wel-ih$_1$-me	uelīmus
3.	*reǵ-ḗ-t(i)	reget	*rego-ih$_1$-t	regat
4.	*-uis-ō	-uerō	*-uis-ih$_1$-m	-uerim

subjunctive. The expected 3rd person singular future of *uolo* would be *uelit* < *uel-et(i)*, but it has replaced this with the future formed in long -*e*, which, as we see in line 3, is regularly derived from the PIE subjunctive for verbs of the 3rd conjugation (representing earlier thematic verbs). The derivation of the thematic optative in Latin is uncertain; it may be possible that the suffix *a* is actually the Latin continuation of *-oyh$_1$*- (see Rix 2002). Line 4 shows the behaviour of the original subjunctive and optative in the perfectum stem, where the form *-uis*- represents the productive stem formation in the perfect (also evident from the perfect infinitive as *amauisse*); here the subjunctive lies behind the Latin future perfect and the optative behind the perfect subjunctive. In Classical Latin the future perfect and the perfect subjunctive look the same except for the first person: perfect subjunctive *amauerim* and future perfect *amauero*, but in Early Latin, the forms were more distinct, with the subjunctive showing a long *ī*, *amauerīs*, *amauerīt* etc., although already in Plautus the vowel is sometimes shortened in the 3rd person.

This pattern can also explain the Latin future formation in -*bō*, used for the 1st and 2nd conjugations, and the 4th conjugation in some verbs in Early Latin. This formation originated from a univerbation of a verbal noun with the original aorist subjunctive of the root *b^huh$_2$*- which survives in Latin *fui* 'I was'. Structurally parallel formations also occur in the older Indo-Iranian languages, for example Vedic *gúhā bab^{h}uva* 'he is hidden' with *gúhā* associated with the verb *gūhati* 'hide' (see Gippert 1999 for details of the supposed PIE background to these forms). The Latin imperfect formation in -*bam* is also a neologism formed from the same univerbation, possibly formed from either an aorist 'injunctive' verb form, or a modal form marked with *-ā*- (in many languages there is an interaction between modal formations and verb forms denoting habitual actions, cf. the English 'would' tenses and the Greek optative). The Latin future in -*bō* is an entirely new formation, only shared by Faliscan, the language spoken in the ancient town of Falerii, and known only from scanty inscriptional sources. The following inscription is found on a Faliscan drinking bowl dated to around 300 BC:

(1) Giacomelli 1963: 49

foied uino   pipafo   cra   carefo
today wine-ACC I-will-drink tomorrow I-will-lack

'Today I will drink wine, tomorrow I'll do without.'
(Latin: *hodie uinum bibam, cras carebo.*)

The Faliscan verb ending *-fo* is clearly exactly the same as Latin *-bo*, with the
-f- rather than *-b-* the outcome of a 'voiced aspirate' *$-b^h$-. This formation
is found nowhere else in Italy and represents a significant shared innovation.

Voice

The PIE verbal system also had a category of voice. As in Latin, there
were two voices, and Latin formally continues the inherited opposition.
However, the precursor to the Latin passive, termed the PIE *medio-
passive* or *middle* appears to have been motivated semantically rather than
syntactically. That is to say, whereas in Latin a passive verb form can
be derived syntactically from its corresponding active verb, by promoting
the object of the active verb to the subject of the passive verb, in PIE no
such syntactic transformation can be made to arrive at the function of
the middle voice. Instead the underlying meaning of the middle appears
to have been affectedness or involvement of the subject, in addition to,
or other than, functioning as the agent. In PIE some verbs could conjugate in both voices, whereas others were restricted either to the active
only (such as *h_1es-* 'be') or to the middle only (such as *sek^w-* 'follow').
The development in meaning from the middle to the passive is straightforward: for most transitive verbs, the object can be seen to be maximally
'affected' by the verbal action, and hence middle forms of transitive verbs
are open to re-interpretation as passives. There are many survivals of the
earlier state of affairs in Latin, notably in the class of deponent verbs, that
is verbs conjugated as passives although having no active counterpart.
These verbs continue the inherited set of verbs which only took middle
endings, note for example *sequor* 'I follow' which in Latin is deponent
and in other IE languages is inflected as a middle.

The Latin personal endings of the passive have clear analogues in other
IE languages. Compare the following 3rd person forms (singular and
plural) in Latin with the Greek and Sanskrit (present and imperfect)
endings:

	Latin	Greek	Sanskrit
3rd singular (present)	agitur	ágetai	ájate
3rd singular (imperfect)		égeto	ā́jata
3rd plural (present)	aguntur	ágontai	ájante
3rd plural (imperfect)		égonto	ā́janta

In all three languages the middle/passive endings are formed from the active endings with a further marker attached. The Greek and Sanskrit secondary (past) endings are formed from the active endings followed by *-o, the primary (non-past) endings of Sanskrit can be derived from final *-oi (i.e. the secondary ending + *-i), and this form is also found in Mycenaean Greek and some Greek dialects (elsewhere in Greek it is replaced by -ai). The Latin endings derive from the active endings followed by *-or. The final *-r of the Latin forms has no equivalent in Greek or Sanskrit, but it is also used to mark the 1st person forms of the passive (*-or and *-mor). There are other IE languages which do, however, show a comparable use of final *-r, and we shall return to discuss the Latin -r forms in detail below when considering Latin's place in the IE language family. The 2nd person forms of the middle are difficult to reconstruct with confidence, and need not detain us here, except to note that the Latin 2nd plural -mini remains unparalleled in other IE languages.

The perfect of the Latin passive is formed by a periphrasis of participle and 'be', actus sum, etc. This formation is not inherited from PIE. Indeed, the PIE perfect does not seem to have made a distinction of voice, since it originally represented the state of the subject and thus was obligatorily understood as 'subject-affected'. In the course of time the original sense of the perfect was lost and it became re-interpreted as a tense parallel to the other active indicative formations, leading to the requirement to create a passive counterpart to perfect forms. The innovation of a new periphrastic perfect passive, formed in exactly the same way, also took place in the Sabellian languages (see Chapter II).

As a summary to the changes discussed above we can represent the differences and similarities between Latin and PIE in a tabular form, using the 3rd person singular as a representative of each paradigm. In Table 1.4 the shaded forms have left no trace in Latin, but the unshaded forms, whether new formations or inherited from PIE have been incorporated into the Latin verbal system. The table shows how much of the Latin verbal system is new, and how much inherited. Note that the arrow signs ⇒ and ⇐ in this table should be taken to indicate that the Latin formation derives from the cited form or from something like it; we are not sure about the exact makeup of the ancestor of the Latin imperfect, for example, as we saw in the discussion.

1.4.5 Syntax

PIE syntax is one of the most difficult areas to reconstruct. However, in recent years scholars have been increasingly turning their attention to syntactic change and we are beginning to get a better picture of what

Table 1.4 Inherited and new elements in the Latin verbal system

(a) The PIE present system ⇒ Latin *infectum*

PIE	Latin	New formations
Injunctive *$h_2eǵ'et$		
Present indicative *$h_2eǵ'eti$ ⇒	Present *agit*	
Imperfect *$e\text{-}h_2eǵ'eti$	Imperfect *agebat*	⇐ *$h_2eǵ'ē\ b^huh_2\text{-}$
Subjunctive *$h_2eǵ'\text{-}ē\text{-}t(i)$ ⇒	Future *aget*	
Optative *$h_2eǵ'\text{-}oih_1\text{-}t$ ⇒	Subjunctive *agat*	
	Imperfect subjunctive *ageret*	⇐ *$\text{-}sē\text{-}t$

(b) The PIE aorist/perfect system ⇒ Latin *perfectum*

PIE	Latin	New formations
Perfect indicative *$d^he\text{-}d^hh_1k\text{-}e$ ⇒	Perfect indicative *vhevhaked*	
Aorist injunctive *$d^heh_1k\text{-}t$ ⇒	Perfect indicative *fecit*	
Aorist indicative *$e\text{-}d^heh_1k\text{-}t$	Pluperfect *fecerat*	⇐ *$\text{-}is\text{-}āt$
Aorist subjunctive *$d^heh_1k\text{-}et(i)$	Future perfect *fecerit*	⇐ *$\text{-}is\text{-}eti$
Aorist optative *$d^heh_1k\text{-}ih_1\text{-}t$	Perfect subjunctive *fecerit*	⇐ *$\text{-}is\text{-}ih_1\text{-}t$
	Pluperfect subjunctive *fecisset*	⇐ *$\text{-}is\text{-}sē\text{-}t$

PIE syntax might have looked like. Here we shall concentrate on just one area where Latin syntactic behaviour can be compared with other IE languages: word order.

Word order in Classical Latin realizes no grammatical information, and poetical or rhetorical texts can show extreme examples of 'scrambled' word placement, with discontinuous constituents, and words removed from their clauses. For example, the following line taken from Vergil (*Aeneid* I.109) shows the relative pronoun occurring after the subject and verb of the relative clause and interrupting a prepositional phrase, which is itself in a non-standard order:

(2)   Vergil *Aeneid* I.109

saxa	vocant Itali	mediis	quae	in fluctibus Aras
rocks-ACC	they-call Italians-NOM	middle-ABL.pl	which-ACC	in wave-ABL.pl altars-ACC

'rocks in the middle of the waves which the Italians call the altars'

This hyperbaton is clearly here used for effect. In Latin prose, scrambling of the word order is rarely so extreme, and sampling and statistical surveys of Latin word order have established a default word order (see Adams 1976). Latin verbs usually come at the end of their clause, but in respect of other constituents heads precede modifiers: Latin has prepositions, not postpositions and the unmarked order for nominal phrases is nouns before dependent adjectives and genitives. Adams (1976) argues that Classical Latin artificially preserves a stage of the language when the word order was changing from 'head-final' (OV) to 'head-first' (VO), and there is certainly evidence (as we shall see in later chapters) from sub-literary texts to suggest that in the spoken language of the first centuries AD, verbs preceded their complements, as they do in the Romance languages.

Extrapolating back from this Classical Latin picture one might expect to find more evidence for head-final constructions in Latin, and that the parent language from which Latin derived was also an SOV language. There is some evidence to support this hypothesis. If we look at verb placement alone, we find that in the earliest lengthy Latin inscription, the *Senatusconsultum de Bacchanalibus* (CIL I² 581, dated to 186 BC, discussed in detail at 5.4), every verb in the 30-line text is clause-final, and in the fragments of Laws of the XII Tables, believed to date from the fifth century BC, verbs always follow their objects and come at the end of the clause, except where followed by afterthoughts or elaboration. There is also evidence that the default word order in PIE was head-final; Hittite is consistently OV, as is the language of the earliest Sanskrit prose texts (although much freer word order is found in Sanskrit metrical poetry).

Some scholars, most notably Winfred Lehmann and his school (see Lehmann 1974, Bauer 2000), accordingly reconstruct PIE as a rigid OV language. However, it seems likely that this oversimplifies the picture of word-order. Verb-final was certainly the unmarked word order in PIE, but textual or pragmatic factors may have led to fronting of the verb, or amplification of the sentence through the addition of extra material after the verb (so-called 'right-detachment'). The very earliest Latin texts we have may give us a glimpse of a period when word-order was not as rigid as it seems in the Laws of the XII Tables or the *Senatusconsultum de Bacchanalibus*. We reproduce below all the inscriptions with verb-phrases longer than two words extant from before *c*.400 BC (with 'translations' into a more recognizable stage of Latin). The verbs are highlighted in **bold** and the sign / is inserted where relevant to show clause breaks. (Note that in these texts square brackets are used to indicate where letters are no longer visible on the original inscription; text inside square brackets is restored by the editors.)

(3)   CIL I² 3 (dated to the seventh century BC, although its authenticity has been doubted, the sign : indicates word or syllable division):

Manios: med: **vhe:vhaked:** Numasioi
Manius me   fecit   Numerio
Manius me-ACC made Numasius-DAT

'Manius made me for Numerius.'

(4)   'Tita Vendia' vase, (seventh century BC, cf. Silvestri 1993, with the reading of Rix 1998: 251 n. 20):

eco urna titas vendias / mamar[cos m]ed **vhe[ced**
ego urna Titae   Vendiae.   Mamarcus me   fecit
I   urn Tita-GEN Vendia-GEN Mamarcus me-ACC made

'I am the urn of Tita Vendia, Mamarcus made me.'

(5)   CIL I² 4 (sixth century BC, the obscure second line is omitted):

iouesat deiuos qoi med **mitat** nei ted endo cosmis virco **sied /**
iurat per deos   qui me   mittit ne in te   comis   uirgo   sit
swears   gods-ACC who me-ACC sends lest to you-ACC kind-NOM girl-NOM is-SUBJ

duenos med **feced** en manom einom duenoi ne med malos **tatod**
bonus   me   fecit   in ? ? bono,   ne me   malus   clepito
good-NOM me-ACC he-made in ? ? good-DAT not me-ACC bad-NOM steal-IMP

'He who gives me swears by the gods that the girl should not be kind to you [. . .] A good man made me for a good man in [two words unclear], let no bad man steal me.'

(6)   CIL I² 2658 (sixth century BC, the reading here follows Wachter
       1987: 80f.)

hoi med **mitat** kauios [. . .]monios qetios d[o]nom pro fileod
hic   me   mittit Gaius   [ ]monius   Cetius   donum   pro filio
here me-ACC sends Gaius-NOM [ ]monius-NOM Cetius-NOM gift-ACC for son-ABL

'Gaius [. . .]monius Cetius places me here as a gift on behalf of his son.'

(7)   CIL I² 2832a (the Lapis Satricanus, sixth–fifth century BC)

]iei **steterai** popliosio ualesiosio suodales mamartei
]ii   steterunt   Publii   Valerii   sodales   Marti
?-LOC they-set-up Publius-GEN Valerius-GEN companions-NOM Mars-DAT

'The companions of Publius Valerius set up [this] to Mars in ?'

(8)   'Garigliano bowl' (fifth–fourth century BC, the reading here follows
       Vine 1998)

esom kom meois sociois trifos audeom duo[m] / nei **pari** med
sum cum meis   sociis   tribus   Audiorum duorum noli me   capere
I-am with my-ABL companions-ABL three-ABL Audii-GEN two-GEN don't me-ACC take

'I am, together with my three companions, (the possession of) the two
Audii. Don't take me.'

Verbs in the above inscriptions are only found clause-finally in the
'Tita Vendia' vase and in the embedded clauses in CIL I² 4. In the other
examples they generally follow directly after their accusative complements
(*med vhevhaked / feced, med mitat*), although in the first clause of CIL
I² 4 and the Garigliano bowl the verbs are fronted to sentence initial position. The subject follows the verb if it is especially long or complex, as
in CIL I² 2658 and 2832a, and dative complements also follow in all the
early inscriptions. The net result is a system where the default word order
is SOV, but where other orders, such as VO and OVS may also be present for reasons of emphasis or contrast. It is possible that the later rigid
SOV system evidenced from sources such as the Laws of the XII Tables
and the *senatusconsultum de Bacchanalibus* is not, in fact, a preservation
of an archaic state, but is itself an artificial 'official' order created for the
specialized discourse of bureaucratic prose (and which later became a
defining marker of 'Classical Latin'). This rigid verb-final pattern may never
have been a feature of spoken Latin. In the plays of Plautus, roughly
contemporary with the *senatusconsultum de Bacchanalibus*, we find a
range of different word-order patterns which fits in with the tendencies
observed in the archaic Latin inscriptions given above. The verb-final order

predominates in subordinate clauses (where emphasis is less of an issue): thus in Plautus's *Captiui* the ratio of VO to OV order in subordinate clauses is 15 : 43, in main clauses 39 : 45 (figures from Adams 1976: 94f.). Verbs almost always follow pronominal objects, as they do in the early inscriptions, and as they continue to do in Romance. The only exceptions to this rule in Plautus's *Captiui* are occasions where the verb is fronted to clause initial position; this is usually the case with imperatives, where the verb is the natural focus, for example 449 *sequere me* 'follow me', and can be compared to the fronting of the imperative in the Garigliano bowl's injunction *nei pari med*. In Plautus subjects are also found following the verb, particularly where the verb is passive, but also where the verb is fronted or the subject is a long constituent; hence the word order of the Lapis Satricanus can be compared to *Captiui* 646, where the focal question word is fronted as would be expected:

(9)   Plautus *Captiui* 646
sed qua   faciest   tuo'   sodalis   Philocrates?
but   what-ABL face-ABL=is your-NOM companion-NOM Philocrates-NOM
'But what does your companion Philocrates look like?'

The more flexible model of Early Latin word order that is formed by looking at the earliest inscriptions and Plautus, with an unmarked head-final order, but the possibility of different orders through verb-fronting or right-detached elements accords well with current models of PIE syntax which incorporate these possibilities (see Clackson 2007, Ch. 6). This account of Early Latin (and PIE) word order will be of relevance to the discussion of changes in Latin word-order patterns in later chapters.

1.5   The Position of Latin within the IE family

The search for the IE language closest to Latin is nothing new, and the place of Latin within the IE family has been discussed since the inception of the discipline of comparative philology. We shall examine the question of the relationship between Latin and the other IE (and non-IE) languages of Italy in more detail in Chapter II. Here we shall briefly review the arguments for special connections between Latin and other IE language groups which lie principally outside Italy. The IE language groups which we know to have been spoken adjacent to the Latin speech area in historic times are Germanic, Celtic and Greek. In the nineteenth century scholars grouped Latin closest to Greek and Celtic. The earliest published 'tree diagram' of the IE family, by Schleicher in 1853, included a branch comprising Greek and Latin, but soon afterwards, in 1858, Carl

Lottner proposed a special relationship between Latin and Celtic (see Schrader 1907: 53–76 and Schmidt 1992 on these early works). It later became apparent that the features shared by Latin and Greek reflected common inheritances from the parent language, lost in other IE languages, rather than new developments, and were thus not significant for their relationship. The 'Italo-Celtic theory', on the other hand, continues to have adherents to the present day. Evidence in support of the reconstruction of an original Italo-Celtic subgroup includes shared phonological and lexical innovations as well as the joint creation of new morphology. Here we shall leave the phonology and vocabulary out of discussion, since it is not uncommon to find vocabulary items or phonological features or processes transferred across neighbouring languages, but it is rare to find borrowing of inflectional morphology through language contact. Unique shared innovations in morphology, particularly in inflectional morphology, are consequently the best indication that two languages earlier formed a subgroup (see Clackson 1994: 1–27).

Of the morphological agreements between Italic and Celtic the most widely discussed is the *o*-stem genitive singular marker *-$\bar{\imath}$, characteristic of Latin, as we saw above, and also found in Celtic (directly attested in, e.g., Archaic Irish (Ogham) *maq(q)i* 'of the son', and Gaulish *Segomari* 'of Segomaros'). This ending is found in none of the other older IE languages and it is possible that both language groups had jointly replaced the inherited ending, *-*osyo* as reconstructed from Sanskrit and Greek. However, a number of recent inscriptional finds show that the evidence in Italic and Celtic is far from straightforward. The early Celtic inscriptions from Italy and Spain show different endings: in Lepontic, three, perhaps four, inscriptions from before 400 BC show an ending *-oiso* (Eska and Wallace 2001: 80, in later Lepontic inscriptions *-oiso* is replaced by *-i*); and the Celtiberian inscriptions regularly show genitive singular *-o*, the origin of which is disputed. The ending *-osio* is attested as a genitive singular in early Faliscan inscriptions, and is now known in one early Latin inscription, the *Lapis Satricanus* (reproduced at 1.4.5 above). The ending *-$\bar{\imath}$ is universal in Latin from inscriptions from 300 BC on (although it is not found in any earlier inscription) and is also widely attested in later Faliscan inscriptions. There is also evidence for the genitive singular *-$\bar{\imath}$ in two other IE languages of Italy: Venetic and Messapic. Since Messapic is usually not reckoned to be part of the Italic language family, and Lepontic has replaced earlier *-oiso* with *-$\bar{\imath}$, and, since Latin and Faliscan seem to have replaced *-osio* with *-$\bar{\imath}$ in historical times, it is now possible to argue (following Eska and Wallace) that the spread of a genitive singular *-$\bar{\imath}$ arose through language contact and took place relatively recently, not at some much earlier period of Italo-Celtic unity. The genitive singular ending may therefore be an example of a borrowed inflectional morph between closely related languages.

Other isoglosses between Latin and Celtic have also had to be revised in the light of new evidence. Nowhere more so, perhaps, than in the case of the verbal endings in *-r. In the Latin passive and deponent endings all forms of the 1st and 3rd person are marked by a morph *-r: *amor*, *amatur, amamur, amantur*. Nothing analogous to this is found in the medio-passive endings of Greek, Sanskrit or Gothic, but there are correspondences in Celtic. In Old Irish, for example, passive and deponent forms also end in -r (outside the 2nd person plural). This seemed a clear indication of a special relationship between Italic and Celtic, until the discovery of new IE languages in the early twentieth century, Tocharian and Hittite, which also have r-endings in the medio-passive conjugation. The presence of these endings in languages not in contact with each other, and on the peripheries of the Indo-European speaking area, argue strongly for r-endings to be a retained archaism, which were lost by a group of innovating languages in the centre of the IE world.

Although the r-endings of Latin and Celtic may not be an innovation, it has been argued that one ending of the medio-passive could represent an Italo-Celtic innovation (see Jasanoff 1997, the idea goes back to Thurneysen 1946: 367). Jasanoff suggests that the 3rd person plural in the Italic and Celtic medio-passive conjugation derives from *-ntro, a compromise between two earlier PIE possibilities *-nto (cf. Greek 3rd person plural imperfect middle ending -nto) and *-ro (an alternative third plural middle form, continued by some forms in Sanskrit such as *duh-ré* 'they milk' < *-ro-i). Jasanoff argues that *-ntro lies directly behind forms such as the Old Irish deponent 3rd person plural (conjunct form) -tar, and Sabellian 3rd person plural -nter (e.g., Marrucinian *ferenter* 'they are carried') – note that in both languages the final vowel has been lost and an anaptyctic vowel inserted in the cluster tr. However, this explanation entails a set of complicated analogical processes in order to explain the form in Latin, -ntur, which appears to derive directly from *-nto-r, a formation which can be exactly paralleled in the Hittite 3rd person plural present medio-passive ending -ndari. And in the Sabellian languages also, the simplest derivation of the different medio-passive endings in -r is from *-nto-r, preserved as a secondary ending in Umbrian **terkantur**, with the 3rd person plural -nter a remodelling by some dialects to make a distinctive primary ending (see Villanueva Svensson 1999).

In summary, the two innovations in inflectional morphology which have been proposed for Italo-Celtic need not represent common developments. The genitive singular marker *-ī, may have been borrowed across different languages, and the reconstruction of a 3rd person plural ending *-ntro is not necessary to explain the Latin deponent/passive ending -ntur. Without good evidence of a shared development in inflectional morphology, it is probably unwise to reconstruct an Italo-Celtic subgroup of PIE.

However, if we examine a wider range of features, including phonological and lexical evidence within the IE context we may get an idea of
whether Italic is more closely related to Celtic than any other language
group. The most comprehensive survey of this type yet to be performed
was carried out by a team led by Don Ringe (Ringe, Warnow and Taylor
2002), who devised a computer programme to examine the best possible fit for a family tree of IE based on analysis of 370 linguistic characters. The results do show a close relationship between Italic and Celtic,
although there are only four features that they share to the exclusion of
any other subgroup. These are:

1   the phonological change of $*pVk^w$- to $*k^wVk^w$-, cf. Latin *quinque* '5'
    < $*penk^we$ (Old Irish *coic*);
2   the productive suffix $*$-$ti\bar{o}n$-;
3   the word for 'lake' $*loku$-;
4   the verb 'sing' $*kan$-.

(see Ringe et al. 2002: 100f., for discussion of these agreements). It seems
to us most likely that these agreements arose through very early contact
between the ancestor of Latin and the Celtic languages, continued through
the common presence of both branches in Italy until historical times, or
perhaps through contact of both with other IE varieties which left no
attestation. Garrett (1999) has suggested borrowing of this sort in the period
following the break-up of the parent language, when the different varieties
were distinct but still very closely related (compare inter-dialectal borrowing
in Greek dialects or among the Sabellian languages which we shall examine
more closely in the next chapter). It is worth noting that Germanic also
shares a number of lexical features exclusively with Italic and with Celtic,
and some examples of these will be discussed at section 2.4 in the next
chapter (Ringe et al. 2002: 86f., Porzig 1954: 123–7).

   In summary, Latin shares more features with Celtic than any other IE
language branch outside Italy. The links to Celtic do not, however, seem
sufficiently close to allow us to reconstruct an 'Italo-Celtic' proto-language,
and Celtic developments can in general shed little light on the development of Latin. Much more important for the history of Latin is the
relationship with other IE languages in Italy, which will be the subject
of the next chapter.

References

Adams, J. N. (1976) 'A typological approach to Latin word order'. *Indogermanische
    Forschungen* 81, 70–99.
Bauer, B. L. M. (2000) *Archaic syntax in Indo-European: The spread of
    transitivity in Latin and French*. Berlin: Mouton de Gruyter.

Clackson, J. (1994) *The Linguistic relationship between Armenian and Greek*. Oxford: Blackwell.

Clackson, J. (2007) *Indo-European linguistics: An introduction*. Cambridge: Cambridge University Press.

Eska, J. F. and R. E. Wallace (2001) 'Remarks on the thematic genitive singular in Ancient Italy and related matters'. *Incontri Linguistici* 24, 77–97.

Garrett, A. (1999) 'A new model of IE sub-grouping and dispersal' in Steve S. Chang, Lily Liaw and Josef Ruppenhofer (eds.), *Proceedings of the Twenty-Fifth Annual Meeting of the Berkeley Linguistics Society*. Berkeley BLS, 146–156.

Giacomelli, G. (1963) *La Lingua Falisca*. Florence: Olschki.

Gippert, J. (1999) 'Das lateinische Imperfekt in sprachvergleichender Hinsicht' in Peter Anreiter and Erzsébet Jerem (eds.), *Studia Celtica et Indogermanica: Festschrift für Wolfgang Meid zum 70. Geburtstag*. Budapest: Archeolingua, 125–37.

Jasanoff, J. (1997) 'An Italo-Celtic isogloss: The 3rd plural Mediopassive in *-ntro*' in Douglas Q. Adams (ed.), *Festschrift for Eric P. Hamp*. I (Journal of Indo-European Studies Monographs no. 23), Washington DC: Institute for the Study of Man, 146–61.

Klingenschmitt, G. (1992) 'Das lateinische Nominalflexion' in Oswald Panagl and Thomas Krisch (eds.), *Latein und Indogermanisch: Akten des Kolloquiums der Indogermanischen Gesellschaft, Salzburg, 23–26 September 1986*. Innsbruck: Institut für Sprachwissenschaft der Universität Innsbruck, 89–135.

Klingenschmitt, G. (1993) 'Die Verwandtschaftsverhältnisse der indogermanischen Sprachen' in Jens Elmegård Rasmussen (ed.), *In honorem Holger Pedersen: Kolloquium der Indogermanischen Gesellschaft vom 25 bis 28 März 1993 in Kopenhagen*. Wiesbaden: Reichert, 235–51.

Lehmann, C. (1979) 'Der Relativsatz vom Indogermanischen bis zum Italienischen'. *Sprache* 25, 1–25.

Lehmann, W. P. (1974) *Proto-Indo-European syntax*. Austin, Texas and London: University of Texas Press.

Lehmann, W. P. (1993) *Theoretical bases of Indo-European linguistics*. London and New York: Routledge.

Meiser, G. (1992) 'Syncretism in Indo-European languages: motives, process and results'. *Transactions of the Philological Society* 90, 187–218.

Meiser, G. (1998) *Historische Laut- und Formenlehre der lateinischen Sprache*. Darmstadt: Wissenschaftliche Buchgesellschaft.

Meiser, G. (2003) *Veni Vidi Vici: Die Vorgeschichte des lateinischen Perfektsystems*. Zetemata Monographien zur klassischen Altertumswissenschaft. Heft 113. Munich: Beck.

Porzig, W. (1954) *Die Gliederung des indogermanischen Sprachgebiets*. Heidelberg: Winter.

Ringe, D. (2000) 'Tocharian class II presents and subjunctives and the reconstruction of the Proto-Indo-European verb'. *Tocharian and Indo-European Studies* 9, 121–42.

Ringe, D., T. Warnow and A. Taylor (2002) 'Indo-European and Computational Cladistics'. *Transactions of the Philological Society* 100, 59–129.

Rix, H. (1965) 'Lat *iecur, iocineris*' *Münchener Studien für Sprachwissenschaft* 18, 79–92.

Rix, H. (1985) 'Das letzte Wort der Duenos-Inschrift', *Münchener Studien für Sprachwissenschaft* 46, 193–220.

Rix, H. (1998) 'Eine neue frühsabellische Inschrift und der altitalische Präventiv'. *Zeitschrift für vergleichenden Sprachforschung* 111, 247–69.

Rix, H. (2002) 'Towards a reconstruction of Proto-Italic: the verbal system' in K. Jones-Bley, M. E. Huld, A. Della Volpe and M. Robbins Dexter (eds.), *Proceedings of the 14th Annual UCLA Indo-European Conference.* Washington, DC: JIES Monograph Series, 1–24.

Schindler, J. (1994) 'Alte und neue Fragen zum indogermanischen Nomen' in Jens Elmegård Rasmussen (ed.), *In honorem Holger Pedersen: Kolloquium der Indogermanischen Gesellschaft vom 25 bis 28 März 1993 in Kopenhagen.* Wiesbaden: Reichert, 397–400.

Schmidt, K. H. (1992) 'Latein und Keltisch: Genetische Verwandtschaft und areale Beziehungen' in Oswald Panagl and Thomas Krisch (eds.), *Latein und Indogermanisch: Akten des Kolloquiums der Indogermanischen Gesellschaft, Salzburg, 23–26 September 1986.* Innsbruck: Institut für Sprachwissenschaft der Universität Innsbruck, 29–51.

Schrader, O. (1907) *Sprachvergleichung und Urgeschichte, Teil I* (3rd edn.). Jena: Costenoble (reprinted in 1980, Hildersheim/New York: Olms).

Schrijver, P. (1991) *The reflexes of the Proto-Indo-European laryngeals in Latin.* Amsterdam/Atlanta: Rodopi.

Silvestri, D. (1993) 'I più antichi documenti epigrafici del latino' in E. Campanile (ed.), *Caratteri e diffusione del latino in età arcaica*'. Pisa: Giardini, 97–118.

Thurneysen, R. (1946) *A grammar of Old Irish* (2nd edn.), translated by D. A. Binchy and O. Bergin. Dublin: Institute for Advanced Studies.

Villaneuva Svensson, M. (1999) 'The Italic simple *R*-endings'. *Glotta* 75, 252–66.

Vine, B. (1998) 'Remarks on the archaic Latin "Garigliano Bowl" inscription'. *Zeitschrift für Papyrologie und Epigraphik* 121, 257–62.

Szemerényi, O. J. L. (1996) *Introduction to Indo-European linguistics.* Oxford: Oxford University Press.

Wachter, R. (1987) *Altlateinische Inschriften.* Bern: Peter Lang.

Watkins, C. (1966) 'Italo-Celtic revisited' in H. Birnbaum and J. Puhvel (eds.), *Ancient Indo-European dialects.* Berkeley and Los Angeles: California University Press, 29–50.

Chapter II

The Languages of Italy

2.1 Latin and the Languages of Italy

Italy was once peopled by speakers of many different languages, but the only variety other than Latin and its descendants to survive into the modern period is Greek, originally brought by colonists, and still spoken in remote parts of Calabria and Apulia. All the other ancient languages of Italy disappeared in the early years of the Roman Empire, leaving only epigraphic remains and occasional words in Roman and Greek literary and sub-literary sources. Even so, enough remains of these languages to piece together much of their grammar and many items of vocabulary, and new discoveries in recent years have resulted in substantial progress in some areas. The South Picene inscriptions, written in an IE language closely related to Umbrian and Oscan, have only been fully deciphered for 20 years, and our understanding of Etruscan has been advanced by the publication of the Pyrgi gold tablets, discovered in 1964, and the Tabula Cortonensis in 2000 (Agostiniani and Nicosia 2000). The importance of the non-Latin languages of Italy for the study of Latin has long been recognized. Ever since antiquity, changes in Latin have been explained as the effect of contact with native speakers of non-Latin languages. The Roman scholar Varro (in the *de lingua Latina*) attempted to explain the meaning and history of a number of Latin words through comparisons with Sabine and Oscan vocabulary, and Cicero's friend Atticus lamented the decline of Latin purity through the influx of speakers from outside Rome (*Brutus* 258, see 6.3). In more recent years, influence from neighbouring languages has been seen as the root of a number of Latin changes, principally in phonology and lexis, and the other IE languages spoken in Italy have been used to help explain Latin morphological and syntactic developments. In order to understand the early history of Latin it is consequently vital to have a good understanding of these languages of Italy, and the nature of the relationship between them and Latin.

The eventual dominance of the Latin language can be seen in the epigraphic record. There are well over 130,000 Latin inscriptions which survive from antiquity, found not just in the Italian peninsula and islands, but throughout the Roman Empire. No other language of Italy can match this number of texts or geographical spread. However, if we take a cut-off point of 100 BC and look at the inscriptions that survive before that date, the picture looks very different. There are over 9,000 Etruscan texts surviving before this date but only around 3,000 in Latin. If we go further back in time the importance of Latin diminishes further. There are only four or five Latin inscriptions datable to before 600 BC and over 150 Etruscan ones in the same period. Etruscan is a non-IE language; there are also IE languages which are better attested than Latin in the early period. South Picene, one of a group of IE languages known as 'Sabellian', is recorded in over 20 inscriptions from a wide area in east central Italy before 300 BC, 19 of them on stone. In the same period there are fewer Latin texts of more than a single word in length, and only six inscriptions on stone. We also have substantial amounts of evidence for other IE languages from before the Roman expansion: Oscan (over 300 texts) spoken over a wide area of southern Italy, Umbrian (attested in the lengthy Iguvine Tables) from central Italy north of Rome, Venetic (around 300 texts) from the north-east and Messapic (around 600 texts) from the 'heel' of Italy.

A number of other languages are known from Italy in the first millennium BC: both IE (Faliscan; minor languages of the 'Sabellian' group such as Marrucinian, Paelignian, Volscian etc.; Gaulish, Lepontic) and non-IE (Etruscan, Raetic, North Picene) – and there are doubtless others which have left no trace. Some linguistic varieties from ancient Italy are attested in such small quantities that it becomes difficult to ascertain whether they are separate languages. Thus the indigenous language spoken in Bruttium, the toe of Italy, before the southward expansion of Oscan speakers in the fourth/third century BC, is known from just a single inscription, of less than 20 letters in length, which is most plausibly interpreted as containing a personal name (Ps 2 in Rix 2002). There are also two inscriptions from south-west Lucania (Ps 1, Ps 20) which have been taken to be the language of the Oenotri (see further Poccetti 1988 and Bugno et al. 2001).

It is not just the number of languages in this period which is remarkable, but also the intermixture of different languages within fairly

restricted areas, particularly in central Italy. An impression of the geographical proximity of a number of different languages can be gained
from examining the finds of inscriptions from an area within a 100 km
radius of Rome. Of course, the presence of an inscription, particularly
one on a portable object such as a jug or a fibula, is no guarantee that
the language was spoken in the area, but the cumulative picture from the
epigraphic finds must bear some relation to the speaker profile of the area.
From within Rome itself Etruscan inscriptions have been found on
vases and on an ivory token, and important Etruscan cities lie in the
immediate vicinity to the north (Veii) and west (Caere) of Rome. There
is evidence for a Greek presence in Rome and the vicinity from the eighth
century on; the earliest inscription from Italy in any language, and one
of the earliest alphabetic Greek inscriptions found anywhere, is the single
word, read as *eulin* and interpreted as *eúlinos* 'spinning well', scratched
on a pot found in the burial of a woman at Osteria dell' Osa, 20 km east of
Rome, dated to around 770 BC (*Supplementum Epigraphicum Graecum*
42 899). Greek inscriptions have also been found at Rome and throughout Latium and southern Etruria, and there are likely to have been Greek
merchant communities at the ports, as we know there were at Graviscae
and Pyrgi in southern Etruria, and elsewhere. At Pyrgi there was also a
community of Punic traders, as evidenced from the discovery of the famous
gold tablets with Punic and Etruscan texts recording a religious donation
in around 500 BC. Faliscan, the language of Italy which has the closest
affinity to Latin, was also spoken in Etruria in the towns of Falerii and
Capena 45 km and 30 km north of Rome with texts surviving from the
seventh to the third century BC.

To the north and east of Rome we have evidence for a number of
different IE languages of the Sabellian group. These all share distinctive
features of phonology and innovations in morphology, which we shall
discuss later in the chapter. Umbrian, the variety for which we have the
longest text, was spoken principally in the area east of the Tiber, and
survives in inscriptions from the fourth to first century BC. Particular
Umbrian linguistic features include a reduction of inherited diphthongs
and the loss of final consonants. There are very few contemporary
inscriptions from the territory of the Sabines, the Aequi and the Marsi,
whose territories lay south of Umbria, but those that do survive show
similar features to Umbrian, and share the same characteristic onomastic
system (see further below). We also have evidence of an earlier Sabellian
linguistic stratum in the South Picene texts, most of which were found east
of the Apennines, except for one text discovered at Cures, 20 km N of
Rome (Sp RI 1 in Rix 2002). South Picene shares some linguistic features
with the later languages, for example, the South Picene word **kuprí/
qupíríh**, plausibly interpreted as an adverb 'well', only has equivalents in

the Sabine word for 'good' *ciprum* (glossed by Varro *de Lingua Latina* V. 159) and Umbrian, *cubra-* / **kupra-** 'good' (note that, conventionally, texts in the Sabellian languages in native alphabets are transcribed in **bold**, texts in the Latin alphabet are transcribed in *italic*). In other respects, however, South Picene is so divergent from Umbrian that it must be taken as a separate language: the 3rd person singular perfect verb form *-út* (as **opsút** 'he made') shows an ending completely at odds with the Umbrian ending *-e* (**dede** 'he gave') etc.

The Hernici and the Volsci are known from Greek and Latin historical sources to have occupied an area just east and south of Rome, which was later to become part of Latium. Both peoples fought for and against the Romans at different times from the fifth century BC until the late fourth century BC when the Hernici were granted Roman citizenship and Roman colonies were established in the Volscian area. Our knowledge of the Hernician and Volscian language is scant, although Latin and inscriptional sources suggest that they were separate. The emperor Marcus Aurelius refers to the *lingua Hernica* in a letter to Fronto (Fronto I. p. 174), and the playwright Titinius writes *uolsce fabulantur* 'they speak in Volscian' (*com.* 104). From Hernician territory there are only two readable inscriptions (He 2 and He 3 in Rix 2002), both short vase inscriptions from Anagnia, one from the sixth and one the third century. The language is clearly Sabellian, although neither inscription shows any particular affinity with Umbrian or South Picene. From the area inhabited by the Volscians there are also only two texts: a three-word inscription from Satricum which dates from the fifth century BC (VM 1 in Rix 2002), and a bronze tablet with four lines of text in the Latin alphabet associated with Velitrae (VM 2 in Rix 2002), although not certainly from there, which is dated to the third century BC. The language of the text from Satricum may be close to Umbrian, but the bronze tablet supposedly from Velitrae shows some important divergences from all other contemporary Sabellian languages; for example, it shows no unambiguous example of the merger of inherited long *$*e$* and short *$*i$* (see further below).

Speakers of the most widespread Sabellian language, Oscan, and the closely related variety Paelignian also came into close contact with the inhabitants of Latium. We do not have evidence for Oscan earlier than the fourth century. Despite this Oscan is phonologically more conservative than South Picene and Umbrian, since all inherited Sabellian diphthongs are preserved. Early Latin texts have also been found in areas within close range of major Oscan settlements, for example a fifth-century Latin inscription, the 'Garigliano Bowl', has recently been found in the vicinity of Minturnae, in the south of Latium and less than 40 km from the major Oscan settlement of Capua, and another inscription (CIL I^2

5) comes from near Alba Fucens in Marsian territory just 20 km west of Corfinum where Paelignian was in use until the first century BC.

2.2 The Central-Italian *Koiné*, 700–400 BC

Numa Pompilius had a great reputation for justice and piety. He lived in the Sabine town of Cures, and was, by the standards of antiquity, deeply learned in all the laws of God and man. It has been said that he owed his learning to Pythagoras of Samos; but this is a mere shot in the dark, and is obviously untrue as it is not until a hundred years later, in the reign of Servius Tullius, that Pythagoras is known to have settled in southern Italy . . . But even if the dates fitted, how could Pythagoras' fame have reached the Sabines all the way from the south? What mutually intelligible language could he have used to awaken amongst them the desire for learning? Under whose protection could a man have travelled alone through so many people differing in language and manner of life? (Livy 1.18, translated by Aubrey de Sélincourt)

In the previous section we saw how diverse the linguistic map of central Italy was, but how much interaction was there between different speech communities? We shall look in the next chapter at the effect of the spread of Roman power in the peninsula on the other languages of Italy, and analyse there the historical sources which relate to the spread of Latin and the motivations for speakers to switch languages. For the period before the first inscriptions in Italy, there is no way of knowing exactly which language was spoken where and by whom. But in the period between the introduction of writing and the rise of Rome we do have some evidence, although meagre, which can help us to build up a picture of linguistic contact.

To the later Romans, such as Livy in the passage cited at the beginning of this section, it seemed inconceivable that Greek learning could have penetrated into Sabine territory, or that there could be any mutual understanding between Greek settlers and the indigenous inhabitants of Italy. But the earliest epigraphic texts tell a different story (see in general, Cristofani 1996). Texts in two (or more) different languages have been found in the same area, even in the same archaeological context. For example, in Capua an early Sabellian inscription recording the gift of a bronze stamnos (Rix 2002 Ps 3) was found in the same tomb as a cup with *mi racus* 'I belong to Racu' in Etruscan written on it (CIE 8680, Rix et al. 1991 Cm 2.67); in another sixth-century tomb, from nearby Pontecagnano, a vase inscribed *mi araθnas* 'I belong to Arathna' in Etruscan (CIE 8843, Rix et al. 1991 Cm 2.19) was found alongside a kylix vase with a Greek inscription (*SEG* 34 1019, Bailo Modesti 1984), and contemporary Sabellian inscriptions have been found in the same burial area. Of course, the presence of texts in different languages side by side does not necessarily mean that both were spoken by the same individual. The Greek vase inscription mentioned above records the Greek owners' names and an injunction not to steal the vase, a message which was presumably either ignored or not understood. True 'bilingual' inscriptions, i.e. those with the same message expressed in two different languages, are uncommon at all periods and usually the product of special circumstances.

Although direct evidence is rare, there is indirect evidence for bilingualism, and language shift. Particularly noteworthy in this regard is onomastic evidence, since the same onomastic system is found in Etruscan, Latin, Faliscan and the Sabellian languages (most likely including South Picene, although the evidence here is not clear-cut). As the onomastic system evolved in Latin, personal names could become quite complex, so that an individual such as Publius Cornelius Scipio Aemilianus Africanus might be identified by a concatenation of five names. However, at the basis of the Latin system is the use of a family name, termed the *gentile*, such as *Cornelius, Iulius* or *Claudius*, and specification of an individual through a *praenomen*, such as *Publius, Lucius* or *Aulus*, of which there were a limited number in the late Republic and Empire. An individual was further specified through mention of his father's praenomen, and the possible addition of one or more *cognomina*. The cognomen originated as a nickname or honorary title for an individual (as *Africanus*, commemorating an African triumph), but then could be developed to specify a branch of a family (as *Cornelius Scipio*), or a special association (as *Aemilianus* which reflects the fact that Publius Cornelius Scipio Aemilianus Africanus was the blood-son of Lucius Aemilius Paulus). As the Roman onomastic system developed in the late Republic and Empire, the cognomen increased in importance, and the praenomen became all but insignificant (see the survey of Roman onomastic practice by Salway 1994 for an overview).

Name formulae in the other languages of central Italy show some variations from the Latin system: in Umbrian, Volscian, Sabine and Marsian texts the indication of the father's name comes before the family name, and it is common in late Etruscan texts to include some indication of the mother's name; but all the languages share the same system of family names combined with a restricted set of praenomina. The use of cognomina is also found in the neighbours of Latin, although their use is never as widespread as in the Latin of the Roman imperial period. The system whereby all citizens have a *gentile* name as well as a praenomen is unique among the older IE languages of Europe. In Greece a (male) individual will be denoted by a single name, frequently a compound, which may be

(in *heluus* *e* remains before velar *l*, rather than developing to *o*, in *rufus* original **d^h* develops to *f* intervocalically, and in *rauus* original **g^h* is lost before *r*) which can be explained if they are loaned from Sabellian. The adoption of colour vocabulary need not reflect a high level of contact; it is possible (as Meiser has argued, 1996: 190 fn. 16) that these were introduced into Latin through the language of traders in animal hides and furs.

Although the level of lexical interchange outside religious language in Italy is generally low, there are other linguistic features that suggest some convergence between the different languages in the period immediately after the introduction of literacy. Most important is the adoption of an initial stress accent and the changes which took place concomitant with this. The accent of Classical Latin followed the so-called 'Law of the Penultimate': in polysyllabic words the penultimate syllable was stressed, unless this syllable was metrically light, in which case the antepenultimate was stressed. In pre-classical Latin, however, the word stress appears to have been placed on the initial syllable. The evidence for this is based principally on the behaviour of vowels in medial syllables: short vowels in open medial syllables are prone to syncope, and low and mid vowels in medial syllables are subject to processes of raising known collectively as 'vowel weakening' (see the fuller discussion of this process in Chapter IV). The effects of these changes can be seen most clearly in compound words and univerbations; for syncope, note *rettulī* 'I brought back' < **retetulai*; for vowel weakening, *reficiō* 'I restore' a compound of *re-* and the verb *faciō* and its passive participle *refectus* < *re-* and *factus*; and *īlicō* 'on the spot' a reduction of the Early Latin phrase *in stlocōd* 'in place-ABL'. In Latin the processes of syncope and vowel weakening do not appear to have taken place at the time of the earliest Latin texts. Thus the *Lapis Satricanus* from around 500 BC shows unweakened forms such as *Mamartei*, which are matched by the evidence of the other seventh- and sixth-century Latin inscriptions.

Etruscan and Sabellian languages also show an initial stress accent, which caused the syncope of short vowels in later syllables. In Etruscan, where we have the greatest amount of documentation for the seventh to fourth century BC, the period at which syncope is reflected in the script can be pinpointed to the first half of the fifth century: in Etruscan texts earlier than this date the name *Aulus* is written *Avile* or *Avele*; in later texts *Avle*. In Sabellian we have direct evidence for the existence of an initial word accent from the writing practice of the Oscans. In texts written in the Oscan script long vowels are sometimes written with a doubled vowel sign; this doubling is only found (with one exception) in word-initial syllables, suggesting a maintenance of vowel length under the word accent, but loss elsewhere. In Sabellian languages syncope of short medial vowels also takes place some time between the sixth and fourth century. For example, the gentile name *Peracis* which is found in a Sabellian inscription from Capua of around 500 BC appears as **perkium** (genitive plural) on a later Oscan text from the same area. Inherited terms in Sabellian and Latin may consequently end up with a similar shape; for example, the word meaning 'right' has a stem **destr-** in Oscan, *destr-* in Umbrian and *dextr-* in Latin, but the form must originally have been more like Greek *dexíteros*.

In this case, we are fortunate enough to have sufficient evidence to be able to assign a likely date to a sound change which affected many of the languages of central Italy. Consequently, we can know that the change which led to the similarity between Latin *dextr-* and Sabellian *destr-* took place when they were separate languages. More often we cannot date a linguistic change, and we may not be able to assess whether a particular development results from contact, or in the case of Latin and the Sabellian languages, reflects an earlier period of unity. We have already seen how some of the agreements in the religious vocabulary can be assigned to a date after contact with Greek speakers, but other changes may be much earlier. Our uncertainty over the chronology of sound changes and other innovations has led to a situation where the same linguistic innovations have been variously accounted as either contact phenomena or evidence that Latin and Sabellian derive from the same subgroup of IE. In section 2.4 we shall assess the arguments on both sides, but before answering this question we need to give a short linguistic account of the Sabellian languages, detailing their salient features, which we shall do through the analysis of text samples.

2.3   The Sabellian Languages

The term 'Sabellian' is now used to refer to the largest group of languages from ancient Italy. Sabellian languages are attested from as far north as the source of the Tiber in Umbria, to as far south as Bruttium. Texts date from the seventh to the first century BC. The languages are IE, and are written in a variety of scripts. As we have seen, the Sabellian group encompasses a number of different varieties, and the assessment of which varieties constitute a separate language is impossible given the evidence we have. Various attempts have been made to position the different varieties within a Sabellian family tree, but again we do not have sufficient data to be able to do this with any certainty. In the most recent edition of the Sabellian texts (Rix 2002), Rix constructs three groups. The first comprises northern varieties: Umbrian, Sabine, Marsian and Volscian; another texts from the centre and south of Italy: Oscan, Paelignian,

Vestinian, Marrucinian, Hernician; another group comprises South Picene and texts from Campania and Lucanian from before 400 BC, which are supposed to predate the expansion of the Oscan tribes to the south. It will be convenient to reproduce that division here, although this does not mean that Rix's alignment of the Sabellian varieties is unproblematic. We remind the reader that Oscan and Umbrian texts are usually reproduced in **bold** if they are written in the native script, and *italic* if written in Latin script. South Picene is written in a unique script, derived from the Etruscan alphabet, and is here reproduced in **bold**.

2.3.1 *South Picene*

The language of the South Picene texts has come under close scrutiny following the full publication in 1985 of three new texts and with them the confirmation that the sign <.> represented /o/, and <:> represented /f/ (Marinetti 1985). Most of the texts are markers of graves or tombs of chiefs, but the language used upon them seems to be highly stylized, incorporating alliteration and marked word order with discontinuous phrasing or interlacing syntax (an example is text (2) below). The interpretation of a number of forms in the small corpus is still uncertain, and we reproduce here four short texts and selections from texts, the meaning of which is generally agreed. We have given Latin equivalents to the first two, complete, texts.

Text (1) below is written on an imposing mid-sixth-century statue of a man, sometimes called 'The Warrior of Capestrano'. The text is unusual among South Picene inscriptions in that it has no indication of word-breaks (which elsewhere we have indicated by a colon), and the division into words here follows that of the editor. South Picene has a much fuller repertoire of signs for vowels than any other language of ancient Italy; unlike Etruscan and the other Sabellian languages it uses the vowel sign <o> and it has innovated new signs for other high vowels alongside /i/ and /u/ which are here transcribed by í and ú. (Note that in reproducing texts we follow the editorial conventions whereby square brackets enclose text which is missing through damage to the original inscription, but restored on the basis of parallels elsewhere.)

(1) Sp AQ 2 (as read by Rix 2002, as are all the texts given here).

ma kuprí koram   opsút aninis   rakinelís   pomp[úne]i
? well memorial-ACC.sg he-made Aninis-NOM.sg Rakinelis-NOM.sg. Pompo-DAT.sg.

'Aninis Rakinelis made this memorial well for Pompo.'
(Latin equivalent: *bene *koram fecit Annius Racinelius Pomponi.*)

(2)   Sp MC 1. A funerary inscription written on a large stone, which
      probably dates from the sixth or fifth century.

apaes: qupat [: e]smin : púpúnis : nír :   mefiín :
Apaes-NOM he-lies   this-LOC.sg=in Púpúnis-NOM chief-NOM middle-LOC.sg=in

veiat : vepetí
he-lies   stone-LOC.sg=in

'Apaes Púpúnis/the Picene lies in this; the chief lies in the middle of the
stone.'
(Latin equivalent: *Apaeus cubat in hoc Pomponius* * *ner in medio* * *lehit
lapide*).
The presence of two verbs in this short inscription is troubling; most
commentators explain the inscription as the amalgamation for 'poetic'
effect of two separate sentences interlaced by a single prepositional phrase.

(3)   Sp TE 1. A fragmentary stone cippus of the same date:

petroh : púpún[is : ní]r: e: súhúh: suaipis :
Petro-NOM Púpúnis-NOM chief.NOM from his-own-ABL.sg. if-anyone-NOM

ehuelí : . . .
he-?wants-OPT

'Petro Púpúnis/the Picene, the chief, from his own resources, if anyone
wants . . .'

(4)   Sp TE 6. A fragmentary stone stela of the late sixth century:

safinúm :   nerf :   persukant
Sabine-GEN.pl chief-NOM.pl they-call

'The chiefs of the Sabines call . . .'

Even from these short fragments, we can gather enough information to
show that these texts are distinctively 'Sabellian'; all of the following phonological developments (a)–(e) are also found in other Sabellian texts:

(a)   Inherited labio-velar consonants have lost the velar element of the
articulation and merged with labial consonants; thus the indefinite pronoun *$k^w is$ > appears as **pis** (cf. **suaipis** in (3)), compare Latin *quis*.

(b)   Inherited voiced aspirates *d^h and *b^h have merged and developed
to fricatives in all positions: note *$med^h yo$- 'middle' > **mefiín** (in (2)),
compare Latin *medius*; and the ethnic adjective *$Sab^h nīno$- > **safinúm**
(in (4)) compare Latin *Sabinus* (and *Samnium*). The South Picene

alphabet, like the Oscan and Umbrian alphabet, uses the same sign to denote a fricative in initial and medial position, but there is reason to believe that the Sabellian *f* was actually voiced between two vowels; note that in Oscan written in Greek letters, the Greek letter <b> is sometimes used in place of <f> as in the divine name *mefitis* written both <mefitei> and <mebitei>, probably representing [meβit-] (Stuart-Smith 2004: 90f.).

The Sabellian development recalls the Latin treatment of original 'voiced aspirates'. As we saw in Chapter I, their outcome in Latin is as fricatives in initial position, but voiced stops in medial position. The picture is complicated by the fact that in Faliscan, the sister language to Latin, the same development as in Sabellian is found: note Faliscan *carefo* = Latin *carebo*, *efiles* = Latin *aediles*. There are also Early Latin examples of *f* < medial $*b^h$, as, for example the 'Garigliano Bowl' (see 1.4.5) if *trifos* = *tribus* three-ABL.PL is correctly read and interpreted (see Vine 1998). (Note that most Classical Latin words with medial -*f*- can be explained as later loanwords from Sabellian languages, as *rufus* 'red' besides inherited *ruber* 'red'.) This suggests that at an earlier period in Latin the word-internal reflexes of voiced aspirates were also fricatives which were then merged with voiced stops. Such a merger of fricatives with voiced stops also helps explain other Latin sound changes, such as the development of $*$-*sr*- > -*br*- (e.g. *funebris* < $*$*funes-ri-*) which presumably took place via $*$-ðr- and $*$-βr-.

The Latin and Sabellian sound changes consequently appear similar – but how should we reconstruct the changes from PIE to the historically attested forms? This is still a matter of dispute, and there are several possible answers to this question. The account given here follows the work of Stuart-Smith (1996 and 2004) and works on the assumption that the reconstructed 'voiced aspirates' were in fact breathy voiced stops (see 1.4.1). In initial position the voiced aspirates were first realized as voiceless aspirates, and subsequently developed to voiceless fricatives. In medial position, voicing was retained, and the sounds developed to voiced fricatives. In Sabellian all fricatives with any front articulation (i.e. labial, dental and labio-velar) merged as /f/, in Latin this merger only affected word-initial forms. Word-internally the fricatives were kept separate, although /ð/ (the reflex of $*d^h$) merged with /β/ < $*b^h$ when in the context of lip-rounding. The developments in tabular form are set out below:

Word-initial position:

PIE	$*b^h$	$*d^h$	$*g^{wh}$	$*g^h$ / $*g'^h$
Stage I	f	θ	χ^w	χ
Sabellian	f	f	f	h
Latin	f	f	f	h

Word-internal position;

PIE	$*b^h$	$*d^h$	$*g^{wh}$	$*g^h$ / $*g'^h$
Stage I	β	δ	γ^w	γ
Sabellian	β	β	β	h
Latin	b	d	u	h

The first step of these developments, labelled Stage I in the above tables, may have been shared by Latin and Sabellian.

(c) Inherited long $*\bar{e}$ and long $*\bar{o}$ vowels raised. The outcome of long $*\bar{e}$ is usually written in South Picene with the letter í, for example nominative singular **nír** < $*n\bar{e}r$ (in (2)), nominative plural **nerf** < $*ner$- (in (4)). Cognate words meaning 'man' or 'hero' in Greek and Vedic show the same alternation between a long and short vowel in the paradigm of this word.

(d) Syncope of short vowels occurred before final $*-s$ in polysyllabic words, as probably in **púpúnis** $*-ios$ (in (2)), and found also in other South Picene texts, for example in a nominative singular **meitims**, perhaps meaning 'gift' with final syllable derived from < $*-mos$. This loss of short vowel before final $*-s$ also occurs in Early Latin following $-r$-, as in *sacer* < $*sakros$ and also following a cluster of consonant and $-t$- (as in *mens* < $*mentis$), although paradigmatic analogy has led to restitutions of the lost vowel in many cases. The Latin change, which occurs in a much more restricted set of phonological environments, must, however, be separate, since an Early Latin inscription (the fragmentary 'forum inscription,' CIL I² 1, dated to the sixth century) shows the unsyncopated form *sakros*.

(e) Final $*i$ was lost, as in the 3rd person verbal forms in -**at** and -**ant** which derive from original forms in $*-ti$ and $*-nti$. This change has also occurred early in the history of Latin (see 1.4.4), although in Latin some instances of final $*-i$ appear to have been retained, as in the locative singular ending of consonant stems $-e < *-i$, and in some neuter nouns and adjectives such as *mare* 'sea' < $*mori$, *omne* 'everything'. The reason for the double development of $*-i$ in Latin is not known for certain, but Rix (1996: 158 n.7 followed by Meiser 1998: 74) has suggested that final $*-i$ was retained if it bore the original accent, as $*ped-i$ the original locative of the PIE word for 'foot', which may lie behind the Latin ablative *pede*. Since not all locatives in $*-i$ carried the accent, and it is unlikely that the final $-i$ of neuter nouns in the nominative singular ever did, this explanation relies heavily on the operation of analogy across nominal declensions to restore final $*-i$ in these nominal paradigms. A further difficulty with this explanation is that the inherited PIE accent seems to have been replaced early in Latin; otherwise it has not had any effect on phonological developments.

2.3.2   Umbrian

Our text samples for Umbrian come from the Iguvine tables, the term used to designate seven large bronze tablets discovered in Gubbio in the fifteenth century. The tables detail the ritual procedure of a college of priests, with some portions written in the native Umbrian alphabet (derived from Etruscan with the addition of two extra letters) and others in the Latin alphabet. The passages in the Latin script show the effects of sound changes which are not found in the portions written in Umbrian script, and must consequently be written later. The first selection is taken from Table Ib line 16–19 (one of the earlier portions written in the Umbrian alphabet, and probably datable to before the second century BC):

(5)   Um 1 Ib 1–19

pune : menes :   akeřuniamem : enumek : etuřstamu :
when   come-2sg.FUT Acedonia-ACC.sg=in then   expel-IMPER

tuta :   tařinate :   trifu :   tařinate :   turskum :
people-ACC.sg of Tadinae-ACC.sg tribe-ACC.sg of-Tadinae-ACC.sg Etruscan-ACC.sg

naharkum : numem :   iapuzkum :   numem :   svepis :
Narcan-ACC.sg people-ACC.sg Iapudican-ACC.sg people-ACC.sg if=anyone-NOM.sg

habe : purtatu   (u)lu : pue : meřs :   est : feitu :   uru :
he-stays carry-IMPER to there where right-NOM.sg is   make-IMPER. there

peře : meřs :   est
what   right-NOM.sg is

'When you come to Acedonia, then they are to expel the people of Tadinae, the tribe of Tadinae, the Etruscan, the Narcan people, the Iapudican people. If anyone stays/is caught, bring him to that place, where it is right, do to him there what is right.'

The second passage of Umbrian is written in Latin Script and comes from Table Vb 8–10; it does not date later than the beginning of the first century BC:

(6)   Um 1 Vb 8–10

clauerniur   dirsas   herti   fratrus   atiersir   posti
Clavernii-NOM.pl give-3pl.SUBJ want-3sg.PASS brother-DAT.pl Atiedi-DAT.pl per

acnu   farer   opeter   p. IIII agre   tlatie
year-ACC.sg spelt-GEN.sg choice-GEN.sg 4 lb   land-GEN.sg Latin-GEN.sg

piquier   martier   et śesna   homonus duir
of-Picus-GEN.sg Martius-GEN.sg and dinner-ACC.sg man.-DAT.pl two.DAT.pl

puri   far   eiscurent   ote a.   VI
who-NOM.pl spelt-ACC.sg ask-3pl.FUT.PERF or   asses 6

'It is required that the Clavernii give the Atiedian brothers 4lb. of choice spelt of the Latin land of Picus Martius per year, and dinner to the two men who will have asked for the spelt or 6 asses.'

Some of the Sabellian features of Umbrian are immediately obvious. Note, for example, the univerbation **svepis** 'if anyone' which corresponds exactly with South Picene **suaipis** in TE 1 (text (3) above). However, Umbrian has undergone a large number of complex sound changes in comparison with most other Sabellian languages, which makes some Umbrian forms difficult to assess at first glance. Some of the Umbrian sound changes are analogous to changes found in Latin, note in particular the following:

1   Rhotacism: intervocalic *-s- changed to -r- as in *puri* 'who' < *$k^w\bar{o}s$-i, an extended form of the nominative plural of the pronoun *$k^w o$-/*$k^w i$-. In the later portions of the text written in Latin script, final *-s underwent the same change if it occurred after a vowel, so **svepis**, for example, appears as *sopir*.

2   Loss of final consonants: all final consonants are prone to loss, although morphological pressures may lead to some restititution of consonants. The writing system is however inconsistent in the representation of final consonants, note **tuta : tařinate : trifu : tařinate :** with loss of final -*m* in every word, immediately followed by **turskum : naharkum : numem: iapuzkum :** with retention of the final consonant. It is likely that these writings represent different strategies for conveying a nasalized final vowel; note that the original final sound of **numem** was *-*n*, and the writing with -**m** is best explained as a representation of nasalization.

3   Palatalization: *k was palatalized in Umbrian before a front vowel to a sound represented by a special letter ç in the Umbrian alphabet, and a modified form of *s* (transcribed *ś*) in the Latin alphabet. Hence *śesna* is an exact cognate to Latin *cēna* 'dinner' (< *kesna*); *g is also palatalized to *i* before a front vowel.

4   Monophthongization of diphthongs; all inherited diphthongs in Umbrian undergo a process of monophthongization. Diphthongs with second member *u* merge as a back vowel (**u**/*o*), those with second member *i* merge as a front vowel (**e**/*e*), except for *oi which follows the pattern of the *u*-diphthongs.

There are also a number of phonological developments which affect Umbrian alone, such as the passage of an intervocalic *d to a sound written with the sign ř in the Umbrian alphabet but by the digraph rs in the Latin alphabet, as **peře** 'what' < *$k^w id$-i, an extended form of the neuter singular of the relative pronoun *$k^w o$- / *$k^w i$-.

The length of the Iguvine tables means that we know a lot more about Umbrian morphology and syntax than we do about South Picene, and several morphosyntactic features found in Umbrian appear to be as characteristic of Sabellian languages as the phonological developments which we found in the South Picene texts:

1 Genitive singular in *-*eis* for consonant stems and *o-stem nouns. This ending is not directly evidenced in Umbrian – but lies behind the ending -**es**/-**er** (for example *farer opeter* < *$b^h ars$-eis $opet$-eis, note that *$b^h ars$- is a consonant stem (cf. Latin *far*) and *$opet$- an o-stem participle formed with the suffix *-to- (cf. Latin -*tus*)). A genitive singular in -**es** is found in South Picene and Oscan -**eís** preserves the original diphthong. The Umbrian and South Picene forms must derive from *-*eis* and not *-*es*, since a short vowel would be lost by syncope before final *-*s* in Sabellian. The ending has usually been explained as a borrowing of the i-stem genitive singular *-*eis*, which spread to consonant stems and o-stems after syncope of short vowels before final -*s* had made the nominative singulars of these three declensions identical.

2 Nominative plural of o-stem and a-stem nouns and pronouns in *-$\bar{o}s$ and *-$\bar{a}s$ respectively. These endings are inherited from IE for the nominal stems, but (as we saw in section 1.4.3) in Latin they have been replaced by the endings *-oi and *-ai which originally were restricted to the pronominal declensions. The Sabellian languages have levelled the different endings of the pronouns and nouns, but in the opposite direction to that taken by Latin. They have retained the original nominal ending and transferred them to the pronouns, as nominative plural *puri* 'who' < *$k^w \bar{o}s$-i.

3 Imperative medio-passive ending *-*mo* as in the deponent **etuřstamu** 'expel', which is matched in Oscan *censamur* (with added 'passive' -*r*) but in no other IE language, although it is possible that the Latin 2nd person plural medio-passive -*mini* may be connected in some way (see Meiser 1998: 219).

4 Remodelling of the verbal system with the creation of new paradigms. These include the 'future' formed with a suffix *-*s*- and the 'future perfect'. The 'future perfect' is the name given to a formation which denotes the priority of a future action in a subordinate clause against another future event in the main clause. In Sabellian,

and no other IE language, the future perfect is formed with a suffix
* -us- (compare the Latin marker -is-, see 1.4.4). In the second
Umbrian passage there is an example of such a verb form in a
relative clause: *eiscurent* 'they will have asked' which is used in order
to specify that it must take place before the action of the matrix clause
verb *dirsas* 'they should give'.

The remodelling of the verbal system can be seen to proceed along
similar lines to those detailed for Latin in 1.4.4. In Sabellian, as in Latin,
the aspect-centred verbal system as reconstructed for PIE, appears to
have been given up in favour of a paradigm with a basic split between
a *perfectum* stem and an *infectum* stem. The two future formations are
associated with different stems, as in Latin: the * -s- future is attached to
the *infectum* and the * -us- 'future perfect' is formed on the perfectum
stem, as can be seen from the following (Oscan) examples:

Infectum	* -s- Future	Perfectum	* -us- Future Perfect
deiua-	*deiuas-*		
tríbaraka-		**tríbarakatt-**	**tríbarakattus-**

Note that although the * *s*-future has clear cognates elsewhere in IE, the
Sabellian languages have innovated in attaching the marker * -s- to a stem
form (that of the infectum). Thus the Umbrian future **menes** given in
text (5) above is derived not from the root *$g^w em$-* + suffix * -s- (+ ending * *s*) but from infectum stem *$g^w emye$-* > * *benie-* + suffix * -s-, just as
the Latin futures *amabo, habebo*, etc. show the infectum stems with a
further marker (the initial *m-* instead of *b-* in **menes** is unexplained, see
Untermann 2000: 144 for various theories). Structurally, then, the
Sabellian future and future perfect are formed in an exactly analogous way
to the Latin future and future perfect, even though the actual morphs
used differ. The significance of the structural similarity of the reshaped
Sabellian verbal system to the Latin verb will be further examined in the
next section.

   Umbrian also shares some morphological developments with other
Sabellian languages which are now recognized to be the result of
parallel changes after the separation of the different Sabellian languages.
A particularly striking example of such a development is the secondary
3rd person plural verbal ending -ns. We have an example of this form in
text (6): *dirsas* (elsewhere written *dirsans*) is the 3rd person plural of the
subjunctive, which, in Sabellian as in Latin, regularly takes secondary endings. The ending -ns is found in all the Sabellian languages later than the
fourth century BC for which we have the appropriate material: Umbrian,
Volscian, Paelignian and Oscan. It was assumed to be a common

Sabellian innovation before the decipherment of South Picene and the discovery of an early Sabellian text from southern Italy (Ps 20 in Rix 2002) which show secondary 3rd person plural endings -**úh** and -*od* respectively, representing direct continuations of PIE *-(o)nt* (via a form *-ōd* with nasalized vowel). The replacement of this ending by -*ns*, which must ultimately derive from a remarked -*n* < *-nt*, must have taken place once the different Sabellian languages had already diversified and spread over a large area of Italy. Developments such as this make it extremely difficult to ascertain what the 'proto-Sabellian' language must have looked like, and leave open the possibility that other Sabellian similarities are also the result of some sort of convergence.

2.3.3 Oscan

There is a greater number of texts written in Oscan than any other Sabellian language, and, if we are to believe Strabo's account, plays in Oscan were performed in Rome (Strabo 5.3.6, see however Adams 2003: 119f. for serious doubt cast on this claim). Speakers of Oscan spread throughout southern Italy in the fourth century BC, and Oscan replaced the former languages spoken in this area. Oscan is far more transparent than the other languages we have considered, since it is generally conservative in phonology, and has a consistent orthography with signs for the two extra vowels written in the native script **í** (the outcome of original *i* and long *ē*) and **ú** (the outcome of original *u* and long *ō*), This linguistic conservativism makes it much easier to apply comparative methods to Oscan vocabulary.

The following text records an agreement between two communities in Campania about the use of a sanctuary of Hercules (Cm 1 in Rix 2002).

(7) Cm 1 A 1–18

maiiúí.   vestirikiíúí.   mai(ieís).   siíl(úí) / prupukid.
Maius-DAT.sg Vestricius-DAT.sg Maius-GEN.sg. Silus-DAT.sg ?

sverruneí. kvaístu/reí. abellanúí.   íním. maiiúí /   lúvkiíúí.
?   quaestor-DAT.sg of-Abella-DAT.sg and   Maius-DAT.sg Lucius-DAT.sg

mai(ieís).   pukalatúí / medíkeí.   deketasiúí. núvla/núí.
Maius-GEN.sg Puclatus-DAT.sg magistrate-DAT.sg ?-DAT.sg of-Nola-DAT.sg

íním. lígatúís.   abellan[úís] / íním. lígatúís.   núvlanúís /
and   legates-DAT.pl of-Abella-DAT.sg and   legates-DAT.pl of-Nola-DAT.pl

pús.   senateís.   tanginúd / suveís.   pútúrúspíd.
who-NOM.pl senate-GEN.sg decision-ABL.sg each-GEN.sg whichever

lígat[ús] / fufans.   ekss. kúmbened. / sakaraklúm.
legates-NOM.pl be(come)-3pl.PAST so   agreed-3sg.PERF sanctuary-NOM.sg

herekleís. [ú]p/ **slaagid. púd.** **íst.** **iním.**
Hercules-GEN.sg in ?-ABL.sg which-NOM.sg is-3sg.PRES and

teer[úm] / **púd.** **úp. eísúd.** **sakaraklúd** [. íst] /
land-NOM.sg which-NOM.sg in this-ABL.sg sanctuary-ABL.sg is-3sg.PRES

púd. **anter. teremníss.** **eh[trúis]** / **íst.** **paí.**
which-NOM.sg between boundaries-ABL.pl. outer.ABL.pl is-3sg.PRES which-NOM.pl

teremenniú. **mú[iníkad]** / **tanginúd.** **prúftú. set.**
boundaries-NOM.pl mutual-ABL.sg decision-ABL.sg approved are-3pl.PRES

r[ehtúd] / **amnúd. puz. ídík.** **sakara[klúm]** / **iním. ídík.**
right-ABL.sg ?-ABL.sg that this-NOM.sg sanctuary-NOM.sg and this-NOM.sg

terúm. **múiník[úm]. múiníkeí. tereí. fusíd.**
land.NOM.sg mutual-NOM.sg mutual-LOC.sg land-LOC.sg be-3sg.IMPERF.SUBJ.

'Maius Vestricius Silus, son of Maius [two words of unclear sense], Quaestor of Abella, and Maius Lucius Puclatus, son of Maius, *meddix degetasis* [?] of Nola, and the legates of Abella and Nola, whoever have become legates by the decision of their respective senates, have agreed as follows: the Sanctuary of Hercules which is on the [word of uncertain sense] and the land which is within this Sanctuary, and which is within the outer boundaries which have been approved by mutual agreement [two words of uncertain reading and sense], [they agreed] that this Sanctuary and this land should be mutual on mutual territory.'

This official record smacks of the language of bureaucracy. However this short text contains two of the most important verbal forms in the whole of Sabellian for the historian of the Latin language. Firstly, the last verb of the text as reproduced above, **fusíd**, shows that the Sabellian languages had undergone the same restructuring of the morphosyntax of dependent clauses that took place in Latin. In Greek and Indo-Iranian, as we saw in 1.4.4, there are two non-indicative modal forms, which are used in a variety of clause types, and there was originally no restriction in using either mood in embedded clauses. By the fifth century BC Greek had developed a rule, termed 'sequence of mood' in traditional grammar, which favoured the optative in subordinate clauses where the verb in the matrix sentence refers to the past. In the Sabellian languages, as in Latin, the difference between two separate modal formations was lost, and only one non-indicative modal category remains. However, Latin and Sabellian have both evolved tense-marked subjunctives, as part of a syntactic process generally termed 'sequence of tenses': a subjunctive in an embedded clause is obligatorily marked also for the tense of the verb in the matrix clause. In Latin the sequence of tense rules are as follows:

Time reference	*Marking of subordinate clause verb*
of matrix clause verb	
Non-past time	present subjunctive/perfect subjunctive
Past time	imperfect subjunctive/pluperfect subjunctive

The 'imperfect' and 'pluperfect' subjunctives are new modal formations marked as 'past', which do not have any analogue in the older IE languages. The imperfect subjunctive is formed from the *infectum* stem and the pluperfect from the *perfectum* stem. We have only a few examples of complex sentence structures in Sabellian which show a subjunctive used in an embedded clause, yet examples such as the Oscan text given above (7) show that the same sequence of tense rules appear to apply in Sabellian as apply in Latin. Thus in the above text:

ekss kúmbened . . .	**puz . . .**	**fusíd**
(Perfect Indic.)	conjunction	(Subjunctive formed with *-sē-)
ita conuenit	*ut*	*esset*
'It was agreed . . . that . . . it should be . . .'		

Compare the construction with a non-past verb in the matrix clause in the *Tabula Bantina* (Lu 1 in Rix 2002), an Oscan text, written in the Latin script:

factud	*pous . . .*	*deicans*
(Imperative)	conjunction	(Subjunctive formed with *-ā-)
facito	*ut*	*dicant*
'See that they say . . .'		

The subjunctive used in the first example, **fusíd**, is marked with a morph -**sí**- which distinguishes it from present subjunctives, marked with a long *ē or long *ā. Since the morph -**sí**- is exactly cognate to the Latin morph used to mark the imperfect subjunctive (as in *esset*, or *amārēs*, both can be derived from *-sē-), it is reasonable to assume that they represent a common innovation of a new subjunctive formation. However, this innovation is difficult to date. If we see it as part of the evolution of a more 'bureaucratic' prose style which took place in the period of the first-millennium Italian *koiné*, it must have spread across the languages of central Italy when they were distinct idioms.

The origin of the marker *sē of this new tense-marked subjunctive is uncertain, and thus offers little help on the date of its innovation. One theory is that it originates as a modal formation of a future stem (Meiser 1993b). In IE, subjunctives could be formed with a suffix *-ē-, and such formations are widespread in Sabellian. The regular means of forming a

subjunctive for the *perfectum* stem, for example, is through the suffix
*$*\bar{e}$; thus the Oscan perfect subjunctive **tríbarakatt-í-ns** < perfect stem
(**tríbarakatt-**) + *$*\bar{e}$ (í) + personal ending (**-ns**). A 'future subjunctive' would
thus be formed by addition of *$*\bar{e}$ to the future stem, formed in *$*-s-$ as
we have already seen. But how does a 'future subjunctive' become used
as a subjunctive form which reflects the past tense of a verb in a higher
clause? The answer may be through use in conditional clauses. In Latin
the imperfect subjunctive is used in counterfactual conditional clauses, as
in the following example:

Plautus *Casina* 811:

si equus esses,   esses   indomitabilis
if horse   you-were-IMP.SUBJ. you were-IMP.SUBJ. untameable

'If you were a horse, you'd be untameable.'

Unfortunately, the scanty Sabellian texts do not contain an example of a
counterfactual condition, but if we hypothesize that the Sabellian languages
also used the imperfect subjunctive, as Latin does, then we may be able
to find a way to explain how a future modal tense may become reinterpreted as a past-marked modal. The development might be thought of
as proceeding in three stages:

1   If *$*fus\bar{e}t$ X, *$*fus\bar{e}t$ Y 'If he were to be X (in the future), he would
   be Y':

   *$*fus\bar{e}t$ = FUT. + MODAL.

2   If *$*fus\bar{e}t$ X, *$*fus\bar{e}t$ Y 'If he were X (now), he would be Y':

   *$*fus\bar{e}t$ = PRES. + MODAL.

3   *$*fus\bar{e}t$ re-interpreted, in the protasis, as preceding the apodosis and
   thus located in the past 'If he had been X, he would be Y':

   *$*fus\bar{e}t$ now has the value PAST + MODAL.

In stage (1) the formation in *$*-s\bar{e}-$ has the original meaning of a future
modal formation, and its presence in protasis and apodosis indicates a remote
possibility in the future. In stage (2) this remote possibility is re-interpreted
as a counterfactual. The re-interpretation may have arisen when the present subjunctive (which in Latin and Sabellian languages derives from the
earlier PIE optative) started to be used to refer to remote future events
even in conditional clauses (Coleman 1996: 405) and encroached on the
original meaning of the *$*-s\bar{e}-$ formation. Once the shift in stage (2) has
been made, the verb in the apodosis may be replaced by other verbal
forms, perhaps to denote a counterfactual in the past ('if he were X, he
would have been Y'). In stage (3) the *$*-s\bar{e}-$ form in the protasis, since it

is logically antecedent to the apodosis, is reinterpreted as also chronologically antecedent, and comes to be felt as having a past sense as well as a modal sense. It is in this function that it is extended to use in embedded clauses.

This chain of events constitutes a significant linguistic innovation, and it is striking that the same formation is found in Latin as well as the Sabellian languages. Another linguistic innovation which appears to be shared by Latin and Sabellian is the creation of a new imperfect tense. That is, a tense which belongs to the *infectum* stem but which refers to action in the past. In Latin, as we have seen in Chapter I, this tense is formed in all verbs except the copula with the morph -*bā*-. There is one formation in Sabellian which appears to show the same development, and that is the verb **fufans** which occurs only in the text sample given in (7) above. The form **fufans** taken at face value appears to show a cognate to the Latin morph -*bā*-, Oscan -*fa*- (both can be directly derived from a preform *-$b^h\bar{a}$-), attached to the stem **fu**- which we have also seen in the verb **fusíd**. The context of the verb supports an interpretation as an imperfect tense verb as well:

pús . . .	lígat[ús]	fufans.
who	legates	were

'who(ever) were legates'

However, since this is the *only* example of this formation in Sabellian we must be careful that we do not build too much on this one form. Note that there is also no Latin equivalent to this verbal form; an imperfect stem *fubam* is nowhere attested. An alternative explanation for the Oscan verb is also available. In Sabellian, there is evidence for a *perfectum* stem *fuf- from the root **fu**-, which derives from a reduplicated PIE stative perfect form (Meiser 2003: 201). Thus a 3rd person plural perfect **fufens** is attested twice in Oscan and an earlier 3rd person plural form *fufuwod* in an early Sabellian text from the far south of Italy (Ps 20 in Rix 2002). The form **fufans** could consequently be explained differently; not as the imperfect of the verb 'to be' but as the pluperfect, formed, like the Latin pluperfect, with a morph *$\bar{a}$, marking 'past', to a verb meaning 'become', which we know to have been the original meaning of this root (this explanation was put forward by Rix 1983: 102 fn. 15). And this interpretation is also supported by the context:

pús . . .	lígat[ús]	fufans.
who	legates	had become

'who(ever) had become legates'

It is of course possible to imagine that **fufans** has become re-interpreted as an imperfect, particularly since most other derivatives of this root have come to be incorporated into the paradigm of the verb 'to be' in Sabellian (as have the *fu-* forms in Latin), and it is possible that the re-interpretation of forms such as **fufans** has led to the spread of a morph -**fa**- to mark the imperfect. However, this question cannot be settled without further evidence from the Sabellian languages of imperfect formations, which is at present lacking.

The second Oscan text that we shall consider (Po 3 in Rix 2002) is a much shorter stone tablet found near a palaestra in Pompeii, recording the donor of building funds and the magistrate responsible for the construction. The original text may date to the second century BC, but was later re-copied in the imperial period (see Poccetti 1982). It is possible to give an exact Latin equivalent for every word in this inscription, which we have included beneath the morphological analysis:

(8) Po 3

v(iíbis).   aadirans.   v(iíbieís).   eítiuvam.   paam /
Vibius   Adiranus   Vibii filius   pecuniam   quam
Vibius-NOM.sg Adiranus-NOM.sg Vibius-GEN.sg money-ACC.sg which-ACC.sg

vereiiaí.   púmpaiianaí.   trístaa/mentud.   deded.   eísak.
reipublicae   Pompeianae   (ex) testamento   dedit   (ex) ea
state-DAT.sg Pompeian-DAT.sg   gave-3.PERF this-ABL.sg

eítiuvad / v(iíbis).   viínikiís   mr.   kvaísstur.
pecunia   Vibius   Vinicius   Mr. filius quaestor
money-ABL.sg Vibius-NOM.sg Vinicius-NOM.sg Mr-GEN.sg quaestor-NOM.sg

púmp/aiians.   tríibúm.   ekak.   kúmben/nieís. tanginud.
Pompeianus   domum   hanc   (de) conuentus   sententia
Pompeian-NOM.sg house-ACC.sg this-ABL.sg senate-GEN.sg   decision-ABL.sg

úpsannam./   deded.   ísídum.   prúfatted
faciendam   dedit   idem   probauit
make-FUT.PASS.PART.ACC.sg gave-3.PERF same-NOM.sg approved-3.PERF

'The money which Vibius Adiranus son of Vibius gave to the Pompeian state in his will, from this money Vibius Vinicius son of Mr., the Pompeian quaestor, arranged for this house to be built by the decision of the senate and the same man approved it.'

This inscription has been taken to show the degree of assimilation between Oscan and Latin in the context of advancing Roman hegemony in the last centuries of the Roman republic. There are clear examples of lexical borrowings for terms relating to law and governance: **kvaísstur** is a loan from Latin *quaestor*, and **trístaamentud** is probably a loan from Latin *testamentum* 'will', although adapted in the first syllable to the native word for 'witness' **tr(i)stus**. The phrase **kúmbennieís tanginud** is equivalent to the Latin formula *de senatus sententia*, and may show the same specialization in meaning of the noun **tanginud** from 'thought' to 'decision' which Latin *sententia* underwent. Note that Oscan here retains the original use of the bare ablative to mark origin or source, whereas Latin has a prepositional phrase; since Oscan still has a fully functioning locative case, there is not the same need to reinforce the ablative meaning with a preposition, as there is in Latin. The closing phrase of the text (which reoccurs in other Oscan building inscriptions) has a close analogy to a common Latin formula: Latin *faciendum curauit eidemque probauit* (CIL I² *passim*). Note also the variant formula *portas faciendas* **dederunt** *eisdemque probauerunt* from an inscription from Formiae (CIL I² 1563).

There is also some syntactic congruence with Latin. The subject and object of the initial relative clause, the name **v(iíbis). aadirans. v(iíbieís)** and the word for 'money', **eítiuvam**, are fronted to initial position in the sentence, and the word for money is repeated again in the matrix clause in a different case. The inclusion of an antecedent to a relative in both the matrix clause and the relative clause is a feature of archaic IE syntax, and may have been inherited in Oscan, but it is perhaps preferable to see the construction here as influenced by Latin legal language, which shows a predilection for topicalizing antecedents and other nouns before preposed relative clauses (see Adams 2003: 137). Compare, for example the *Lex Cornelia de XX questoribus* (CIL I² 587) II 31f. (from 81 BC): *uiatores praecones, quei ex hac lege lectei sublectei erunt, eis uiatoribus praeconibus magistratus proue magistratu mercedis item tantundem dato* . . . In this Latin law, as in the Oscan text, we find the antecedent to the relative fronted before the relative clause (*uiatores praecones*), and then picked up in the matrix clause in a different case (*eis uiatoribus praeconibus*).

This Oscan text also shows an equivalent to the Latin gerundive construction. However, here the similarity is not just in the syntactic equivalence of the construction, i.e. the use of a quasi-participle (termed 'the gerundive' in Latin grammar) **úpsannam** in agreement with the object of the verb in order to designate the purpose of the gift, but also in the formation of the gerundive. Oscan **úpsannam** is formed through the addition of a suffix -**nn**- to the present stem of the verb. The only possible cognate for this suffix in any IE language is the Latin suffix -*nd*- used to form the gerundive in Latin (in Oscan *-nd-* becomes -*nn*-, and Oscan -**nn**- and Latin -*nd*- could also both derive from *-dn-*). It is very unlikely that the suffix is borrowed from Latin, since it is also found in Umbrian and in Oscan names, such as **Heírens** (gen. *Herenneis*) lit. 'the wished for one' and **Perkens** 'the prayed for one' (see Meiser 1993a). In these cases a calque from Latin is unlikely, and these names are in any case attested from well before the spread of Roman influence (note that *herine*, an Etruscanized form of **Heírens**, is attested already in fifth-century Etruscan sources). The formation of the gerundive is consequently another area where Latin and Sabellian may have made a common morphological innovation, not shared by other IE languages.

Finally, we shall consider an important area where Latin and the Sabellian languages differ: the formation of the perfect. The last word in the text **prúfatted** is an exact semantic match for Latin *probauit*, a verb which also occurs at the end of many building inscriptions to signify that the person responsible for the building inspected the completed work and was satisfied. Oscan **prúfatted** is also formed in exactly the same way as Latin; both derive most probably from an earlier adverb. In Sabellian the adverb is attested in Umbrian **prufe** meaning 'in order', in Latin as *probe* 'satisfactorily'. Oscan **prúfatted** and Latin *probo* probably originally arose as delocutives from the utterances indicating official approval **prufe!** or *probe!* 'OK!' (Campanile 1993: 31f.). Although **prúfatted** is an exact morpheme-by-morpheme match for *probauit*, there is a different choice of marker for the perfect stem: -**tt**- in Oscan, the productive marker for perfects from denominative verbs, but -*u*- in Latin, again, the productive marker of the perfect. This discrepancy between the languages may not seem that important in itself, particularly since the Oscan -**tt**- perfect is not even found in all Sabellian languages, being absent in Umbrian and South Picene. Yet it gains in significance when we start comparing other means of forming the perfect stem in Latin and Sabellian. Both language groups show a variety of different stem-forming types, some inherited from PIE (in both Latin and Sabellian the 'perfect' represents an amalgamation of the PIE aorist and the PIE perfect, see Chapter I), some innovative. However, none of the innovative formations are the same in Sabellian and Latin, and where cognate verbs use inherited formations for the perfect, in the majority of cases they choose a different option from those available (Meiser 1993b: 170f. and 2003 *passim*). Compare the following cases:

1 Latin chooses the aorist stem, Sabellian the Perfect stem:

    Latin *feci* (pres. *facio*) 'make'   : Oscan *fefacid* (pres. **fakiiad**)
    Latin *fui* 'be'   : Oscan **fufens**
    Latin *dixi* (pres. *dico*) 'say'   : Umbrian *dersicurent* < **dedik-*
                                        (pres. < **deik-e-*)
    Latin *fi(n)xi* 'make'   : Oscan **fifikus**

2 Latin chooses a perfect stem, but Sabellian the aorist stem:

    Latin *pepuli* (pres. *pello* < *pel-ne-*)   : Umbrian **apelust** (pres.
    'push'   **apentu** < **-pel-ne-*)

Latin *tetuli* (pres. *tollo* < *tl-ne-*)   : Umbrian **entelust** (pres.
'raise'   **ententu** < *-tel-ne-*)
Latin *legi* 'read'   : Paelignian *lexe* < *leg-s-*

3   Latin and Sabellian agree on the formation:

Latin *dedit* 'give'   : Oscan **deded**

2.4   Sabellian and Latin

We have already discussed two significant morphological innovations which may have been made both in Sabellian and in Latin, and this naturally leads to the question of the nature of the relationship between Latin and the Sabellian group. Latin and the Sabellian languages all belong to the IE family, and they all share the same confined geographical space and they have all been in contact with Etruscan, Greek and other Mediterranean languages as we have already seen. It is not surprising, therefore, that there should be many similarities between them. But these similarities have been explained in two different ways by linguists in the last century. The earlier model of their relationship, which was put forward by German scholars in the nineteenth century, and is still held by the majority of scholars today, is that Latin and the Sabellian languages all form a sub-group of IE which has been named 'Italic'. A rival theory, proposed by Devoto and followed largely in Italy in the twentieth century, denies any earlier genetic unity between Sabellian and Latin other than their shared development from PIE and explains the similarities between the languages as the result of later convergence within the Italian peninsula.

It is worth here grouping together the arguments for the opposing theories, in list form.

2.4.1   Arguments for the Italic theory

Firstly, in support of the Italic theory there are a number of linguistic changes which have been argued to have been made in a period of common unity (the following list follows Heidermanns 2002: 186–9 with some modifications and additions):

Phonology

1   'Thurneysen's Law', long $*\bar{u} > *\bar{\imath}$ before a following $*y$:

Latin *pius*, Sabellian $*p\bar{\imath}o$- (Oscan dative singular **piíhúí**, Volscian *pihom*) < $*p\bar{u}$-*yo*- 'pious'

The number of etymologies in support of this change is small, and forms in Celtic and Germanic make it uncertain whether this change actually had more general application in western IE languages.

2   Loss of intervocalic *y. This change must post-date Thurneysen's Law. The same change is found in other IE languages, such as Greek and Celtic.

Latin *trēs* 'three', Sabellian **trēs* (Oscan nominative plural **trís**) < **treyes* '3'

3   PIE vocalic **r* and **l* > **or* and **ol*. These changes are well attested for Latin, but there are few watertight examples in Sabellian.
4   PIE **-tl-* > **-kl-* in the middle of a word:

*-tlom (PIE suffix) > Latin *pia-culum*; Umbrian *piha-clu*

The change here is not startlingly unusual across the world's languages. In clusters of stops and laterals (as *tl* and *kl*), the stop consonants may be released laterally, leading to merger of the dental and velar in this environment (as happens frequently in spoken English). The cluster **-tl-* is not frequent in reconstructed PIE, and the significance of this change is small.

5   Merger of PIE **bʰ-* and **dʰ* as *f-* at the beginning of a word:

*bʰer- > Latin *fero*, Marrucinian *feret*
*dʰh₁k- > Latin *facio*, Oscan **fakiiad**

6   Loss of original final **-i* in verbal primary endings:

*esmi > Early Latin *esom*, South Picene **esum**
*esti > Latin *est*, Oscan **íst**

Morphology

1   The spread of the ablative singular marker with long vowel followed by *-d*, originally limited to the *o*-stem declension, to the *ā*- (1st) declension (ablative singular **-ād*), *i*-declension (ablative singular **-īd*), and to the *u*- (4th) declension (ablative singular **-ūd*). The treatment of ablative singulars in the consonantal (3rd) declension is various: in Early Latin there is inscriptional evidence for the endings *-ed* and *-id* (*leged*, *loucarid*), presumably with long vowels, but the Classical Latin ending *-e* (a short vowel) is not derivable from either of these, but from the original locative ending (see 1.4.3). In Oscan the consonant stems sometimes borrow the ending *-ud* of the *o*-stems wholesale, as in *ligud*. The same spread of the ablative singular marker and case is also found in Celtiberian, the early form of Celtic attested in inscriptions from Spain, and in later forms of the Iranian language Avestan.

2 The spread of a marker *-*ēd* on adverbs: Latin -*ēd*, Oscan -**íd** and possibly South Picene -**íh**. This change has been explained as the re-marking of an original instrumental ending *-*ē* with final -*d* transferred from the ablative ending, and representing the outcome of a merger of the ablative and instrumental in proto-Italic. The competing end-ings *-*ēd* and *-*ōd* were then refunctionalized with *-*ēd* used as the adverbial marker (Meiser 1992: 201). However, it is possible that the appearance of forms with -*d* could result from later interaction between ablatives in -*d* used adverbially and original instrumentals in -*ē*, together with the archaizing tendency in Latin inscriptions to write in -*d*, even when etymologically incorrect. Note also that the South Picene form **kuprí** 'well', given in text (1) above shows no trace of an original final *-*d* (the South Picene form **qupíríh** in SP AP 2 (in Rix 2002), is taken as equivalent to **kuprí** with final -**h** < *-*d*, but it occurs in a text in which every word ending in a vowel has the letter -**h** added). In Germanic also adverbs are found in both *-*ēd* and *-*ōd* (Old English *lange* but Old High German *lango* (Klingenschmitt 1992: 94)).

3 The remodelling of the plural of the *-*ā*- (1st) declension through the extension of the genitive plural in *-*āsom* from pronominal declen-sions and the creation of a dative/ablative plural in *-*āis* on the model of the *o*-stem ending *-*ois*:

	Old Latin	Oscan
Genitive plural	*ros-ārum*	*egm-azum*
Dative/Ablative plural	*colon-eis*	**kerssn-aís**

We have already discussed some of the innovations in the verbal systems above. Innovations here include:

4 The common use of a suffix *-*sē*- to form a new 'imperfect subjunc-tive'. See discussion above at 2.3.3.

5 The use of a suffix *-*bʰā*- to form the imperfect indicative. We have seen in our discussion at 2.3.3 that the interpretation of the one relevant Oscan form is open to question.

6 The creation of verbal adjectives from the present stem (termed gerundives). In Latin these are formed with a suffix -*ndus*, in Oscan with a suffix -*nn*- as in **úpsannam** (equivalent to Latin *faciendam*). These two suffixes can both be traced back to a common origin, although the exact formation (and origin) of the forebear of the Oscan and Latin forms remains open to doubt. As we have seen in our dis-cussion of the formation of the imperfect subjunctive, morphological innovations also entail syntactic innnovations; the development of new gerundive formations also involves the development of gerundive syntax.

7   The remodelling of the paradigm of the copula verb, in particular
    the formation of a 1st person singular form *esom* where other
    Indo-European languages have *esmi*.

Word-formation

Heidermanns argues that word-formation is also a fertile field for Italic
innovations, and gives the following specific innovations which have only
been made in this branch of Indo-European:

8   a diminutive suffix *-kelo-*;
9   a suffix *-āno-* used to form secondary adjectives;
10   a suffix *-āli-* used to form secondary adjectives;
11   a suffix *-āsio-* used to form secondary adjectives;
12   a parallel restriction of the inherited types of compound formation.

Vocabulary

We have also discussed some of the shared vocabulary unique to languages of Italy earlier in this chapter, and we list here some further
vocabulary items, with relevant cognates in other IE languages where
they exist:

	Latin	Sabellian
'earth'	*terra*	Oscan **terúm**
		specialization of the root *ters-* 'dry' also found in Celtic (Old Irish *tír* 'land')
'hand'	*manus*	Oscan *manim* (accusative)
		possibly related form *mņt-* found in Germanic (Old Norse *mund* 'hand')
'lie, recline'	*cubare*	South Picene **qupat**, Marrucinian *cibat*
'other'	*alter*	Oscan **alttram** (feminine accusative)
		suffixed form of widespread root *al-* (Greek *állos* etc.)
'road'	*uia*	Oscan **víú**, Umbrian **via**, South Picene **viam** (accusative)
		may be related to forms in Germanic (Gothic *wigs*, German Weg, and English *way*)
'say'	*dico*	Oscan *deicum*, Umbrian *deitu*
		specialization of widespread root *deik'-* meaning elsewhere 'show'

'sing'	*cano*	Umbrian **kanetu**
		root **kan-* which is also used used as a verb in Celtic (Old Irish *canim*)
'stone'	*lapis*	Umbrian **vapeře** (locative)
'year'	*annus*	Oscan *aceneis* (genitive), Umbrian *acnu* (accusative)
		the same form occurs in Gothic *apna-* 'year', from **atno-*

2.4.2 Arguments against the Italic theory

Alongside this list of features which could represent innovations made at a period of common unity, there are also a number of features which separate Latin from the Sabellian languages, which have been emphasized by Devoto (1944: 59f.) and others. Again, for ease of reference and exposition we shall give these in list form.

Phonology

1 Development of labio-velar consonants, which are partly retained in Latin but which become labials in Sabellian:

$*k^w$ > Latin *qu* but Sabellian $*p$ Latin *quid*   Oscan **píd**
$*g^w$ > Latin *u* but Sabellian $*b$ Latin *uiuus*   Oscan **bivus**
                                                           (nom. pl.).

2 Development of vocalic $*n$, which gives $*en$ in Latin initial syllables (raised to *in* before velars), but $*an$ in Sabellian:

$*dng^hu\bar{a}/*d^hng^hu\bar{a}$ 'tongue' > Latin *dingua/lingua*, Oscan **fangvam**.

Morphology

3 The formation of the nominative plural of *ā*- and *o*-stems. Latin has generalized the pronominal endings $*-ai$ and $*-oi$ to nouns and pronouns; Sabellian has generalized the nominal endings $*-\bar{a}s$ and $*-\bar{o}s$ to nouns and pronouns.

4 The formation of the genitive singular of *o*-stems. Latin (and Faliscan) shows two alternative endings, long *ī* and *-osio*. The Sabellian languages have all extended the original *i*-stem genitive ending *-eis* (which is lost in Latin) to the *o*-stem declension.

5 The future tense is formed differently in Latin from Sabellian. In Latin, and in Faliscan, the future is formed with a suffix **-b-* or with $*\bar{e}$, whereas Sabellian languages employ the suffix **-s-*: Umbrian *habiest* 'he will have', **ferest** 'he will carry'.

6 The formation of the verbal 'infinitive'. Latin forms infinitives with a suffix *-si, Sabellian with a suffix *-om. Compare the different infinitives formed for the verb 'to be' (stem es- (*$h_1$es-)), and 'to fine' (stem moltā-):

Latin *esse* < *es-si   Sabellian *esom > Oscan *ezum*, Umbrian **eru**
Latin *multare* < *moltāsi   Sabellian *moltāom > Oscan *moltaum*

7 Although Latin and Sabellian share the creation of a *perfectum* stem through the amalgamation of PIE perfect and aorist stems, the actual creation of individual stems is at variance for most verbs for which we have both Latin and Sabellian examples (see 2.3.3 above).

Vocabulary

Finally, the difference between Latin and Sabellian is most marked in the choice of vocabulary. The following list presents some of the differences the two groups show in their basic vocabulary items:

	Latin	Sabellian
'son'	*filius*	Oscan **puklum** (accusative), Paelignian *puclois* (dative plural)
'daughter'	*filia*	Oscan **futír**
'man'	*uir*	South Picene **nír**, Oscan **niir**, Umbrian *nerf* (accusative plural)
'fire'	*ignis*	Umbrian **pir**, Oscan **pur-asiaí**
'water'	*aqua*	Umbrian **utur**
'all'	*omnis*	Oscan **sullus** (nominative plural), Paelignian *solois* (dative plural)
'house'	*domus*	Oscan **trííbúm**
'people'	*populus*	South Picene **toúta**, Umbrian *tot-*, Oscan **túvt-**
'justice, judge'	*ius, iudex*	Umbrian *mers*, Oscan **meddíss**, Volscian *medix*, Marsian *medis*

The choice between the two rival theories has generated much discussion among linguists, and it has been held to have important ramifications for the historian of the Latin language. For if Latin and Sabellian were once united as 'Italic' languages then we should be careful that any explanations of Latin phenomena pay due attention to Sabellian phenomena, whereas if the similarities between them are secondary, then we should seek to avoid following an explanation which uses Sabellian data which may in fact be misleading. The explanation of the Latin imperfect ending *-bā-* is a case in point. Should we attempt to use Oscan **fufans** as a means to arriving at the origin of this formation, or should we be wary of seeing a similarity between the forms?

We have already seen in this chapter that there are reasons for supposing that Latin and the Sabellian languages shared some common phonological developments around the middle of the first millennium BC, including the syncope of short vowels owing to a word-initial stress accent, and phenomena such as the change of intervocalic $*s > r$ in Latin and the north Sabellian language Umbrian (but not in the southern Oscan) may also be related. We have also seen how the spread of Roman power led to the borrowing of some Latin vocabulary and may have also contributed to the creation of Oscan formulae and syntactic structures towards the end of the Republican period. There are therefore some developments that can be explained through contact. Is it possible, however, to explain all the similarities between Latin and Sabellian as convergence phenomena? Could the shared innovation of morphological markers, such as the new past-marked subjunctive formant $*-s\bar{e}-$, have arisen through contact and bilingualism? We suggested above at 2.3.3 that the creation of a past-marked subjunctive accords well with the shared development of a legalistic, bureaucratic and religious idiom which took place in the cultural contact of the first millennium BC. Does the linguistic evidence support this hypothesis?

Comparative linguistic studies on living languages have shown that inflectional markers are only borrowed between languages where there is a prolonged period of bilingualism or extraordinary social conditions. Well-known cases of morphological borrowing include those of Asia Minor Greek which borrowed Turkish morphemes through centuries of bilingualism, and mixed languages such as Menyj Aleut (Copper Island Aleut) or Mitchif which both originated as the language spoken by the offspring of fathers speaking a common language (respectively Russian and French) and mothers speaking another (Aleut and Cree) (see Thomason and Kaufman 1988 for these examples). The periods of linguistic contact that we know about between the speakers of Latin and Sabellian language do not seem to have been of this intensity. We have seen already that onomastic evidence suggests that from the seventh century onwards, speakers of languages other than Etruscan adopted Etruscan citizenship and, presumably, they or their descendants also switched to speaking Etruscan. It is possible that such 'sideways mobility' also took place among the other communities of Italy. However, in the case of Etruscan, the influence of non-native speakers on the language seems not to have been profound. There is no evidence for any morphological borrowing between Etruscan and any other language of Italy that we know about, except in the case of some derivational suffixes. Rix (1994) has argued that the absence of any morphological borrowing between Etruscan and Latin or Etruscan and Sabellian makes it more difficult to accept that the Latin and Sabellian agreements arise through contact. This is a valid point, but we should note that morphological borrowing takes place more easily among closely related languages, as Latin and the Sabellian varieties were. Moreover, closely related languages in contact may also extend the use of shared inherited material in similar ways. We might also question the assumption that the level of contact between Etruscan and Latin was similar to that between Latin and Sabellian. In the absence of concrete data, we may consider the picture of the origin of Rome as presented by the Romans themselves. The Roman sources for the history of early Rome are nowadays considered with a healthy scepticism, and their value as evidence has been largely discredited by methodologically unsound attempts to relate them to archaeological findings. However, the treatment of Etruscan and Sabellian in the Roman tradition is of interest. Prominent Etruscans, such as Lucumo and Mastarna, do feature in the traditional stories of early Rome, but the Sabines play a much more important role, and the story of the rape of the Sabine women is indicative that the Romans themselves thought that there had once been an especially intense interaction between the Romans and a Sabellian people (and may recall to us the scenarios sketched out above for the creation of 'mixed languages').

The conclusion to these arguments must therefore remain disappointingly vague. On the available evidence, it is possible that at some point in their prehistory Latin and Sabellian did form a subgroup of Indo-European, but this cannot be the only explanation for all the similarities between them, since some developments, such as the adoption of an initial stress accent and concomitant vowel weakening or syncope, clearly reflect more recent phenomena. Every shared feature found in Latin and Sabellian must be examined closely to see whether it is better explained as the result of contact or earlier genetic unity – or indeed, whether it does reflect a shared feature at all. As we have seen, some of the phonological agreements between the languages could in fact be independent developments.

Most of the discussion of the relationship between Latin and Sabellian concentrates on explaining their similarities. But since all the varieties are descended from PIE, and none has features which are at odds with other western IE languages, and they are attested at around the same point in time in close proximity, the similarities perhaps do not so much require an explanation as the dissimilarities. This is especially the case if Latin and Sabellian derive from Proto-Italic. In order to answer the question of how the divergences between the languages evolved one must first ask how old the divergences are. Devoto's famous dictum (1944: 67) 'le affinità fra latino e osco-umbro sono recenti, le diversità sono antiche' ('the affinities between Latin and Osco-Umbrian are recent, the divergences are old') cannot tell the whole story. We have seen that one of the principal areas of divergence is in the formation of the *perfectum* stem; Latin generally chooses a different stem form for the *perfectum* than Sabellian, even when they share the same inherited verb. We argued in the last chapter that the merger of the aorist and the perfect as the new *perfectum* in Latin was likely to be late, since there were still survivals of aorist stems alongside perfect stems in Early Latin. There is nothing to suggest that the formation of the future is not a late divergence either, particularly if we follow the explanation for the Latin imperfect subjunctive marker *-sē- sketched out above, which entails that Latin at one time also had futures formed with *-s- (these may survive in an altered form as the *faxo* formations of Early Latin). None of the other divergences listed above is easily dated with any confidence, but there is no need to see any of them as extremely old either.

If the differences between Latin and Sabellian are in fact relatively recent, how should we explain this? Rix (1994) sets up a complex model of pre-history. By this theory, both Latin and Sabellian derive from Proto-Italic, but this language was spoken not in Italy, but in southern Austria. Three subsequent waves of migration, each separated by a century or more from the last, led to the separate branches Latin, Venetic and Sabellian entering Italy. It is not clear, however, that the data really justify such a radical hypothesis of migration, with each language group patiently waiting its turn to move into Italy. Recent studies of ancient Italy have tried to explain ethnic diversity in ways other than through 'waves of invaders', a model which itself derives from ancient accounts of prehistory (Dench 1995: 186f.). An alternative explanation for the Latin/Sabellian differences could be based on sociolinguistics. In Roman accounts of their own history there is a self-conscious distancing from the peoples who lived in and beyond the Apennines, who are generally por-trayed as wild men of the mountains, or inhabitants of an Arcadian idyll (Dench 1995: 67–108). We cannot say how ancient this tradition is, but it may have its origins in the eighth century BC. Urban settlements arose earlier in Latium than in the central Apennines, and the inhabitants of Rome came into very early contact with the Etruscans and Greeks and with them a very different cultural environment from that of the peoples to the east. The earliest Greek accounts of the inhabitants of Italy occurs in Hesiod (*Theogony* 1011ff.) who names the two sons of Odysseus and Circe who ruled over the 'Tyrrhenians' as *Latínos* and *Ágrios*. These lines may be a post-Hesiodic interpolation (West 1966: 436 judges them to be sixth century BC on the basis that this is when the Mainland Greeks are likely to have known about the Etruscans), but it is significant that the names of the kings translate as 'Latin' and 'wild man' reflecting a perceived division between the Latins (and/or Etruscans) and their neighbours. If the notion that the speakers of Sabellian languages were wild and uncivilized goes back as far as the eighth century, it could help explain some of the linguistic divergences between Latin and Sabellian. A Roman desire to differentiate themselves from their neighbours may have led to their choice of linguistic forms which were not found in Sabellian, and the innovation of new linguistic features.

The above account must be treated with caution. As we have already seen, there are also many areas of linguistic convergence in central Italy from the seventh–fifth century BC, and not all the divergences between Latin and Sabellian can be dated as late as the beginnings of Greek contact and the rise of urbanism in Latium in the eighth century. Some features may well be explained in this way – the development of voiced stops from voiced aspirates in medial position in Latin, for example; we have already noted the presence of medial -f- in Faliscan texts from the seventh century on and in Latin dialects outside Rome (see also Devoto 1944: 97f. on 'anti-Sabine' developments in archaic Latin). But for other features, we do not have sufficient evidence to judge. It is possible that we are projecting back into the archaic period a dichotomy between *urbanitas* and *rusticitas*, which, as we shall see in the following chapters, was to become of importance in the definition of Latin in the last centuries of the Republic.

References

Adams, J. N. (2003) *Bilingualism and the Latin Language*, Cambridge: Cambridge University Press.

Agostiniani, L. (1982) *Le 'Iscrizioni Parlanti' dell'Italia Antica*. Florence: Olschki.

Agostiniani, L. and F. Nicosia (2000) *Tabula Cortonensis*. Roma: Bretschneider.

Bailo Modesti, G. (1984) 'Lo scavo nell' abitato antico di Pontecagnano e la coppa con l'iscrizione *amina[. . .]*'. *AION-ArchStAnt* 6, 215–45.

Bugno, M., C. Masseria and P. Poccetti, (2001) *Il Mondo Enotrio Tra VI e V Secolo a.C.: Atti dei Seminari Napoletani (1996–1998)*. Napoli: Loffredo.

Campanile, E. (1993) 'L'uso storico della linguistica italica: l'osco nel quadro della koiné mediterranea e della koiné italiana' in Helmut Rix (ed.) *Oskisch-Umbrisch: Texte und Grammatik*. Wiesbaden: Reichert, 26–35.

Coleman, R. G. G. (1996) 'Conditional clauses in the Twelve Tables' in H. Rosén (ed.), *Aspects of Latin: Papers from the Seventh International Colloquium on Latin Linguistics, Jerusalem, April 1993*. Innsbruck: Institut für Sprachwissenschaft der Universität, 403–21.

Cornell, T. J. (1995) *The Beginnings of Rome: Italy and Rome from the Bronze Age to the Punic Wars (c.1000–264 BC)*. London: Routledge.

Cristofani, M. (1996) *Etruschi e Altre Genti nell' Italia Preromana: Mobilità in Età Arcaica*. Roma: Bretschneider.

Dench, E. (1995) *From Barbarians to New Men: Greek, Roman, and Modern Perceptions of Peoples from the Central Apennines*. Oxford: Oxford University Press.

Devoto, G. (1944) *Storia della Lingua di Roma* (2nd edn.). Bologna: Capelli. (Reprinted with new introduction by A. L. Prosdocimi, 1983, Bologna: Capelli.)

Heidermanns, F. (2002) 'Nominal composition in Sabellic and proto-Italic'. *Transactions of the Philological Society* 100.2, 185–202.

Klingenschmitt, G. (1992) 'Das lateinische Nominalflexion' in O. Panagl and T. Krisch (eds.), *Latein und Indogermanisch: Akten des Kolloquiums der Indogermanischen Gesellschaft, Salzburg, 23–26 September 1986*. Innsbruck: Institut für Sprachwissenschaft der Universität, 89–135.

Marinetti, Anna (1985) *Le Iscrizioni Sudpiceni I*. Florence: Olschki.

Meiser, G. (1992) 'Syncretism in Indo-European languages: Motives, process and results'. *Transactions of the Philological Society* 90, 187–218.

Meiser, G. (1993a) 'Das Gerundivum im Spiegel der italischen Onomastik' in F. Heidermanns, H. Rix and E. Seebold (eds.), *Sprachen und Schriften des antiken Mittelmeerraums: Festschrift für Jürgen Untermann zum 65 Geburtstag*. Innsbruck: Institut für Sprachwissenschaft der Universität, 255–68.

Meiser, G. (1993b) 'Uritalische Modussyntax: zur Genese des Konjunktiv Imperfekt' in Helmut Rix (ed.), *Oskisch-Umbrisch: Texte und Grammatik*. Wiesbaden: Reichert, 167–95.

Meiser, G. (1996) 'Accessi alla protostoria delle lingue sabelliche' in *La Tavola di Agnone nel Contesto Italico: Convegno di Studi, Agnone, 13–15 aprile 1994*. Firenze: Olschki, 187–209.

Meiser, G. (1998) *Historische Laut- und Formenlehre der lateinischen Sprache*. Darmstadt: Wissenschaftliche Buchgesellschaft.

Meiser, G. (2003) *Veni Vidi Vici: Die Vorgeschichte des lateinsichen Perfektsystems*. Zetemata Monographien zur klassischen Altertumswissenschaft. Heft 113. München: Beck.

Poccetti, P. (1982) 'Il testamento di Vibio Adirano'. *RAAN* 57, 237–45.

Poccetti, P. (1988) 'Lingua e cultura dei Brettii' in P. Poccetti (ed.), *Per un'Identità Culturale dei Bretti*. Napoli: Istituto universitario orientale, Dipartimento di studi del mondo classico e del Mediterraneo antico, 11–158.

Rix, H. (1963) *Das Etruskische Cognomen*. Wiesbaden: Harrassowitz.

Rix, H. (1972) 'Zum Ursprung des römisch-mittelitalischen Gentilnamen-systems' in H. Temporini et al. (eds.), *Aufstieg und Niedergang der Roemischen Welt* I, 2. Berlin/New York, 700–58.

Rix, H. (1983) 'Umbro e Proto-Osco-Umbro' in Edoardo Vineis (ed.), *Le Lingue Indoeuropee di Frammentaria Attestazione = Die indogermanischen Restsprachen: atti del Convegno della Società italiana di glottologia e della Indogermanische Gesellschaft, Udine, 22–24 settembre 1981*. Pisa: Giardini, 91–107.

Rix, H. et al. (1991) *Etruskische Texte: Editio Minor*. Tübingen: Narr.

Rix, H. (1994) 'Latein und Sabellisch: Stammbaum und/oder Sprachbund'. *Incontri Linguistici* 17, 13–29.

Rix, H. (1996) Review of P. Schrijver (1991) *The Reflexes of the Proto-Indo-European Laryngeals in Latin*, *Kratylos* 41, 153–63.

Rix, H. (2002) *Sabellische Texte: Die Texte des Oskischen, Umbrischen und Südpikenischen*. Heidelberg: Winter.

Salway, B. (1994) 'What's in a name? A survey of Roman Onomastic Practice from c.700 B.C. to c.700 A.D.' *Journal of Roman Studies* 84, 124–45.

Smith, C. J. (1996) *Early Rome and Latium*. Oxford: Oxford University Press.

Steinbauer, D. (1993) 'Etruskisch-ostitalische Lehnbeziehungen' in H. Rix (ed.), *Oskisch-Umbrisch: Texte und Grammatik*. Wiesbaden: Reichert, 287–306.

Stuart-Smith, J. (1996) 'Phonetic constraints on breathy voiced stops as a cause of their development'. *Oxford University Working Papers in Linguistics, Philology and Phonetics* 1, 100–110.

Stuart-Smith, J. (2004) *Phonetics and Phonology: Sound Change in Italic*. Oxford: Oxford University Press.

Thomason, S. G. and T. Kaufman (1988) *Language Contact, Creolization and Genetic Linguistics*. University of California Press: Berkeley and Los Angeles.

Untermann, J. (2000) *Wörterbuch des Oskisch-Umbrischen*. Heidelberg: Winter.

Vine, B. (1998) 'Remarks on the archaic Latin "Garigliano Bowl" inscription'. *Zeitschrift für Papyrologie und Epigraphik* 121, 257–262.

Watkins, C. (1995) *How to Kill a Dragon: Aspects of Indo-European Poetics*. New York/Oxford: Oxford University Press.

Watmough, M. M. T. (1997) *Studies in the Etruscan Loanwords in Latin*. Florence: Olschki.

Whatmough, J. (1937) *The Foundations of Roman Italy*. London: Methuen.

West, M. L. (1966) *Hesiod Theogony, Edited with Prolegmena and Commentary*. Oxford: Oxford University Press.

Chapter III

The Background to Standardization

3.1 Introduction

The story of Latin in the centuries following its earliest attestations provides one of the first, and certainly one of the most important, examples of how the prestige of a 'standard language' and the benefits deriving from its use in the context of a rapidly expanding imperialist state can not only put great pressure on other varieties (thereby encouraging convergence in the direction of the norm), but also hasten the wholesale abandonment of other languages spoken by minorities within a larger political structure. The adoption or imposition of such a superordinate variety across ethnically, culturally and linguistically diverse communities may therefore have a dramatic impact, both in matters of language choice and ethnic identity, and in terms of shifting attitudes towards language, typically reflected as a growing resistance to change in the dominant language. The history of Latin offers many insights into these and related issues, and it is often revealing to compare the role of Latin in the western Roman Empire with the role of English today as a 'global language' (for which see Crystal (1997)).

In order to prepare the ground for the detailed discussion of later chapters we must first examine the notion of a standard language a little more carefully (see Joseph 1987, Hudson 1996: ch. 2, Downes 1998: ch. 2, Milroy and Milroy 1999 for a range of views), and then outline the long-term impact of the geographical spread of Latin occasioned by centuries of Roman conquest (see Dalby 2002: ch. 2, and especially Adams 2003).

3.2   How and Why Standard Languages Develop

Living, spoken languages are networks of continua, lacking clearly demarcated boundaries between their different varieties, whether geographical or social. Synchronic heterogeneity and diachronic change are, and have always been, the norm for most varieties of most languages for most of human history, though this basic fact has to a great extent been obscured in a world where the existence of, and need for, standard written languages is increasingly taken for granted.

But standard languages, often functioning specifically as 'national' or 'imperial' languages, are far from universal, and are by definition anomalous with respect to more regular, i.e. historically related, varieties, which, as spoken media, have typically evolved quite freely in the communities that use them under a range of essentially local linguistic and social pressures. It is precisely the establishment of a standard that first motivates the idea of a 'language' distinct from, and superordinate to, its (substandard) 'dialects', and which in turn leads to all the familiar notions of correctness and prestige deemed to characterize the former to the detriment of the latter. Standard languages emerge and are maintained through the conscious and protracted intervention of elites seeking to privilege a particular version of a language (i.e. the one based on the way they speak and, above all, write), and to this end they will usually employ all the resources of a centralized state to impose and reinforce their linguistic preferences and prejudices. The motives for doing this are, in practice, quite variable, but a fully developed standard is always autonomous with respect to all other varieties, existing on a higher level and, given a context of formal instruction and at least limited literacy, increasingly shaping their evolution as a norm imposed 'from above'.

The emergence of a standard is most naturally associated with state formation, or with the prosecution of imperial ambitions on the part of a state, in combination with the pressure for cultural innovation that the acquisition of empire typically engenders. A good example of this from the ancient world is provided by the development of the Attic dialect of ancient Greek as a standard (viz. the Koine, i.e. 'common dialect') in the context of the Athenian, Macedonian and Roman empires (Horrocks 2010: chs 3, 4 and 5). One obvious characteristic of such standard languages is the very high level of innovative vitality and functional elaboration that follows directly from their central role in law, government and education, and, in artistically modified variants, in literature, science and philosophy.

The prestige that arises from this association with high-level administrative and cultural activity attaches also to those able to deploy them effectively, i.e. the ruling classes and those who aspire to power and influence under their patronage. In these circumstances a standard language may readily evolve into an important symbol of a state and of what it represents, at least in the minds of those in whose interests it is organized, but often also more generally, as a trickle-down effect of elite dominance of the political and cultural agenda. To participate fully in the life and work of the state it becomes essential to be able to use the standard, with consequential loss of status for other, increasingly parochial, languages and dialects with correspondingly restricted functional domains. The existence of a standard may therefore have the effect of encouraging communities to abandon their linguistic inheritance, as speakers and their families come to appreciate the advantages associated with the acquisition and use of the norm, a process which, over time, then contributes directly to the development of a sense of political unity and shared identity at the expense of more traditional, local sentiment.

A common, if irrational, consequence of the role and status of standard languages is a belief that these alone have the 'precise, logical structure' or 'aesthetic excellence' required for philosophy or literary composition. In truth all varieties have coherent grammars (otherwise they would be unlearnable and unusable), even if only the standard is thought worthy of formal codification; and any dialect is in principle capable of elaboration into a literary medium (cf., for example, the various literary dialects of ancient Greece before the emergence of Attic as a standard), even if the establishment of a standard language before, or in tandem with, the emergence of a literary culture may prevent this from occurring in specific cases. Those who interview candidates for admission to read Classics in British universities are still often told that much of the appeal of Latin as a language lies in its 'precision' and 'elegance'. To the extent that these qualities are indeed characteristic of Latin, they are characteristic of standardized Latin in the form in which it was codified in antiquity, a form of the language in which a great deal of earlier phonological, morphological, lexical and syntactic variety had been consciously suppressed by the 'great' authors of the late Republic and early Empire (thereby creating, *inter alia*, a higher than usual level of precision and consistency) whose works were then taken to constitute a literary canon at the heart of a great cultural tradition (a corpus therefore embodying, by virtue of its 'classic' status, the essence of correct and elegant usage).

Codification of a language, in the form of written grammars and lexica, coupled with the establishment of a canon illustrating the 'best' usage, typically leads to a growing resistance to change; if best practice is thought to be contained in and defined by such books, then any change must, by definition, be change for the worse, a view routinely endorsed by educational establishments with a vested interest in managing perceptions of language so as to highlight their own role as guardians and purveyors of 'true' knowledge. (Kaster 1988 provides much illuminating discussion of the role of the grammarian in late antiquity in this regard). In time, then, a standard may come to be seen as the instantiation of a language in its 'ideal' form, and a whole linguistic ideology may evolve that runs entirely counter to what, in reality, is the natural state of affairs, viz. a world of linguistic heterogeneity and change.

It should be emphasized here that none of these developments is likely to occur unless a language has first been written down; the very idea of standardization, involving a lengthy process of selection, elaboration, codification and dissemination, presupposes that language is seen first and foremost as a tangible and permanent 'thing' rather than as manifesting itself primarily in a transitory stream of sound. The extent to which modern states prioritize the written over the spoken is obvious ('can I have that in writing?'), and this perception is reflected in many different ways, not least in an instinctive tendency to talk about 'pronouncing letters', or in casually dismissive attitudes to languages that have never been written, or have only marginal written functions. It has been estimated that such languages are currently being lost at the rate of approximately two per week as standardized languages with international, even global reach undermine their role in the communities that use them. As we shall see below, *mutatis mutandis*, things were not so very different in the Roman Empire.

3.3 The Roman Context

3.3.1 Rome and Italy

Even in the regal period, before the supposed foundation of the Republic in 509 BC, Rome had begun to expand at the expense of the city's neighbours, but the process gathered momentum under the Republic, and by the beginning of the third century only the Gauls in the north still posed any kind of threat to Roman dominance (see Cornell 1995 for a thorough and up-to-date account of Rome's beginnings). One major consequence of Roman expansion, notwithstanding the economic and political crises of the later Republic, was the gradual emergence of a sense of common purpose and common identity throughout Italy. This is a remarkable outcome when one recalls that Italy in the earliest period of Roman conquest was still extraordinarily diverse in terms of ethnicity, social and political organization, religion, language and material culture (see Chapter II). One significant feature of central Italian society at this time, however, was an apparent freedom of movement between local communities and their mutual openness to outsiders, as stories about the seizure of power at Rome by Etruscan kings and, shortly after the fall of the monarchy, the admission of the Sabine aristocrat Appius Claudius to the Roman community suggest. This openness largely persisted, partly out of enlightened self-interest, in the years that followed. Thus those living in Rome were either Roman citizens, whether of patrician or plebeian origin, or slaves, but slaves freed by Roman citizens became citizens themselves, and Roman citizenship was soon made available to, or in some cases imposed on, first the other Latin communities and then progressively other Italian peoples, albeit often after ruthless conquest and the founding of defensive *coloniae* in newly acquired territories (David 1996).

But even though Roman power had extended throughout Italy, including the Po valley, by the early second century BC, it had not yet effaced the many differences, cultural, political and linguistic, that traditionally separated the many peoples of the peninsula and its neighbouring islands. Nonetheless, the virulent opposition to Roman power characteristic of the early period of Roman expansion in the fifth and fourth centuries had already started to give way to a growing sense of unity. Consider, for example, Hannibal's failure in the Second Punic War of 218–201 BC to drive any serious wedge between Rome and her Italian allies, despite the defection of Capua. In this evolving context we find communities voluntarily adopting Latin alongside, or instead of, their own languages, in recognition of changes in their status or in pursuit of the advantages that the use of Latin might bring, politically and commercially. Thus the multi-ethnic Italian trading community operating on Delos in the last centuries of the Republic very naturally used Latin for the conduct of its affairs (albeit alongside Greek, see Adams 2002, 2003: ch. 6 for details), while in 180 BC the town of Cumae formally asked the Roman Senate for permission to use Latin rather than Oscan as its official language.

(1)   Livy 40.42

Cumanis   eo   anno   petentibus permissum ut publice Latine
Cumaeans-DAT that-ABL year-ABL asking-DAT (was-)permitted that publicly in-Latin

loquerentur   et praeconibus   Latine uendendi ius
speak-3pl.IMPF.SUBJ and auctioneers-DAT in-Latin selling-GEN right

esset.
be-3sg.IMPF.SUBJ.

'That year permission was granted to the Cumaeans, at their request, to speak on official matters in Latin, and for their auctioneers to have the right to sell in Latin.'

Cumae had been the first Greek colony on the mainland of Italy, but it was conquered by the Oscan-speaking Samnites during the fifth century before finally being made a *ciuitas sine suffragio* in 338 BC (i.e. its citizens then had the 'private' rights of Roman citizenship, plus the duty to serve in the army, but lacked the 'public' right to vote). Since citizenship automatically entailed a closer political and cultural affinity with Rome, presumably including the wider use of Latin on an informal basis, we might be tempted to interpret Livy's account in (1) as pointing to some issue of public law. But given that there was no legal requirement to ask for permission to use Latin, the request seems rather to have a more symbolic function, namely to confirm that the Cumaeans' attitude to Latin was a strongly positive one and that they wanted the Romans to know they were using Latin, as an expression of their new identity and allegiance.

Other evidence in this period for the spread of Roman cultural influence, always reinforced by the realities of Roman power, is provided by the obvious competence of Italian writers in Latin. The spectacular overseas conquests of the third and second centuries (see 3.3.2 below) created a new self-confidence in the Roman ruling class which led some, for the first time, to lend their patronage to literary composition in Latin. The so-called 'Scipionic circle' of the later second century, supposedly comprising a group of eminent Roman aristocrats with Hellenizing interests and a commitment to making the ruling class less 'provincial' and more 'worthy' of its imperial mission, may well be the product of wishful thinking in Cicero's time, but the fact remains that, even though Rome itself produced the first prose writers in Latin, all the earliest poets writing in Latin were Italians enjoying Roman patronage, with Naevius and Lucilius coming from Campania, Ennius and Pacuvius from the far southeast (Calabria to the Romans, but now part of Apulia/Puglia), Plautus (probably) and Accius from Umbria, and Caecilius from Cisalpine Gaul.

Inscriptions too provide significant information about the progress of Romanization, including changes in the use of language reflecting the impact of Roman institutions (such as the introduction of Roman titles for local magistrates), the appearance of Latin in official functions alongside or instead of local languages, and changes in onomastic usage marking the adoption of Roman-style civic status. Nor should we forget the role of Latin as the sole language of command in the Roman army, in which large Italian contingents served during the Punic wars and continued to serve in the wars of overseas conquest of the second century BC. Furthermore, the wider use of Latin greatly facilitated trade and communication across Italy, and this was later reinforced by large-scale population movements, especially in the first century, when many new colonies were established in order to give military veterans the land promised by their commanders.

Slowly, and with varying rates of success, the use of Latin therefore spread. Initially learned as a second language, it soon became a first language for many Italians, as younger generations began to turn their backs on the traditional languages of their communities in favour of the only language that promised access to the means of advancement on the 'national' stage. In Umbria, for example, the Latin alphabet probably replaced the native alphabet during the late second century BC, when Latin inscriptions also begin to appear, and Umbrian itself quickly disappears from the written record after the Social War (91–87 BC, fought between Rome and its allies – *socii* – over the issue of full political rights, the granting of which was crucial to the eventual Roman victory). Though this almost certainly does not imply the immediate demise of Umbrian as a spoken language, it reflects directly the consequences of the granting of the full Roman franchise and the associated adoption of Latin as the official language of a newly 'Roman' community (cf. Bradley 2000 for an extended treatment of this and other related issues). Similar observations apply in Oscan-speaking areas, where Latin again replaces the local language in official written documents during the first half of the first century, though in this case there are a handful of graffiti from Pompeii that are certainly later (a couple may even have been scratched after the first earthquake in 63 AD), thus confirming its continued informal use for a while at least.

In Etruria, by contrast, despite a few Latin inscriptions from Veii from the third century BC (viz. a collection of dedications on altars to individuals and Roman deities), most cities seem already to have adopted the official use of Latin by the end of the second century, with Latin again becoming dominant after the Social War (see Bonfante and Bonfante 2002). Though formal bilingual inscriptions continue into the first century (e.g. the funerary dedications from Arretium (Arezzo), *c*.40 BC or later), these are all largely onomastic in character and there is good reason to think the language was no longer properly understood. Similar remarks apply *a fortiori* to later references to the practices of Etruscan priests (e.g. in AD 408 Etruscan *fulguriatores* offered to avert the threatened Gothic sack of Rome by reciting special prayers). Unsurprisingly, there is also good epigraphic evidence for the tenacity of Greek in some areas, e.g. Locri, where inscriptions continue beyond the end of the Social War, though Greek, of course, had the unique advantage of continuing prestige as a written medium (in the form of the standardized Koine and its literary variants), and the language was in any case extremely well-entrenched as a spoken medium in Sicily and the South, continuing in use in remote parts of (modern) Calabria and Apulia to the present day.

The acquisition of full Roman citizenship did not therefore entail the immediate abandonment of local languages, even as written media. Over time, however, Roman norms and standards were adopted almost everywhere, as Italians joined the community of Roman citizens and the former city states lost their old importance. No doubt self-interested aristocrats, particularly in areas where the local identity lacked prestige, very quickly associated themselves with the 'superior' culture of those who governed the growing empire, while elsewhere others continued to take a genuine pride in their local history and traditions. But by the end of the first century BC, under the influence of Hellenistic and Roman models and the impact of Roman realpolitik, the peoples of Italy as a whole had effectively united under a single identity, that of a conquering nation with Latin as its national language, now the common language of trade, law, literature and government. We may usefully note here Quintilian's approach to defining what was 'native' in Latin: *licet omnia Italica pro Romanis habeam* (1.5.57), 'I am allowed to regard all Italian (words) as Roman.'

3.3.2   Rome and the Mediterranean

The last two centuries of the Roman Republic saw not only the transformation of Italian society and its economy but also the extension of Roman power throughout the Mediterranean. It has often been argued that the conquests of the third and second centuries BC were the unplanned result of a series of defensive campaigns fought against the Carthaginians and the Hellenistic monarchies, even if allowance is made for a more ruthless approach in the final period of the Republic, after the dictatorship of Sulla (*c.*138–78 BC, appointed dictator 82 BC), when personal greed and political corruption supposedly came to the fore. More recently, however, others have argued that greed and ambition were major factors all along, and that the changes observable in the late Republic reflect the fundamental shift of power from the senate and people to individuals such as Pompey and Caesar (see Beard and Crawford 1999 for some helpful discussion).

Whatever the actual motivations, and these are likely to have been both varied and complex, it has been fairly noted that the one-year term of office legally available to Republican generals positively encouraged aggressive pursuit of the material rewards and personal prestige to be derived from a victorious short-term campaign outside Italy. Such campaigns required armies to be raised, as did the subsequent control of conquered provinces (even if formal annexation did not always follow immediately), and these armies were in large part demanded from, and supplied by, the Italian allies in recognition of Roman leadership of the peninsula. Maintenance of a leadership manifested primarily in the right to demand troops rather than taxes therefore required conquest if those troops were to be usefully deployed, and conquest brought enormous benefits to both Rome and Italy in the form not only of personal wealth for the ruling senatorial elite but also of profitable tax-collecting contracts for the *publicani* (men of equestrian status), while the recycling of this vast new wealth in the form of building contracts and increased trade created many business and employment opportunities further down the social scale. This new level of economic activity was in turn stimulated by the fact that provincials, who in the period of the Principate were increasingly able to acquire citizenship (a process culminating in the granting of citizenship to all free inhabitants of the Empire by Caracalla (Aurelius Antoninus) in AD 212), were obliged to sell a proportion of their produce in order to pay their taxes, a situation which prompted urbanization in so far as towns provided the necessary facilities for the efficient exchange of goods and services. The economic unity of the Empire, based on the growing interdependence of Rome and its provinces, thus quickly took shape, and the kind of cultural and linguistic influences described above in the Italian context also began to take hold further afield – though in the East, as we shall see, Latin more than met its match in Greek.

3.3.3 Language diversity and language 'death' in the Roman Empire

It is hard to assess the number of languages spoken around the Mediterranean at the beginning of the first century BC, since it is certain that many were never written, while the records of others are often sparse, and difficult or impossible to interpret; some 'survive' only in the form of place names etc., a notoriously difficult form of evidence to work with. What follows is therefore only a partial survey, which also ignores the many languages of Italy south of the Po (for which see Chapter II, and 3.2.1 above; Adams 2003: ch. 2 provides a detailed treatment).

Beginning in the Iberian peninsula, much of the centre and north was occupied by Celtic peoples commonly referred to as Celtiberians. There are some written texts, including the famous bronze tablet of Botorrita, which can now be partly read. The Mediterranean coast (including part of southern France), apart from the Greek and Punic (Carthaginian) colonies there, was occupied by a people known as Iberians. There are a number of texts in Iberian, and the phonetic values of the characters used to write it are now known, though the language itself (non-IE) remains uninterpretable. In the southwest there is also some evidence for a language known as Tartessian, while further north, in much of the territory of modern Portugal, a language called Lusitanian was spoken (which some have sought, with little supporting evidence, to classify as Celtic).

In Gaul (France) the majority population was of Celtic origin, and Gaulish varieties of Celtic had already displaced a number of earlier languages. Celtic languages had also spread into northern Italy (Cisalpine Gaulish and Lepontic), where Venetic (IE, possibly Italic), Raetic (non-IE, conceivably related to Etruscan) and Ligurian (only vestigially attested) were also spoken. But southwestern Gaul together with part of north-eastern Spain (Navarre bordering the Pyrennes) was inhabited by a non-Celtic people whom the Romans called Aquitani. After the Roman conquest the Aquitani began to write in Latin, but the surviving texts (mainly votive and funerary inscriptions) contain many Aquitanian names. These are unmistakably Basque in their morphological structure and phonology, and it is now generally accepted that Aquitanian (sometimes also called Vasconian) was an ancestral form of that language.

In the Balkans, apart from Greek in the south, which by this time had also become, as a result of the Macedonian conquests of the later fourth century BC, the principal administrative and cultural language as well as the spoken *lingua franca* of much of the eastern Mediterranean, we find Illyrian in the northwest (of which almost nothing is known, though some see it as the ancestor of Albanian), and Thracian and Dacian in the northeast (each taken by others to be the ancestor of Albanian); ancient Macedonian (unrelated to the modern Slavonic language of that name), if this was not simply an aberrant Greek dialect, may also have still been spoken in parts of northern Greece and modern Macedonia, along with Paeonian further north and Epirot to the south (of which, once again, virtually nothing is known).

Further east, in Asia Minor, Greek had long been established in the major coastal cities, and had then spread inland with the Hellenization of the interior, where a bewildering variety of peoples and languages co-existed alongside it, including Lydian, Carian, Lycian, Milyan, Sidetic (all related to ancient Hittite), Phrygian, Lycaonian, Isaurian, Cappadocian, Cilician and Galatian (the language of Celtic migrants).

To the south, Syriac (the *lingua franca* of the Persian Empire) and other Aramaic dialects extended from western Mesopotamia down through Syria and Palestine as far as the borders of Egypt, confining Greek mainly to the major cities, while the great urban centres of the Phoenician coast (Byblos, Beirut, Sidon and Tyre), despite very intensive Hellenization, had successfully maintained Phoenician alongside Greek. We may also note here the presence of speakers of Arabic in parts of Syria and Palestine.

In Egypt too, though Greek had become the chief language of Alexandria and the other Hellenistic foundations, and some degree of bilingualism was routine, the local Egyptian language (later written in a Greek-based alphabet and known as Coptic) had continued to enjoy high prestige because of its religious significance and long written tradition, and had remained the dominant medium overall. Elsewhere in north Africa, from the borders of Egypt to the Atlantic coast, the native population spoke a continuum of language varieties known variously as Libyan, Numidian or Massylian (the ancestor of modern Berber), though the great city of Carthage (destroyed by Rome in 146 BC, but later refounded) and the other Phoenician colonies of the seaboard, together with their hinterland, spoke a variety of Phoenician known as Punic (spoken also in colonies in Spain, see above).

By the time Roman rule spread eastwards, therefore, Greek was already established as the official language of government, education and high culture in the affected territories, while the long-term presence of important Greek colonies in southern Italy and Sicily had, from the late fourth century onwards, already introduced the Romans and their Italian allies to the many tantalizing possibilities opened up by Greek culture, a culture which became increasingly influential as Rome became more and more involved in the East. Widespread Roman respect and admiration for the Greek language and Greek culture, at least in its 'higher' forms, therefore meant that the eastern part of the Empire was never required to change its established linguistic habits. While Roman provincial officials and colonists naturally communicated with Rome and with one another in Latin, much of the day-to-day business of local administration involving Greek-speaking communities continued to be carried out, using both original and translated documents, in the standardized Koine, just as new developments in Greek intellectual life continued to play a major role in the evolution of Roman culture. In the end Greek was, in effect, appropriated as 'the other' Roman language alongside Latin, albeit with periodic reservations and misgivings. By the second and third centuries AD, in a period of philhellenism that had culminated in AD 212 with the political equalization of the two halves of the Empire, the linguistic 'border' between East and West in terms of language choice for official purposes had become rather less sharply defined, though it should be stressed that the role and status of Greek in the East were never seriously threatened. We may note, in particular, the later position of Greek as the sole official and dominant cultural language of the East Roman (Byzantine) Empire following the formal split between East and West in late antiquity.

But despite the high cultural status of Greek and its continuing official role in the East, Latin was the 'true' native language of the seat of Roman power and of the institutions of its government, including the law, just as it remained in theory the universal language of command in the Roman army once non-Italian contingents began to be recruited (we might compare the role of French in the Légion étrangère). In practice, however, Greek was tolerated in Greek-speaking units just as it was in day-to-day dealings with Greek-speaking civilians, with Latin often used only 'symbolically', and incomprehensibly, as a reminder of the fact of Roman rule. But in general Latin spread and took root with the consolidation of Roman power, Roman culture and Roman citizenship, most obviously in the West, where there was no language with the status of Greek to rival it, and its long-term impact, as earlier in Italy, eventually proved fatal to many of the languages previously in use there. In the East the continuing use of Greek in high-prestige functions and as a *lingua franca* had a similar effect, though on a smaller scale, most dramatically in Asia Minor.

Consequently, of the 60 or so languages spoken around the Mediterranean in *c.*100 BC, only Latin, Greek, Coptic, Aramaic (including Syriac), Arabic, Libyan (Berber), Basque, the ancestor of Albanian (?Illyrian) and Punic remained in general use by *c.*AD 400, and Punic would very soon join the ranks of the lost. We may simply note that, leaving Latin and Greek aside, the long-term survivors fall into three subgroups: the languages of small populations in inaccessible regions, those of nomadic peoples at the margins of the Empire, and those of large, long urbanized populations with deep-rooted literate cultures of their own.

3.4   Conclusion

In this chapter we have set the scene for much of what is to follow. Chapters IV–VI will deal with the progressive standardization of Latin from the mid-fourth century down to the period of the early Empire, examining the emergence and development of both official and literary written varieties. Chapter VII will then redress the balance by examining the evidence for sub-elite Latin in various regions, and considering in more detail the complex issues associated with growing bilingualism and the spread of Latin as a spoken as well as a written language. Finally, Chapter VIII will examine the fate of Latin in later antiquity, including a brief assessment of its spectacular 'afterlife' as a cultural language in the context of the development of local vernaculars.

References

Adams, J. N. (2002) 'Bilingualism at Delos', in J. N. Adams, M. Janse and S. Swain (eds.), *Bilingualism in Ancient Society*. Oxford: Oxford University Press, 103–27.

Adams, J. N. (2003) *Bilingualism and the Latin Language*. Cambridge: Cambridge University Press.

Beard, M. and M. Crawford (1999) *Rome in the Late Republic* (2nd edn.). London: Duckworth.

Bonfante, G. and L. Bonfante (2002) *The Etruscan Language* (2nd edn.). Manchester: Manchester University Press.

Bradley, G. (2000) *Ancient Umbria*. Oxford: Oxford University Press.

Cornell, T. (1995) *The Beginnings of Rome*. London/New York: Routledge.

Crystal, D. (1997) *English as a Global Language*. Cambridge: Cambridge University Press.

Dalby, A. (2002) *Language in Danger*. London: Penguin.

David, J.-M. (1996) *The Roman Conquest of Italy*. Oxford: Blackwell.

Downes, W. (1998) *Language and Society* (2nd edn.). Cambridge: Cambridge University Press.

Horrocks, G. (2010) *Greek: A History of the Language and its Speakers* (2nd edn.). Wiley-Blackwell, Malden Mass. and Oxford.

Hudson, R. (1996) *Sociolinguistics* (2nd edn.). Cambridge: Cambridge University Press.

Joseph, J. E. (1987) *Eloquence and Power: The Rise of Standard Languages and Language Standards*. London: Pinter.

Kaster, R. A. (1988) *Guardians of Language*. Berkeley: University of California Press.

Milroy, J. and L. Milroy (1999) *Authority in Language: Investigating Standard English* (3rd edn.). London: Routledge.

Chapter IV

'Old' Latin and its Varieties in the Period *c.*400–150 BC

4.1 Introduction

If we now recall the factors that promote the emergence of a standard language in the specific context of the formation of a Roman state in Italy and of the subsequent extension of Roman power in the Mediterranean, and bear in mind the associated commitment of progressive elements among the Roman elite to forge a 'higher' culture based on Greek models and precedents, it should be no surprise that the dramatic historical developments of the middle and later Republic very largely coincided with the period in which Roman Latin was progressively elaborated, regularized and imposed as the official language of the expanding state. It is therefore categorically not the case that the process of standardization belongs exclusively to the final years of the Republic and the early Empire, even if this was a particularly important, even climactic, phase in the development of the language in its higher written forms (see Chapter VI). On the contrary, the contact with Greek culture and the need for an efficient medium of imperial administration had already led to a considerable elaboration of form and function by the mid-third century, together with the emergence of many genre-conditioned conventions for writing. This is particularly apparent in the tendency to retain traditional spellings and older grammatical forms in a period of rapid language change engendered by growing urbanization and much greater mobility, a tendency that can only be explained in terms of an already well-established tradition of official writing on the one hand, and an impulse to emulate the archaizing styles of much 'classic' Greek literature on the other.

But the progressive standardization of the written language and, to a lesser extent, of the formal speech of the elite, should not lead us to imagine that 'substandard' Latin simply disappeared, either in the original Latin-speaking territory of Latium or elsewhere in Italy and the Empire. On the contrary, local and popular spoken varieties continued and evolved (albeit increasingly towards a norm set by the standard), even if this is largely concealed behind the increasingly uniform linguistic facade of official documents and literary texts. Indeed, periods in which languages undergo rapid geographical expansion typically produce high levels of bilingualism (the use of two languages with some degree of competence) and/or diglossia (the use of two varieties of the same language, one the standard, or at least the dominant, variety), as well as other forms of social interaction between people from different regions, as a result of the foundation of new colonies, increased trade, common service in a single army, etc. Such circumstances almost inevitably lead, and indeed, in the specific case of Latin, led, to rapid evolution, especially in the popular speech of developing urban centres with mixed populations. But diversity and change eventually came to affect even the speech of the conservative elite at the heart of the expansion process as the higher spoken varieties of 'provincial' areas, previously only partly reflecting the top-down imposition of the developing standard, became increasingly familiar, and accepted, through the routine appointment of leading provincials to senior positions. There was therefore an inherent tension between the obvious need for standardized written forms of Latin and the continuing development of its spoken varieties at all levels, and we shall see much evidence of this in the material to be examined below: even the highest written varieties tend to show a progressive compromise with natural change, at least until such time as the most intensive period of empire-building had peaked and relatively stable borders, with relatively stable lifestyles, institutions and forms of governance had emerged. The final fixing of the grammar and orthography of 'correct' (written) Latin therefore belongs to the comparatively settled period of the early Empire.

In this chapter we shall first outline some of the distinctive characteristics of 'Old Latin' between the fourth and second centuries BC, and also present the evidence for regional and social variety in this period. Against this background Chapter V will examine the elaboration of elite (Roman) Latin in the same period, both in its role as the official language of the Empire and as a literary language with the potential to rival Greek, and so serve as the vehicle of a culture commensurate with Rome's new-found status in the world. The final stages of standardization and the further refinement of specifically literary forms of Latin will then be discussed in Chapter VI, while evidence for the character of sub-elite Latin in the late Republic, in the Empire at its height, and in later antiquity is considered in Chapters VII and VIII.

4.2   Some Characteristic Markers of 'Old Latin'

In order to provide a convenient reference section for the following chapters, we summarize here some of the major phonological/orthographic and grammatical features of 'Old' (i.e. preclassical) Latin, especially Roman Latin, tracing their development as necessary (see in particular Baldi 2002, Dangel 1995, Giacomelli 1993, Meiser 1998 for a range of up-to-date treatments of the key issues). Much of the evidence comes directly from 'early' inscriptions (see Chapter I for 'archaic' Latin pre-400 BC), but this may often be supplemented, given due caution, with evidence taken from the extant texts of the earliest surviving writers in prose and verse. As already noted, some of these features persisted as conventional archaisms, at least in certain genres, down into the imperial period. Unfortunately, however, there is almost no Roman epigraphic material from the fourth century, and only a subset of the Roman inscriptions before 150 BC can be securely dated, so many uncertainties remain, especially when trying to establish the chronology of the key linguistic changes. The earliest dated attestation of a phenomenon from Rome may very easily postdate the actual change, and even when we have earlier evidence from other areas (as sometimes from Praeneste), the same principle applies, and it would in any case be unrealistic simply to assume that the relevant change occurred at the same time throughout Latium. Much argument is therefore based on plausibility rather than demonstration, though we can at least be certain that once evidence for a given change has been attested graphically on a datable inscription, any later documents retaining 'older' forms and/or orthography are clearly 'archaizing' in character (throughout, Wachter 1987 is the indispensable guide).

4.2.1   *Phonology and orthography*

Vowels and diphthongs

Vowel weakening in medial and final syllables   It is plausibly assumed that Early Latin, like other languages of central Italy in the same period, including both Oscan and the unrelated Etruscan, had primary stress on the initial syllables of words, since there was a growing tendency, beginning around 450 BC (recall that in the earliest Latin texts the vowels inherited from PIE are mainly preserved), for non-initial, and so *ex hypothesi* unaccented, short vowels and certain diphthongs to undergo a process of 'weakening', i.e. a loss of quality through raising (Oscan and Etruscan typically go further than Latin, showing extensive syncope of such vowels). Note, however, that the evidence of Plautine accentuation (in a period, non-coincidentally, when verse in Saturnians ceased to be composed, see Chapter V) shows that a different accentual system, with primary stress falling on one of the last four, later three, syllables of a word, had superseded this Old Latin system by the latter part of the third century. The result is that the shifted accent of the classical language could then fall on previously weakened syllables. The main effects of vowel weakening, affecting unaccented short vowels and diphthongs, are as follows:

1 /a/ > /e/ in closed syllables, but developed further > /i/ in open ones (e.g. *reficio* 'restore', *refectus* 'restored', beside *facio* 'make/do').

2 /e/ > /i/ in open syllables and in final syllables generally (e.g. *retineo* 'keep' beside *teneo* 'hold', *cepit* 'took' beside *feced* 'made' on the Duenos vase, 1.4.5. text (5), etc.); the first attestations of the latter are probably from the mid-third century, though the period is characterized by lingering orthographic uncertainty.

3 /o/ and /u/ > /ə/ > /i/ in open medial syllables (e.g. *memini* 'remember' beside *moneo* 'warn', *capitis* 'head' (genitive) beside *caput* 'head' (nominative)), and /o/ > /u/ in final syllables except after /w/ (*bonus* 'good' beside earlier *duenos* etc., but *equos* 'horse' (unless this is simply a graphic convention)); this latter change took place at the end of the third century, though with some archaizing spellings persisting for a time after the sound change.

4 /ai/ and /oi/ > /ei/ [then > /e:/ > /i:/ by monophthongization] and /au/ > /ou/ [then > /u:/ by monophthongization] (e.g. *occīdō*, 'kill' beside *caedo* 'cut/slaughter', 2nd-declension nominative plural *-oi* > *-ei* [> *-e* > *-i*], *inclūdō* 'shut in' beside *claudo* 'close').

There was, however, much analogical interference on expected outcomes, as well as a range of specific, contextually conditoned, variants. For example, both original /i/ and other vowels that would normally have weakened to /i/ were reduced to a central vowel in a labial environment: this was noted first as *u*, = [ʉ], and then, from the late second century, as *i*, = [ɨ], with the latter becoming standardized by imperial times (e.g. *maxumus* vs. *maximus* 'biggest/greatest' etc.). In other cases, and under circumstances that are hard to define precisely (Exon's law, postulating deletion of the first of the short vowels in a tetrasyllabic sequence [x ˘ ˘ x], accounts for many examples, but there are exceptions), there was outright loss, as in *rettuli* 'brought back' < **re-te-tul-ai*, *legit* 'chooses/reads' < **lege-ti* (where, however, the loss of the final vowel was probably very much earlier than that of the medial vowel in *rettuli*). Such syncopation/apocopation was largely prehistoric, but many other aspects of the weakening process are directly reflected in the changing orthography of inscriptions from the fourth, third and second centuries, albeit with many uncertainties and inconsistencies.

Monophthongization   Independently of vowel-weakening effects, i.e. even in initial syllables, original diphthongs show a tendency to become simple long vowels (see Coleman 1986/7):

1   /au/ and /ai/ persist in Roman Latin, though with the latter becoming /-ai̯/, i.e. with a more open articulation of the second element, probably in the early second century to judge from the associated orthographic change of *ai* > *ae* after 187 BC (*ai* finally dies out by around 120 BC). However, /au/ and /ai/ were monophthongized > /ɔː/ and /ɛː/ quite early in some non-urban dialects, perhaps in part under the influence of neighbouring Italic languages of broadly Umbrian type, and monophthongization eventually became quite general in the later vulgar Latin of the imperial period (i.e. the period of rule by emperors initiated, according to one convention, by Augustus in 27 BC, following the collapse of the Roman Republic, which by tradition had replaced a monarchical form of government in 509 BC), though the evidence of many Romance varieties shows that it was never completed for /au/. In non-final syllables, however, /ai/ > /ei/ by weakening, with subsequent treatment as for original /ei/.

2   /oi/ > /uː/ in initial syllables during the third century (e.g. *oinos* > *ūnus* 'one'), though examples of the old spelling (modified to *oe* on the analogy of *ae*) persist into the mid-first century. There is also a small set of regularly archaizing exceptions that were perhaps originally purely orthographic in character but which eventually led to spelling pronunications (e.g. *poena* 'penalty' beside *pūnīre* 'punish', and cf. French *peine* vs. *punir* confirming that surviving examples of /oi/ developed to /ɛː/ in vulgar Latin). Elsewhere /oi/ > /ei/ by weakening, then with the same development as for original /ei/ (e.g. dative-ablative plural of the second declension *-ois* > *-eis* > *-īs*).

3   /ei/, both original and as the product of weakening, > a close /ẹː/ during the third century, and was then raised > /iː/ in Roman Latin by the middle of the second century, though with the intermediate stage persisting in many non-urban varieties (e.g. *deico* > *dīcō* 'say', *scribeis* > *scrībīs* 'scribes' (dat/abl. pl.), *castreis* > *castrīs* 'camp'

(dative-ablative plural)). The close mid-vowel resulting from mono-phthongization must have been distinct from original /eː/, at least in Roman Latin, since the latter does not undergo the subsequent raising > /iː/. The old orthography *ei* survived, however, into the late Republican period and beyond, especially in official documents, and this was sometimes then erroneously used to represent original /iː/. Occasional spelling mistakes involving *-ei-* to represent even original /eː/ in the period prior to raising (e.g. *pleib(ei)* CIL I² 22, *c*.300 BC from Rome) presumably reflect a purely orthographic uncertainty in the spelling of two very similar mid-vowels (by the same token /ẹː/ is also occasionally spelled *-e-* rather than *-ei-* in early Roman Latin, e.g. *ploirume* in CIL I² 8/9, though the spelling *-e-* is quite normal for both original /eː/ and /ẹː/ in dialect inscriptions).

4 /eu/ merged with original /ou/ at a very early date, and then all examples of /ou/, both original and secondary, > close /ọː/ > /uː/, probably by the end of the third century (e.g. *leucos, though note the name *Leucesie* in the *Carmen Saliare*, > *loucos* > *lūcus* 'grove', *douco* > *dūcō* 'lead' etc.), though archaizing spellings again persist. Dialectally, however, the development is often arrested at the inter-mediate stage, through which Roman Latin must also have passed (cf. the parallel Roman treatment of /ei/, via /ẹː/, to /iː/). Note that this close mid-vowel must again have been distinct from original /oː/, which was not raised at the same time as /ọː/ in Roman Latin.

Marking of vowel length Vowels are sometimes doubled to indicate length in the period *c*.135–75 BC, though sporadically also later, and the 'apex' (e.g. *á*) is also used in a similar function from the end of the second century BC, though again without consistency.

Long /iː/, however, is rarely noted as *-ii-*, perhaps because two vertical strokes could be used to represent /e/ in some forms of writing; *-ii-* was in any case sometimes used in Cicero's time to note the geminate semivowel in words like *ei(i)us* ['ejjus] 'his/her/its'. Whatever the reasons, from around 110 BC the so-called 'i longa', i.e. *I*, perhaps in origin an adaptation of *í*, is sometimes used instead to note /iː/ (both original, and the product of monophthongization or compensatory lengthening, i.e. the lengthening of a vowel 'in compensation' for the loss of one of a pair of following consonants – for examples see 'Some sound changes and their consequences for spelling' below), though some stonecutters also used this symbol for decorative effect as a simple vari-ant of *i*. 'I longa' also appears on occasion before another vowel to mark the close articulation of short /i/ in this environment (elsewhere /i/ was more open, and somewhat retracted, by comparison with close /iː/): note the treatment of Latin short /i/ in Italian *dì* < *die(m)* 'day' beside *pera*

< *pira(m)* 'pear', and the frequent misspellings of words containing long /eː/ and short /i/, which were clearly similar enough in quality to allow the 'same' symbol, whether *e* or *i*, to be used for both long and short 'varieties' (just as *a* was used for both /aː/ and /a/), e.g. *minsis* for *mēnsis* 'month', *menus* for *minus* 'less', etc. Early examples appear in CIL I² 610 (200 BC) from near Rome, which has *Aurilius* for *Aurelius* and *didit* for *dedit* ('gave').

Consonants

Letter forms and spelling conventions   The letter *g* (i.e. G = C with a diacritic) is first used in the third century; prior to that *c* was used to represent both voiced /g/ and voiceless /k/ (having spread at the expense of *q* and *k*, which were originally used before back rounded vowels and /a/ respectively, with *c* written before front vowels and consonants), though some archaizing spellings continue.

Double consonants first begin to be written double very late in the third century, the single spelling finally disappearing by the end of that century.

The writing of aspirated plosives (*ch*, *ph*, *th*) first begins to be noted around 150 BC.

Some sound changes and their consequences for spelling   Intervocalic /s/ was rhotacized > /r/ some time before the mid-fourth century, via voicing from the neighbouring vowels > [z] and the addition of a trilled articulation which eventually predominated at the expense of frication (*Lases* > *Lares* 'household gods', *iouesat* > *iurat* 'swears', etc.): L. Papirius Crassus is recorded as the first member of his gens to spell traditional *Papisios* with an *-r-*. Final /s/, however, was weakly articulated in Old Latin, at least preconsonantally after a short vowel, and is sometimes not written in Roman inscriptions of the third century and in regional Latin documents more generally (as well as failing to make position pre-consonantally in poetry pre-200 BC); but it was quickly restored graphically and also phonetically in elite Roman Latin, and this reform may also have had some limited impact in certain popular varieties (cf. French *fils* 'son' < *filius*, which exceptionally derives from the Latin nominative rather than the usual accusative, even though Italian itself shows no trace, implying that the loss was permanent in many long-established sub-elite spoken varieties).

Final *-m* is much more regularly omitted in early inscriptions (especially in regional Latin and in early verse inscriptions composed in Saturnians), and it is well known that a final vowel + /m/ is regularly 'elided' prevocalically in classical poetry (whatever this means in strictly phonetic terms), even though such syllables are treated as heavy before a consonant. It must be assumed, then, that early weakness and partial loss had been at least partly reversed in elite Roman Latin by the beginning of the second century, both graphically and phonetically, with a pronunciation perhaps involving nasalization and concomitant length-ening of the preceding vowel, (e.g. *donum* = [do:nū:] 'gift', etc.). This allows for normal elision/synizesis when word-final and word-initial vowels come into contact, while the lengthening explains the heavy status of these syllables (creating the illusion of a consonantal value for final /m/) before a word-initial consonant. To judge from the Romance reflexes of relevant word forms, however, near-complete loss persisted in many sub-elite varieties (French *rien* 'nothing' < the accusative form *rem* 'thing' is a notable exception), and later commentators and grammarians make it clear that in their time the sound was also very weakly articulated even in higher varieties before being lost altogether (Quintilian IX.4.40, Velius Longus, K. VII.54).

Final /d/ disappears after long vowels from late in the third century (e.g. in ablative singular case endings, adverbs in -*ē(d)*, and -*tō(d)* imperatives), though archaizing spellings persist until around 125 BC, especially on official documents and in the personal pronouns *mēd* 'me', *tēd* 'you', *sēd* 'him/her/it-self', where /d/ may have continued to be pronounced longer, especially before word-initial vowels.

Certain clusters of consonants preserved in the oldest texts are simpli-fied in various ways, most notably initial /dw-/ > /b-/, with a corres-ponding shift in the orthography from *du-* to *b-*, though some archaizing spellings persist as always, particularly in proper names. Thus original *duenos* > *duonos* (by the third century at the latest) > *bonus* 'good'. The cluster /-ns-/ was also simplified to /-s-/, and the preceding vowel was then lengthened 'in compensation' (thus maintaining the syllable quantity). Although this was for a time reflected in the orthography (so *cosol*, *cesor* 'consul', 'censor', etc.), spelling with -*ns*- was quickly restored, and spelling pronunciations ensued, with the consequence that the long vowel was retained even in the presence of the restored /-n-/, so *con-sul* ['co:nsul], *censor* ['ce:nsor] etc.

4.2.2   Morphology

Turning now to morphology, even official Roman Latin tolerated a much greater variety of formations prior to the final selection of 'favoured' variants in the final years of the Republic (see especially Meiser 1998). Some of these variants also occur in regional Latin inscriptions, and since such forms often survived longer in the speech of country areas, many had come to be viewed not merely as archaic but as specifically 'rustic' or 'substandard' by Cicero's time. A range of relevant phenomena is illustrated below, for both verbal and nominal morphology.

Verbal morphology

Stem forms There is some residual variety in stem-formation, particularly in forms of the Latin perfect, which, as noted in Chapter I, represents a relatively 'recent', but none the less prehistoric, formal merger of original aorist and perfect forms, with one or other stem normally prevailing, albeit now with both functions: cf. sigmatic *dix-i* 'I said/have said' with Greek aorist *é-deiks-a* 'I showed', and reduplicated *ded-i* 'I gave/have given' with Greek perfect *dédō-ka* 'I have given'.

Earlier, however, there seems to have been more uncertainty and variation, partly the result of the continuing co-existence of perfect and aorist stems. Occasional traces of this remain even in Classical Latin (thus *pepigi*, *pegi* and *panxi*, for example, are all attested as perfects of *pango* 'fix'), but Old Latin has rather more examples. Thus the putative *s*-aorist stem of **fax-i* (from *facio* 'make/do', cf. also the original reduplicated perfect type *vhe-vhak-ed* on the Praenestine fibula (text (3) at 1.4.5), if this is genuine) is apparently retained in the future and subjunctive formations *faxo/faxim*. Such *s*-futures/subjunctives (e.g. *ax-o/-im* 'do', *caps-o/-im* 'take', and, from the 1st and 2nd conjugations, forms like *indicass-o/-im* 'proclaim', *prohibess-o/-im* 'prohibit') are not strictly speaking 'classical', since they survive in regular use only in a few fossils like *haud ausim* 'I would not dare'. They are, however, particularly characteristic of early comedy and the archaizing diction of laws and religious texts. Note that on this analysis, since the *s*-aorist is in origin an athematic formation (i.e. one lacking the thematic, or stem-forming, vowel *-e/o-*), and since Latin futures and subjunctives are normally derived from PIE subjunctives and optatives respectively (cf. Chapter I), the *s*-future will continue the short-vowel subjunctives of PIE athematic stems (i.e. **fax-e/o-*), while the *s*-subjunctive will naturally employ the athematic optative marker *-i-*. This suffix originally showed ablaut, but the weak forms were eventually generalized, cf. *s-ie-m* 'be', later replaced by *s-i-m*, beside plural *s-i-mus*, with /-ie:-/, /-i:-/ < **-ieh₁-*, **-ih₁-*, and the characteristic Latin shortening of long vowels before final /-m/ (1st person singular), /-t/ (3rd person singular), /-nt/ (3rd person plural) and /-r/ (1st person singular passive); note that the shortenings before /t/ and /r/ were relatively late, with long vowels often still attested in early poetry. By contrast, the fossilized *dumtaxat*, lit. 'until it touches' (so > 'as far as', 'at least', 'only'), apparently contains a thematic subjunctive, i.e. with /-a:-/, < **-o-(y)a- < **-o-ih₁-*, as in *legam* 'choose/ read', etc.; this may therefore go back to a thematic type of future stem *$*taxe/o-$, formed from the root *tag-* of *tango* 'touch' with the originally desiderative suffix *$*-(h_1)se/o-$ seen also in Greek futures. Perhaps, then, *s*-futures/subjunctives have two different origins (sigmatic aorists and desideratives), but with a variety of analogical levellings taking place amid the growing confusion as the morphological transparency and awareness of the original purpose of these various types declined.

On the other hand, original thematic aorist stems, as seen also in Greek *élipon* 'I left', *ébalon* 'I threw', may be the ultimate origin of the so-called 'root subjunctives' seen in forms like *tagam* 'touch', *attigam* 'touch/arrive', *(ad-/per-)uenam* 'come', *fuam* 'be' etc., even if some of these are not genuine archaisms but simply modelled on existing forms. Thus putative 1st person singular aorists like *$*tag-o-m$ might conceivably have had thematic subjunctives (originally optatives) such as *tagam* < *$*tag-o-ih_1-m$, a pattern which might then have led to the reanalysis of an originally athematic root aorist like *$*tola-m$ 'I carried/bore' (cf. dialectal Greek *é-tlā-n*) as *tul-a-m*, with a 'modal' suffix *-a-*, and later even prompted a set of analogical formations. Whatever the ultimate origins of such marginal forms in Old Latin, they were eliminated in the subsequent standardization of the language.

Inflection Many inflectional endings seen in the earliest Latin inscriptions have already evolved by this period, while others, though still in general use in the third and second centuries, are subsequently eliminated as part of the process of standardization.

As an example of the first category, recall that the old PIE system of verbal endings was continued in the earliest Latin, with the so-called primary endings (with a final *$*-i$ marking temporal reference to the here-and-now or the immediate/predictable future) distinguished from secondary endings (used otherwise, i.e. in past tenses and subjunctives). Traces of this contrast in fact remain only in 3rd person singular verb forms, where the original primary ending *$*-ti$ survived long enough for still prefinal *-t-* to escape the effects of the prehistoric sound change by which final [-t] was voiced; thus when its final vowel was eventually lost, primary *$*-ti > -t$, while secondary *$*-t$ had already shifted to *-d*. Early documents therefore show 3rd person singular perfects like *fec-e-d* 'did/made' (the *e*-vowel of 3rd person singular thematic aorists was generalized) and subjunctives like *kapi-a-d* 'take' alongside presents such as *iouesa-t* 'swears' and *mita-t* 'sends' (see 1.4.4). By the early third century, however, the primary endings had already been generalized and the former (already very limited) contrast was wholly lost; vowel weakening then led to progressive replacement of *-et* by *-it* (the first datable example is from 217 BC). We may also note here the alternative ending for 3rd person singular perfects, namely *-eit*. This developed first to *-it* [-i:t] by monophthongization, and then to [-it] by the usual shortening before *-t*, thereby falling together with aorist *-it* (< *-et*). This form may reflect the original 3rd person singular perfect ending *-e*, with very early addition of the primary suffix *-i* (to emphasize the present-time reference of the true perfect) and subsequent recharacterization as a 3rd person singular by the further addition of *-t(i)*; we should not, however, discount the possibility that the form is simply analogical, with substitution of *-eit* for *-et* on the basis of 1st person singular *-ei* (< *-a* + *-i*), 2nd person singular *-istei* (< *-is-ta* + *-i*). Examples with [-i:t] are sometimes metrically guaranteed in work of the early dramatists (as well as occasionally in later poetry), and *-eit* is also attested epigraphically. Unfortunately, the paucity of evidence for the crucial period of development means that we have no clear idea of how these two endings interacted prior to their formal merger.

As an example of the second category, the 3rd conjugation passive infinitive in *-ier* is still widely used in even the most official documents of the second century (e.g. *gnoscier* 'to be learned' on the *Senatus-consultum de Bacchanalibus*, on which see 5.4), but then gradually gives way to its rival in *-i*. In Classical Latin prose only the latter is acceptable. The longer form is perhaps in origin an early recharacterization of *-i*, < dative *-ei* of a neuter root noun, through the addition of a 'typical' infinitival ending *-er(e)* < *-ese*, < the locative *-es-i* of a neuter *s*-stem (though with later segmentation of *-se* as a suffix in its own right, as in *es-se* 'be', *ama-re* 'love' < *ama-se*, etc.). Note that the development of a systematic opposition of voice in such verbal nouns is likely to have been a secondary development, motivated in part by their growing use in indirect statements, where replication of the grammatical categories of the finite forms of direct speech was semantically important. But if, prehistorically, such verbal nouns were typically governed, and their cases assigned accordingly, 'voice' would normally be contextually determined by the semantics of the relevant phrasal head: contrast 'Marcus is keen for-eating' (= 'for him to eat something') with 'these fish are good for-eating' (= 'for someone to eat them'). The subsequent functional specialization may well reflect the fact that originally locative expressions of this type, such as the infinitival forms in *-ere*, are characteristically active in meaning (cf. 'keen on-eating', 'good at-fighting', etc.), thus leaving the dative type to take on the passive role by default.

Similarly, the ending *-ere* (i.e. [-e:re]) of the 3rd person plural perfect indicative, still very much a marker of the 'high style' in official documents of the early second century as well as in Cato's historical and rhetorical works, gradually gives way to its originally less valued rival *-erunt*, though in this case the former was not ousted until very much later, partly because of its obvious metrical usefulness in poetry. Apart from the Saturnian (see 5.3.1), Latin metres, borrowed and adapted from Greek, involve patterns of metrical 'feet' composed of fixed combinations of light and heavy syllables, the former involving short vowels in open syllables (those not ending in a consonant), the latter long vowels and diphthongs in open syllables and both short and long vowels, or diphthongs, in closed syllables (those ending in a consonant). Note, however, that syllabification crosses word boundaries, so that *fēcit*, for example, would be syllabified *fē-ci-tV-* before a word beginning with a vowel, but as *fē-cit-CV-* before a word beginning with a consonant. Since light syllables are a regular element of many types of feet, the option of having *-ēre* (with a naturally light final syllable as opposed to the heavy final syllable of *-ērunt*) is therefore extremely helpful.

It is perhaps worth noting here that *-erunt* may be scanned in verse with both long /e:/ and short /e/, i.e. with either a heavy or a light initial syllable. The latter variant is < *-is-ont(i)*, where the original secondary thematic (aorist) ending has again been replaced by the corresponding primary ending (i.e. originally in *-i* before loss). This has been added to a perfect stem incorporating the *-is-* element seen elsewhere in the perfect system (cf. the perfect infinitive *amau-is-se* 'to have loved', etc.); *-is-* then > *-er-* by rhotacism and the regular lowering of /-i-/ before /-r-/. This is the form that is reflected directly in Romance, and it was presumably the 'popular' form throughout. It seems, then, that the 'standard' variant, with the long vowel, was in origin a blend of this Early Latin innovation with its older rival *-ēre*, which reflects an alternative inherited 3rd person plural ending *-ēr* + primary marker *-i* ([i] is always lowered in final position when not lost, cf. *mare* 'sea' < *mari*). The rise of *-ērunt* may well therefore date from the advent of this long-vowel variant and its adoption by the Roman elite.

Nominal morphology

Many alternative endings and declensional patterns are in evidence in Old Latin inscriptions as well as in early literature and in ancient documents partly preserved as quotations in later writers (such as the Twelve Tables and various *carmina*, on which see 5.5). A few examples will suffice here (see Klingenschmitt 1992 for a thorough, if sometimes idiosyncratic account).

Ablative singulars; partial merger of i-stems and consonant-stems in the 3rd declension The inherited ablative singular of the 2nd declension in *-od* [-o:d] gave rise prehistorically to a set of analogical ablative singulars containing long vowels in the other declensional patterns involving vowel-stems, so -*ad* (1st declension), -*id* (3rd declension *i*-stems), -*ud* (4th declension). The traditional spelling persists in inscriptions of the third and second centuries, even after the loss of final /-d/ (cf. 4.2.1 under 'some sound changes and their consequences for spelling'). Obviously consonant-stem nouns of the 3rd declension had no vowel to be lengthened, and the classical ending of the ablative singular is -*e* ([-e]), variously explained as a normal phonological reflex of the inherited locative ($*$-i), which is, however, hard to account for functionally, or of the instrumental ($*$-eh_1), which is fine functionally, but requires special pleading to account for the phonology (? a shortening of [-e:] < $*$-eh_1 or an odd reflex of the zero-grade variant $*$-h_1).

Even in Classical Latin, however, the 3rd declension terminations represent a blend of consonant-stem and *i*-stem forms, a confusion prompted in part by the prehistoric syncopation of the characteristic stem-vowel in many deverbal nouns originally ending in -*ti-s*, such as *mors* 'death', *pars* 'part', *gens* 'clan/race', *mens* 'mind', etc.: thus the consonant-stem (C-stem) accusative singular -*em*, < syllabic $*$$m$, very largely replaced the *i*-stem ending -*im*, the *i*-stem nominative plural -*es* /-e:s/, < $*$-ei-es (by loss of the intervocalic semivowel [j] and contraction), replaced the original C-stem ending $*$-es /-es/ (with short vowel), while the C-stem accusative plural -*es* /-e:s/, < $*$-ens < $*$$ns$ (through the normal Latin treatment of the syllabic nasal followed by simplification of the consonant cluster and compensatory lengthening of the vowel), eventually replaced the *i*-stem form in -*is* /-i:s/, < $*$-i-ns, etc. The establishment of stable paradigms clearly took some time, and it is therefore no surprise that Old Latin shows possibilities that were later rejected in the classical language. Most notable among these is the continuing uncertainty about the choice of -*um* or -*ium* in the genitive plural of many nouns (e.g. *marum* 'of the seas', etc.), and the use of the *i*-stem ablative singular in -*id* with C-stem nouns in inscriptions of the third and second centuries (e.g. *couentionid* 'gathering', etc.). It is worth noting, however, that there is also very limited evidence for alternative C-stem ablatives in -*ed* from inscriptions of the late third and second centuries (e.g. *dictatored* CIL I² 25, *c]osoled* CIL I² 19, *leged* M. Mello and G. Voza *Le Iscrizione de Paestum*, number 139). Wachter (1987: 424–5) treats these as false archaisms of a purely graphic nature (recall that the pronunciation of original final /-d/ after long vowels ceased in the latter part of the third century), arguing that the occasional addition of -*d* to ablative -*e* in official documents, a combination which he believes was actually pronounced [-e], was motivated by a desire to identify C-stem ablatives visually in a period when the final -*m* of accusative singulars was also frequently not written (and presumably not pronounced either: see 4.3 below for further discussion of CIL I² 25).

Genitive singulars Serious forms of Early Latin poetry, such as epic and tragedy, show a particular tendency to deliberate archaism in morphology, motivated in part by the model of Homeric Greek, where the integral archaism reflects not only the antiquity of the tradition but also the continuing metrical usefulness of archaic forms. Recall in this connection that the first true Latin poem is a 'translation' of the Odyssey by Livius Andronicus, a Greek slave from Tarentum who came to Rome as a prisoner of war after the surrender of his city to the Romans in 272 BC. Thus we find genitive singulars of the first declension in original *-as* [-a:s], routinely retained only in the fossilized *paterfamilias* 'father of the family', but now attested epigraphically on the Tita Vendia vase of the late seventh century (see (4) at 1.4.5). Around the beginning of the third century this ending was remodelled into disyllabic *-a-i* [-a:-i:], with *-i* taken from the 2nd declension, perhaps as part of a levelling promoted by the regular association of 1st- and 2nd-declension forms in adjectival paradigms (*-us, -a, -um*), and/or by the asymmetry of syntagmatic structures such as **agricolas boni* 'of a good farmer', where a masculine noun of the first declension was modified by a 2nd-declension adjective. Whatever the motivation, [-a:i:] had evolved into the regular diphthong [-ai] (later [-ai̯]) by around 200 BC. However, the disyllabic form is often still attested in poetry of the third and second centuries, and occasionally even in classical verse, largely for metrical reasons (many examples appear at the line end, where a sequence of two long vowels, forming two heavy syllables, was particularly useful), and it may even appear in some early inscriptions, if *-ai* does not already represent a diphthong there.

The PIE genitive singular of C-stems showed qualitative ablaut variation (under now unrecoverable conditions), with reflexes going back to both **-es* and **-os*. Though the former prevailed in Latin (eventually > *-is* by vowel weakening), *-os* (> *-us*) is also still attested in Old Latin, particularly in certain traditional names and formulae in the case of official documents, but also more generally in regional Latin, e.g. *nominus Latini* 'of the Latin name', etc.

Some nouns of the 4th declension (*u*-stems) also have alternative 2nd-declension (*o*-stem) genitives, so *senati* 'senate' rather than *senatus*, etc. *Domus* 'house' remains a 'mixed' type even in Classical Latin, but many more of these survived in popular varieties, and eventually the 4th declension was fully merged with the 2nd by late imperial times, as the Romance languages show. Nouns of the 4th declension may also have genitive singular in *-u-os* (or *-u-is*) rather than *-us* [-u:s] (e.g. *senatuos*, etc.). Both reflect inherited patterns of declension, the former showing a 'weak' form of the stem with a 'full' ending, the latter, < *-ou-s*, showing a 'full' form of the stem and a 'weak' ending, the original distribution in PIE having perhaps been accentually determined.

Pronominal forms Some pronouns in Classical Latin combine both *o*-stem (2nd declension) and *i*-stem (3rd declension) forms in a single paradigm, e.g. nominative singular *i-s* 'that one' beside accusative singular *e(i)-u-m*, nominative plural *qui* (< **quoi*) 'who' beside dative-ablative plural *quibus*, etc. Old Latin shows a greater variety of such forms, including an accusative demonstrative *im*. This extended variety is particularly apparent in the interrogative/indefinite and relative pronouns, however, where the former show more *i*-stem forms than survive in Classical Latin, the latter more *o*-stem ones: e.g. nominative plural *ques* (interrogative/indefinite) beside *quei* (relative), dative/ablative plural *queis* (relative) beside *quibus* (interrogative/indefinite). But partial merger was already in place, and a number of 'redundant' case forms are already fossilized in special uses, e.g. accusative singular *quom* (*cum*) = 'since/when', replaced by *i*-stem *quem*, neuter plural *quia* = 'because', replaced by *o*-stem *quae*, ablative singular *qui* = 'how?/whereby/so that', replaced by *o*-stem *quo*.

There is also a wider range of pronominal roots still in use in Old Latin, most notably accusative forms like *som, sam, sas, sos*, which are attested, for example, in the XII Tables and in early poetry and go back to the PIE demonstrative that is the source of the Greek definite article *ho* (masculine), *hē* (feminine), *tó* (neuter); this element is preserved later only in *si(c)* (< **sei(-ce)*, i.e. locative with optional deictic suffix, = 'in that (case)', developing to both 'if' and 'thus'), *sed* 'but' (< ablative **sed* [se:d], lit. 'without this'), and *tum* ('then', remodelled as a conventional 2nd-declension neuter – the original form was **tod*), as well as in *ille* 'that one (there)' (< *olle* < **ol-so*, where the initial vowel of the Classical Latin forms is the result of remodelling after *is/iste* 'that one/that one (by you)', the second of which itself perhaps comes from *is-to*).

4.2.3 *Syntax, lexicon and style*

The surviving inscriptions of the third century are mainly brief and syntactically very simple, but second-century epigraphic material, especially that with an official function, is often much more complex, and already provides clear evidence of a very sophisticated set of syntactic rules and conventions, some of which will be discussed in detail below. On the literary side, however, we have quite extensive fragments of a number of early poets and prose writers, the surviving comedies of Plautus (*c.*254–184 BC) and Terence (*c.*185–159 BC), and the *de Agri Cultura* of Cato (234–148 BC) as a basis for building up a fuller picture of the state and variety of written Latin from the later third century onwards, always allowing for the fact that the texts in question have been partly modernized, most obviously orthographically, in the process of transmission. Here we may simply note that many features of traditional religious and legal *carmina* (assuming that the few surviving examples are indeed typical of the most ancient practice) are carried over and developed in various ways in early varieties of both official and literary Latin prose, and to some extent also in verse (see (h) below). This reflects the natural exploitation of an existing 'source' for the dignified stylization of diction appropriate to a range of newly emerging higher functions, though this source is from the first combined with other stylistic and rhetorical devices adopted from the more sophisticated traditions of writing in Greek, elements which, as time goes on, come to predominate in all but the most official styles (where indigenous 'Romanness' was naturally at a premium). A few examples of traditional Roman practice will suffice here (see also Bennett 1910–14 and Courtney 1999):

(a)   Changes of subject are not always clearly indicated grammatically/ lexically, a feature that seems to have its roots in the language of the law (see, for example, surviving quotations from the famous XII Tables, whose origin perhaps goes back to the fifth century BC: thus I.1, *si in ius uocat, ito* 'if (he = a plaintiff) calls (him = a defendant) to law, (he = the defendant) shall-go').

(b)   The standard phrasal and sentential connective is *-que* 'and', with *atque* still highly marked (and as such typical of literary rather than official styles); there is also heavy use of simple temporal (e.g. *tum* 'then') and anaphoric (*is, ea, id* 'that one') elements rather than logical conjunctions (e.g. *enim* 'for', *igitur* 'therefore', etc.) and connecting relatives (very much the marker of a higher style in Old Latin) to provide textual cohesion, though asyndeton also remains common, not only between sentences but also between sets of co-ordinated words (the latter is probably very old: note that the names of consuls, for example, never have connecting *-que*).

(c)   Topic-comment-afterthought structures are routine, with much 'loose' syntax between the component parts of sentences (of the type 'as for X, he must do Y, and Z as well'). This sort of layout is quite unlike that of the carefully integrated structure of a Ciceronian 'period' (developed later under the influence of Isocratean rhetorical practice), though a refined version of it survives in the trope of prolepsis. It is particularly apparent in the frequent preposing of relative clauses, again with anaphoric resumption in the main clause (e.g. '(he) who does X, that (one) shall Y', etc.), a structure much favoured in legal/official styles and often retained in that context into the Empire.

(d)   The basic word order is already standardized to (S)OV in simple narration and in official edicts, though literary styles in general and naturalistic dialogue in particular admit of much more variation, both for dramatic effect and/or linking purposes (for which see (f)).

(e)   There is still some considerable heterogeneity in syntactic usage. For example:

(i)   Many deponent verbs that impose 'marked' cases on their comple-ments in Classical Latin may take the unmarked accusative, at least as an option (*utor* 'use', *fungor* 'perform', *fruor* 'enjoy', etc.). Some also alternate freely with 'regularized' active counterparts, as *arbitro/arbitror*, etc.

(ii)   The indicative may be used in subordinate clauses in indirect speech, in circumstantial *cum*-clauses (= 'since'), and in indirect questions (perhaps still with a difference of meaning in this case, denoting questions of fact, e.g. 'I wonder what he is doing', rather than questions with potential or deontic force, e.g. 'I wonder what he can/should do').

(iii)   Deverbal nouns in -*tus* and -*tio* retain a much closer relationship with their verbal roots, the latter in particular often taking an accusative rather than a genitive 'object' (e.g. *quid istum tactio?* 'why the touching (of) him?'). Note too the use of neuter perfect passive participles as verbal nouns, especially in the phrase *quid opus est?* (e.g. *quid opus est facto?* lit. 'what is the need of action?', i.e. 'what needs to be done?').

(f)   By classical standards there is little apparent concern for variation in the use of vocabulary, and repetition is sometimes used deliberately to provide textual cohesion, often through chiastic structures (e.g. 'X (subject) must Y (verb), and Y (verb) must also Z (subject)'), some-thing else which may reflect the traditional usage of *carmina* (on which see (h)).

(g)   Some vocabulary has a 'colloquial' feel from the point of view of Classical Latin, though this is often the result of later stigmatization resulting from the standardization process. For example, diminutives may be used rather freely, compound adverbs are quite common (*derepente/desubito* 'suddenly' etc., many of which then 'resurface' in later vulgar Latin and in Romance), and *nimis* 'too' and *bene* 'well' may be used as adjectival intensifiers meaning little more than 'very'.

Particularly characteristic of Old Latin, however, is the productive use, often well beyond their original functional distribution, of certain derivational suffixes that were later strongly disfavoured or at least highly restricted; we find, for example, many more abstract nouns in *-tudo*, adjectives in *-eus, -osus* and *-bundus*, and adverbs in *-ter* and *-im* than survive in the classical language. This reflects directly a period of experimentation (quite a lot of the relevant forms are *hapax legomena*, and we often find whole sets of formations with no apparent difference in meaning, e.g. *squalor, squalitas, squalitudo, squales*) when the need to develop new vocabulary was beginning to be felt quite acutely as the range of functions the language was called upon to perform expanded, and Latin writers came to feel increasingly 'under-resourced' when faced with the lexical exuberance of their Greek models. Particularly noteworthy in this connection is the revival of (especially adjectival) compounding under Greek influence, at least in belletristic writing (especially poetry): otherwise in Early Latin compounding is severely restricted, the only truly common type being negative exocentric compounds beginning with *in-* (e.g. *inermis* 'unarmed', etc.).

(h) Certain syntactic structures, such as the framing of injunctions with *uti* (positive) or *ne* (negative) + the subjunctive, as well as certain stylistic devices, such as a liking for *figura etymologica* (i.e. the use in a construction of a noun and a verb from the same root), the repetition of key phrases and vocabulary, and the frequent use of short rhythmical cola involving pairs/triples of alliterative and/or assonant synonyms (*congeries*) or the exhaustive enumeration of options, seem to reflect the traditional language of ancient legal and religious 'texts' (*carmina*).

This 'padded style' was perhaps first motivated by the need to cover all the options when framing a successful injunction or an efficacious prayer, but it was quickly institutionalized by precedent and tradition. The associated rhythmical special effects, which often impart a strongly incantatory quality, must originally have enhanced the memorability of such texts in a still largely oral culture, but they must also have been felt to help convey the absolute seriousness of their purpose by distancing the language from everyday usage. These traditional functions are to some extent retained in official documents of the second century, where the relevant techniques may still be used to underline the importance of the content and the authority of the issuing body, though their use in contemporary literary compositions is already more conscious and selective, often marking a high level of emotional commitment on the part of the writer, and so constituting no more than one of many devices exploited for the demarcation of specifically poetic/belletristic styles.

4.3 An Example: The *Columna Rostrata*

As an illustration of some of these features, and of the problems raised by attempts to maintain a traditional (i.e. archaizing) style, whether in restoring an older text or in composing an original document, we may consider here the famous honorary inscription of C. Duilius (CIL I² 25) from the *Columna Rostrata*, so named because part of the column in question comprised the *rostra*, or 'beaks', of Carthaginian ships. Duilius was consul in 260 BC during the first Punic War, and the document celebrates his naval victory over the Carthaginians in that year.

Unfortunately, the text we have was either recut and heavily restored, or, in the opinion of some, even first composed, during the early imperial period, as the letter forms and various false archaisms clearly show (see below). But even if the text was indeed composed under Augustus or Claudius (this was, after all, a period for reconnecting the present with Rome's 'glorious past'), it must at least have been modelled on genuine inscriptions of the era to which it relates, and to that extent may still provide a plausible illustration of the 'simple' narrative style used to commemorate the achievements of Roman commanders, and later employed on a far grander scale in Augustus's *Res Gestae* (*Monumentum Ancyranum*). The style should not, however, obscure the fact that the subject matter of such texts is always very carefully selected and organized, and often given a politically motivated 'spin'. Note here the explicitly 'heroic' character of Duilius's ground-breaking exploits, and the fact that the events are not chronologically ordered, but organized according to whether they took place on land or sea; we know that Segesta, for example, was relieved after the sea battle. The rather extensive restorations, included here to give the whole a clear meaning, are largely the work of Mommsen, based in part on Polybius's account (I.23ff.) of the events in question:

(1)   CIL I² 25
[. . . Secest]ano[s . . .
    Segestans-ACC

opsidione]d exemet   lecione[esque Cartacinienses omnes
siege-ABL   deliver-3sg.PG troops-and-NOM Carthaginian-NOM all-NOM

ma]ximosque macistr[a]tos l[uci   palam post dies
greatest-and-NOM magistrate-NOM light-LOC openly after days-ACC

n]ouem castreis exfociont, Mace[lamque opidom
nine   camp-ABL flee-3pl.PRES, Macella=ACC   town-ACC

p]ucnandod cepet.   enque eodem mac[istratud bene
fighting-ABL   take-2sg.PF in-and same-ABL magistracy-ABL well

r]em   nauebos marId consol   prImos c[eset   copiasque
thing-ACC ships-ABL sea-LOC consul-NOM first-NOM do-3sg.PF forces-and-ACC

c]lasesque nauales prImos ornauet   para[uetque],
fleets-ACC   naval-ACC first-NOM equip-3sg.PF prepare-and-3sg.PF,

cumque eis   nauebos claseis   Poenicas omn[is item   ma-
with-and   these-ABL ships-ABL fleets-ACC Punic-ACC all-ACC likewise

-x]umas   copias   CartaciniensIs praesente[d Hanibaled]
greatest-ACC forces-ACC Carthaginian-ACC present-ABL   Hannibal-ABL

dictatored ol[or]om inaltod   marId pucn[andod uicet]
dictator-ABL them-GEN on-high-ABL sea-ABL fighting-ABL   beat-3sg.PF,

uique   naue[is cepet]   cum socieis   septer[esmom I, quin-
force-and-ABL ships-ACC take-3sg.PF with associates-ABL septireme-ACC   one,

-queres]mosque triresmosque   naueis X[XX, merset   XIII.
quinqueremes-ACC triremes-and-ACC ships-ACC 30,   sink-3sg.PF 13

au]rom   captom   numei . . .
gold-NOM taken-NOM coins/pieces-NOM . . .

arcen]tom captom   praeda   numei . . .
silver-NOM taken-NOM booty-NOM coins/pieces-NOM . . .

omne] captom   aes . . . [
all-NOM taken-NOM money-NOM . . .

[. . .]   . . .   [. . . prI-

-mos   qu]oque naualed praedad poplom [donauet   prI-
first-NOM also   naval-ABL booty-ABL people-ACC present-3sg.PF

-mosque]   Cartacini[ens]is [ince]nuos d[uxet   in
first-and-NOM Carthaginians-ACC free-born-ACC lead-3sg.PF in

triumpod]   . . .
triumph-ABL

'. . . the Segestans . . . he delivered from blockade, and all the Carthaginian troops and their greatest magistrate [Hamilcar] fled from their camp openly in daylight after nine days; and he took the town of Macella by force of arms. And in the same magistracy he was the first to perform an exploit at sea with ships as consul, and the first to equip and prepare naval forces and fleets; and with these ships he defeated on the high seas by force of arms all the Punic fleets, likewise the greatest Carthaginian forces, in the presence of Hannibal their supreme commander, and by force he seized ships with their complements, 1 septireme, 30 quinqueremes and triremes, (and) sank 13. Gold taken – . . . pieces. Silver taken, booty – . . . pieces. Total money taken . . . He was also the first to present the people with booty from a sea-battle and the first to lead free-born Carthaginians in triumph . . .'

Genuine features of Duilius's period include the use of *c* to represent /g/ (*macistratos, pucnandod*), the retention of [-oi-] (*Poenicas*, though the contemporary spelling was -*oi*-), the absence of double consonants (*numei, olorum*: note too the retention of *ol*-) and of vowel weakening (*maximos, macistratos, consol, exfociont, exemet/cepet/ornauet*), the retention of *ei*-spellings (*castreis, socieis*), the use of ablative singulars in -*d* (*pucnandod, marId, inaltod*, though note *uique*, where the restorer perhaps had doubts about using -*d* before the clitic connective), and the relentless use of the connective -*que*. Though the prepositions used in *enque eodem* and *inaltod* might be thought to belong to different periods, the first, as host to enclitic -*que* must in fact be a 'stronger' form phonologically, with the second perhaps representing a contemporary proclitic reduction (note the spelling as one word, and contrast unweakened *en manom* on the 'Duenos vase', probably of the sixth century). Unfortunately, it is unclear whether proclitic weakening had already occurred in Roman Latin by the first half of the third century, so the status of the variants here must remain uncertain.

By contrast with the certainly archaic features noted above, the completely regular use of final -*m* is rather odd in the context of the orthographic practice of other third-century Roman documents, though it may be that the heavy hand of officialdom had already standardized the spelling in this respect, as most of the examples of omission come either from poetic texts in Saturnians or regional/personal inscriptions (on which see 4.4 below). But the addition of a final -*d* to 3rd-declension C-stem ablative singulars (*dictatored, naualed*, the latter in fact an *i*-stem adjective with the C-stem ending, as sometimes elsewhere outside classical prose) seems to involve no more than a generalization of the archaism; as already noted, such forms are not very well attested and may simply have been motivated to distinguish ablatives from accusatives graphically (cf. 4.2.2 'Ablative singulars' above). Further confusion is apparent in the forms *clases nauales, claseis* (*Poenicas*), and *naueis*, all of which, like *CartaciniensIs*, are *i*-stem accusative plurals, though only the last shows the expected ending (and even that is spelled anachronistically with 'i longa'). It seems that the final levelling of the C-stem and *i*-stem accusative plural endings to -*es* [-e:s], characteristic of the Augustan period, has affected the spelling of the first example, while in the others -*ei*- has been wrongly substituted for -*i*- [-i:-] in the mistaken belief that this ending, like many other forms by then containing [-i:-], was earlier spelled with the diphthong (as ablative *castreis*). Compare also the substitution of -*e*- for original -*i*- in *nauebos* and of -*o*- for original -*u*- in the root of *exfociont*, both based on the false assumption that the relevant vowels would have been 'unweakened' in the period of Duilius (as in 3rd person singular -*et* and 3rd person plural -*ont* respectively). (It is assumed here that *exfociont* is indeed an earlier version of *effugiunt* ('flee from') rather than a careless spelling of *exfodiont* ('dig out'), thus making *macistratos* a nominative singular rather than accusative plural of the 2nd declension – either way, this is a variant of the usual 4th declension form, as evidenced elsewhere for *senatus* etc.)

Another interesting issue here is the shift of tense from perfect to present in the non-initial member of the closely linked conjuncts *Secestanos . . . exemet, lecionesque . . . exfociont*, where the second event is a consequence of the first, perhaps partly overlapping with it in time, and not merely one of the series of discrete occurrences marked by perfects. This usage may well already involve a deliberate imitation of a similar Greek practice, while also providing us with a clue as to the origins of the so-called 'historic present', i.e. as a tense originally employed as a grammatically 'reduced form' in a thematically linked context in which the leading verb has set the necessary temporal parameters (so replacing the PIE injunctive in this function). The classical use of the present indicative in *dum* 'while' clauses may well be related.

4.4   Dialectal Variation in Latin in the Period *c.*400–*c.*150 BC

4.4.1   Latin outside Latium

To complete the background necessary for the study of the early development of specifically Roman Latin, we must also consider here briefly the rather limited evidence for regional and social variation in this period. Some of the non-Roman Latin inscriptions of this era provide tantalizing glimpses of what, given the very recent spread of the language and the correspondingly high incidence of imperfect bilingualism, must have been very considerable diversity in local speech, especially in areas beyond Latium. Unfortunately, most of the relevant texts are isolated, and, in the absence of comparable material, are often difficult, sometimes impossible, to interpret. We should also bear in mind that, while some of the poorly understood phenomena in evidence may represent long-term substrate effects that had become established in the local Latin patois, others may simply reflect ephemeral developments, induced by interference from a first language on the imperfect learning of Latin by particular individuals; unfortunately, we often have no secure basis for distinguishing between the two cases when dealing with 'odd' features in specific texts (see Adams forthcoming, chs 2 and 3) for full discussion and evaluation of the evidence).

Consider now the following selection of documents (2–5 below), from a variety of areas beyond Latium, and dating from the fifth to the second centuries BC:

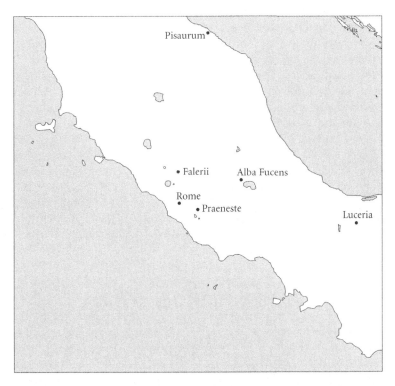

Map 4.1 Places where inscriptions discussed in Chapter IV were found

(2) CIL I² 5: the bronze 'Fucine Lake inscription' (found near Alba
     Fucens in Marsian territory and first published in 1877, but now
     lost), probably of the very late fourth century BC. This inscription
     has long resisted satisfactory interpretation because of probable
     errors of transcription in the published versions, but the new text
     proposed by Crawford (2006), based on careful examination of
     relatively recently recovered photographs of the original, at last
     provides the basis for a meaningful translation that relates well
     to the likely context of 'archaic' Italian raiding and warfare. The arrows
     indicate the direction of writing:

Caso   Cantouio   →
Casus-NOM Cantouius-NOM
Aprufclano   cei-   ←
of-Aproficulum-NOM took-3sg
p(et) apud finem   →
     by   boundary-ACC

Calicom   en ur- →
?Gallic-ACC in city-ABL
bid Caiontoni ←
   Caiontonius-GEN
socieque   dono- →
allies-NOM-and gift-ACC
m atolere Anctia ←
   took-3pl Angitia-DAT
pro l[ecio]nibus Mar- →
for   ligions-ABL   Marsic-ABL
tses ←

'Casus Cantouius of Aproficulum captured (this) near the *finis Gallicus* in the city of Caiontonius, and his *socii* brought it as a gift to Angitia on behalf of the Marsic troops [probably not yet "legions", levied to fight with the Romans, but rather men in the private army of Casus Cantouius].'

Though some details remain uncertain (e.g. what exactly is the *finis Gallicus*?), the text clearly refers to booty seized by Casus Cantouius of Aproficulum (cf. del Tutto, Prosdocimi and Rocca 2002: 55), which his *socii* brought to the shrine of Angitia, perhaps following his death in battle. Note the characteristic markers of Latin as opposed to those of an Italic language (in this case Marsian), namely *-que* (not *-pe*) < * *-k^we*, with retention of the labio-velar, and *-b-* (not *-f-*) < * *-bh-* in *-ibus* (also with early vowel weakening). Note also, however, the non-Latin development of *-ti-* to an affricate in *Martses* (= ablative plural *Marsis*: the Latin word is *Martius*, so the name *Marsi* is clearly not of Latin origin), and the early monophthongization of /ei/ > /e:/ (as also in *socie*), both characteristic of Marsian and Paelignian; the name *Aprufclano(s)* is also Sabellian, as the medial *-f-* and syncopation of short unstressed vowels show. *Ceip*, with mistakenly written *-i-* (recall that the monophthongization of /ei/ led to a close mid-vowel similar to original /e:/, with some consequential spelling errors), is plausibly taken to be an abbreviation of *cepet*; *en urbid* shows the still unweakened form of *in* plus an *i*-stem ending for the ablative of a consonant-stem noun, as often in Old Latin, while *Anctia*, with long final /a:/ and syncopation of /i/, is the 1st declension dative singular of a divine name = *Angitiae*. This form involves an alternative treatment of the original long diphthong /a:i/, originally occurring only prevocalically, i.e. with loss of the final element in hiatus, but then generalized: the shortening seen in the regular Classical Latin paradigm represents the preconsonantal variant in origin. Curiously, Classical Latin eventually generalized the long-vowel variant of the dative singular in the *o*-stems (i.e. /-o:/ < /-o:i/) alongside the diphthongal variant in the *a*-stems. Such datives in *-a* are more commonly found outside Rome, but the examples are almost all of divine names or attributes of divinities, leading to the possibility that the form was already an archaism, and one that may also have been characteristic of 'traditional' Roman Latin generally in a period for which there is little relevant Roman evidence (see (a) under 'Possible collateral features *vis-à-vis* Roman Latin' in 4.4.2 below for a full discussion).

(3)   CIL I² 401: the *Lex Lucerina*, from Luceria (Apulia), perhaps from the late third century BC:

In hoce   loucarid stircus
in   this-ABL grove-ABL dung-ACC

ne[qu]is   fundatid neue cadauer
no one-NOM dump-?   nor   corpse-ACC

proiecitad neue parentatid
cast-?   nor   perform-sacrifices-for-a dead-relative-?.

sei quis   aruorsu hac   faxit   [ceiu]ium
if   anyone-NOM against   this-ABL act-3sg.FUT citizens-GEN

quis   uolet   pro   ioudicatod   n.   [L]
whoever wish-3sg.FUT, by-way-of judgement-ABL sesterces [50]

manum iniect[i]o   estod   seiue
hand-ACC laying-on-NOM be-3sg.IMP If-or

mac[i]isteratus uolet   moltare
magistrate-NOM   wish-3sg.FUT fine-INF

[li]cetod
be-allowed-3sg.IMP.

'In this grove let no one tip dung nor cast a dead body nor perform sacrifices for a dead relative. If anyone acts contrary to this, (and) if any citizen wishes, let there be, by way of a judgement, a laying of hands upon him in the sum of 50 sesterces. Or if a magistrate wishes to impose a fine, let this be allowed.'

Unfortunately, the original has again been lost since it was first copied, and the transcription may be less than wholly accurate (a possibility of some significance, as we shall see). Luceria is in northern Apulia adjacent to Samnite (Oscan-speaking) territory, and was probably under Samnite control until Roman colonisation in the late fourth century. Vowel weakening in *aruorsu(m)*, and perhaps in *macisteratus* if this is a 2nd- rather than 4th-declension form, suggests, however, that this document postdates the period of colonization.

There are many familiar features of Old Latin in evidence here, reinforced by the archaizing tendencies characteristic of legal documents throughout history. Note in particular the 'verbal' syntax of the accusative after *iniectio* (a usage common enough in Plautine Latin, e.g. *Curculio* 626, *quid tibi istum tactio est* 'what business do you have touching him?'), and the double conditional protasis with asyndeton, so characteristic of early laws. We may compare the following instance from the XII Tables: *si nox furtum faxsit, si im occisit, iure caesus esto* (VIII.12), 'if he [= someone] commits a theft at night, (and) if he [= someone else] kills him, let him be lawfully killed', where the use of *s*-forms in the protases and an imperative in *-to(d)* in the apodosis anticipates very nicely the form of the first conditional sentence above. Note, however, that by the late third century the *s*-form had come to be regarded as equivalent to a future indicative (cf. *uolet*). We may speculate, nonetheless, that prehistoric Latin had used present or perfect (= aorist) subjunctives quite generally in this context (= 'if on any occasion X'), much in the manner of Greek, which in fact provided the model for Early Latin law codes, but that these were progressively replaced by a mish-mash of presents, perfects and futures (or future perfects) after vowel weakenings and shortenings obliterated earlier formal distinctions (see Coleman 1996). Consider, for example, 3rd person singular indicatives like present *facit* ('make'/'do') or perfect *ru:pit* ('burst'), versus hypothetical athematic 3rd person singular subjunctives like present **faci:t* (cf. *faci:mus*, the transmitted reading of Plautus *Truculentus* 60, and *uelit* 'wish'/*edit* 'eat'/*duit* 'give'), and perfect **ru:pi:t*. The sole exception would appear to have been those cases involving 'distinctive' *s*-forms (originally functioning as aorist subjunctives), with the result that these soon came to be regarded simply as 'old-fashioned' futures/future perfects in the relevant cases.

What is particularly interesting here, however, is the evidence for Oscan substrate effects on Latin. Though the text is probably too early for the Oscan preservation of diphthongs to be a distinguishing influence on local Latin, we may note the raising of [-e-] before a group [-rC-] in *stircus*, and the anaptyxis in *macisteratus*, both very characteristic of Oscan. The strange verb forms *fundatid*, *proiecitad* and *parentatid* are also potentially important in this connection, although there is no wholly satisfying explanation for them (see Wallace 1988). There are three possible accounts, as follows. They may represent a local development within Latin, involving a conflation of present subjunctive and imperative forms motivated by overlapping use in commands and prohibitions: thus *fundassid/fundatod* > new imperative *fundatid*, *proieciad/proiecitod* > new imperative *proiecitad*, etc. But though *ne* + present subjunctive does indeed overlap with *ne* + imperative (and *ne* + perfect subjunctive) as a means of expressing prohibitions in Old Latin, and while subjunctives and imperatives similarly overlap in commands, it is probably significant that both the commands here have only the conventional imperatival form (*estod, licetod*). Why should the supposed contamination have been so 'selective', and affected only the prohibitions? Alternatively, we may be dealing with a local Oscan development, again based on functional overlap between subjunctives and imperatives, which then influenced the Latin dialect: thus the Oscan style present subjunctives **funda-id, *proieci-ad* might have led to similarly modified forms of the normal imperatives *funda-tud, proiec-tud*, etc. But in roughly contemporary Oscan texts, the subjunctive is rarely used in commands and prohibitions, and all examples are in any case perfect, while imperatives are not used at all in prohibitions. There seems, therefore, to be little distributional basis for the supposed contamination. Finally, then, we may be dealing with straightforward adoption of Oscan forms into local Latin: thus the standard perfect subjunctives *fundatt-id/parentatt-id*, representing the normal usage in Oscan prohibitions, may simply have been carried over into Latin (though with characteristic single spelling of the double consonants). This, however, fails to account for *proiecitad*, which is not an Oscan perfect subjunctive form. One possibility, and it is no more than that, is that this is a graphic error for *proiecat(t)id* (assuming local Latin *proiecare* for *proiecere*, cf. parallel *fundare* for *fundere*), either original, or introduced when the document was first transcribed: recall that the original is lost and cannot now be checked. Whatever the true story, these forms, taken with the other evidence for Oscan substrate influence, may perhaps be taken to point to a form of contact-induced change, possibly first occurring in Samnite Latin but perhaps eventually passing into the substantard speech of local Latins too. Alternatively, we may be dealing with an essentially ephemeral phenomenon, reflecting the partial competence in Latin of a particular Samnite speaker. In the absence of comparable evidence, these issues must once again remain unresolved.

(4) CIL I² 378 and 379: inscribed on stone pillars from Pisaurum in Umbria, probably from the early second century BC:

(a) Iunone   Reg(ina)
     Juno-DAT Queen-DAT

     matrona
     matrons-NOM

     Pisaurese
     from-Pisaurum-NOM

     dono   dedrot
     gift-ACC gave-3pl

     'To Queen Juno, matrons from Pisaurum gave [this] as a gift.'

(b) Matre
     Mother-DAT

     Matuta
     Morning-DAT

     dono   dedro
     gift-ACC gave-3pl

     matrona
     matrons-NOM

     M'. Curia
     Mania Curia-NOM

     Pola   Liuia
     Pola-NOm Livia-NOM

     deda
     ?nurses-NOM/give-3pl.PRES

'To Mother Morning, matrons gave [this] as a gift – Mania Curia
and Pola Livia, nurses/are the donors.'

Just as the women in (4b) still have praenomina, showing that they
were not yet fully integrated 'Romans', so too the Latin in these
examples may well display some Umbrian characteristics, especially in its
morphology and in the loss of final consonants. Note first the possible
1st-declension nominative plurals *matrona (Pisaurese)* and *deda*, which
perhaps involve an Italic-style formation in [-a:s] but with characteristically
Umbrian loss of the final consonant, as also seen in *Pisaurese < Pisaurenses*
(which, incidentally, shows a surprising retention of /au/, given *Pola <
Paula*; since Umbrian monophthongized its inherited diphthongs very
early, and much rustic Latin followed suit, this spelling could reflect the
refounding of Pisaurum as a Roman colony in 184 BC). The argument
is not altogether compelling, however. Since Umbrian Latin attests
1st-declension dative singulars in *-a* [-a:] (< original *-a:i*) that do not
correspond to Umbrian datives in *-e* (monophthongized < shortened
-ai), cf. *Matuta*, we might instead argue that these nominative plurals
are also just local Latin, and that both the dative singular and nominative plural endings involve the generalization of forms originally resulting from a local loss of the regular final [-i] before words beginning
with a vowel (i.e. *-a(:)i > -a(:)j > -a(:)*). In 379 there is the further
possibility of taking *matrona* as a singular epithet of *Mania Curia* and
deda as a singular epithet of *Pola Liuia*, with the two phrases arranged
chiastically in asyndeton. *Deda*, however, could also be a 3rd person
plural verb form < an original *di-da-nt* 'give-3pl.PRES', with loss of both
final consonants as sometimes attested in Umbrian (see also on *dedro*

below), provided that we do not find the repetiton of 'giving' redundant. We might even take both instances of *matrona* as datives modifying *Iunone/Matre*, particularly as *matrona* is a common appellation of protecting goddesses including Juno, though in this case the resulting cumulation of epithets would be relatively unusual and the dislocation of word order in 379 rather awkward.

These two inscriptions are perhaps too early for the 3rd-declension datives in *-e* < **-ei* (*Matre, Iunone*) to be taken as distinctively 'rustic' Latin influenced by Umbrian speech habits (even if the retention of such forms, i.e. after the Roman shift of secondary /ẹ/ > /i:/, was clearly regarded as a rustic feature in later times). But with regard to the clear 1st-declension dative singular in *-a* (*Matuta*), we should recall that Umbrian has only the formerly diphthongal *-e* (< **-ai*), and note that Latin inscriptions from Pisaurum actually show variation in this respect, with e.g. *Diane* (with *-e* < **-ai* by monophthongization) on CIL I² 376 alongside *Loucina* on CIL I² 371. Thus even if the former type in local Latin inscriptions does reflect specifically Umbrian influence in its early monophthongization of this diphthong, there are also features elsewhere which point to the language and practice of Latin-speaking immigrants.

The apparent syncopation of /e/ in *dedro(t)* (< *dederont) is another candidate-Umbrianism, though these could simply be examples of abbreviated spelling analogous to that seen elsewhere in forms like *lubs* = *lubens* (see example (7) below). If we continue to take them at face value, however, the fact that the Umbrian primary 3rd person plural ending is regularly written *-ent* (< **-enti*) suggests that this was not phonetically identical to Latin *-ont* in its coda and so could not provide a basis for the apparent reduction of the secondary Latin forms here. (The Umbrian secondary 3rd person plural ending *-es*, perhaps < **-en(d)-s* with analogical *-s* from the first or second person plural forms, or possibly directly from **-ent* via some sort of assibilation, was presumably too remote from *-ont* to provide such a basis either.) In the case of *dedrot*, then, we may simply be dealing with the weakened articulation of preconsonantal /n/ that is also attested in other country areas (e.g. *aged[ai]* = *agendae* '(time) to-be-passed' on CIL I² 364 from Falerii, *lubetes* = *lubentes* 'willing' on CIL I² 1531 from near Tarentum, etc.). In *dedro*, however, it remains possible that we see the same omission of final *-(n)t* that is also attested, albeit rarely, in Umbrian: thus Um 1 VIb 48 has *sururo* for normal *sururont* 'likewise', IIb 22 has **eruhu** 'with the same' rather than the usual **-hunt**, and most relevantly here, IIa 4 has the 3rd person plural verb form **fefure** 'they will have been' in place of the expected future perfect form with primary ending *fefurent.

(5) CIL I² 365: a bronze tablet from Falerii Novi (Southern Etruria), perhaps from the second half of the second century BC:

Menerua   sacru   ←
Minerva-DAT sacred-NEUT.NOM

[L]a.(rs) Cotena La.(rtis) f.(ilius) pretod de   ←
Lars   Cotena Lars-GEN son   praetor according-to

zenatuo   sententiad uootum   ←
senate-GEN vote-ABL   vowed-NEUT

dedet. cuando datu   rected   ←
gave-3sg When   given-NEUT correctly

cuncaptum   ←
formulated-NEUT

'Sacred to Minerva, Lars Cotena son of Lars, praetor, gave [this dedication], vowed [to her] in accordance with a vote of the senate. When it was given, it was correctly formulated.'

Particularly striking here is the apparent topic-comment structure of the first sentence, with a further descriptive afterthought sandwiched between the subject and verb forming the second of these components, almost as if each element was written down before the whole had been properly thought through, thereby creating the impression of a series of loosely juxtaposed formulae.

Once again, however, we shall focus here on those forms and features that may have been influenced by the local language, in this case Faliscan. Unfortunately, the period following the destruction of the old city of Falerii in 241 BC was one of steadily increasing Latinization/ Romanization, and by the time of this inscription it is often hard to draw a clear line between what is Faliscan and what is local Latin as the former gradually adopts the characteristics of a 'normal' Latin dialect. Thus monophthongization (*pretod*), the omission of some instances of final -*m* and -*s* (*sacru, zenatuo, datu*), and 1st-declension datives in -*a* (*Menerua*) are not features specific to Faliscan and/or to the Latin of the region; indeed, since the last of these is again not shared by the local language at all (which always has -*ai*), we may be confident that this is in fact a Latin text. Confirmation comes from the writing of other final consonants (*uootum, dedet, cuncaptum*), the archaizing retention of spellings with final -*d* (*sententiad, rected*), and the partial adoption of the then novel Latin practice of writing long vowels double (*uootum*, something otherwise first attested in 142 BC), all of which point to influence from official Roman practice of the period, and all of which are alien to Faliscan.

Nonetheless, the text is still written right-to-left in the Faliscan manner, with Faliscan letter forms and mainly Faliscan orthography (e.g. no Q, as in *cuando*), so we might reasonably expect to find some residual Faliscan linguistic traits as well. Possible candidates include the interchange of *z-/s-* at the beginnings of words (*sacru/zenatuo*), a feature that is replicated in Faliscan texts and suggests a lack of distinctive voicing in at least the dental fricative, and the apparent absence of vowel weakening in *cuncaptum*, another feature which has possible parallels in Faliscan (*cun-/con-* sometimes alternate before velars even in second/first-century Roman Latin, perhaps reflecting the raising effect of the assimilated velar nasal [ŋ]). Unfortunately, the specific examples available for comparison, a compound ending in -*pater* and the genitive of the god Apollo's name, *apolonos*, might involve an etymological spelling and a form with a long /o:/ respectively; in fact *cuncaptum* itself might be an etymological spelling, since the practice was motivated precisely by the fact that changes such as vowel weakening and consonant assimilation had led to 'incorrect' spellings. Note finally the odd spelling of *pretod* with -*d* (before *de*). If this is not just the result of graphic confusion of D and R (many local Italian alphabets used an inverted D = R), it could conceivably reflect a local difficulty in pronouncing final -*r*, which was routinely dropped in Faliscan. This problem would be acute when the sound occurred in preconsonantal position, as here, and an inability to produce a rolled or flapped sound in this environment might have resulted in a *d*-like closure (in fact a double [dd], released only with the vowel of *de*). But once again, the overall picture is one in which relatively little can be attributed to the influence of the local language with any degree of certainty.

4.4.2   Latin within Latium: Praenestine

Turning now from such inherently problematical documents, our best evidence for 'dialect' Latin, simply because there are reasonable numbers of inscriptions, including examples from the fourth and third centuries (a period for which we have very little, and only late, Roman evidence), comes from the Latin town of Praeneste, a major urban centre 23 miles east of Rome where the onomastic data suggest that up to 30 per cent of the population may have been of Sabellian origin in the third and second centuries BC. The city was defeated by Rome in the so-called Latin war of 341–338 BC, when the Latini, together with their allies the Volsci and Campani, took up arms against the very real threat of Roman territorial ambition signalled *inter alia* by the annexation of Tusculum in 381 BC. Though the evidence, as always, is inconsistent, and, after *c*.200 BC, subject to steadily growing influence from Rome (orthographic change in particular effectively obliterates the evidence for many local features), we are still able to build up a partial picture of the local dialect (see Coleman 1990). It should be emphasized at the outset, however, that almost all the features noted below are also attested in inscriptions from elsewhere in Latium, and that, as far as we can tell, the local varieties spoken in areas outside Rome where Latin had been established prehistorically seem to have been rather weakly differentiated from one another, even in the period before Roman influence became decisive. Furthermore, in the absence of comparably early material from Rome, even the supposed contrast between Roman and rustic Latin may have been less than it seems in the fourth and third centuries, despite growing polarization later:

Possible conservative features *vis-à-vis* Roman Latin

(a)   As in neighbouring Sabellian languages, [o] was apparently retained before the velar nasal [ŋ] + velar where Roman Latin raises to [u] (cf. *uncus* 'hook' beside Greek *ónkos*): Coleman cites *tongitio* (= *notio* 'acquaintance/idea/examination'), which is noted as Praenestine (beside *tongent* in an illustrative quotation from Ennius) in Paul the Deacon's abridgement of Festus (P.F. 489.5 (L)). However, one of our earliest Roman inscriptions, CIL I^2 8/9 (the epitaph of L. Cornelius Scipio, son of Scipio Barbatus), still has *honc*. Unfortunately, the exact dating of this and related Scipio epitaphs remains controversial, but we may be sure that they are later than much of the commonly cited epigraphic material from Praeneste. It is vital therefore to identify 'late' (second/first century) evidence from Praeneste, and there is in fact no such epigraphic support for this retention as far as we can determine. The absence of words that might show retention of /o/ (or even of the change to -*u*-) in this context is of course accidental, but as things stand the evidence for conservatism here is slender.

(b)   As in many country areas of Latium, and in those Sabellian languages that had undergone monophthongization (e.g. Umbrian, Marsian), the long vowel -*e*- /ẹ:/ < earlier /ei/ was maintained after Roman Latin had raised this to /i:/ during the first half of the second century BC: e.g. dative *Hercule* 'Hercules' (CIL I^2 1458, late second/first century BC). This feature was taken in Cicero's time to be a clear marker of 'rusticity' (see, for example, *de Oratore* 3.46). The same is perhaps true of the /ọ:/ < /ou/ once Roman Latin had raised this to /u:/, though there is too little supporting evidence from non-urban Latin that is late enough to confirm this.

(c)   As in Faliscan, and in some dialectal Latin outside Latium, the variant genitive singular of the 3rd declension in *-us* was apparently retained at Praeneste, at least in dedications: e.g. *nationu* (CIL I² 60, with omission of final *-s*) 'birth', *Salutus* (CIL I² 62) 'Salvation', both from the third century BC. But this 'traditional' and highly formulaic context at least raises the possibility that *-us* was already a genre-conditioned archaism. And though Roman Latin eventually opted for *-is* except in certain traditional legal formulae (e.g. *nominus Latini* 'of the Latin name' in the *Senatusconsultum de Bacchanalibus* of 186 BC, where the connection with Latins may, however, be significant), we should recall that the lack of third-century Roman epigraphic material makes straightforward comparisons difficult: for earlier periods, therefore, this apparent 'difference' between urban and rustic Latin may turn out to be illusory. There is, however, the possible single form *Labeonus* on CIL I² 1865 (mid-second century BC), admittedly alongside *Labeonis* in CIL I² 1478 (second/first century BC), and this 'later' example of *-us* in a cognomen at Praeneste may just be sufficient to make the point.

By Cicero's time, of course, clearly conservative features like (b) had been largely identified with 'rusticity', and were therefore stigmatized and carefully avoided by the urban elite in a period of marked linguistic polarization. But overall, the remaining evidence cited by Coleman for Praenestine conservatism is perhaps, in the end, less than compelling.

Possible collateral features *vis-à-vis* Roman Latin

(a)   The dative singular endings of the 1st and 2nd declensions derive from *[-aːi] and *[-oːi] respectively. Originally we may assume loss of final [-i] prevocalically and shortening of the diphthong preconsonantally, but Latin dialects sooner or later made a choice between these positionally determined variants, with Roman, as noted, eventually selecting *-ai* (later *-ae*) in the 1st declension and *-o* in the 2nd. At Praeneste, however, as in many areas outside Rome as well as in the central Italic languages (e.g. Marsian, Marrucinian and Paelignian), the long-vowel variants were apparently generalized in both declensions: e.g. dative *Fortuna* 'Fortune' (CIL I² 1445, third/early second century BC). Once again, however, the fact that most examples occur in divine names and/or descriptors of divinities on dedications allows for the possibility that this form too was already an archaism, even at Praeneste. As before, the shortage of comparable epigraphic material of a private nature from Rome in this relatively early period makes any meaningful comparison very difficult, and it therefore remains possible that the usage of Roman Latin was not significantly different in earlier times. Roman examples such as

[Me]nerua (CIL I² 460), admittedly beside *Meneruai* (CIL I² 34), and *Flaca* (CIL I² 477, this a personal rather than a divine name), both undated but certainly belonging to the period before 150 BC, provide food for thought, even though both are on portable objects (a fragment of a dish and an ointment jar respectively), thus raising the possibility that they may have been imported into Rome from elsewhere. The absence of guaranteed examples of datives in *-a* from later Praenestine inscriptions is also problematical.

(b)   In the nominative plural of the 2nd declension, the ending *-ei*, or its monophthongized equivalent *-e* (as regularly in Praenestine spelling), sometimes acquires a final *-s* in Republican Latin (see Vine 1993: ch. 8 for a full discussion). The form is most commonly used for gentilicia and/or cognomina shared by two individuals (e.g. *Q.M. Minucieis Q.f. Rufeis* = 'Quintus and Marcus Minucius Rufus' on the archaizing CIL I² 584, the *Sententia Minuciorum* of 117 BC, found in the Vale of Polcevera near Genoa) and then, by extension, for descriptors characterizing groups of individuals – i.e. official titles (esp. *magistre(i)s*), occupations, other indicators of status, and the names of peoples. The origin and development of this rather strange feature remain entirely unclear. Perhaps there was some kind of analogy with syntactically and/or thematically linked nominative plurals of the 3rd- and 4th-declensions ending in *-s*, or we may be dealing with the influence of neighbouring Sabellian languages with 2nd-declension nominative plurals in *-os*. But both accounts fail to explain the observed distribution, and we must ask further why internal-Latin analogy apparently fails to affect 1st-declension nominative plurals in the same way, or why evidence for parallel influence from Italic 1st-declension nominative plurals in *-as* is so limited (only *matrona(s)* of CIL I² 378, 379 from Pisaurum, where, always assuming that these are not in fact datives, Umbrian influence is possible, see above). It has therefore been suggested by Vine that in origin *-eis* is an orthographically motivated borrowing based on Sabellian onomastic conventions, whereby Oscan combinations of a praenomen in *-s/-is* and a gentilicium in *-is/-iis* (*-ies*), both showing loss of prefinal **-o-*, with an expression of filiation using a genitive in *-eis* (e.g. **Marahis Rahiis Papeis**, Cm 14), and/or Umbrian combinations of a praenomen in *-s/-is*, a patronymic adjective in *-is* and a gentilicium in *-ies* (e.g. **Vuvçis Titis Teteies**, Um 1 Ib 45), all with loss of prefinal **-o-*, might have served as a purely visual/graphic model, in outlying contact areas, for the expression in Latin of two nominative singular praenomina in *-us/-ius* (i.e. identifying two different individuals) with a shared nominative plural gentilicium in *-e(i)s*.

Whatever its origins, the phenomenon is more common in inscriptions from outside Rome, while the only sign of its possible penetration into non-epigraphic, and so necessarily Roman, varieties of Latin is in the occasional use of pronominal nominative plural *his(ce)* and *illis* in Roman comedy (with Roman treatment of original /ei/), a development motivated in part by their convenience as metrical variants, though surely providing testimony to their relatively 'normal' status *vis-à-vis* the corresponding nominal forms. It is important to note, however, that epigraphic evidence for *-e(i)s* in nominal forms is all from a later period and in inscriptions of a legal/official character, so it may well be that these apparent pronominal parallels are of a quite different origin. Examples of nominal *-e(i)s* from Praeneste include *Coques Atriensis . . .* 'the Cooks of the Hall' and *Magistres . . .* 'Foremen' (both on CIL I² 1447, second/first century BC). But the fact that there are a good number of examples from Roman legal documents of the Gracchan era and later, e.g. CIL I² 583 (14), the *Lex Acilia de Repetundis* of 122 BC, and CIL I² 585 (28, 29), the *Lex Agraria*, strongly suggests that the usage of official Roman Latin was not significantly different from that of rural varieties in this era.

(c)   Certain lexical items were apparently characteristically Praenestine: e.g. *conea* (for *ciconia* 'stork'), Plautus *Truculentus* 691, where the dialect is mocked (cf. also *Captiui* 882–4); *tongitio* (for *notio* 'acquaintance, idea, examination', see (a) under 'Possible conservative features *vis-à-vis* Roman Latin' above); and perhaps *nefrones* (for *nefrendes* = *testiculi* 'testicles'), P.F. 157.12 (L). Any such egregious markers of rusticity were naturally eschewed in elite Roman Latin.

Once again, therefore, it must be admitted that much of the evidence cited by Coleman for collateral developments supposedly distinguishing Praenestine from Roman Latin in the relevant periods is in fact less than demonstrative.

Innovative features *vis-à-vis* Roman Latin

(a)   Original /i/ was lowered to /e/ prevocalically, as also in Faliscan and Faliscan Latin: Coleman cites *fileai*, 'daughter' (the Cista Ficoroni, CIL I² 561, possibly late fourth century). We should note, however, that the object in question is in fact originally from Rome (cf. *Nouios Plautios med Romai fecid* 'N.P. made me at Rome'), and further that we also once find *filios* in CIL I² 555 (a Praenestine mirror, fourth/third century BC) beside *filea* (CIL I² 60, a Praenestine dedication of the early third century, see below). Caution is clearly in order here, even if general tendencies are clear.

(b)   Original /e/ was raised to /i/ before /r/ and a consonant (as also in Oscan and Faliscan, and apparently in Faliscan Latin): e.g. *Mirqurios* (CIL I² 553), *Mircurios* (CIL I² 564) 'Mercury', both perhaps of the late fourth century. Raising seems also to have affected [o] in the same context, so some 'standard' Latin words, such as *hircus* 'goat', *firmus* 'firm', *furca* 'furrow', *furnus* 'oven', must be of non-Roman origin.

(c)   As in many Italic languages to the north and west of Rome, as well as in the varieties of Latin spoken in those regions, the diphthongs /ai/ and /au/ probably monophthongized relatively early to /ɛ:/ and /ɔ:/ at Praeneste. For example, the names *Grecia* (CIL I² 530) and *Ceisia* (CIL I² 559, where *ei* may represent the first stage in the development of /ai/, namely to /ɛi/), both on inscriptions of uncertain date. Though words and names with *-ai-* are also attested, it is possible that these represent earlier, or at least archaizing, spellings. Unfortunately, nothing can be said with certainty because even the relative dating of many of the crucial Praenestine inscriptions remains highly problematical. However, the following quotation from the late second-century writer Lucilius (fragment 1130, cited in Varro, *de Lingua Latina* VII.96) probably satirizes the speech of the Praenestine Caecilius Metellus Caprarius, consul in 113 BC, and if so, shows that the feature was well-established in the dialect by that period: *Cecilius pretor ne rusticus fiat*, 'lest Caecilius become *praetor rusticus*' (i.e. not *praetor urbanus*, an official title). For examples of /au/ > /ɔ:/ from Praeneste, note the names *Polia* (CIL I² 83) and *Lorelano* (CIL I² 181), though again words/names spelled with *au* are also attested, with the same problems and uncertainties of chronology. Varro (*de Lingua Latina* V.97) makes it clear, however, that these monophthongizations were regarded as rustic in the late Republic, even though they subsequently affected Latin more generally, as many Romance reflexes make clear (e.g. Italian *fieno* < *fēnum* rather than *faenum*, 'hay').

(d)   Final /-t/ and /-(n)t/ seem to have been lost early (though loss of final /-t/ at least affects Latin generally at a later date): e.g. 3rd person singular *dedi* 'gave' (CIL I² 60), 3rd person plural *coraueron* 'superintended' (CIL I² 59)/*dedero* 'gave' (CIL I² 61), all probably from the mid-third century, though once again there are Praenestine texts of a similar period with forms in which the final consonant is retained, a situation perhaps pointing to very recent loss and orthographic uncertainty, or even to earlier loss with deliberate orthographic archaism. A similar form occurs at Tibur (viz. *dede* 'gave', CIL I² 47, perhaps third/early second century BC), and this loss is, of course, routine in Umbrian (and Umbrian Latin), though sporadic in Faliscan (and not attested for Faliscan Latin).

The evidence for innovation in Praenestine (and other rural dialects) is therefore stronger overall than that for elements of conservatism or collateral development. Though many such innovatory features were again tagged as 'rustic', their lasting impact is sometimes reflected in later Latin and Romance, as noted, thus showing that some at least had successfully infiltrated Roman speech, cf. the appearance of doublets such as *faenus/fēnus* 'interest, profit', *saepēs/sēpēs* 'hedge, fence', *lautus/lōtus* 'clean, sumptuous', *cauda/cōda* 'tail', and of socially motivated hypercorrections such as *scaena* for *scēna* 'stage/scene', *plaudere* for *plōdere* 'clap', *ausculor* for *ōsculor* 'kiss'. Indeed, almost all the innovatory features which distinguish Praenestine Latin from (elite) Roman Latin also turn up in private inscriptions found at Rome. This overall situation is perhaps to be explained as reflecting a new, socially defined, form of speech variation whereby features of the old country dialects had become increasingly characteristic of the language of the urban poor as large numbers moved to the city with the expansion and consolidation of Roman control, thus setting in motion the urbanization process that culminated in the second and first centuries (see Joseph and Wallace 1992). If we abstract away from the fact that Rome was now unquestionably the dominant power, with the speech of the Roman elite duly assigned a privileged status, the linguistic consequences of the mobility of population in this period are otherwise analogous to those evidenced for an earlier time by legends about the fusion of Sabine and Latin tribes and the period of Etruscan monarchy, and confirmed by the clear contribution of Etruscan and Sabellian languages (and perhaps of non-Roman Latin too) to the 'standard' vocabulary of Latin (see Chapter II).

4.4.3   *Some examples*

We may complete this chapter with two illustrative examples of Praenestine Latin:

(6)   CIL I^2 60: A dedication on a bronze plate, first half of the third century BC:

Orceuia   Numeri
Orceuia-NOM Numerius-GEN

nationu cratia
birth-GEN gratitude-ABL

Fortuna   Diouo   filea
Fortune-DAT Juppiter-GEN daughter-DAT

primo.ɔenia
?acting-as-genius/protectress.at-the-beginning-DAT (see Wachter 1987: 216–19)

donom dedi
gift-ACC give-3sg.PF

'Orgeuia wife of Numerius, in gratitude for a birth gave [this] as a gift to Fortune Primogenia, daughter of Juppiter.'

(7)   CIL I² 62: A dedication on a block of tufa, third century BC:

L(ucio)   Gemenio   L(uci)   f(ilius)   Pel- / t
Lucius-NOM Gemenius-NOM Lucius-GEN son-NOM of-Peltuinum

Hercole   dono
Hercules-DAT gift-ACC

dat   lubs merto- / d
give-3sg.PRES willing deservedly

pro   sed   sueq
on-behalf-of himself his-own-and

ede   leigibus
same-ABL conventions-ABL

ara   Salutus
altar-ACC Wellbeing-GEN

'Lucius Gemenius, son of Lucius, of Peltuinum, gives [this] as a gift to Hercules, willingly and deservedly, on behalf of himself and his family. By the same conventions, an altar of Wellbeing.'

Given what we know about the size of the population of Italic-speaking origin at Praeneste, we should not be surprised by the syncopation in *mer(i)tod*, though we should also emphasize here that *lubs* (also attested elsewhere) is not an extreme example of this phenomenon but simply an abbreviated writing for *lubens*. Most of the other relevant points have already been discusssed above. Note in particular: the regular monophthongization of -*ei*- > -*ē*-, as probably still in Roman Latin at this time (*Hercole*, *sueq(ue)*, *ede*; *leigibus* is perhaps no more than a spelling error); the weakness of final -*s* and -*m* (*nationu/Diouo/Gemenio*, *dono/ara/ede*, but *Salutus*, *donom*), and especially of final -*t* (*dedi* – the 1st person singular form in Praenestine would be *ded-e* < -*ei* < *-ai*); the lowering of -*i*- prevocalically (*filea*); the inconsistency in writing final -*d* (*cratia/mertod*) and in noting vowel weakening (*Gemenio/dono(m)*, but *nationu/ leigibus/Salutus*); the 3rd-declension genitive singulars in -*o(s)/-u(s)* (*nationu/Diouo/Salutus*); and finally, the 1st-declension dative singulars in -*a* (*Fortuna/filea/Primo.ɔenia* – the purpose of the reversed letter form here is unclear, since C is used to note both /g/ (*cratia*) and palatalized velars before high front vowels (*Orceuia*), but the spelling

Primo- rather than *Prim(i)-* is perhaps an archaism or an etymologically motivated restoration.

4.5 Conclusion

Enough has now been said about our (very limited) early evidence for 'dialects' of Latin outside Rome, and we must now turn in the next chapter to the detailed examination of the earliest evidence for Roman Latin, the already dominant variety that would soon evolve into a fixed written standard and eclipse all other varieties from the written record.

References

Adams, J. N. (forthcoming) *Regional Diversity in Latin*. Cambridge: Cambridge University Press.

Baldi, P. (2002) *The Foundations of Latin* (2nd edn.). Berlin/New York: Mouton de Gruyter.

Bennett, C. E. (1910–14) *Syntax of Early Latin*. Boston: Allyn and Bacon.

Coleman, R. G. G. (1986/87) 'Some remarks on Latin monophthongizations'. *Cuadernos de Filología Clásica* 20, 151–62.

Coleman, R. G. G. (1990) 'Dialectal variation in Republican Latin, with special reference to Praenestine'. *Proceedings of the Cambridge Philological Society* 36, 1–25.

Coleman, R. G. G. (1996) 'Conditional clauses in the XII Tables', in H. Rosén (ed.), *Papers from the Eighth International Colloquium on Latin Linguistics (Jerusalem, April 1993)*. Innsbruck: Institut für Sprachwissenschaft der Universität Innsbruck, 403–21.

Courtney, E. (1999) *Archaic Latin Prose*. Atlanta, GA: Scholars Press.

Crawford, M. (2006) 'Caso Cantouio'. Unpublished manuscript, London.

Dangel, J. (1995) *Histoire de la langue latine*. Paris: Presses Universitaires de France.

del Tutto Palma, L., A. L. Prosdocimi and G. Rocca (2002) *Lingua e cultura intorno al 295 a.C.: tra Roma e gli Italici del nord*. Rome: Il Calamo.

Giacomelli, R. (1993) *Storia della lingua latina*: Rome: Jouvence.

Joseph, B. and R. Wallace (1992) 'Socially determined variation in ancient Rome'. *Language Variation and Change* 4, 105–19.

Klingenschmitt, G. (1992) 'Die lateinische Nominalflexion', in O. Panagl and T. Krisch (eds.), *Latein und Indogermanisch: Akten des Kolloquiums der Indogermanischen Gesellschaft (Salzburg 23–26 September 1986)*. Innsbruck: Institut für Sprachwissenschaft der Universität Innsbruck, 89–135.

Meiser, G. (1998) *Historische Laut- und Formenlehre der Lateinischen Sprache*. Darmstadt: Wissenschaftliche Buchgesellschaft.

Sihler, A. (1995) *New Comparative Grammar of Greek and Latin.* Oxford: Oxford University Press.

Vine, B. (1993) *Studies in Archaic Latin Inscriptions.* Innsbruck: Innsbrucker Beiträge zur Sprachwissenschaft.

Wachter, R. (1987) *Altlateinische Inschriften.* Bern: Peter Lang.

Wallace, R. (1988) 'Dialectal Latin *f undatid, proiecitad, parentatid*'. *Glotta* 66, 211–20.

Chapter V

The Road to Standardization: Roman Latin of the Third and Second Centuries BC

5.1 The Typology of Roman Inscriptions

Before tackling specific texts, it will be useful to begin with a summary of the conventional typology of inscriptions, distinguishing inscriptions proper (*tituli*), inscribed on monuments and other objects to denote their purpose or relation to named individuals, from public or private documents (*acta, instrumenta, tabulae*), inscribed on durable material in order to publish, and indirectly to preserve, the contents (see, for example, Keppie (1991) for a brief introduction). The former subclass includes epitaphs, dedications, honorary inscriptions, inscriptions on public works, and inscriptions on portable objects; the latter, treaties, laws, decrees of official bodies and organizations (e.g. the Roman Senate, *coloniae, municipia, collegia* and *sodalicia*), decrees of magistrates and emperors, other public and religious documents, private documents, and graffiti. Needless to say, the boundaries are not always watertight, and many documents fall under more than one heading, e.g. epitaphs that include various legal provisions, or which honour the individual concerned, such as that of Scipio Barbatus (CIL I² 6/7, see (2a) below, where the original text is supplemented by an *elogium* in Saturnians). Clearly decrees of official bodies or high-ranking magistrates will typically display the benefits of more or less competent drafting by a professional secretariat, while private documents may well reflect variation in the educational level of the individuals who commissioned and/or composed them. Both types were, in varying degrees, at the mercy of the technical and linguistic competence of the craftsmen employed to produce them, and provincial copies of even senatorial decrees may contain errors absent from the originals.

5.2   Dated Roman Inscriptions of the Third and Second Centuries BC

In the absence of epigraphic material from Rome datable to the fourth century BC, we must begin our discussion of the development of Roman Latin with the still rather limited corpus of inscriptions available to us from the third and second centuries (Wachter (1987: ch. IV.B) provides comprehensive commentary). All but one of the 17 dated Roman inscriptions within the period down to 150 BC have an official character; the earliest is from 217 BC (CIL I² 607), and the latest from 155 BC (CIL I² 623). Most are also quite short, apart from two *senatusconsulta* (CIL I² 581, 586), which will be examined in detail in 5.4 below. Unsurprisingly, some of the first examples of a number of the key shifts from the 'older' to the more 'modern' orthography of Roman Latin appear in this corpus (see Wachter (1987: 285, 358): in some cases there are earlier examples from outside Rome, especially Praeneste, e.g. CIL I² 561 for final *-it*, thought to date from the fourth century):

1	[-i-] < [-e-]	217 BC	(CIL I² 607, *uouit*)
2	[-us] < [-os]	211 BC	(CIL I² 608/9, *Claudius*)
3	double C written	211 BC	(CIL I² 608, *Hinnad*)
4	[-um] < [-om]	200 BC	(CIL I² 610, *iterum*)
5	loss of [-d] in ablative singular	?192/189 BC	(CIL I² 613/614, *?[Le]ucado/turri Lascutana*)
6	[-ae] < [-ai]	187 BC	(CIL I² 616/617, *Aetolia/ Aemilius*)

As noted in Chapter IV, any associated phonetic changes (recall that the writing of double consonants is a purely orthographic change) may well have occurred much earlier than the first written evidence for them, even though we *can* be sure that any later texts using the older spellings are archaizing to the extent that they fail to reflect these sound changes. Nor does the first attestation of a modern spelling necessarily imply that this was already the 'standard' orthographic practice, thus making any continuing archaism deliberate (self-conscious) rather than merely conventional. Indeed, the writing of double consonants and the omission of final *-d* were certainly not routine at the time of their first datable occurrence, at least at the highest levels of the Roman bureaucracy, since the orthography of CIL I² 581, the famous *Senatusconsultum de Bacchanalibus* of 186 BC (text (3) below), remains 'traditional' in these two respects; the corresponding modern spellings only became acceptable in this lofty domain somewhat later in the second century, as probably shown by the equally famous *senatusconsultum* paraphrased in a letter of the praetor Lucius Cornelius to the people of Tibur, CIL I² 586, of 159 BC (see text (4) below). It is interesting, however, that CIL I² 614, a decree of Lucius Aemilius Paullus, proconsul of Further Spain in 189 BC, freeing a local community from the control of its neighbours three years before the issuing of the *Senatusconsultum de Bacchanalibus*, already lacks final -*d*'s and has four of seven double consonants so written (and two instances of the older spelling occur in just the one word, *posedisent* 'they should possess', which appears after *essent* 'they should be' and before *possidere* 'to possess'). The only other relevant evidence from Roman documents before 186 BC is *Hinnad* 'from Enna' (a town in Sicily) on a dedicatory inscription of the consul Marcus Claudius Marcellus (CIL I² 608, 211 BC), but we might be tempted to speculate that the late third and early second centuries saw a short-lived period of contrast between inconsistent attempts to modernize the orthography on the part of Roman officials acting in their own capacity and the time-honoured archaisms still felt necessary for formal decrees of the Senate.

5.3   Two Undated Inscriptions: The Scipio Epitaphs CIL I² 6/7 and I² 8/9

5.3.1   Old Latin prosody and the Saturnian verse

Since what are probably our earliest undated Roman inscriptions of this period, namely the two Scipio *tituli* discussed below in 5.3.2, also provide our earliest examples of the Saturnian metre, we must first say something about this ancient verse form. The most recent, and most illuminating, approach to a better understanding of its rhythms is provided by Parsons (1999), who rejects attempts to characterize it exclusively on a quantitative or syllabic basis, and exploits the insights of modern metrical phonology to develop an alternative analysis based on what we know about the rhythmical properties of Old Latin (particularly word-initial stress), linking his findings to the shift in accentual patterns towards the classical model, as already evidenced in the verse of Plautus (*c*.254–184 BC).

The comparative simplicity and overall predictive power of Parsons's stress-based account of the Saturnian as a stylization of native Latin prosody argue rather persuasively against a quantitative foundation of Greek origin, a position that is not well supported even on external grounds. Thus the fact that the Scipio epitaphs show Greek influence in content (as well as in the novel practice of putting a poem over a tomb, not to mention the iconography of the sarcophagus itself) tells us nothing about the verse form *per se*, while the two alleged metrical 'parallels' cited by Fraenkel (1951), from Euripidean lyrics (*Troades* 529–30) and a Cretan cult hymn (Diehl *Anthologia Lyrica* vol. 2, p. 131), are far too quantitatively regular, involving a metrical unit with a first colon of three and a half iambic feet and a second of three trochaic feet (with spondaic variants and resolutions), to be compared with the quantitatively and syllabically much more variable Saturnian: indeed the unsystematic complexity of Courtney's quantitative account (1995: 28–30) serves only to emphasize the wrong-headedness of this approach. Ultimately, the only thing that these verse forms have in common is a clear dicolonic structure, which is manifestly insufficient to demonstrate borrowing from Greek practice.

Parsons's account (somewhat adapted and developed here) rests upon a prior analysis of the lexical accent of early spoken Latin in terms of a hierarchical system of units, namely *moras* (the minimal units of syllabic duration), *syllables* (of one or two moras' duration according to whether the syllable is light or heavy), *prosodic feet* (comprising one heavy syllable/two light syllables [= 'bimoraic feet'] or one light syllable [= 'monomoraic feet'], with the first or only mora serving as the dominant element or 'head'), and *prosodic words* (each comprising a number of prosodic feet). The primary word accent of Old Latin then falls on the head of the first prosodic foot, whether bimoraic or monomoraic; if the word is long enough, a secondary accent also appears on the head of the last accessible bimoraic foot (i.e. excluding the final foot, which is extraprosodic, see below), but accents cannot fall on immediately adjacent feet.

Before illustrating these rules, however, it is important to emphasize that this definition of 'foot' is quite distinct from that familiar to Classicists. The representation of the *metrical* feet of quantitative verse indicates their composition in terms of combinations of light and heavy syllables (and so only indirectly in terms of their moraic composition), while the representation of *prosodic* feet indicates their temporal duration directly in terms of moras: a 'trochaic' prosodic foot, for example, is two moras long, with the first, i.e. potentially accent-bearing, mora serving as its head, whether the foot contains one heavy or two light syllables. Parsons's point is that it was the moraic composition of prosodic feet that controlled word stress, and that the normal rhythm of connected speech was marked by sequences of such stressed syllables separated from one another by groups of unstressed syllables, and not by patternings of syllable quantities. The Saturnian is taken to be an artistic stylization of such 'natural' rhythms, as we shall see.

The rules for the analysis of prosodic words into prosodic feet are as follows:

1 The right-most syllable of a word forms an 'extraprosodic' foot, and is invisible to the rules assigning stress.
2 The residue is then 'parsed', from left to right, into prosodic feet (monomoraic or bimoraic): non-initial monomoraic feet are not, however, available for stress assignment.

The examples listed below should help to clarify the principles involved: recall that the primary accent falls on the head of the first prosodic foot (i.e. on the first syllable), and that a secondary accent is placed on the head of the last accessible bimoraic prosodic foot (i.e. on the last heavy syllable or the first of two light syllables preceding the final extraprosodic foot) provided that the two affected feet are not adjacent. In the analyses given below, the prosodic feet are enclosed in [ ], and extrametrical final feet are enclosed in ( ). It will be seen that accented feet regularly alternate with unaccented feet in longer words, except that a non-initial monomoraic foot cannot be accent-bearing, making for a long unaccented 'tail' in the affected words (recall that ˘˘ here = 'bimoraic', and does not indicate two 'shorts'):

1	[cápe]-(re)	[˘́˘](˘)
2	[fár]-[ci:]-(re)	[˘́˘][˘˘](˘)
3	[ádo]-[ri:]-(ri:)	[˘́˘][˘˘](˘˘)
4	[fáci]-[li]-(us)	[˘́˘][˘](˘)
5	[ób]-[si]-(de:s)	[˘́˘][˘](˘˘)
6	[dé]-(dit)	[˘́](˘)
7	[tém]-[pes]-[tá:]-[ti]-(bus)	[˘́˘][˘˘][˘́˘][˘](˘)
8	[ín]-[sidi]-[á:]-(tor)	[˘́˘][˘˘][˘́˘](˘)
9	[ád]-[simi]-[li]-(ter)	[˘́˘][˘˘][˘](˘)
10	[Síci]-[li]-[é:ns]-(e:s)	[˘́˘][˘][˘́˘](˘˘)
11	[í]-[nu:]-[ti]-(lis)	[˘́][˘˘][˘](˘)

Or perhaps better with a conventional bimoraic accented foot, assuming 'iambic shortening' (i.e. the less forceful articulation of an unstressed heavy syllable when the accent fell on a preceding light syllable, as in *cítŏ, égŏ, módŏ, uólŭptátem* – a process which presumably eliminated a perceived prosodic oddity):

[ínu]-[ti]-(lis) [˘́˘][˘](˘)

The shift from this Old Latin system to the Classical one can perhaps best be explained on the basis that the secondary accents on longer words were at some point reanalysed as dominant, leading eventually to the generalization of the last rather than the first potentially stress-bearing foot as 'the' accent bearer in **all** words, so that those with a non-initial bimoraic foot, like *farcire*, would have the stress transferred to the second syllable, just as in Classical Latin. This change would not, of course, affect words with only one potentially stress-bearing foot, and we may note in support that cases like *facilius* remain accented on the initial (rather then the second) syllable in the iambo-trochaic verse of Plautus and Terence, always assuming that verse ictus is a broadly reliable guide to lexical stress. Similarly, though the stress on words like *adsimiliter* would now fall on the second syllable, again as attested in comedy, this too does not yet correspond to the classical position (the antepenultimate). The final stage in the transition to the classical system was possibly due to an inherent ambiguity in the analysis of a large number of words like *facilis* (*[faci]-(lis)*) or *imperator* (*[im]-[pe]-[ra:]-(tor)*), where the accentual result is the same whether the parsing is carried out left-to-right or right-to left. If we suppose that this situation led to the eventual substitution of a right-to-left analysis, the effect on *facilius* and *adsimiliter* would be to shift the accent in each case to the classical position, since these would now be analysed as *[fa]-[cili]-(us)* and *[ad]-[si]-[mili]-(ter)* respectively.

With this background, we are now in a position to consider the probable structure of the Saturnian in more detail. Parsons argues that the verse can be analysed into a set of hierarchically organized binary metrical constituents, with the left-hand member serving as the 'head' at each level. The line therefore comprises two *cola* (C), each of which consists of two *dipodes* (D) separated by the principal caesura. Each dipode in turn consists of two *metrical feet* (F, distinct from prosodic feet, see below)), each comprising a *strong position* (S, the head) and a *weak position* (W):

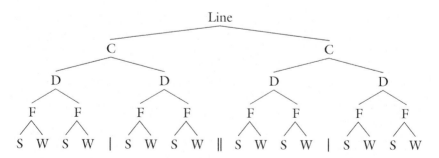

Each *position* in a *metrical foot* may contain one prosodic foot (bimoraic or monomoraic) or one 'extrametrical' foot (bimoraic or monomoraic), all feet being integral to the verse rhythm, though dipode-final weak positions may be left unrealized, functioning like rests in musical notation. The alternation of strong and weak positions corresponds roughly to the alternation of feet containing accented and unaccented syllables within the prosodic phrases of ordinary discourse, though things are inevitably more complex, since the purpose of the Saturnian is to define a regular 'metre' by imposing a set of restrictions on the inherently more variable rhythms of natural speech.

Elaborating and extending the detail of Parsons' treatment, the main principles regulating the content and accentuation of the positions shown above are as follows:

1   All strong positions are regularly filled (but see 2(b)).
2   (a)   Weak positions are also regularly filled, but at least one dipode-final weak position within each colon must be unrealized and both may be: if only one is unrealized, it is usually that in the second dipode of the first colon, but always that in the second dipode of the second colon: the strong position preceding an unrealized weak position must be filled by an extraprosodic (i.e. word-final) foot.
    (b)   This condition obviously cannot be met if the end of a word coincides with the end of the first foot of an affected dipode: such coincidence is allowed only in the second colon, usually in its second dipode (though sometimes in the first or even in both), and the whole second foot is then unrealized, including its strong position.
3   Strong positions alone may contain word accents, subject to the following conditions:
    (a)   the strong position in the first foot of each dipode must contain an accented syllable;
    (b)   when a dipode-final weak position is realized, the preceding strong position must also contain an accented syllable;
    (c)   when a dipode-final weak position is unrealized, the preceding strong position is unaccented (since it contains an extrametrical foot, cf. 2(a)).
4   Syllables in verb forms which would normally bear an accent may, when the verb is in clause-second position following a stressed conjunction, pronoun or focal constituent, fall in weak positions, in which case the lexical accent is suppressed. This may, however indirectly, continue the PIE rule that verbs here were regularly enclitic (cf. Watkins (1964)).

A few examples (the final three lines of the Scipio epitaph in (2a) below) should make these principles clearer.

(1)   [cón](sol) [cén](sor) | [aíd][i](lis)   ‖
      [[[s   w] [s   w]] [[s   w][s   w]]]
         [queí] [fu](it) | [á](pud) [uos]
      [[[s   w][s   w]] [[s w   ] [s   w]]]
      [Taú] [rasi](a) | [Cí][sau](na)   ‖
      [[[s   w][s w]] [[s   w   ][s   w]]]
         [Sám] [ni](o) | [cé](pit)
      [[[s   w][s   w]] [[s   w] [s w]]]

      [súbi][gi][t óm](ne) | [Loú][ca](nam)   ‖
      [[[s   w][s   w]] [[s   w][s   w]]]
         [óp][si][dés](que) | [áb][dou](cit)
      [[[s   w][s   w]] [[s   w][s   w]]]

Word accents always occur on the first (or only) syllables of metrically
strong positions, and accented positions are always followed by realized
weak positions. There must be at least one such accent per dipode, falling
on the first (or only) syllable of the strong position of its first foot, and
one dipode of each colon may also have a second accent on the first (or
only) syllable of its second foot: but there can never be more than three
accents in a colon, since the final strong position in at least one of its
dipodes (regularly the second, giving a 'falling' cadence as the default case)
must be filled by a prosodically extrametrical (word-final) foot followed
by an unrealized weak position. Thus pauses of one weak position are
routine before the caesura and obligatory at the line end, and pauses of
one weak position are also permitted before an intracolonic dipode
boundary if the second metrical foot of the first dipode is headed by an
extrametrical syllable.

Each of the strong positions containing the four obligatory stresses in
a line is therefore followed by three metrical positions, the first weak, the
second strong, the third weak. When both strong positions within a dipode
contain accented syllables, the interval between the two stresses is one weak
position; and since there can then be no pause before the following dipode
boundary (recall that the weak position after a strong position containing
a stressed syllable must be realized), the interval between the last stress-
bearing position in the first dipode and that in the second is also one weak
position. When only the first strong position in a dipode is accented,
however, the second strong position can only be filled, as noted, by an
extrametrical (word-final) syllable followed by a pause of one weak position;
this excludes words with 'overlong' tails (in conformity with the restriction
that the interval between obligatory stresses is of three metrical positions).
The framework also excludes Cole's (1969) 5- or 6-syllable words with
various disallowed quantitative sequences, all of which necessarily violate
the restrictions on the permissible intervals between stresses.

It is important to note that, metrically speaking, all stressed positions play the same role regardless of their syllabic makeup, and that the timing of the intervals between stressed positions is based solely on the number of intervening unstressed positions, again without reference to their internal composition. In other words, all accented positions are equal in being 'loud', and all intervening unaccented positions are equal in their lack of such articulatory dynamism. The audible reduction of certain unstressed heavy syllables is reflected directly in the phenomenon of iambic shortening or *brevis brevians* (see above), which is most familiar from Roman comedy but was characteristic of the spoken language in general. Similarly, the relative freedom, *vis-à-vis* Greek practice, in the makeup of certain weak positions in the iambo-trochaic parts of Roman comedy almost certainly represents a residual effect of a preceding word accent in the period of transition to strictly quantitative verse forms: e.g. word-finally, one heavy or two light syllables are admissible as alternatives to a single light syllable at the beginning of the second or fourth foot of iambic senarii ('in thesi') if the immediately preceding strong position in the first or third foot ('in arsi') contains the word accent (see Gratwick 1982). Note too that prosodic phenomena like cliticization (e.g. of unemphatic pronouns, the copula, monosyllabic prepositions, connective *-que*, etc.) and elision, which naturally occur within the prosodic phrases of natural speech, are permissible only within, and not across, each of the four dipodes, which therefore represent metrically stylized prosodic phrases, as expected. The overall effect is to create a regular stress-timed rhythm, shaped by the permitted intervals betweens word stresses and modulated by the optional or obligatory pauses of fixed duration at the various metrical boundaries. It is important to appreciate that these optional and obligatory pauses, alongside the regular, metrically determined, patterning of stressed and unstressed syllables, were an integral part of the rhythm of the Saturnian, articulating its natural internal and external boundaries and imparting much of its variety. It should not be surprising, therefore, that when the accentual rules of Latin started to shift towards the classical model (see above) this metre, apparently now lacking any regular prosodic properties of any kind, whether stress-timed or syllable-timed, should very quickly have been abandoned as an increasingly incomprehensible anachronism.

5.3.2   *The earliest Scipio epitaphs*

With this background, we are ready to examine two of the most important undated documents illustrating the Latin of the period before 150 BC, namely the *tituli sepulcrales* (in fact epitaphs-cum-*elogia*) of Lucius Cornelius Scipio Barbatus, consul in 298 BC and censor in 290 BC, and of his son Lucius Cornelius Scipio, consul in 259 BC and censor in

258 BC. In the first case, the epitaph (CIL I² 6) is painted on the lid of the tomb, with the *elogium* (CIL I² 7) cut on its front, while in the second, though the epitaph (CIL I² 8) is again painted on the tomb itself, the *elogium* (CIL I² 9) is cut on a separate tablet. Both *elogia* are in the Saturnian metre, as already noted.

The texts run as follows (with expansions of abbreviations in ( ), likely restorations of damaged text in [ ], and, in CIL I² 6/7 only, the ends of the actual lines of the inscription marked |, since these do not correspond with the lines of Saturnians:

(2) (a) CIL I² 6/7 (Father)

[L.(oucio) Corneli]o.   Cn.(aiui) f.(ilio) Scipio
Lucius-NOM Cornelius-NOM Gnaeus-GEN son-NOM Scipio-NOM

[...]
[..........] Cornelius.   Lucius.   Scipio.   Barbatus.
　　　　　　Cornelius-NOM Lucius-NOM Scipio-NOM Barbatus-NOM

Gnaiuod. patre | prognatus. fortis.   uir.   sapiensque
Gnaeus-ABL father-ABL child-NOM. Brave-NOM man-NOM wise-NOM-and

quoius. forma.   uirtutei.   parisuma | fuit
whose   form-NOM courage-DAT most-equal-NOM be-3sg.PF

consol.   censor.   aidilis.   quei.   fuit.   apud. uos
consul-NOM censor-NOM aedile-NOM who-NOM be-3sg.PF among you-ACC

Taurasia.   Cisauna. | Samnio.   cepit
Taurasia-ACC Cisauna-ACC Samnium-ACC take-3sg.PF

subigit.   omne. Loucanam.   opsidesque.   abdoucit.
subjugate-3sg.PRES all-ACC Lucanian (land)-ACC hostages-ACC-and carry-off-3sg.PRES.

'Lucius Cornelius Scipio, son of Gnaeus.
Cornelius Lucius Scipio Barbatus ('Longbeard'), offspring of his father Gnaeus, a brave and wise man whose beauty was quite the equal of his courage. He who was consul, censor and aedile among you took Taurasia, Cisauna, indeed [all] Samnium, subjugating all of Lucanian territory and carrying off hostages.'

(b) CIL I² 8/9 (Son)

L.((o)ucio). Cornelio.   L.((o)uci) f.(ilio)   Scipio
Lucius-NOM Cornelius-NOM Lucius-GEN son-NOM Scipio-NOM

aidiles.   cosol.   cesor
aedile-NOM consul-NOM censor-NOM

honc.   oino.   ploirume. cosentiont. R[omane]
this-man-ACC alone-ACC most-NOM agree-3pl.PRES Romans-NOM

duonoro. optumo. fuise.   uiro
good-GEN best-ACC be-PF.INF man-ACC

Luciom.   Scipione. filios.   Barbati
Lucius-ACC Scipio-ACC. Son-NOM Barbatus-GEN

consol.   censor.   aidilis.   hic.   fuet.   a[pud. uos]
consul-NOM censor-NOM aedile-NOM this-man-NOM be-3sg.PF among you-ACC

hec.   cepit.   Corsica. Aleriaque.   urbe
this-man-NOM take-3sg.PF Corsica-ACC Aleria-ACC-and city-ACC;

dedet.   Tempestatebus. aide.   mereto[d]
give-3sg.PF Weather-goddesses-DAT temple-ACC deservedly.

'Lucius Cornelius Scipio, son of Lucius, aedile, consul, censor.
This man alone most Romans agree was the best of good men, namely
Lucius Scipio. Son of Barbatus, he was consul, censor and aedile among
you. He took Corsica and the city of Aleria (its capital); he gave to the
Weather Goddesses a temple in return for benefits received.'

Both are already 'literary' in character (cf. Rosén 1999: 37f.), as
marked first and foremost by the fact that the *elogia* are in verse, as well
as by the conciseness and overall simplicity of their language (we may
compare in this regard the *Columna Rostrata*, 4.3), the freedom of order
with respect to the position of the verb, and the use of simple relative
clauses without 'resumptive' correlatives (of the type 'who does X, he will
Y'). By contrast, our first extended examples of 'official' Latin, though
also stylized and elaborated in specific ways, already display a characteristic verbosity, while their language shows rigid verb-final order and employs
preposed relatives with anaphoric resumption as a key 'marker' of the
style, see 5.4 for details. Note too the liking for appositive structures with
asyndeton, where more official Latin typically favours linkage with -*que*
or -*ue*, and, most importantly for the development of a literary style,
the early occurrence on the father's *titulus* of the Greek-inspired *topos*
linking wisdom and beauty with courage.

The key linguistic facts can be summarized as follows (see 4.2 for more
detailed information on the language of these and the other Old Latin texts
discussed below). First, it is generally assumed that the epitaphs in each
case are earlier than their associated *elogia*: note in particular the absence
of vowel weakening and final -*s* in *Cornelio* in each case beside *Cornelius*
in the father's *elogium* and *filios* in the son's, together with the absence
of -*n*- before -*s*- in *cosol/cesor* in the son's epitaph beside *consol/censor*,
the latter showing 'later' restoration of the original nasal, in his *elogium*.

The father's *elogium*, however, unlike the son's, shows consistent vowel weakening, which has led many scholars to assume that it must be relatively 'late', and in fact later than the son's, where such weakening is noted only sporadically (thus final *-o(m)* and *-os* are retained, but we have alternation between *hec/hic* and *fuet/cepit*). We may also note here that the son's tomb itself actually looks older: the much more elaborate iconography and superior workmanship of the father's tomb have therefore been taken by many as supporting the assumption of relative lateness. Alongside its more 'modern' features, however, the father's *elogium* also shows regular graphic preservation of diphthongs (*uirtutei/quei*, *Loucanam/abdoucit*, though note the exception in *Lucius*, confirming that this monophthongization had taken place despite the use of the traditional spelling elsewhere). In this respect, therefore, the son's *elogium* might be seen as the more 'modern' in the light of *ploirume* and *Luciom* (*oino* and *ploirume* are not relevant here, since *oi* -spellings were the norm until around 170 BC, long after the monophthongization of /oi/ to /u:/). The real problem, of course, is that we have no independent evidence in Roman Latin for the chronology of the different phonetic and/or graphic changes associated with most of these key phenomena prior to the earliest datable attestations listed in (5.2) above. Since archaizing spellings often persist, at least as an option, long after the relevant sound changes, especially in documents that aim for a 'high' style, it therefore remains a possibility that the father's *elogium* is in fact earlier than the son's, and that the latter is merely more traditional in some aspects of its orthography, e.g. in not noting vowel weakening (albeit with one or two tell-tale lapses), even though, on this analysis, it would also have to be assumed that the equally traditional diphthongal spellings of [ẹ:] and [u:] resulting from the monophthongization of [ei] and [ou], still generally used in the putatively 'earlier' text (though once again with a tell-tale lapse), had subsequently fallen out of favour and had not yet been routinely restored (we can at least be sure that they persisted for a time in later official Latin, cf. 5.4). In other words, different spelling reforms might well have been introduced at different times in different text types, and fashions might have changed during the course of the third century, with periodic 'reviews' of the various trends towards a more modern orthography – note, for example, that the near-routine omission of final *-m* in these two verse *elogia* is not replicated in our earliest dated 'official' texts from Rome. All in all, therefore, given our almost total ignorance of the chronological detail of orthographic reform, it is hugely ironic that, *faute de mieux*, these two texts still provide much of the basis for the conventional dating of many of the key sound changes that took place in the transition from Old to Classical Latin. The simple fact is that the dating of the documents themselves remains, and indeed must remain, controversial, with obvious consequences for the dating of the phenomena they exemplify (see Wachter (1987: ch. 4.B.2) for a more positive, if also controversial, view).

Other points worthy of mention here include, as already noted, the combination of traditional Latin with more 'philosophical/aesthetic' qualities in the father's *elogium*, as well as the highly marked 'neutralization' of tenses after perfect *cepit*, both perhaps showing Greek influence (cf. 4.3 once again for some discussion of the latter phenomenon, though the presents *subigit* and *abdoucit* both show signs of later tampering involving the addition of marks over the first *i* of the former and the *c* of the latter, perhaps in an effort to convert them into perfects (= *subegit, abdoucsit*)). In the son's epitaph/*elogium* we may also note the possibility that, alongside genuine *e/i* fluctuation in *aidiles/aidilis, Tempestatebus*, etc., the perfects in -*et* rather than -*it* may just reflect the first stage of the Roman monophthongization of the alternative 3rd person singular perfect ending -*eit* (cf. 4.2, 'Inflection', and see *ploirume*), though the apparent randomness of the choice probably tells against this. *Ploirume*, incidentally, looks like a false archaism in which, on the analogy of forms like *oino(m)*, an *oi*-spelling has been employed incorrectly to represent the contemporary pronunciation [u:]. The expected form is *plourume* (attested on a later Scipio epitaph), a remodelling of *$pleirumei$ (< *$pleh_1\text{-}is\text{-}mmoi$, with zero grade of the *-*yos* suffix characteristic of comparatives) on the basis of the neuter comparative *plous* 'more' (< *$pleus$, itself apparently modified prehistorically, under the influence of *u*-stem *minus* 'less', from an earlier *$ple(i)os$ < *$pleh_1\text{-}yos$, cf. *pleores*, as attested in the *Carmen Aruale*).

5.4   Dated Inscriptions of the Second Century: The Official Latin of *Senatusconsulta*

Since Rome was the political heart of the growing Empire, it was naturally the Latin of the Roman elite which provided the base for the standardization of the language for official purposes. As noted earlier, progressive Romanization of culture and language quickly obliterated local varieties of Latin from the written record, both from the regions of Latium outside Rome, where in earlier times non-Roman dialects had been used for writing, and from other Italian territories, where local languages had influenced the forms of spoken Latin that had begun to rival or replace them (see Chapter IV for examples). Once established, official epigraphic Latin became remarkably homogeneous throughout the Empire, with even the deviations from the standard (so-called 'vulgarisms'), observable in documents produced by the less well-educated, showing a surprisingly even distribution (cf. Chapter VII). Even after the collapse of central Roman authority in the West in the fifth century AD there is only very limited evidence for significant local variation (see Chapter VIII).

The actual steps by which the Latin of Rome developed into an official standard in the period between the fourth and the second centuries BC is unfortunately now beyond detailed investigation because of the absence of relevant evidence. The earliest surviving documents of any length already show clear signs of an established official practice, while Roman writers of later periods, though often discussing issues relevant to standardization *en passant*, are concerned almost exclusively with rhetorical, technical and literary varieties, and in any case bring a strongly contemporary perspective to their theorizing (see Chapter VI).

Here we shall focus on the official Latin of two early *senatusconsulta* ('decrees of the senate': see Courtney 1999: 93ff. for a very helpful commentary). The first is the famous *Senatusconsultum de Bacchanalibus* (CIL I^2 581, 186 BC, henceforth *SCB*), embodying measures to control the activities of Bacchanalian houses in Italy (see Livy 39, 8–19 for a full account of the background). The actual text of the senate's decree is quoted in a letter of the consuls of the year to the people of the Ager Teuranus in Bruttium (modern Calabria), and was inscribed on a locally made bronze tablet, containing one or two careless errors of execution, found at Tiriolo. The document concludes with the consuls' own instructions to the local officials, and also contains, at the very end, an order about where the plate is to be located. Note that the introductory formula, giving the names of the consuls together with the date of their consultation of the Senate and the names of those who witnessed the record, is omitted here:

(3)   CIL I^2 581, 186 BC: *Senatusconsultum de Bacchanalibus*

. . . de   Bacanalibus, quei   foideratei   esent,   ita
about Bacchic-festivals, who-NOM bound-by-treaty-NOM be-3pl.IMPF.SUBJ, thus

exdeicendum censuere:
to-be-proclaimed decree-3pl.PF

---

neiquis eorum   [B]acanal   habuise   uelet;   sei ques
noone   them-GEN shrine-of-Bacchus have-PF.INF wish-3sg.IMPF.SUBJ; if   any-NOM

esent,   quei   sibei   deicerent   necesus ese
be-3pl.IMPF.SUBJ, who-NOM themselves-DAT say-3pl.IMPF.SUBJ necessary be-INF

Bacanal   habere, eeis   utei ad pr(aitorem) urbanum Romam   5
shrine-of-Bacchus have-INF, they-NOM that to praetor-ACC of-city-ACC Rome-ACC

uenirent,   deque   eeis   rebus,   ubei eorum   u[e]r[b]a audita
come-3pl.IMPF.SUBJ, about-and those-ABL things-ABL, when them-GEN words-NOM heard

esent, utei senatus noster decerneret, dum ne minus
be-3pl.PLPF.SUBJ, that Senate-NOM our-NOM decide-3sg.IMPF.SUBJ, provided not less

senator(i)bus C adesent [quom e]a res cosoleretur.
senators-ABL 100 be-present-3pl.IMPF.SUBJ when that thing discuss-3sg.IMPF.SUBJ.PASS.

Bacas uir nequis adiese uelet
Bacchic-women-ACC man-NOM none-NOM visit-PF.INF wish-3sg.IMPF.SUBJ

ceiuis Romanus neue nominus Latini neue socium quisquam, nisei 10
citizen-NOM Roman-NOM nor name-GEN Latin-GEN nor allies-GEN anyone-NOM, unless

pr(aitorem) urbanum adiesent isque [d]e senatuos sententiad,
praetor-ACC of-city-ACC approach-3pl.PLPF.SUBJ he-and by Senate-GEN vote-ABL,

dum ne minus senatoribus C adesent, quom ea res
provided not less senators-ABL 100 be-present-3pl.IMPF.SUBJ, when that-NOM thing-NOM

cosoleretur, iousisent. censuere.
discussed-3sg.IMPF.SUBJ.PASS, order-3pl.PLPF.SUBJ. Resolve-3pl.PF.

sacerdos nequis uir eset; magister neque uir neque
priest-NOM no-NOM man-NOM be-3sg.IMPF.SUBJ; master-NOM neither man-NOM nor

mulier quisquam eset. neue pecuniam quisquam eorum comoine[m 15
woman-NOM any-NOM be-3sg.IMPF.SUBJ. nor money-ACC anyone-NOM them-GEN common-ACC

h]abuise ue[l]et; neue magistratum neue pro magistratu[d]
have-PF.INF wish-3sg.IMPF.SUBJ; neither holder-of-mastership-ACC nor pro-holder-of-mastership-ABL

neque uirum [neque mul]ierem qui(s)quam fecise uelet,
neither man-ACC nor woman-ACC anyone-NOM make-PF.INF wish-3sg.IMPF.SUBJ,

neue posthac inter sed conioura[se neu]e comuouise
neither hereafter between themselves-ACC swear-together-PF.INF nor vow-together-PF.INF

neue conspondise neue compromesise uelet, neue
neither pledge-together-PF.INF nor promise-together-PF.INF wish-3sg.IMPF.SUBJ, nor

quisquam fidem inter sed dedise uelet. 20
anyone-NOM faith-ACC between themselves-ACC give-PF.INF wish-3sg.IMPF.SUBJ.

sacra in [o]quoltod ne quisquam fecise uelet, neue in
Rites-ACC in secret-ABL not anyone-NOM make-PF.INF wish-3sg.IMPF.SUBJ, neither in

poplicod neue in preiuatod neue exstrad urbem sacra quisquam fecise
public-ABL nor in private-ABL nor outside city-ACC rites-ACC anyone-NOM make-PF.INF

uelet, nisei p[r(aitorem) urbanum adieset, isque
wish-3sg.IMPF.SUBJ, unless praetor-ACC of-the-city-ACC approach-3sg.PLPF.SUBJ, he-and

de senatuos sententiad, dum ne minus senatoribus C adesent,
by Senate-GEN vote-ABL, provided not less senators-ABL 100 be-present-3pl.IMPF.SUBJ,

quom ea res cosoleretur, iousisent. censuere. 25
when that-NOM thing-NOM discuss-3sg.IMPF.SUBJ.PASS, order-3pl.PLPF.SUBJ. Resolve-3pl.PF.

homines plous V oinuorsei uirei atque mulieres sacra ne
people-NOM more 5 in-all-NOM men-NOM and women-NOM ceremonies-ACC not

quisquam fecise uelet, neue inter ibei uirei plous duobus
anyone-NOM do-PF.INF wish-3sg.IMPF.SUBJ, nor among there men-NOM more two-ABL

mulieribus plous tribus arfuise uelent, nisei de pr(aitori/us)
women-ABL more three-ABL be-present-PF.INF wish-3pl.IMPF.SUBJ, unless by praetor-GEN

urbani senatuosque sententiad, utei supra scriptum est.
of-the-city-GEN Senate-GEN-and decision-ABL, as above written be-3sg.PRES.

---

haice utei in couentionid exdeicatis ne minus trinum 30
these-ACC that in public-meeting-ABL proclaim-2pl.PRS.SUBJ not less three-each-GEN

noundinum; senatuosque sententiam utei scientes
periods-between-market-days-GEN; Senate-and-GEN vote-ACC that cognisant-NOM

esetis (eorum sententia ita fuit: 'sei ques esent
be-2pl.IMPF.SUBJ (them-GEN vote-NOM thus be-3sg.PF: 'if any-NOM.PL be-3pl.IMPF.SUBJ

quei aruorsum ead fecisent quam suprad scriptum est,
who-NOM.PL against that-FEM.ABL do-3pl.PLPF.SUBJ than above written be-3sg.PRES,

eeis rem caputalem faciendam. censuere'), atque utei
them-DAT matter-ACC capital-ACC to-be done-ACC. Resolve-3pl.PF'), and-furthermore that

hoce in tabolam ahenam inceideretis, ita senatus 35
this-ACC onto tablet-ACC bronze-ACC inscribe-2pl.IMPF.SUBJ, thus Senate-NOM

aiquom censuit; uteique eam figier ioubeatis ubei
proper-NEUT.ACC resolve.3sg-PF; that-and it-ACC fix-PRES.PASS.INF order-2pl.PRES.SUBJ where

facilumed gnoscier potisit, atque utei ea Bacanalia, sei qua
most-easily read-PRES.PASS.INF can-3sg.SUBJ, and that those Bacchanalian-houses, if any

sunt, exstrad quam sei quid ibei sacri est, ita utei
be-3pl.PRES, outside than if anything-NOM there consecrated-GEN.SG be-3sg.PRES, thus as

suprad scriptum est, in diebus X quibus uobeis tabelai datai
above written be-3sg.PRES, in days-ABL 10 which-ABL you-DAT tablets-NOM given-NOM

erunt, faciatis ✦ utei dismota sient. 40
be-3pl.FUT, do-2pl.PRES.SUBJ that dispersed be-3pl.PRES.SUBJ.

---

in agro Teurano.
In territory-ABL of-the-Teurani-ABL

'. . . Concerning Bacchic festivals, with regard to those who were bound to Rome by treaty [i.e. the Italian *socii*], they [i.e. the senators] passed a resolution that the following proclamation should be issued:

That none of them should (wish to) keep a shrine of Bacchus. That if there were any who said it was necessary for them to keep a shrine of

Bacchus, they should come to Rome to the praetor of the city, and that our senate should decide about these things when their words had been heard, provided that no less than 100 senators were present when the matter was debated.

That no man should (wish to) attend a meeting of Bacchic women, [neither] a Roman citizen nor someone of the Latin name nor one of the allies, unless they had approached the praetor of the city and he with the Senate's vote – provided that no less than 100 senators were present when the matter was debated – had authorized them. Resolved.

That no man should be a priest; that no man or woman should be a *magister* [i.e. head lay administrator]. That none of them should (wish to) hold money in common; that no one should (wish to) appoint either a man or a woman as either the holder of a *magistratus* [i.e. head lay adminstratorship] or as a deputy for such, or hereafter (wish to) offer reciprocal oaths or vows, undertakings or promises to one another, nor should any (wish to) pledge good faith to one another. In the matter of ceremonies, that no one should (wish to) perform these in secret, nor should anyone (wish to) perform them in either a public or a private capacity or outside the city, unless he had approached the praetor of the city, and he with the Senate's vote – provided that no less than 100 senators were present when the matter was debated – had authorized them. Resolved.

With regard to groups of people more than five in all, men and women, that no one should [wish to] hold ceremonies, and that men no more than two, [and] no more than three women, should [wish to] attend in that company, unless in accordance with the decision of the praetor of the city and the Senate, as written above.

You shall proclaim these orders at public meetings during a period of not less than three separate market days; and with regard to the vote of the Senate, the Senate decreed it proper that you should be aware of its content (their vote was as follows: 'If there were any who had acted otherwise than has been written above, proceedings for capital offence were to be taken against them. Resolved'), and furthermore that you should inscribe this order on a bronze tablet; you shall also give orders for it to be fastened up where it can most easily be read; and in addition you shall arrange for those Bacchanalian houses that may exist to be dispersed in the manner written above within ten days from the time when the dispatches are given to you, except if there is anything duly consecrated therein.

In the territory of the Teurani.'

The second example is the equally famous bronze *Epistula ad Tiburtes* ('Letter to the Tiburtines', CIL I² 586, henceforth *ET*), now lost, in which the praetor Lucius Cornelius reports to the people of Tibur the import of a *senatusconsultum* concerning them. The document probably dates to 159 BC:

(4) CIL I² 586, ?159 BC: *Epistula ad Tiburtes*

L(ucius)   Cornelius   Cn(aei)   f(ilius)   pr(aetor)   sen(atum) cons(uluit) a(nte)
Lucius-NOM Cornelius-NOM Gnaeus-GEN son-NOM praetor-NOM senate-ACC consult-3sg.PF before

d(iem) III   Nonas   Maias   sub   aede   Kastorus.
day-ACC third-ACC Nones-ACC of-May-ACC beneath temple-ABL Castor-GEN.

scr(ibundo) adf(uerunt)   A(ulus)   Manlius   A(uli)   f(ilius),   Sex(tus)
writing-DAT be-present-3pl.IMPF Aulus-NOM Manlius-NOM Aulus-GEN son-NOM, Sextus-NOM

Iulius.....   L(ucius)   Postumius   S(puri)   f(ilius).
Iulius-NOM..... Lucius-NOM Postumius-NOM Spurius-GEN son-NOM.

quod Teiburtes   u(erba)   f(ecistis), quibusque   de   rebus   5
because Tiburtines-NOM words-ACC make-2pl.PF, which-ABL-and about things-ABL

uos   purgauistis,   ea   senatus   animum aduortit ita utei aequom
you-ACC exculpate-2pl.PF, those-ACC senate-NOM mind-ACC turn-3sg.PF thus as fair-NOM

fuit;   nosque   ea   ita audieramus ut uos   deixsistis uobeis
be-3sg.PF; we-NOM-and those-things-ACC.pl thus hear-1pl.PLPF as you-NOM say-2pl.PF you-DAT

nontiata   esse. ea   nos   animum nostrum non indoucebamus
announced-ACC.pl be-INF. those-things-ACC we-NOM mind-ACC our-ACC not bring-1pl.IMPF

ita facta   esse propterea   quod scibamus   ea   uos   merito
thus done-ACC.pl be-INF on-this-account that know-1pl.IMPF those-things-ACC you-NOM desert-ABL

nostro facere non potuisse;   neque uos   dignos   esse quei   ea   10
our-ABL do-INF not be-able-INF.pf; nor   you-ACC worthy-ACC be-INF who-NOM those-things-ACC

faceretis   neque id   uobeis neque rei poplicae uostrae oitile
do-2pl.IMPF.SUBJ nor   that-thing-ACC you-DAT nor   state-DAT   your-DAT useful-ACC

esse facere. et postquam uostra   uerba   senatus   audiuit,   tanto   magis
be-INF do-INF. and after   your-ACC words-ACC senate-NOM hear-3sg.PF, so-much-ABL more

animum nostrum indoucimus, ita utei ante arbitrabamur, de   eieis   rebus   af
mind-ACC our-ACC bring-1pl.PRS, thus as   before think-1pl.IMPF, about those-ABL things-ABL by

uobeis peccatum   non esse. quonque de   eieis   rebus   senatuei purgati
you-ABL sinned-ACC.sg not be-INF. since-and about those-ABL things-ABL senate-DAT cleared-NOM.pl

estis,   credimus,   uosque   animum uostrum indoucere oportet,   15
be-2pl.PRES, believe-1pl.PRES, you-ACC-and mind-ACC your-ACC bring-INF   behove-3sg.PRES,

item   uos   populo   Romano   purgatos   fore.
likewise you-ACC people-DAT Roman-DAT cleared-ACC be-INF.fut.

'Lucius Cornelius, praetor, son of Gnaeus, consulted the Senate on 5th May at the Temple of Castor.

Present at the drafting were: Aulus Manlius son of Aulus, Sextus Iulius . . . , Lucius Postumius son of Spurius.

Inasmuch as you Tiburtines made a verbal report, and concerning the matters about which you justified yourselves, the Senate took note of these just as was proper; and we had heard these charges just as you said they had been reported to you. We were not inclined to take the view that these things had been done in this way because we knew that, given what we deserved from you, you could not have done them; nor was it worthy of you to do them, nor was it advantageous for you or your polity to do them. And now the Senate has heard your own words we take the view all the more, just as we thought before, that there was no fault on your part with regard to these matters. And since you have been cleared of these charges in the eyes of the Senate, we believe, and you must take the view, that you will likewise be cleared in the eyes of the Roman People.'

The rigid format of these documents is eloquent testimony to an already lengthy tradition of such official writing, and indeed to the rigorous training of the senatorial draftsmen who prepared them. Two obvious indicators of the existence of established conventions are the archaizing orthography (note especially the regular diphthongal spellings, aside from *nontiata* (l. 8) and *purgati* (l. 14) in *ET*, of what were now long vowels) and the rather tortuous syntax and phraseology so characteristic of legal-official documents in most cultures throughout the ages. Independent evidence for a protracted process of development behind the fully fledged official Latin of the second century BC is, however, provided by the Greek historian Polybius (*c*.200–118 BC), who was deported to Italy in 168 BC, and became a friend of Scipio Aemilianus. His history of Rome in the period 264–146 BC includes a tentative translation (given the difficulties already experienced with archaic Latin) of the text of a treaty made between Rome and Carthage in 508/7 BC (3.22.3).

Beginning with the orthography of these two texts, it should be no surprise that, after a period of rapid and extensive sound change (see Chapter IV for details), there should still be some uncertainties of spelling, either because no relevant convention had yet become fully established, e.g. the treatment of medial -*ns*- in *SCB*, perhaps reflecting the relative novelty of the graphic restoration of the nasal (cf. *censuere* (l. 2) vs. *cosoleretur* (l. 8)), or because of sporadic hypercorrection. Thus the conjunction *cum* continued to be written *quom* (e.g. *quon-que* (l. 14) in *ET*, with assimilation) at least until the middle of the first century BC, long after [o] > [u] before nasals or [l] + consonant (cf. *hunc* for *honc* 'this (man)', *multa* for *molta* 'fine') and the consequential dissimilatory loss of lip rounding in [kʷ] had led to the pronunciation [kum]: but the homophony is reflected in the misspelling of the preposition *cum* 'with', which never had a labio-velar, as *quom* in a contemporary Scipio epitaph (CIL I² 11, *c.*160 BC), and we have a very similar hypercorrection in *oquoltod* (l. 21) (for *ocultod*) in *SCB*.

In general, however, the traditional rules are correctly and consistently applied in *SCB*. In *ET*, by contrast, we already see a partial tendency to modernize spelling in line with earlier changes in pronunciation. Whether such practice had already been generalized, or is merely a function of a possible continuing contrast between 'senatorial' and 'personal' styles is uncertain: but recall that *ET* is an individual official's report of the Senate's decree (note, *inter alia*, that, unless this simply records the words addressed directly to Tiburtine representatives in the Senate, the 3rd-person verb forms of the official record of those words have been turned back into 2nd-person forms), and compare the more modern spellings already used in the personal decree of Aemilius Paullus of 189 BC, mentioned above, with the traditional spellings employed by the consuls in their appendix to *SCB*, the content of which presumably carried senatorial backing.

Orthographic innovations in *ET* include the shift of *ai* to *ae* (*aequom* (l. 6), but cf. also *aedem* in the preamble to *SCB*, not reproduced above), the use of etymological *ad-* before *-fuerunt* (l. 3) for earlier *ar-* (cf. *SCB* (l. 28), reflecting a contextually conditioned pronunciation as an alveolar flap in the context of a labio-dental fricative or bilabial continuant, probably as a precursor to full assimilation, e.g. [affu'e:runt]), the noting of double consonants (*peccatum* (l. 14)), and the omission of *-d* in ablatives like *merito nostro* (ll. 9–10), all in contrast with *SCB* (the *d*-less ablative in the final instruction to the local officials (l. 41) is not part of the official document). If not already standard, such changes were quickly endorsed by the central bureaucracy and became characteristic of all subsequent official documents (always allowing for sporadic archaism, see the discussion of text (6) below).

By contrast, certain aspects of the morphology and syntax remain traditional in both documents. *Kastorus*, for example, in *ET* (l. 2) exemplifies the variant form of the 3rd-declension consonant-stem genitive singular in *-us* < *-os*, still normal at this time in the names of deities and in traditional formulae such as *nominus Latini* 'of the Latin name', as employed in *SCB* (l. 10). There has been much confusion about such alternative forms (as also about certain traditional spellings like *ar* [aɾ]] (= *ad*) and *af* [av] (= *ab*, cf. *ET* ll. 13–14), marking loss of occlusion before fricatives/continuants), because they typically appear for longer and/or with greater frequency in regional Latin inscriptions. From the perspective of a Roman aristocrat of the mid-first century BC, these would indeed seem 'rustic', but in reality, as these official Roman documents make clear, they were once characteristic of Latin in general, only disappearing from elite styles as standardization progressed (though *af* enjoyed a restricted after-life in the technical Latin of accounting and surveying).

Turning now to issues of syntax, a number of points in *ET* deserve specific mention, including the preclassical use of the indicative rather than the subjunctive in a circumstantial (causal) *cum*-clause (*quonque . . . purgati estis* ll. 14–15), the simplicity of the forms of connection between sentences (*-que* and *neque* are used repeatedly, though linking is also achieved by repetition of an element from one sentence in the initial position of the next, cf. *nosque ea ita audiueramus . . . ea nos animum non indoucebamus ita facta esse* ll. 7–8), and the regular placing of verbs in final position in their clauses, a key feature of official Latin seen also in *SCB* (where the only exception is *exdeicatis* in the consuls' appendix (l. 30)). We should also note that the accusative and infinitive construction, the classic Latin instrument for introducing a complement clause after verbs of 'saying/thinking/believing/knowing' etc., is already well in evidence in both texts, as might be expected in a context where the reporting of what was said or thought is routine. The repeated use in *SCB* of *ne* + subjunctive of *uelle* ('wish') + perfect infinitive to express a prohibition is another characteristic 'marker' of administrative decrees, serving as the oblique equivalent of imperative *noli/nolite* (lit. 'be unwilling') + infinitive, but with the perfect infinitive conveying the perfective aspect of prohibitions of the type *ne* + perfect subjunctive.

But perhaps the most important issue here concerns the overall structuring and presentation of information. It has been suggested that the structure of the initial sentence of *ET* proper (beginning *quod* . . . (l. 5)) is clumsy, even contorted, from the point of view of the norms of classical literary prose (Courtney 1999: 102). However, the context of traditional orthography, in combination with the repetitive diction (e.g. *de eieis rebus* (ll. 13, 14), *animum indoucere* (ll. 8, 13)) and the use of self-consciously 'weighty' periphrastic phraseology (*u(erba) f(ecistis)* (l. 5), *animum aduortit* (l. 6), *animum indoucere* (ll. 13, 15)), suggests that the syntax too follows an established legal-official style designed both to achieve clarity and to convey the seriousness of the message. This sentence in fact first presents the key issues (the topic), then states what was done about them (the comment). The topic component begins with a conflation of two formulaic beginnings, the first introduced by a 'causal' conjunction (*quod* (l. 5)) motivating the Senate's deliberations, the second by a relative clause (beginning with *quibusque de rebus* (l. 5)) outlining the issue discussed, with the two together picked up by a 'resumptive' demonstrative pronoun in the main clause (*ea* (ll. 6, 7)).

Both types of rubric are well attested in other official documents, the formula *quod uerba fecit/fecerunt . . . , de ea re ita censuerunt* ('inasmuch as X made a verbal report, [the senators] decreed as follows on that matter') being in fact the standard beginning of a *senatusconsultum* (e.g. the Latin-Greek bilingual CIL I^2 588 of 78 BC, though the poorly preserved Latin has been extensively restored on the basis of the Greek text). But a clause beginning with a noun phrase headed by a relative pronoun, often followed by a counterpart phrase beginning with a correlative demonstrative in the main clause ('which X . . . , that X . . .'), is also routinely employed, sometimes following a general heading of the form *de X* ('concerning X'), as a rubric for introducing the provisions of a law regarding the specified person or thing (e.g. CIL I^2 583, the *Lex Acilia* of 122 BC on extortion; CIL I^2 585, an agrarian law of 111 BC; CIL I^2 582, a law from Bantia of the late second century BC; CIL I^2 587, the *Lex Cornelia de XX Quaestoribus* of 81 BC). The specific expression *quibus de rebus* is not employed in laws, however, and appears to be used here as an alternative to the *quod* option (though see the discussion of text (9) below for its likely official status in *senatusconsulta*). There is a clear parallel to this 'dual' topic structure in *SCB* (l. 1), though there the draftsmen have employed a version of the formulaic combination often used in laws, viz. *de X . . . , quei . . .* (though without resumption of the relative in the main clause), 'concerning X . . . , (the people) who . . .', as in CIL I^2 583.

In this connection, it is interesting to note that, from the fourth century BC onwards, decrees of the Athenian people almost always begin either with *epeidé* 'inasmuch as' or with a relative clause introduced by *perì hôn* 'about what' (though the relative pronoun appears alone, in contrast with *quibus de rebus*, and there is no main-clause correlative). The decision itself is then put in the form of a 'report' by means of the accusative and infinitive construction, used to express what it was agreed should be done by the relevant parties (e.g. *Inscriptiones Graecae* II^2 111, II^2 107, among many examples). Though 'preposed' relative clauses, with or without explicit resumption in the main clause, are an inherited feature of all ancient IE languages, the formal parallelism of these two types of introductory formula at least invites the suspicion that Roman officialdom had partly modelled its own linguistic usage on established Greek practice in a period when exposure to Greek culture and practice was becoming increasingly routine. Similarities to archaic Greek laws in matters of expression and syntax can already be detected in the famous XII Tables, originally dating from the fifth century BC, and one may also note here a common liking for periphrases involving a neutral verb of 'making/doing', as already mentioned above (see Horrocks 2010: 29, 45 for comparable Greek examples).

Nonetheless, there are also clear differences: main-clause correlative demonstratives are regular (if not obligatory) in Latin, and, more importantly, there is an alternative, preferred, construction for main clauses: while the accusative and infinitive may be used, as in Greek, to record what should be done, this is largely confined to semantically passive gerundives with *esse* (the latter often omitted) or, more rarely, passive infinitives, both of which carry the necessary 'modal' associations (e.g. CIL I² 588, 78 BC: *ita censuerunt: Asclepiadem . . . , Polystratum . . . , Meniscum . . . , uiros bonos et ameicos appellari,* 'voted as follows: for A, P and M to be known as "good men and friends" '). The regular form of expression is a subjunctive clause introduced by *utei* (positive) or *ne(i)* (negative), corresponding to what would have been expressed directly in such a context by a 3rd-person imperative (i.e. forms in *-to(d)*, = 'let X do Y'). This is not a native Greek practice. Furthermore, such non-infinitival main clauses demonstrate from the first the application of the classical sequence-of-tense rules, and subordinate clauses may also show the conversions of tense and mood characteristic of *oratio obliqua* ('indirect speech'), as familiar from classical literary Latin. Again Greek has nothing to parallel this.

SCB illustrates these points very clearly, where, unlike in *ET*, which gives the praetor's summary of the Senate's decree as addressed directly to its recipients, the actual text of the *senatusconsultum* is quoted. Since the document reports the Senate's deliberations as past events, the relevant commands and prohibitions all contain 'past' (i.e. imperfect) subjunctives, in accordance with the grammatical principles of *consecutio temporum* ('sequence of tenses'). Subordinate clauses are also affected in Latin at this level, so that what would have been a future perfect indicative in a temporal clause in direct speech (*audita erunt,* 'when their words *will have been heard*') appears here as a pluperfect subjunctive (*audita esent* (ll. 6–7), '[they decreed that] when their words *had been heard*'). Here the subjunctive has no independent semantic force, but is used simply to mark the clause grammatically as part of what is reported, just as the pluperfect tense is required to mark its anteriority to the prospective action of the main clause, which, as noted, contains a past (imperfect) subjunctive. Very similar usage is in evidence in CIL I² 614, the decree of Aemilius Paullus already mentioned above.

None of this has any parallel in Greek, and it seems likely that the rules for converting direct into indirect discourse had a purely Roman origin, evolving with the growing need for the decrees of public bodies and magistrates to be recorded and reported. A context for such a development can perhaps be found in the social struggles of early Rome and the city's subsequent imperial expansion, when the issue of citizen rights, the negotiation of treaties, and an ever-wider range of legal and administrative responsibilities must have led to the rapid evolution of a complex official form of the language. From the point of view of the linguistic historian, however, it is unfortunate that these rules are already fully developed in the earliest surviving documents that require the operation of such a convention.

It is interesting at this point to compare what we have seen so far of official Latin with the Greek translation of a *senatusconsultum* (*Sylloge Inscriptionum Graecarum*[3] II, number 646) concerning the city of Thisbae in Boeotia, dating from 170 BC (see also Sherk 1969, Horrocks 2010: 86–8):

(5) *Senatusconsultum de Thisbensibus*

perì hôn   Thizbeîs lógous epoiésanto, perì tôn kath' hautoùs
about which-things Thisbians   words   made-3pl;   about the   by   themselves

prāgmátōn, hoítines en têi philíāi   têi hēmetérāi enémeinan, hópōs
affairs,   whoever   in the friendship the ours   remained-3pl, that

autoîs dothôsin   hoîs   tà kath' hautoùs prágmata eksēgésōntai,
to-them be-given-3pl.SUBJ by-which the by   themselves affairs   conduct-3pl.SUBJ,

perì toútou toû prágmatos hoútōs édoksen;   hópōs Kointos Mainios
about this   the matter   thus   was-resolved-3sg; that   Quintus Maenius

stratēgòs tôn   ek   tês synklétou pénte apotáksēi,   hoì àn autôi
magistrate of-those from the Senate   five   delegate-3sg.SUBJ, who ever to-him

ek tôn dēmosíōn-prāgmátōn kaì tês idíās písteōs phaínōntai. édokse.
from the republic   and the private faith   seem-3pl.SUBJ. Resolved-3sg.

'Concerning the matters about which the citizens of Thisbae made verbal representations; concerning their private affairs; [regarding] those who remained true to our friendship, [regarding the proposal] that facilities should be given to them by means of which they might conduct their own affairs; concerning this matter the following decision was taken; that our magistrate Quintus Maenius should delegate five members of the Senate who[se selection] seemed to him consistent with the interests of the republic and his personal integrity. Resolved.

The Latinate quality is immediately apparent in the elaborate sequential refinement of the topic (compare the double topics of *ET* and *SCB*: normal official Greek would use only the first of these clauses), in the use of a relative clause with the subjunctive to express purpose ('(facilities) by means of which they might conduct their own affairs'), in the use of a subjunctive clause (with *hópōs* for *utei*) rather than an accusative and infinitive to present the Senate's decision, and in the close rendering of the formulaic *ita utei/quei ei e re publica fideque sua uideatur/uideantur (esse)*, 'just as/who seemed to him (to be) advantageous to the republic and consistent with his personal integrity' (see, for example, the ending of the *senatusconsultum* CIL I² 588 of 78 BC). Note too the use of preposed relatives followed by resumptive demonstratives, both to define the set of people concerned, and to specify what should be done in their case with regard to the specified proposal. In this overall context of 'translationese', it seems reasonable to infer that *perì hón ... lógous epoiḗsanto, ... perì toútou toû prágmatos hoútōs édoksen* translates an original *quibus de rebus ... uerba fecerunt, ... de ea re ita censuerunt*, given that *epeidḗ* was available in principle to translate *quod*; the grammatical mismatch between plural relative and singular correlative, actual in the Greek, presumed for the Latin, is explained by the long hyperbaton and the fact that the last element of the rubric is a singular proposal, presumably expressed in the original text as an *utei* clause. This document therefore provides indirect support for the formulaic status of *quibus de rebus ...* (+ *uerba fecit/fecerunt* or other predicate) in official Latin of the period. It also confirms that any apparent 'clumsiness' of the beginning of the *Epistula ad Tiburtes* was in fact a routine property of official Latin, in which the topic of a decree was often cumulatively specified through a series of a loosely juxtaposed, or conventionally conjoined, rubrics.

There is, however, one necessary concession to Greek over and above the indicators of familiarity with normal Greek practice of the period, such as the use of prepositional phrase possessives (like *tà kath' hautoùs prágmata*) and of the impersonal *édokse(n)* 'it seemed good' for 3rd person plural *censuere*, etc. Given that the language had no rules of the Latin type for regulating the sequence of tenses in indirect discourse and since, in its contemporary form, it had only one set of modal verb forms, namely tenseless subjunctives (the optative, which had earlier fulfilled the role of a 'past' subjunctive in certain contexts, having by now disappeared from all but the most archaizing styles), the subjunctive clause used to convey the Senate's *sententia*, unlike those in *SCB*, cannot be made 'past' to mark its reported status in a past-time context.

Returning now to *SCB*, it is important to note that, when the consuls start to improvise their own instructions (ll. 30ff.), the format changes and a distinction is drawn between reports of what the senate decreed should be done (all the relevant clauses have imperfect subjunctives) and what the consuls themselves now require (the clauses concerned have present subjunctives). The use of apparently non-dependent present subjunctives to express these orders, marked by 'jussive' *utei* without a governing main verb analogous to the senatorial *censuere/censuit*, is very characteristic of official Latin, and interesting questions arise with regard to its interpretation. These may be 'real' independent clauses (with *utei* used as the positive equivalent of *ne* rather than as a subordinating conjunction), or, by convention, a verb of 'ordering' etc. is to be 'understood' (we may compare here the similar Greek use of *hópōs*, literally 'how', + future indicative without an overt verb of 'taking precautions'). In favour of the latter interpretation, note the many literary examples where ellipsis of such a verb is strongly implied by the preceding context: e.g. Cato, *de Agri Cultura* 1.2, *et uti eo introeas et circumspicias* ('then you should go in there and look around'), immediately preceded in 1.1 by *sic in animo habeto, uti* . . . ('keep this in mind, that . . .). It is therefore at least arguable that the 'independent' use of such clauses is simply an extension of this covertly dependent use, in which an appropriate (non-past) main verb has been omitted from all but the first of a list of injunctions. That true subordination was already well established is, after all, demonstrated by the fact that the overtly reported senatorial commands and prohibitions contain grammatically controlled past-tense subjunctives after past-tense main verbs. This therefore seems preferable to assuming that imperatival *utei*-clauses in second-century texts are residual examples of an ancient main-clause construction in which *utei* was originally, say, an indefinite manner adverb (meaning 'somehow/anyway', cf. preclassical *neutiquam* 'not in any way'), even if such a construction is indeed the ultimate origin, via parataxis, of the subordinating structure.

Whatever the truth of this particular matter, it is important to appreciate that the practice of reporting senatorial decisions as past events becomes increasingly inconsistent in the decrees of subsequent periods. Thus already in CIL I² 591 (the *Senatusconsultum de Pago Montano*, second half of the second century BC) and probably in CIL I² 588 (a fragmentary *senatusconsultum* of 78 BC heavily restored on the basis of its Greek translation, as noted) we find shifts between reported (past-time) clauses and direct statements of the Senate's decisions in conjoined contexts that make clear the dependent status of all the clauses involved. Consider the *Senatusconsultum de Pago Montano*:

(6)   CIL I² 591, second half of second century BC: *Senatusconsultum de Pago Montano*

. . . curarent   tu[erenturque   ar]bitratu   aedilium   pleibeium
. . . care-3pl.IMPF.SUBJ keep-watch-3pl.IMPF.SUBJ discretion-ABL aediles-GEN of-plebs-GEN

[quei]comque essent;   neiue ustrinae   in eis   loceis
whoever-NOM   be-3pl.IMPF.SUBJ; nor   burning-grounds-NOM in those-ABL places-ABL

recionibusue niue foci   ustrinae<ue> caussa fierent   niue
regions-or-ABL nor fireplaces-NOM burning-GEN for   be-made-3pl.IMPF.SUBJ nor

stercus   terra[m]ue intra ea   loca   fecisse   coniecisseue
dung-ACC earth-or-ACC within those-ACC places-ACC make-PF.INF throw-together-or-PF.INF

ueli[t]   quei   haec   loca   ab paaco   Montano
wish-3sg.PRES.SUBJ who-NOM these-ACC places-ACC from hamlet-ABL Mountain-ABL

[redempta   habebit,   quod si stercus in eis   loceis   fecerit
repurchased-ACC have-3sg.FUT, but   if dung-ACC in those-ABL places-ABL make-3sg.FUT.PF

terramue in ea]   loca   iecerit, . . .   [ma]nus iniectio
earth-or-ACC into those-ACC places-ACC cast-3sg.FUT.PF, . . . hand-GEN laying-on-NOM

pignorisq(ue) cap[tio   siet.]
pledge-and-GEN taking-NOM be-3sg.PRES.SUBJ

'[The senators decreed as follows: that] . . . they should take care and guard [the burial ground] at the discretion of the aediles of the plebs who were in office, and that no burning-grounds should be made in those places or areas and no fireplaces for burning [the dead], and that no one shall (wish to) make a dung heap or throw down earth within those places who shall hold these places by redemption from the Mountain Hamlet, but if anyone shall have made a dung heap in those places or cast earth into those places, . . . there shall be a laying of hands [on him] and the taking of a pledge.'

As expected, the orthography is less archaizing in general than in *SCB*. Thus double consonants are written but not final *-d*, and *ei* is inconsistently noted (contrast *neiue . . . in eis loceis* with *niue foci*). In one respect, however, the orthography is actually more archaic: in *recionibusue* and *paaco* the letter *c* represents [g], even though *g* had been available from the third century (though the innovatory convention of writing vowels double to mark length, prompted in part by established Oscan practice despite the tradition that it was introduced by the poet and grammarian Accius (170–*c*.85 BC), becomes common only towards the end of the second century, continuing thereafter, at least as an option, to the end of the Republic).

But the key feature here is the seemingly unmotivated shift from imperfect to present subjunctives half way through: contrast *curarent*, etc. with *uelit*, etc. Assuming a uniformly subordinating structure throughout (cf. the conjoined sequence of *n(e)ive*-clauses: *neiue . . . fierent, niue . . . uelit*), the explanation lies in an ambiguity inherent in the meaning of the formulaic introductory verb *censuerunt* (assumed here for the missing rubric). On the one hand, it could be taken as a perfective past tense ('[the senators] resolved'), with the force of a verb of reporting, and with the following *ut*-clause then used by a third party to convey to readers of the document what the senate had agreed, as in *SCB*. On the other hand, it could equally naturally be taken as a present perfect ('[the senators] have resolved'), with what follows merely defining the terms of the senators' decree directly (i.e. not involving a report of it by a third party). The sequence of tense rules for dependent clauses differ according to whether the governing main verb is past (secondary sequence) or non-past (primary sequence). In the latter case present subjunctives are naturally employed; and since the *ut*-clause now simply spells out the content of the order rather than representing a reported command in *oratio obliqua*, the other subordinate clauses are not understood as forming part of a report either, and the use of indicatives is therefore natural: thus the subordinate clauses that are part of the 'reported' part of the document contain past subjunctives, as expected in *oratio obliqua*, while those in the 'direct' part have future-referring indicatives: contrast [*quei*]*comque essent* (imperfect subjunctive) with *quei haec loca . . . habebit* (future indicative) or [*quod si stercus*] . . . *iecerit* (future perfect indicative), and with the latter pair compare examples like *censeo ut iis, qui in exercitu M. Antonii sunt, ne sit ea res fraudi, si . . .* , 'I take the view that this affair should not be damaging to those who are in Mark Antony's army, if . . .' (Cicero *Philippic* 5.12.34), where the *ut*-clause once again merely expresses the content of Cicero's view, and the relative clause is similarly understood not to be within *oratio obliqua*. It is probably worth observing that the fact that the antecedent in the indicative relative clause in the *SC de Pago Montano* is generic, while that in the Cicero example is specific, is probably not relevant to the choice of mood here, since the relative clause within the direct (non-reported) command of the consuls in the *SCB* (text (3) above) has a specific antecedent but once again contains an indicative verb (*in diebus X quibus uobeis tabelai datai erunt* (ll.39–40)).

It seems, then, that with the passage of time the interpretation of such documents vacillated in the minds of those who drafted them: texts of the later second and first centuries BC reflect some hesitation and uncertainty, while those of later periods reveal that the 'direct' type of reading had become the norm to the exclusion of the 'reported' reading. Consider, for example, the following clauses of the *Lex de Imperio Vespasiani* ('Law concerning the Imperial Powers of Vespasian') of AD 70 (CIL VI 930), which, though described as a *lex*, in fact takes the form of a *senatusconsultum*, with each clause, apart from the final *sanctio* ('penal clause'), introduced by *uti(que)* dependent on *censuerunt*:

(7)   CIL VI 930, AD 70: *Lex de Imperio Vespasiani*
. . . .

4:   utique, quos   magistrum   potestatem imperium
      that-and, who-ACC.pl magistracy-ACC authority-ACC power-ACC

curationemue   cuius   rei   petentes   senatui   populoque
management-or-ACC any-GEN thing-GEN seeking-ACC.pl Senate-DAT People-and-DAT

Romano   commendauerit,   quibusque   suffragationem
Roman-DAT commend-3sg.FUT.PF, who-and-DAT.pl support-ACC

suam   dederit   promiserit,   eorum   comitis   quibusque
his-ACC give-3sg.FUT.PF promise-3sg.FUT.PF, they-GEN assemblies-ABL each-ABL

extra ordinem ratio   habeatur;
outside norm-ACC enrolment-NOM have-3sg.PRES.SUBJ.PASS;

. . . .

7:    utique, quibus   legibus plebeiue   scitis   scriptum   fuit,
       that-and, which-ABL laws-ABL plebs-or-GEN decrees-ABL written-NOM. be-3sg.PF,

ne diuus   Aug(ustus), Tiberiusue   Iulius   Caesar   Aug(ustus),
lest divine-NOM Augustus,   Tiberius-or-NOM Julius-NOM Caesar-NOM Augustus-NOM,

Tiberiusque   Claudius   Caesar   Aug(ustus)   Germanicus
Tiberius-and-NOM Claudius-NOM Caesar-NOM Augustus-NOM Germanicus-NOM

tenerentur,   iis   legibus plebisque   scitis   imp(erator)
hold-3sg.IMPF.SUBJ.PASS, those-ABL laws-ABL plebs-and-GEN decrees-ABL emperor-NOM

Caesar   Vespasianus solutus sit,   quaeque   ex quaque
Caesar-NOM Vespasian-NOM free-NOM be-3sg.PRES.SUBJ, which-and-ACC by each-ABL

lege   rogatione diuum   Aug(ustum), Tiberiumue   Iulium
law-ABL proposal-ABL divine-ACC Augustus-ACC, Tiberius-or-ACC Julius-ACC

Caesarem Aug(ustum), Tiberiumue   Claudium   Caesarem Aug(ustum)
Caesar-ACC Augustus-ACC, Tiberius-or-ACC Claudius-ACC Caesar-ACC Augustus-ACC

Germanicum facere oportuit,   ea   omnia imp(eratori) Caesari
Germanicus-ACC do-INF behove-3sg.PF, those-ACC all-ACC emperor-DAT Caesar-DAT

Vespasiano Aug(usto)   facere liceat;
Vespasian-DAT Augustus-DAT do-INF allow-3sg.PRES.SUBJ;

. . . .
' . . . .

4:    and that, whomever seeking magistracy, authority, power or right of
management over any thing he has (lit. will have) commended to the Senate
and Roman People, and to whomever he has (lit. will have) given or
promised his support, of those there shall be an extraordinary enrolment
in each of the assemblies (for electing magistrates);

. . . .

7:    and that, by whichever laws or decrees of the plebs it was written
that the divine Augustus, or Tiberius Julius Caesar Augustus, and
Tiberius Claudius Caesar Augustus Germanicus should not be bound, from
those laws and decrees of the plebs the emperor Caesar Vespasian shall
be exempt, and whatever by each law or proposal the divine Augustus,
or Tiberius Julius Caesar Augustus, or Tiberius Claudius Caesar
Augustus Germanicus was obliged to do, all those things it shall be
permitted to the emperor Caesar Vespasian Augustus to do.

. . . . '

Despite the thoroughly 'modern' orthography, the essentially traditional format is immediately apparent, most obviously in the verb-final word order, the continued use of clause-connective *-que*, asyndeton between coordinated verb forms, introductory *uti*, and preposed relative clause 'rubrics' with resumptive demonstrative phrases in the following main clauses. But this document is now drafted entirely in the form of a direct statement of the Senate's will (even though in reality it now had little or no autonomy); there are therefore no past subjunctives dependent on the assumed *censuerunt* to indicate that this is a report of the Senate's wishes, and all subordinate clauses contain indicatives as expected (the imperfect subjunctive *haberetur* in the *ne*-clause of paragraph 7 is controlled by the 'local' past-tense verb *scriptum fuit*).

We may reasonably conclude, then, that though there were significant changes in the orthography over time, and even changes in the conventional 'view' of a *senatusconsultum* (as a direct statement of the Senate's decisions rather than as a report of them), a generally archaic form of syntactic structure and a traditional framework for organizing information were largely preserved in documents written in 'high' official Latin from the time of the earliest surviving texts down into the Empire. There may have been marginal influences from the practice of Greek official-dom, but this style, overall, was of an essentially Roman character, as might be expected of material emanating from the highest Roman authorities. In the long period of Roman expansion in the East we should not under-estimate the importance of the need constantly to assert, at least at the diplomatic level, the new realities of Roman dominance: Greek might be useful for practical purposes (cf. the translation in (5)), but whenever a given body or individual represented the state in a situation requiring a demonstration of Roman authority, Latin alone had to be employed. We may recall in this connection Livy's account (45.8, 29) of the defeat of the Macedonians by Lucius Aemilius Paullus at Pydna in 168 BC: the philhellenic consul is reported first to have addressed King Perseus kindly, but privately, in Greek, and then publicly to have informed the Macedonian senate of his terms in Latin, with a bilingual praetor trans-lating. Even in Cicero's time it was still possible for the famous orator, who had addressed the Syracusan senate in Greek, to be accused of an *indignum facinus* ('unworthy deed'), doubtless with some exaggeration in an adversarial context, but the point clearly retained enough resonance to be worth making (*in Verrem* II.4.147). Only in the Empire, as social and economic stability returned and Roman self-confidence peaked, did a more relaxed, and pragmatic, attitude to language choice in such contexts emerge and finally predominate (cf. 3.3.3).

But even if, in the absence of relevant documentary evidence, we can-not trace the earlier evolution of this official form of Latin directly, there are important indirect indications of the sources from which some of its salient properties were drawn, and these will be considered briefly in the next section. As we shall see, these sources also had an important role to play in the early development of more literary varieties of Latin.

5.5 *Carmina* and their Impact on Early Latin Prose

It seems likely, then, that official written Latin evolved as the demands imposed upon the language grew with the expansion of Roman power, and that this evolution took place very largely 'internally'. Furthermore, since the earliest surviving documents already exhibit a demonstrably mature format, it is reasonable to assume that, by the time distinctively literary forms of Latin had begun to emerge, from the late third century BC, as part of the wider cultural awakening inspired by Hellenistic models, a partly elaborated written language was already available to provide something of a native foundation, both grammatical and stylistic, on which to build, even if belletristic Latin quickly reveals the impact of an increasingly sophisticated literary sensibility and a corresponding shift away from the rigidly conventionalized topic-comment structures, verb-final word orders, and archaizing formulaic phraseology of the official 'high' style.

It is important to appreciate, however, that many of the stylistic resources available to Early Latin, both official and literary, are also strikingly in evidence in our surviving examples of archaic, or in some cases archaizing, Roman *carmina*, whose rhythmic qualities (of which the Saturnian may represent one particular formalization, to judge from the *carmen Arvale*) and balanced colonic structures were doubtless once important aids to memory in an oral society: the English translation of the Lord's Prayer perhaps gives something of the relevant flavour. The characteristic formal traits of these ancient laws (including the XII Tables), treaties, oaths, spells and prayers, many of which were later learned by heart at school, had become deeply ingrained through transmission from generation to generation, and their use in the language of official administration, in documents which fulfilled much the same range of legal and religious functions in their own era, is surely no accident; *carmina* provided the only native model of a stylized and elaborated form of diction appropriate to the recording of business at the highest levels. But given their powerful associations with the Roman past, these same markers were, from the first, just as naturally exploited in more literary compositions, as an indicator of an author's stylistic ambition and seriousness of intent: once established in this domain, they then remained available, albeit as an increasingly marked resource, in even the most sophisticated prose and verse of later times (see Williams 1982).

One particularly important structural property of our surviving *carmina* is the regular use of dicolonic or tricolonic phrases (with the third element often displaying a 'weightier' structure – 'tricolon crescendo'). The elements are often all but synonymous, leading to much apparent redundancy, but may also, in the case of dicola, express a polar complementarity. This property of exhaustiveness is traditionally, and perhaps plausibly, ascribed to a desire, in legal and religious contexts, to avoid loopholes (in Roman religion men struck a deal with their gods just as they did with other men), though the technique undeniably underlines key points in an emphatic fashion. Linkage within cola is often reinforced by rhetorical and phonetic devices such as anaphora, alliteration and assonance, which, along with the occasional use of *figura etymologica* (construction of a verb with a noun from the same lexical root), must have further enhanced memorability while distancing the language from that of everyday discourse. Interestingly, a wider Italian context is suggested by the selective use of such stylistic devices in the Umbrian Iguvine Tables (e.g. the coupling of synonyms in VIa 5 and the alliterative pairs in VIb 60, and compare also the invocation to Jupiter Grabovius in VIa 22ff. with that in text (8) below), though it is not clear whether this reflects a common prehistoric tradition or simply indicates later Roman influence.

To illustrate these points in more detail, we may now compare the text of the most extensive surviving *carmen* (from Cato's *de Agri Cultura* 141. 2–3) with elements of the *SCB* and extracts from Cato's speech *Pro Rhodiensibus*, later incorporated in his historical treatise the *Origines* (the relevant sections of Courtney 1999 provide, as always, insightful commentary):

(8)

Mars pater, te precor quaesoque,
Mars-VOC father-VOC, you-ACC pray-1sg.PRES beseech-1sg.PRES-and,

uti sies uolens propitius
that be-2sg.PRES.SUBJ willing-NOM well-disposed-NOM

mihi domo familiaeque nostrae;
me-DAT house-DAT household-DAT-and our-DAT;

quoius rei ergo
which-GEN thing-GEN for-the-sake-of

agrum terram fundumque meum 5
ground-ACC land-ACC farm-ACC-and my-ACC

suouitaurilia circumagi iussi;
suouitaurila-ACC lead-around-PRES.INF.PASS order-1sg.PF;

uti tu   morbos   uisos   inuisosque
that you-NOM illnesses-ACC seen-ACC unseen-ACC-and

   uiduertatem uastitudinemque, calamitates intemperiasque
   barrenness-ACC destruction-ACC-and, disasters-ACC intemperate-weather-ACC-and

   prohibessis   defendas   auerruncesque;
   keep-off-2sg.SUBJ ward-off-2sg.PRES.SUBJ avert-2sg.PRES.SUBJ-and;

utique tu   fruges   frumenta uineta   uirgultaque   10
that-and you-NOM crops-ACC grain-ACC vineyards-ACC plantations-ACC-and

   grandire   beneque euenire   siris,
   grow-tall-INF well-and   come-out-INF allow-2sg.PRES.SUBJ,

   pastores   pecuaque salua   seruassis
   shepherds-ACC flocks-ACC safe-ACC keep-2sg.PRES.SUBJ

   duisque   bonam   salutem   ualetudinemque
   give-2sg.PRES.SUBJ good-ACC health-ACC soundness-ACC-and

   mihi   domo   familiaeque   nostrae.
   me-DAT house-DAT household-DAT-and our-DAT.

harumce rerum   ergo   15
these-GEN things-GEN for-the-sake-of

   fundi   terrae   agrique   mei
   farm-GEN land-GEN ground-GEN-and my-GEN

   lustrandi   lustrique   faciendi   ergo,
   being-purified-GEN purification-GEN-and being-made-GEN for-the-sake-of,

   sicuti dixi,
   just-as say-1sg.PF,

macte   hisce   suouitaurilibus lactentibus immolandis   esto.
increased-VOC these-ABL *suouitaurilia* -ABL suckling-ABL being-sacrificed-ABL be-2sg.IMP.

Mars   pater,   eiusdem rei   ergo   20
Mars-VOC father-VOC, same-GEN thing-GEN for-the-sake-of

   macte   hisce   suouitaurilibus lactentibus esto.
   increased-VOC these-ABL *suouitaurilia* -ABL suckling-ABL be-2sg.IMP.

'Father Mars, I pray and beseech you:
   that you be gracious and well-disposed
   to me, our house and our household;
for which reason
   I have ordered sacrifical victims comprising piglet, lamb and bullock
                                                   to be led around
   my ground, land and farm;
[I pray and beseech you] that you keep away, ward off and avert
   diseases seen and unseen,
   barrenness, destruction, disasters and intemperate weather;

that the crops, corn, vineyards and plantations
   you permit to grow tall and come to good issue,
   that you keep the shepherds and flocks safe
   and give good health and strength
   to me, our house and household.
For these reasons,
   because of performing a purificatory rite and purifying
   my farm, land and ground,
   just as I have said,
be increased by the sacrifice of these suckling victims comprising piglet,
                                  lamb and bullock.
Father Mars, for the same reason
   be increased by these suckling victims comprising piglet, lamb and
                                  bullock.'

It is now generally agreed that this is not a genuinely ancient prayer but one composed, or at least adapted, by Cato himself. Be that as it may, there can be little doubt that it reflects the norms of 'real' ancient examples if we accept that similar material quoted by later writers (see, for example, the rites presented in Livy 1.32.6–14 and Macrobius *Saturnalia* 3.9.6–11, or the charm in Marcellus Empiricus *de Medicamentis* 15.11) more or less accurately reproduces the authentic formulations of antiquity. Note here in particular the repeated use of *uti* (best taken as marking subordination to *precor quaesoque* (l. 1), rather than serving as a jussive particle, see 5.4 above) to introduce a series of things to be done, a practice now familiar from senatorial decrees and presumably adopted on the basis of traditional models such as this: here too the relevant 'main verbs' are introduced only once at the beginning and not then repeated before subsequent injunctions (just like *censuere/-unt* in *senatusconsulta*).

The demarcation of the compositional units in (8) is effected by the means already described: in particular, the polar expression (*uisos inuisosque* (l. 7)) and the regular di- and tricolonic combinations of near-synonyms (*precor quaesoque* (l. 1), *uolens propitius* (l. 2), *mihi domo familiaeque* (l. 3), *agrum terram fundumque meum* (l. 5), the last chiastically reversed in the second half (l. 16), etc.) are immediately apparent, with the pairs regularly displaying 'linking' alliteration (*uiduertatem uastitudinemque* (l. 8), *fruges frumenta* (l. 10), *pastores pecuaque salua seruassis* (l. 12)) or assonance based on parallel or similar inflection (*uisos inuisosque* (l. 7), *grandire . . . euenire* (l. 11)). Note too the chiastic structure of the whole, comprising invocation *Mars pater . . .* (ll. 1ff.), + reason *quoius rei ergo . . .* (ll. 4ff.), + injunction (negative in spirit, comprising three paired sets of disasters to be kept off and three synonymous verbs in a tricolon, *prohibessis defendas auerruncesque* (l. 9)) *uti tu morbos . . .* (ll. 7ff.) followed by injunction (positive in spirit and triclausal in structure, with each of the three clauses containing either one or two pairs of benefits to be granted and a verb ending in -*is* (ll. 11–13)) *utique tu fruges* ... (ll. 10ff.), + reason *harumce rerum ergo* ... (l. 15), + invocation *macte* ... *Mars pater* ... (ll. 19ff.). Finally, it should be observed that verbs are again normally placed last in their cola, with the exception of *sies* (l. 2) in the initial request dependent on *te precor quaesoque* and *duis* (l. 14) in the last. In each of these cases the verb in question is followed by a complex complement incorporating the phrase *mihi domo familiaeque nostrae*, and it seems that this chiastic structure, involving [(shared) object + paired main verbs] + *uti* + [verb + (partly shared) complement], formally marks the beginning and the end of the series of 'obligations' imposed upon the god. Marked orders therefore remained available for special purposes, as expected.

Though the orthography of the prayer, like that of the text as a whole, has been modernized in transmission (if not always systematically, e.g. *uti* (l. 2), etc. but *quoius* (l. 4), etc.), some striking morphological and lexical archaisms have been retained. Such features include the subjunctive *duis* (l. 14) and the consistent use of -*que* as a linking conjunction to the exclusion of *et* (originally enumerative) and *atque* (emphatic, 'and in addition'). But particularly notable here are those features that remained, from the time of the XII Tables onwards, key markers of legal Latin, most obviously the sigmatic subjunctives (*prohibessis* (l. 9), *seruassis* (l. 12)) and -*to* imperatives (cf. *esto* (l. 19)), though this particular verb form, along with *scito* and *memento*, remained in regular use in Classical Latin. Forms of both types are used by Cicero in the 'laws' proposed in *de Legibus*, which, even if written in the author's own brand of 'legalese' (cf. *de Legibus* 2.18), clearly reflect what was then still thought appropriate for traditional legislation.

We should note, however, that such forms were probably not yet fully 'archaic/legal' in tone in Cato's time (234–148 BC), since they recur not only in contemporary high-style poetry but also in the more 'naturalistic' dialogue of comedy. Thus sigmatic and non-sigmatic subjunctives are still used side by side in Plautus:

(9)

(a)   at ita me   machaera et clupeus
         but thus me-ACC blade-NOM and shield-NOM

         bene iuuent . . .
         well   help-3pl.PRES.SUBJ

         'so help me well blade and shield . . .'   (*Curculio* 574–5)

         at ita me   uolsellae,   pecten,   speculum, calamistrum
         but thus me-ACC tweezers-NOM, comb-NOM, mirror-NOM, tongs-NOM

meum   bene me   amassint . . .
my-NOM well   me-ACC love-3pl.SUBJ

'so love me well my tweezers, comb, mirror, curling tongs . . .'

(Curculio 577–8)

(b)   ut illum   di   immortales omnes . . . perduint!
    <small>that him-ACC gods-NOM immortal-NOM all-NOM . . . destroy-3pl.SUBJ!</small>

    'may all the immortal gods destroy him!'   (Aulularia 785)

    qui illum   di   omnes . . . perdant!
    <small>that him-ACC gods-NOM all-NOM . . . destroy-3pl.PRES.SUBJ!</small>

    'may all the gods . . . destroy him!'   (Casina 279)

(c)   ita di   faxint!
    <small>thus gods-NOM make-3pl.SUBJ!</small>

    'may the gods make it so'   (Aulularia 149)

    ita di   faciant!
    <small>thus gods-NOM make-3pl.PRES.SUBJ!</small>

    'may the gods make it so'   (Aulularia 789)

Clearly the second example in (9a), spoken sarcastically by a pimp, is intended as a parody of the first example, spoken by a pompous soldier, but the other examples of 'archaic' forms seem to be used interchangeably with their 'modern' equivalents; note in particular the co-occurrence of 'modern' ut with 'archaic' perduint (originally from the root of facio, i.e. $*d^h(e)h_1$-, rather than that of do, though with much subsequent confusion) and of the functionally equivalent but soon-to-be-superseded qui with 'modern' perdant. The most that can be said is that the 'archaic' type appears to be increasingly confined to formulaic or semi-formulaic expressions (many precative/imperative in character, cf. also caue siris . . . 'mind you don't let . . .', Bacchides 402, Epidicus 400), and that this is a sure sign of its decline in the ordinary Latin of the period, as confirmed by the obvious reduction in their use by around 160 BC compared with even 40 years before. In all probability, then, the forms in question were still used conversationally in certain clichés, particularly to convey the seriousness of an appeal to the gods (or to parody such an appeal), but in spoken Latin were largely confined to such environments, where competition from their 'modern' equivalents was already well established. Subsequently, they survived only in specialized legal/religious written contexts and in a few expressions such as haud ausim 'I would not be so bold (as to . . .)'.

With this background in mind, we may return for one last time to the *SCB* (text (3) above), where certain verbal and stylistic similarities with the *carmen* in (8) are immediately apparent. In particular, the polar pairs (*neque uir neque mulier* (ll. 14–5), *neue in poplicod neue in preiuatod* (ll. 21–2)) and other dicola (*neue magistratum neue pro magistratud* (l. 16), *neue ... coniourase neue comuouise* ‖ *neue conspondise neue compromesise* (ll. 18–19)) stand out, the last set involving a characteristic covering of the eventualities by means of two pairs of synonyms, of which the final three seem to have been formed *ad hoc* to achieve the desired formal and phonological parallelism with the first. It is also generally assumed that a phrase such as *neue in urbid* 'neither in the city' has been omitted before *neue extrad urbem* (l. 22) in our copy (compare Livy 39, 18.8), as being irrelevant to the distant Teurani. Clearly the traditional resources for emphasizing the seriousness of an injunction remained available to Roman officialdom when the need arose.

As already noted, however, these same markers of stylistic elevation are also exploited in early examples of rhetorically elaborated 'literary' prose. Cato the Elder (Marcus Porcius Cato, 234–148 BC) is the first Roman orator whose rhetorical writings survive in sufficient quantity (in the form of extracts quoted by later writers) to enable us to form a reasonable impression of his style and use of language. As well as being the author of the handbook *de Agri Cultura*, he was a famous patron and legal expert, and has been presented to modern audiences as the archetypal old Roman, relentlessly austere and anti-Greek in outlook, who instigated litigation against the philhellenist Scipios and any others who fell short of his exacting standards. While there can be little doubt that he represented a conservative school of thought that saw danger to the 'Roman way' in the extreme wealth, cultural innovation and enticing intellectual freedoms offered by the conquest of the Greek East, it is clear from his control of Greek rhetorical technique and his use of Greek sources and models in his technical and historical writing that his overall position was rather more balanced, revealing a pragmatic willingness to exploit what seemed to him useful (cf. Plutarch, *Cato* 2.4), while rejecting what he judged to be pretentious and decadent faddery detrimental to the dignity and future well-being of the Roman state (see, for example, Gruen 1992).

The following extract, quoted by the second-century AD antiquarian Aulus Gellius (*Noctes Atticae* 6.3.1ff.), is taken from the speech Cato delivered in the Senate in 167 BC on behalf of the Rhodians, who had wavered in their loyalty to Rome and shown some sympathy towards the recently defeated King Perseus of Macedon. This was later incorporated into Cato's Roman history, the *Origines* (cf. Livy 45.20–5), now almost entirely lost:

(10) Malcovati 163–4

scio	solere	plerisque hominibus rebus	secundis
know-1sg.PRES	be-customary-PRES.INF	most-DAT men-DAT things-ABL	favourable-ABL

atque prolixis	atque prosperis	animum excellere	atque superbiam
and expansive-ABL	and prospering-ABL	spirit-ACC exult-PRES.INF	and pride-ACC

atque ferociam	augescere	atque crescere.	quod	mihi	nunc
and ferocity-ACC	increase-PRES.INF	and grow-PRES.INF.	what-NOM	me-DAT	now

magnae curae	est,	quom haec	res	tam secunde
great-GEN concern-GEN	be-3sg.PRES,	since this-NOM	thing-NOM	so favourably

processit,	nequid	in consulendo aduorsi	eueniat	5
advance-3sg.PF,	lest-anything-NOM	in deliberating-ABL adverse-GEN	come-about-3sg.PRES.SUBJ	

quod	nostras secundas	res	confutet,	neue
which-NOM	our-ACC favourable-ACC	circumstances-ACC	check-3sg.PRES.SUBJ,	and-lest

haec	laetitia	nimis luxuriose	eueniat.	aduorsae
this-NOM	happiness-NOM	too immoderately	turn-out-3sg.PRES.SUBJ.	Adverse-NOM

res	edomant	et docent	quid opus siet	facto,
circumstances-NOM	tame-3pl.PRES	and teach-3pl.PRES	what need be-3sg.PRES.SUBJ	act-ABL,

secundae	res	laetitia	transuorsum trudere	solent
favourable-NOM	circumstances-NOM	gladness-ABL	across push-PRES.INF	be-apt-3pl.PRES

a	recte consulendo	atque intellegendo.	quo	maiore-opere	10
from	correctly deliberating-ABL	and understanding-ABL.	Which-ABL	more-strongly	

dico	suadeoque	uti haec	res	aliquot dies
say-1sg.PRES	urge-1sg.PRES-and	that this-NOM	thing-NOM	some days-ACC

proferatur,	dum ex tanto	gaudio in potestatem
postpone-3sg.PRES.SUBJ.PASS,	until from so-great-ABL	joy-ABL into control-ACC

nostram	redeamus.
of-ourselves-ACC	return-1pl.PRES.SUBJ.

atque ego	quidem arbitror	Rodienses	noluisse	nos
and I-NOM	indeed think-1sg.PRES	Rhodians-ACC	not-want-PF.INF	us-ACC

ita depugnare	uti depugnatum est,	neque regem Persen	15
thus fight-it-out-PRES.INF	as fought-out-NOM be-3sg.PRES,	nor king-ACC Perseus-ACC	

uinci.	sed non Rodienses	modo id noluere,	sed multos
defeat-PRES.INF.PASS.	But not Rhodians-NOM	only that not-want-3pl.PF,	but many-ACC

populos	atque multas	nationes idem	noluisse	arbitror.
people-ACC	and many-ACC	nations-ACC same-ACC	not-want-PF.INF	think-1sg.PRES.

atque haud scio	an	partim eorum	fuerint	qui	non
and not know-1sg.PRES	whether	part-ACC them-GEN	be-3pl.PF.SUBJ	who-NOM	not

nostrae contumeliae causa	id	noluerint	euenire,
our-GEN disgrace-GEN	for-sake-of	that-ACC not-want-3pl.PF.SUBJ	happen-PRES.INF,

sed enim id metuere, si nemo esset homo quem 20
but indeed that fear-3pl.PF, if no-NOM be-3sg.IMPF.SUBJ man-NOM whom-ACC

uereremur, quicquid luberet faceremus, ne sub
fear-1pl.IMPF.SUBJ, whatever-ACC please-3sg.IMPF.SUBJ do-1pl.IMPF.SUBJ, lest beneath

solo imperio nostro in seruitute nostra essent; libertatis
alone-ABL power-ABL our-ABL in servitude-ABL our-ABL be-3pl.IMPF.SUBJ; freedom-GEN

suae causa in ea sententia fuisse arbitror. atque
their-own-GEN for-sake-of in that-ABL opinion-ABL be-PF.INF think-1sg.PRES. And

Rodienses tamen Persen publice numquam adiuuere. cogitate
Rhodians-NOM however Perseus-ACC publicly never help-3pl.PF. Reflect-2pl.IMP

quanto nos inter nos priuatim cautius facimus. 25
how-much-ABL we-NOM among ourselves-ACC privately more-cautiously act-1pl.PRES.

nam unusquisque nostrum, siquis aduorsus rem suam
for each-one-NOM us-GEN, if-anyone-NOM against interest-ACC his-own-ACC

quid fieri arbitratur, summa ui contra nititur
anything-ACC do-PRES.INF.PASS think-3sg.PRES, utmost-ABL force-ABL against strive-3sg.PRES

ne aduorsus eam fiat; quod illi tamen perpessi.
lest against it-ACC do-3sg.PRES.SUBJ.PASS; which-ACC they-NOM however endured-NOM.

'I know that it is customary for the majority of men, when circumstances are favourable and expansive and prospering, for their spirits to rise and for pride and ferocity to increase and grow. This is of great concern to me at present – since this matter has turned out so favourably – in case anything untoward should take place in our deliberations to check our own good fortune, and this happiness culminate too immoderately. Adverse circumstances tame and teach what action is to be taken, favourable circumstances, through happiness, are apt to push us aside from right deliberation and understanding. So still more strongly do I say and urge that this matter be postponed for some days until we return from such great joy to self-control.

For my part I do not think the Rhodians wanted us to fight to the end as the battle was fought to the end, nor did they want King Perseus to be defeated. But it was not only the Rhodians who had this negative desire, but many peoples and many nations had the same negative desire, I think. Furthermore, I wonder whether there may have been some of them who wanted this negative outcome not in order to secure our disgrace, but actually were afraid that, if there were no one whom we feared, if we were to do whatever we liked, they would be under our sole rule in servitude to us; it was for the sake of their own freedom that I think they were so minded. And yet the Rhodians never helped Perseus publicly. Consider how much more cautiously we act amongst ourselves even in a private capacity. For each one of us, if any thinks anything is being done against his interests, strives with all his might to obstruct this being done against them; yet this is what they endured.'

It is clear that Cato was no pioneer in the field of oratory, despite the fact that no significant fragments of the work of earlier orators survive, since Cicero (*Brutus* 53ff.) mentions not only the funeral orations traditionally delivered for members of noble families but, more importantly, predecessors of Cato's with a recorded reputation for eloquence, including Appius Claudius Caecus (consul in 307 and 296 BC; *Brutus* 61 implies that his speech against peace with Pyrrhus, king of Epirus, in 280 BC could still be read) and M. Cornelius Cethegus (consul in 204 BC). It therefore seems reasonable to conclude that Cato was not the first to combine traditional Latin exponents of the 'high style' with elements of Greek rhetorical technique to achieve the conscious stylization of diction on display in the passage above (cf. also the evidence provided by the 'literary' and Hellenizing qualities of the Scipionic *tituli* of the late third century BC): as with official Latin, so with the Latin of oratory, the early history is simply unavailable to us, and it is only the later stages of linguistic and stylistic development that can now be traced in any detail.

In (10) the constant accumulation of synonyms in di- and tricola, with some supporting alliteration and/or assonance, is by now too familiar to require further comment, though here, of course, the function is merely to add 'dramatic' emphasis. Other noteworthy features include the habitual use of *atque* in preference to the traditional, but banal, *-que*, both as a phrasal and a sentential connective (e.g. it introduces each new topic in the second paragraph), and the selection of the 3rd person plural perfect ending *-ere* rather than *-erunt* (*noluere* (l. 16), *metuere* (l. 20), *adiuuere* (l. 24), cf. *censuere* in the *SCB*), both evidently markers of stylistic ambition for Cato. Thus *atque* occurs only four times as a connective in *de Agri Cultura*, where, like other prose writers of the third and second centuries, he also uses *-erunt* systematically: this ending is already the normal choice not only of the poet Ennius (239–169 BC) in his 'simple' prose translation of Euhemerus's *Sacred Chronicle* (where, assuming that the extracts preserved by Lactantius are not a later paraphrase of a composition in verse, the style, given the occasional rhetorical flourishes, is again a matter of choice rather than necessity), but also of orators and historians such as Scipio Aemilianus, C. Gracchus, L. Calpurnius Piso and, somewhat later, Q. Claudius Quadrigarius (all of whose works are again preserved only fragmentarily in the form of quotations).

What mainly distinguishes the use of language in (10) from a more 'classical' style, however, is the infrequency of logical connectives to link the thought between sentences (here only *tamen* (l. 24) and *nam* (l. 26), *enim* (l. 20) being used in its traditional sense of 'indeed' after *sed*), the corresponding frequency of asyndeton, the apparent lack of interest in varying key vocabulary (*eueniat/euenire* (ll. 5, 7, 19), *aduorsi/aduorsae* (ll. 5, 7), *noluisse/noluere/noluerint* (ll. 14, 16, 19), motivated in part by the role of repetition in textual cohesion, see immediately below), the minimal variation in the position of the verb (almost always clause-final), and the tendency not to build up to a weighty 'climax' at the end of phrases or clauses (cf. *augescere atque crescere* (l. 3)), all reflecting a traditional organization of material based on a non-periodic conception of sentence structure, seen also in official documents, in which previously mentioned (or implied) 'topics' and novel/contrastive 'foci' tend to be placed first in a clause (in the order topic + focus if both are present), and much inter- and intrasentential linkage is effected asyndetically by topic continuity (cf. the repetitions of *secundae/aduorsae res* (+ *secunde, aduorsi*), *laetitia, consulendo, noluisse/noluere/noluerint*), or by focal contrastiveness (*aduorsae res . . .* (l. 7) *secundae res . . .* (l. 9), *ego quidem* (l. 14), *non nostrae contumeliae causa* (ll. 18–19), *libertatis suae causa* (ll. 22–3)). Particularly noteworthy to later critics such as Gellius (*Noctes Atticae* 6.3.53), however, was the general absence of rhythmical smoothness, a 'fault' commented on earlier by Cicero (*Brutus* 65–9), who clearly missed the characteristic sentence-final cadences (*clausulae*) that had become the norm in his own time (see 6.5.1).

The question of the extent to which Cato made use of formalized Greek rhetorical theory, as opposed to relying on a 'natural eloquence' informed by traditional Latin practice, has been much debated. But given the pervasiveness of Greek culture in Cato's time, including the routine presence in mid-second-century Rome of Greek rhetoricians and grammarians, and in view of the fact that Cato himself wrote a treatise on rhetoric (Quintilian 3.1.19), it seems likely that part at least of the rhetorical elaboration seen in his speeches is indeed due to the influence of Greek learning. He had, after all, spent a great deal of time in Greek-speaking provinces and employed a Greek tutor for his son, while Plutarch (*Cato* 2.4) observes, apparently uncontroversially, that his writings generally were ornamented with Greek thought, with the great fourth-century Athenian orator Demosthenes cited as a major influence on his style. In (10) we may note the clear contrast between the rhetorically developed *exordium* (first paragraph) and the less elevated style of the following paragraph. In particular, the initial *sententia* ('men are inclined to get over-confident when things go well') is almost certainly of Greek inspiration (cf. the theme of many a tragedy), and the twice-used form of argument, from general principle to particular case (*haec res*), together with the antithetical structuring of the second *sententia* (*aduorsae res . . .* , *secundae res*, with asyndeton), both have a long history in Greek rhetorical practice. By contrast, the repeated underlining of key points by means of alliteration (*scio solere . . . secundis/secundae . . . solent, prolixis atque prosperis, laetitia . . . luxuriose, transuorsum trudere*) and assonance, especially homoeoteleuton (*secundis atque prolixis atque prosperis, superbiam atque ferociam, augescere atque crescere, consulendo atque intellegendo*) probably has more traditional roots, even though both phenomena are familiar enough, albeit far less densely deployed, in Greek writing.

But leaving such questions of style to one side, there is in fact not a great deal to distinguish this passage grammatically from Classical Latin. One major difference concerns the distribution of indicative and subjunctive verb forms in subordinate clauses: e.g. the use of an indicative in a circumstantial *quom* (*cum*)-clause (ll. 4–5) (though here 'causal' *quod*, which naturally takes the indicative, is the transmitted reading, and *quom* is an editorial emendation); retention of the indicative in a subordinate clause in indirect speech (*uti depugnatum est* (l. 15)); and the use of indicatives in indirect questions (*cogitate quanto . . . cautius facimus* (ll. 24–5)) alongside subjunctives (*docent quid opus siet facto* (l. 8), *haud scio an partim eorum fuerint . . .* (l. 18)).

In the specific case of indirect questions, there is a widely held view that these resulted, prehistorically, from the optional reanalysis of paratactic direct questions as dependent clauses (e.g. *rogo te – quid agit?* = 'I'm asking you – what is s/he doing (indicative)?' > *rogo te quid agit* = 'I'm asking you what s/he is doing (indicative)'), so that indirect questions of fact should retain the original indicative, while indirect questions containing what were originally deliberative/jussive ('what is s/he to do?') or potential ('what can s/he do?') subjunctives should retain the subjunctive (see, for example, Woodcock (1959: sections 131ff. and 177ff.)). During Cato's lifetime, however, it became increasingly routine for all indirect questions to contain a subjunctive verb, a situation which duly became the rule in Classical Latin. Rosén (1999: 111) therefore argues that the residual distinction between indicative and subjunctive in Old Latin was no longer based simply on whether an embedded question was one of fact or conveyed modal notions of duty or possibility, but crucially on whether or not the main verb introduced a genuine inquiry, so that clauses dependent on verbs of asking or replying, or on the imperatives of verbs of declaring, thinking or perceiving, already have the subjunctive as a matter of routine, while those introduced by non-imperative verbs of declaring/thinking/perceiving or by verbs of knowing/not-knowing may still optionally have the indicative. But though there are many cases to bear this out (e.g. *scire uolo quoi reddidisti*, Plautus *Curculio* 543, 'I want to know to whom you gave it back (indicative)'), there are also counterexamples. Compare, for example, the following sentences, one with the indicative, the other with the subjunctive, but both dependent on imperatives of *cogitare* 'think': *cogitate quanto . . . cautius facimus* (Cato *Origines* (Malcovati 163–4)), 'think how much more cautiously we have acted (indicative)', and *cogitatoque hiemis quam longa siet* (Cato *de Agri Cultura* 30), 'and think about how long winter is/can be (subjunctive)'. Thus while it is clear that the use of the subjunctive in indirect questions is already spreading beyond strictly modal contexts in Old Latin (cf. the conjoined indicative and subjunctive in *cuius iussu uenio et quam ob rem uenerim dicam* (Plautus *Amphitryo* 17) 'I shall tell you on whose orders I come (indicative) and for what purpose I have come (subjunctive)'), Rosén's hypothesis, even if it is broadly correct, does not constitute an absolute rule.

Since, therefore, the situation was still fluid in Cato's time (and remained so in subliterary varieties of Latin), it is at least possible that some subjunctives in indirect questions were not yet purely conventional and were intended to be read with a modal force; this possibility is reflected, perhaps erroneously, in the translations of the relevant cases above. Thus *cogitatoque hiemis quam longa siet* ('and think about how long winter is/can be') may well be factual, but could also reasonably be taken as potential in force (though clearly not as deliberative/jussive). Similarly, *quanto peiorem ciuem existimarint feneratorem quam furem, hinc licet existimare* ('how much worse a citizen they considered the usurer than the thief one may estimate from the following', *de Agri Cultura*, Preface 1) is very naturally taken factually, but a potential reading ('they could consider'), if not a deliberative/jussive one ('they were to consider'), is again possible, if perhaps rather unlikely.

Eventually the subjunctive rule was extended by convention across the board, even to finite subordinate clauses following 1st-person verbs of 'saying' or 'asking', where the speaker/writer could not, strictly speaking, disclaim responsibility for what was stated or asked (so *rogo te quid agat* = 'I'm asking you what he is doing (subjunctive)'). This obviously created a situation in which indirect questions of fact became indistinguishable from indirect questions with 'modal' content, and so led to the growing use of various clarificatory periphrases in the latter (e.g. 'deliberative/jussive' *rogo te quid agere debeat*, lit. = 'I'm asking you what s/he ought to do'; 'potential' *rogo te quid acturus/actura sit*, lit. = 'I'm asking you what s/he is going to do'). This particular trend was, of course, part of a more general development whereby the subjunctive came to be used as a marker of all 'reported' statements or questions containing finite verbs, i.e. of those finite clauses whose 'factual' content the speaker/writer could not be held personally responsible for. Since, however, reported statements in indirect speech, unlike reported questions, were expressed by the accusative and infinitive construction, the rule in this case applied only to finite clauses subordinated to the main clause of the report.

Other grammatical differences are more minor. The linking use of a relative adjective or pronoun is, of course, familiar from Classical Latin, but in Early Latin the regular function, as in (10) (*quod* (ll. 3, 28)), *quo* (l. 10)), is to summarize the content of a preceding sentence, while in the classical language it is more common for the relative to have a specific antecedent with which it agrees (and indeed for such relatives to appear in subordinate clauses, including ablative absolutes, rather than, as here, in main clauses). This use of a connecting relative as opposed to a demonstrative (contrast the resumptive use of sentence-initial *ea* in the *Epistula ad Tiburtes*, (4) above, l.8) appears once again to have been a device for 'raising' the stylistic level; the *carmen* in (8) uses both options (*quoius rei ergo* (l. 4), *harumce rerum ergo* (l. 15), but the connecting relative is not a regular feature of the more down-to-earth style of *de Agri Cultura* (where only the preface and the 'hymn to the cabbage' (156ff.) show evidence of any conscious elaboration). In this connection note too that, in his rhetorical writing, Cato already prefers the 3rd-conjugation present passive infinitive in *-i* (*uinci* (l. 16)) over the variant in *-ier* (as used, for example, in the *SCB* text (7), (ll. 36, 37)); the choice here of the 3rd person plural perfect indicative in *-ere* has already been mentioned.

In conclusion, the close examination of just one extract has shown that even the earliest surviving examples of prose writing reveal a language that is already grammatically 'developed' to a high degree, with significant stylistic resources at its disposal. Though the surviving examples of early prose writing do not all involve the same degree of rhetorical elaboration, it is clear that nearly all the grammatical fundamentals of what would later be codified as 'classical' Latin are essentially in place by the mid-second century BC. Later developments therefore fall under three main headings. The first is stylistic, involving the progressive elaboration of a more varied range of 'high' styles under the continuing influence of Greek models, a process that also led to some grammatical extension of existing Latin usages. The second involves a further development of the lexical resources of the language to meet a range of new needs, with certain patterns of word formation then becoming the norm, others falling out of favour. The last involves the selection, from among still competing morphological and syntactic variants, of forms and constructions which, for whatever reasons, were deemed to be 'correct' by the urban elite. But the earlier use of many such rejected forms and constructions in both official and artistically elaborated compositions shows that these should not be taken as a mark of the 'colloquial' foundations of Old Latin prose writing, despite their undoubtedly sub-standard status in later times: the bulk of *de Agri Cultura* is 'colloquial' because of its subject matter and purpose, not because there were no other options. These issues will be explored further in the next chapter, but we must first take a brief look at some of the earliest examples of non-epigraphic Latin verse composition.

5.6   Early Latin Poetry

With the exception of the comedies of Titus Maccius Plautus (*c*.254–184 BC, though his 'reality' as a single individual has been questioned) and Publius Terentius Afer (Terence, *c*.185–159 BC), Old Latin poetry is preserved only as series of brief quotations in later writers, which modern editors have endeavoured to collate and organize as sets of extracts from specific books and plays. Fortunately, however, at least from the point of view of the historical linguist if not from that of the literary critic, the reason for such quotation is more often than not the 'odd' grammatical or lexical usage of the writers in question from the standpoint of later 'classical' practice. The principal authors in question are Lucius Livius Andronicus (third century BC: epic, tragedy, comedy, satire, hymns), Gnaeus Naevius (*c*.270–201 BC: epic, comedy, historical drama), Quintus Ennius (239–169 BC: epic, tragedy, comedy, historical drama, satire, and other works), Gaius Caecilius (d. 168 BC: comedy), Marcus Pacuvius (220–*c*.130 BC: tragedy, historical drama, satire), Gaius Lucilius (*c*.180–102 BC: satire) and Lucius Accius (170–*c*.85 BC: tragedy, historical drama, erotic poems, and other works), all of whom were 'outsiders' of Italian origin for whom Latin may not have been a first language. Their work is therefore eloquent testimony to the progress of Romanization/Latinization in the period, and to the increasingly central role of Rome in the political and cultural affairs of Italy. See the relevant chapters (all by Gratwick) in Kenney and Clausen (1982) for a brief introduction to poets and poetry in the early Republic.

Since the generic range of surviving fragments is wide, including epic (in both Saturnians and hexameters), tragedy, several varieties of comedy, and satire, generalization is difficult, though some commonalities may be established. First and foremost, with the possible exception of satire (though there is in fact little evidence for Roman satire before Ennius, while the fragments of his minor works, including the miscellaneous *Saturae*, are strongly reminiscent of similar, low-key Alexandrian poetry), the genres involved are all of Greek origin. Similarly, with the probable exception of the Saturnian (see above), the metres used are also Greek, albeit with skilful adaptations dictated by the prosodic properties of a language with a strong stress accent. Indeed, the skill with which these typologically alien metres were appropriated and the creative confidence with which they were already deployed in a range of styles represent a remarkable achievement. The extent to which the early poets established the norms of rhythm and diction for Latin poetry is still greatly under-estimated: they took great pride in their technical expertise and compe-tence, and though their successors sometimes modified and restricted the conventions they had refined, such changes mainly reflect shifts in taste and fashion rather than demonstrate progress towards some imaginary ideal.

Secondly, with the partial exception of comedy (see below) and satire, Old Latin poetry typically displays some clear linguistic and stylistic markers. One obvious trait is the exploitation of archaic morphology and lexicon, sometimes metrically motivated but also, as often in epic and tragedy, reflecting a desire to distance the language from everyday usage and to validate the enterprise through partial imitation of the stylized archaizing dictions of Homeric/Hellenistic epic and Athenian tragic drama. Thus we find a number of ancient forms, often drawn from the language of ritual and law and already obsolete or obsolescent in con-temporary Latin, such as *indu-/endo* for *in-/in*, the genitive singular of the 1st declension in *-as* (rare) or disyllabic *-ai* [-a:i:] (quite frequently), the genitive plural of the 2nd declension in *-um*, and the 3rd-person pronominal stem seen in *sum/sam* 'him/her' etc., all of which offer useful metrical variants to the more usual forms as well as bringing with them an air of solemnity and tradition. Such forms are, of course, to be carefully distinguished from the many usages which were normal in the Latin of the period and simply look old-fashioned from the perspective of 'classical' norms.

Further evidence of the efforts made to develop a range of 'artistic' registers capable of emulating the distinctiveness, richness and variety of their Greek counterparts is provided by the combination of increasingly restrictive lexical choice with considerable experimentation in word-formation. Thus the identification of a 'high' poetic vocabulary (e.g. *ensis* for *gladius* 'sword', *tellus* for *terra* 'land', etc.) went hand in hand with derivational innovations designed to dissociate the language of poetry from normal lexical usage: the methods employed include the creation of new compounds and/or the use of simplex forms in place of an established compound (e.g. *conglomero* rather than *glomero* 'pile up', but *fligo* for *affligo* 'throw down/crush'), the invention of unusual by-forms (e.g. novel adverbs in *-im*, *-atim*, *-itus*), the use of innovative adjectival forma-tions (most notably in *-bilis*, *-ficus*, *-osus*, *-bundus*), and the formation of Greek-inspired compounds (of the type *altiuolans* 'high-flying', *taurigenus* 'bull-born', etc.). We may also note here the conspicuous freedom of word order in evidence in these early fragments (with considerable artificiality already permissible in the 'higher' genres, as, for example, in the convention allowing wide separation of adjectives from the nouns they modify), as well as the expected redeployment for literary ends of the traditional stylistic devices for marking out 'important' texts (e.g. alliteration, assonance, homoeoteleuton, anaphora, tricolon, congeries, figura etymologica, etc.), as discussed above in connection with ancient *carmina* and early prose writing.

By contrast, spoken comic dialogue (in iambo-trochaic metres) aims for a more 'natural' and 'colloquial' style than either epic or tragedy, but even here we should have no illusions that we are simply dealing with a variety of the contemporary vernacular, not least because the language is, first and foremost, metrical. Though the manuscripts of Plautus's surviving plays derive from a compilation made *c.*AD 100, and show a random mix of older and 'classical' spellings, the colloquial (rarely 'vulgar') basis for the language of spoken dialogue is very much in evidence in the frequent choice of 'emotive' vocabulary characteristic of street banter (e.g. 'cuddly' diminutives, exclamations, 'emphatic' superlatives), the regular use of phonetically reduced allegro forms, the heavily paratactic and often informally structured syntax (though relative and adverbial subordinate clauses are by no means uncommon, and lengthy complex sentences may appear in expository passages or for parodic purposes), the high incidence of 'clarificatory' demonstratives in both deictic and anaphoric functions, and the rather free word order (especially with regard to verb position, though any preposing or postposing of elements is almost always pragmatically motivated). Furthermore, since many of the plays were translated or adapted from Greek originals and have a Greek setting, it should be no surprise that Greek words and expressions are also admitted, though this is generally put only into the mouths of Greek slaves and in fact reflects the sort of Greek heard on the streets of Italian cities (typically of a west Greek character, reflecting the speech of many of the great cities of Magna Graecia), rather than the Attic of the originals (familiar from the comedies of Menander).

But woven into this colloquial foundation we also find many of the 'poetic' markers typical of other forms of contemporary verse. Thus Plautus, when he wishes to add emphasis or express heightened emotion, may employ all the devices of verbal inventiveness – archaizing/tragic phraseology, figura etymologica, repetition, accumulation of synonyms, assonance and alliteration – in a manner that often undermines any impression of real-life conversation. Even in more routine exchanges we often find, alongside their modern counterparts, a number of obsolescent (though not yet archaic) forms artificially exploited, especially at line-ends, for metrical purposes, e.g. the longer forms of the singular of the present subjunctive of *esse* (*siem, sies, siet*), or the passive infinitive in *-ier*, though we should also note here the continued use in other positions of *s*-futures and subjunctives (*faxo/faxim*), forms such as *attigas* (2nd person singular subjunctive) and *ipsus*, the conjunction *qui* (ablative) for *ut*, etc., all of which were presumably still in at least limited use, e.g. in particular phrases or contexts.

All such forms and devices are significantly rarer in the work of Terence, who, by retreating from the unfettered verbal and stylistic exuberance of his predecessor, established a more restrained and formally consistent style that reflects, as far as we can tell, the Latin usage of the upper classes of the period, and as such still includes many forms and features that Cicero's generation would not have accepted (e.g. 4th-declension genitive singulars in -*i*, active forms of deponent verbs, 4th-conjugation futures in -*ibo*, indicatives in indirect questions, etc.). This style is characterized overall by terseness, simplicity and the absence of archaism (by the standards of the time), but still exhibits, when required in the interests of 'realism', the exclamations, false starts, emphatic preposings, paratactic structures and incoherences of ordinary dialogue, though not the variations associated with age, sex or social class that must have existed then in Rome, as in all places at all times. It was clearly intended as an imitation of the 'educated colloquial' of Menander's Attic Greek, and as such won the admiration of later generations as an early example of good Latinity (Caesar, for example, describes Terence as *puri sermonis amator*, 'lover of pure speech', at the end of Suetonius's *Life of Terence*, part of a compilation drawn by Donatus from the original work *de Poetis*), even if the plays themselves often lacked the sheer sense of fun required to command the unqualified enthusiasm of their audiences and readers.

Thus in even the earliest surviving fragments of Latin poetry, whatever the genre, there is already clear evidence of a conscious effort to blend together and exploit both Greek and native resources, not only thematically but also linguistically and rhetorically, in order to develop 'literarized' varieties of Latin as vehicles for forms of poetic expression which, though novel in their Roman context, might be seen as continuations of the various Greek traditions that had in part inspired them. A few short extracts should help to illustrate these points. The first set (11a–c) is taken from Naevius's *Belli Poenici Carmen* (an epic of the first Punic War composed in Saturnians), the second example (12) from Ennius's *Annales* (an epic of Rome from its origins, written, like all epic thereafter, in hexameters), and the third (13) from Plautus's *Epidicus* (a comedy):

(11)   Naevius *Bellum Punicum*
(a)   amborum uxores
                      both-GEN   wives-NOM

   noctu   Troiad   exibant   capitibus opertis,
   by-night-ABL Troy-ABL go-out-3pl.IMPF heads-ABL covered-ABL,

flentes   ambae abeuntes   lacrimis cum multis.
weeping-NOM both   leaving-NOM tears-ABL with   many-ABL.

fr. 4

'The wives of both were passing out from Troy, heads veiled, both weeping, departing with many a tear.'

(b)   eorum   sectam sequuntur   multi   mortales . . .
       them-GEN.PL path   follow-3pl.PRES many-NOM mortals-NOM

       multi   alii   e   Troia   strenui   uiri . . .
       many-NOM others-NOM from Troy-ABL vigorous-NOM men-NOM

       ubi foras   cum auro   illi[n]c exibant.
       when outdoors with   gold-ABL there   go-out-3pl.IMPF.

fr. 6

'Many mortals follow their path . . . Many other strong men from Troy . . . When they were passing outdoors there with the gold.'

(c)   senex   fretus   pietati   deum   adlocutus
       old-man-NOM relying-NOM piety-DAT/?ABL god-ACC calling-upon-NOM

       summi   deum   regis   fratrem   Neptunum
       highest-GEN gods-GEN king-GEN brother-ACC Neptune-ACC

       regnatorem marum . . .
       ruler-ACC   seas-GEN

fr. 10

'The old man, trusting in his piety, addressed the god, Neptune, brother of the highest monarch of the gods, ruler of the seas . . .'

A quick comparison of these passages with more or less contemporary inscriptions reveals the orthographic modernization that has taken place in the process of textual transmission, particularly as regards vowel weakening, monophthongization and the omission of final -*d* (except where this would lead to hiatus, cf. *Troiad exibant* in (11a)). Otherwise many of the features referred to above are clearly in evidence: archaic or archaizing lexicon and morphology (*noctu, deum*), frequent assonance and alliteration within cola, and even an example of (pseudo-)figura etymologica (*sectam sequuntur*, in fact from different roots). There are also variant forms and/or constructions that were not acceptable in later periods: e.g. *marum* (for *marium*), and *pietati*, which is either a dative or a *d*-less ablative with *i*-stem suffix, the former representing an 'unclassical' construction after *fretus* (the later historian Livy's use of the dative rather than the ablative perhaps reflects his supposed provincialism), the latter a variant form disallowed in Classical Latin. The now familar lack of concern for lexical variation (*deum . . . deum . . .*) together with the optional use of prepositions with descriptive ablatives, later generally regarded as rather unpoetic (contrast *capitibus opertis* with *lacrimis cum multis*), are also in evidence.

Similar remarks apply to the following extract from Ennius's *Annales,* where we once again find emphatic use of alliteration alongside archaic case endings (*siluai frondosai*). But particularly important here are the examples of the elision of final -*s* after short -*u*- (*securibu', fraxinu'*), a metrically very convenient option, presumably still reflecting phonetic realities, that was firmly rejected in Cicero's time as 'rather rustic' (cf. *Orator* 161), even by the newer generation of poets, who might have found it a useful archaism had it not by then sounded so irredeemably clownish and old-fashioned:

(12)   Ennius, *Annales* (6) 175–9 SK

incedunt   arbusta   per   alta,   securibu' caedunt.
pass-3pl.PRES groves-ACC through high-ACC, axes-ABL   cut-3pl.PRES.

percellunt   magnas   quercus, exciditur   ilex;
strike-down-3pl.PRES mighty-ACC oaks-ACC, cut-down-3sg.PRES.PASS holm-oak-NOM;

fraxinu' frangitur   atque abies   consternitur   alta;
ash-NOM break-3sg.PRES.PASS and   fir-NOM lay-low-3sg.PRES.PASS high-NOM;

pinus   proceras peruortunt.   omne   sonabat
pines-ACC lofty-ACC overturn-3pl.PRES. all-NOM sound-3sg.IMPF

arbustum fremitu siluai   frondosai.
grove-NOM noise-ABL forest-GEN leafy-GEN.

'They pass through tall groves, they fell with axes. They strike down mighty oaks; the holm-oak is slashed; the ash is broken and the tall fir laid low; they overthrow lofty pines. The whole grove resounded with the murmur of the forest rich in foliage.'

The final extract, from Plautus, illustrates a typical 'conversational' passage, in which colloquial diminutives (*muliercula, grauastellus, unguiculum*), Greek loans (*danista*), emotive vocabulary (exclamations, superlatives), allegro forms (*haecinest, summumst, sicin*), heavy use of demonstrative pronouns, emphatic displacements (e.g. *meum futurum corium pulchrum praedicas*, where a form of 'be', as often, has been attracted to the focal element in initial position), and generally simplified syntax (note in particular *sicin iussi ad me ires?* in the penultimate line, without conjunction) sit alongside more traditional 'literary' features of the now familar kind (cf. Palmer 1954: 88, Rosén 1999: 19), most notably alliteration, assonance and the repetition of key words, the cumulation of synonyms (*aspecta et contempla*), and the use of figura etymologica (*pingent pigmentis*), though none of these 'devices' is overused here in ways that would draw special attention to the literary quality of the language:

(13)   Plautus *Epidicus* 620–8

EPIDICUS.

sed quis haec   est muliercula   et ille grauastellus   qui   uenit?
but who this-NOM is   woman-DIM.NOM and that grey-hair-DIM.NOM who-NOM come-3sg.PRES?

STRATIPPOCLES.

hic est danista,   haec illa   est autem, quam [ego] emi   de praeda. EP.
this is money-lender, this that-one is however, whom   buy-1sg.PF from booty-ABL.

haeci-ne-st?
This -Q-is?

STR.

haec   est. est-ne   ita ut tibi   dixi?   aspecta et contempla, Epidice:
this-NOM is. Is-NEG.Q thus as you-DAT say-1sg.PF? Gaze-IMP and observe-IMP, Epidicus-VOC:

usque ab   unguiculo   ad capillum summum-st festiuissuma.
right   from finger-nail-DIM.ABL to hair-ACC topmost-ACC-is delightful-SUPERL.NOM.

est-ne   consimilis quasi quom signum   pictum   pulchre aspexeris?
is-NEG.Q just-like-NOM as   when   picture-ACC painted-ACC beautifully look-at-2sg.PF.SUBJ?

EP.

e   tuis   uerbis   meum futurum   corium pulchrum praedicas,
from your-ABL words-ABL my-ACC about-to-be-ACC hide-ACC beautiful   predict-2sg.PRES.SUBJ,

quem   Apelles   ac Zeuxis   duo   pingent   pigmentis ulmeis.
which-ACC Apelles-NOM and Zeuxis-NOM two-NOM paint-3pl.FUT paints-ABL   of-elm-ABL.

STR.

di   immortales! sici-n iussi   ad me   ires?   pedibus plumbeis
gods VOC immortal-VOC! thus-Q order-1sg.PF to me-ACC come-2sg.IMP.SUBJ? Feet-ABL of-lead-ABL

qui   perhibetur   priu' uenisset   quam tu   aduenisti mihi.
who-NOM endow-3sg.PRES.PASS before come-3sg.PLPF.SUBJ than   you-NOM come-2sg.PF me-DAT.

'EPIDICUS (*a slave of Stratippocles' father Periphanes, an Athenian gen-tleman*). But who's the slave girl and the grey-haired chap coming along here? STRATIPPOCLES (*son of Periphanes*). He's the money-lender – she's the one I bought from the booty sale. EP. That's her? STR. That's her. Isn't she just like I described her to you? Gaze and admire, Epidicus. Right from the ends of her nails to the tips of her hair she is utterly delightful. Isn't she just like when you look at a beautifully painted picture? EP. From what you're saying one might hazard a guess that what's about to be beautiful is my hide, which that pair Apelles and Zeuxis (*the names of two famous Greek painters used here ironically to refer to Periphanes and his friend, who are currently scouring the town for Epidicus*) are going to paint with paints of elm wood. [*The money-lender enters*]. STR. (*to the money-lender*). Good God! Is this how I told you to come to me? A man with lead feet could've got here before you turned up.'

5.7   Conclusion

In this rather lengthy survey of 'preclassical' Roman Latin, we have seen that much of what we now regard as standard, both grammatically and stylistically, was in fact already in place by the time of our first texts of any significant length. But while official Latin, other than in matters of orthography, evolved only slowly in subsequent generations, thereby retaining all the useful validating associations of traditional practice, literary varieties continued to be developed and extended more rapidly, leading to greater differentiation by genre and much stricter conventions about what was 'acceptable' to its elite creators and readers. The two sides of this process, the rigorous selection from available options and the development of new lexical and grammatical resources, form the subject of the next chapter.

References

Cole, T. (1969) 'The Saturnian verse'. *Yale Classical Studies* 21, 3–73.

Courtney, E. (1995) *Musa Lapidaria: A Selection of Latin Verse Inscriptions*. Atlanta: Scholars Press.

Courtney, E. (1999) *Archaic Latin Prose*. Atlanta: Scholars Press.

Fraenkel, E. (1951) 'The pedigree of the Saturnian metre'. *Eranos* 49, 170–1.

Gratwick, A. S. (1982) 'Drama', in E. J. Kenney and W. V. Clausen (eds.), *The Cambridge History of Classical Literature, Vol. II Part I: The Early Republic*. Cambridge: Cambridge University Press, 77–137.

Gruen, E. S. (1992) *Culture and National Identity in Republican Rome*. Ithaca NY: Cornell University Press.

Horrocks, G. (2010) *Greek: A History of the Language and its Speakers* (2nd edn.). Wiley-Blackwell, Malden Mass. and Oxford.

Inscriptiones Graecae (1873–), various editors. Berlin: G. Reimer (later editions, De Gruyter).

Kenney, E. J. and W. V. Clausen (eds.) (1982) *The Cambridge History of Classical Literature, Vol. II, Part I: The Early Republic*. Cambridge: Cambridge University Press.

Keppie, L. (1991) *Understanding Roman Inscriptions*. Baltimore, MD: The Johns Hopkins University Press.

Palmer, L. R. (1954) *The Latin Language*. London: Faber and Faber.

Parsons, J. (1999) 'A new approach to the Saturnian verse and its relation to Latin prosody'. *Transactions of the American Philological Association* 129, 117–37.

Rosén, H. (1999) *Latine Loqui: Trends and Directions in the Crystallization of Classical Latin*. Munich: Wilhelm Fink Verlag.

Sherk, R. (1969) *Roman Documents from the Greek East*. Baltimore, MD: The Johns Hopkins Press.

Sylloge Inscriptionum Graecarum[3] (1915–24), edited by W. Dittenberger and F. Hiller von Gaertringen. Leipzig: S. Hirzel.

Wachter, R. (1987) *Altlateinische Inschriften*. Bern: Peter Lang.

Watkins, C. (1964) 'Preliminaries to the reconstruction of Indo-European sentence structure', in H. G. Lunt (ed.), *Proceedings of the Ninth International Congress of Linguists (Cambridge, MA, August 27–31 1962)*. The Hague/London: Mouton, 1035–42.

Williams, G. (1982) 'The genesis of poetry in Rome', in E. J. Kenney and W. V. Clausen (eds.), *The Cambridge History of Classical Literature, Vol. II, Part I: The Early Republic*. Cambridge: Cambridge University Press, 53–59.

Woodcock, E. C. (1959) *A New Latin Syntax*. London: Methuen (reprinted 1985, Bristol: Bristol Classical Press).

Chapter VI

Elite Latin in the Late Republic and Early Empire

6.1 Introduction

It has become a commonplace to regard the aristocracy of the late Republic as the driving force behind the final stages of the formation of literary Latin (e.g. Rosén 1999: 11). Though many people contributed to this process of refinement and elaboration, the bulk of our surviving evidence, at least as regards explicit comment and discussion, derives directly from the works of Marcus Tullius Cicero (106–43 BC), and it is his compositional practice above all, especially in maturity, that has traditionally been seen as encapsulating the essence of 'correct' syntax and 'good' style. This is so not only because of the widespread acceptance of much of his very extensive technical and philosophical neologism, but also because of his elaboration of periodic sentence structure, his formalization of the principles of euphony for prose composition (most notably with regard to the establishment of rhythmic *clausulae*, on which see 6.5.1 below), and his implicit definition, through the careful selection and promotion of particular variants, of 'best practice' in grammar and usage. Notable syntactic innovations of the 'classical' Latin style include the elaboration of participial and infinitival syntax, the refinement of rules regulating the form of subordinate clauses, especially the use of the subjunctive, and the regular use of 'logical' connective particles and connecting relatives in extended discourse. This style, which, as expected, was largely developed on the basis of already established grammatical principles, including those controlling the sequence of tenses in subordinate clauses, had a profound long-term impact, as revealed not only through its emulation by Latin writers of the Carolingian period and Renaissance but also by the transfer, *mutatis mutandis*, of many of its characteristic traits to the standard written forms then being developed for the European vernaculars. Its influence finally waned only with the advent of Romanticism and the shift of focus away from traditional humanistic pursuits engendered by the industrial and technological revolutions of the nineteenth and twentieth centuries.

The testimony relating to Cicero's activity, e.g. in matters of selection, innovation, and the establishment of Greek standards of stylistic elegance, therefore provides a helpful window on what must have been a period of considerable linguistic and literary controversy and experimentation. But before considering Cicero's contribution in detail (6.3), it will be useful first to examine briefly the Greek background to the final impetus towards the standardization of Latin.

6.2   The Encounter with Greek

6.2.1   Background

Though the evolution of Latin as an official and literary language in part reflected internal factors peculiar to the language, the changing circumstances of its use, including ever closer involvement with the Greek-speaking world, had a particularly profound impact on Roman culture and attitudes, not least in matters of language, and above all in promoting the use of language as a medium for technical, philosophical and artistic discourse. One obvious consequence of the encounter with Greek was a period of turmoil characterized by invention, translation and calquing, out of which various accepted genre 'markers' eventually emerged, differentiating a range of styles and conventions associated with particular contexts of use (see 6.5 below). Less obviously, however, the way in which the Greek language was learned by Romans, and perceived as a *system*, had an equally dramatic effect.

The Greek *Koine*, or 'common dialect', which evolved as an international variety of Attic, the dialect of ancient Athens, during the period of the Athenian empire and the Macedonian expansion (fifth and fourth centuries BC), had become the sole official, technical and scientific language of the extensive Greek-speaking community of the eastern Mediterranean, and as such had remained the 'standard' form of Greek in Roman times, a status which it retained into late antiquity and beyond. Even though belletristic writers increasingly looked towards older forms of Greek to provide the norms for literary composition, and especially towards ancient Attic as a model for prose writing (cf. below), the reality was that 'normal' Hellenistic Greek still provided much of the basis for such literary elaboration, with many writers doing little more than substituting key Attic grammatical markers and lexical items into fundamentally *Koine* structures reflecting the contemporary standard.

At the highest levels of usage the *Koine*, widely learned as a second language but also taught to native speakers as a formal written language, was soon reduced to sets of rules and paradigms, and, once established as a language with 'fixed' grammatical properties, quickly came to represent an unchanging ideal in the minds of its users, the primary vehicle of a universal Greek culture: actual practice was, of course, subject to change under pressure from natural developments in the spoken language on the one hand and the Atticizing tendencies of literary writers on the other. Didactic considerations, soon refined by more systematic philosophical and philological enquiry into the nature of language and the concept of linguistic correctness, therefore led to Greek becoming the first language to be subject to the kind of normative principles of good usage characteristic of a true standard. According to Stoic grammatical theory, at least as reported by Diogenes Laertius (VII, 59), correct usage, or *Hellenismós*, meant speech/writing that was 'free of faults in grammar and without careless usage', though there was inevitable tension between the expectation of formal regularity (leading sometimes to the artificial imposition of a supposed norm) and the acceptance, in the case of irregular forms, of established written practice or even contemporary educated usage as the final criterion of correctness in specific cases.

Against this background, it was inevitable that the prestige of a language endowed with remarkable lexical resources and characterized by rules imposing clarity, consistency and precision of expression (involving *inter alia* the specification and differentiation of word meanings, the elimination of grammatical variation and the partial regularization of morphology), should have had a profound impact on Roman thinking, even if many key grammatical concepts actually remained controversial in the period in which Roman thinkers first began to apply them to Latin. The *Koine*, increasingly familiar to a Roman aristocracy instructed by Greek orators, philosophers and grammarians, therefore influenced the development of Latin in its higher registers in two very different ways. First, it helped to promote a vast enrichment of the lexicon and to consolidate the role of particular native modes of expression: an example of the latter is perhaps provided by the growing use of periphrases comprising nouns and 'light' verbs such as *facere* 'make/do', *dare* 'give', *habere* 'have', which correspond structurally, if not routinely in their specific lexical makeup, with similar Greek expressions using *poieîsthai* 'make/do' that had long been a key marker of the *Koine* as an official language: e.g. *mentionem facere* 'make mention', *uerba facere* 'make a verbal report', *iter habere* 'have a journey (to make)', etc. The increasing use of Latin as an administrative language had doubtless led very naturally to the formation of a bureaucratic 'nominalizing' style, but the parallels with established Greek practice in this domain are at least suggestive of reinforcement, even if internal motivations can also be found for specific instances (e.g. in the case of *mentionem facere* Latin does not generally favour denominative verbs derived from nouns ending in *-tio* and in any case *mentiri* 'lie' already existed with a different meaning). Secondly, and even more importantly, the *Koine* helped to establish the notion that 'real' languages were those that had been given a unique and definitive form in a rule book. The two processes identified here were in no sense contradictory, since both had the effect of shaping Latin on the model of the *Koine*, even if the period of experimentation with novel word formation had the temporary effect of enhancing lexical redundancy and overlap before new norms were firmly established.

In consequence, the notion of *Latinitas* soon emerged as the Roman equivalent of *Hellenismós*, with all that this implied for the regulation of the language and the establishment of 'good practice'. Interestingly, the Roman scholar Marcus Terentius Varro (116–27 BC) was already in a position to present a developed grammatical theory, emphasizing the notion of regularity, in book X of his *de Lingua Latina*, published in 43 BC. This provides us with a useful *terminus ante quem* for the constitution of an autonomous approach to grammar in the Greek world, albeit one exploiting earlier Stoic theorizing and Alexandrian textual scholarship, that served as Varro's inspiration. Direct evidence of this may be provided by the famous *Grammatikḗ Tékhnē (Ars Grammatica)* attributed to Dionysius Thrax (*c.*170–*c.*90 BC), though there are reasons to think that this work may in fact have originated in a later period, and been attached to Dionysius's name through the reworking of an earlier treatise (see Matthews 1994, Law 2003, for a thorough survey of Greco-Roman linguistic theory).

But grammar was only one aspect of the Greek tradition. Rhetorical technique also played an important role at Rome, especially in a society that was striving not only for correctness but also for elegance and *urbanitas* (see 6.3 below). During the third century BC there had been a reaction in the Greek-speaking world against the long-established norms of rhetorical composition, embodied prototypically in the work of the Athenian orator Isocrates (436–338 BC), which were felt to have become 'stale' through over-rigid teaching methods. The reaction, which began in Asia Minor and was therefore known as Asianism, involved the partial abandonment of the carefully crafted period, and the reintroduction of more obviously emotive techniques, including the deliberate accumulation of vocabulary items, often with a 'poetic' pedigree, and the frequent use of short antithetical clause structures characterized by metaphor, word-play and various rhythmical special effects. But this approach in turn had led to problems of mechanical over-use and a consequential vacuity of content, and during the first century BC a counter-reaction eventually set in, involving a return to the 'leaner' practice and norms of the great Athenian orators and prose writers of the past, who were also increasingly seen as embodying the 'true' nature of Greek in their grammatical usage, a nature that was felt to have become confused and obscured by the process of linguistic evolution that had led to the *Koine*.

This Atticist movement was to have a profound effect on the subsequent history of Greek by establishing what was already an ancient form of the language as a rival to the *Koine* in the field of literary prose composition (see Horrocks 2010: chs 3–5), but it should be no surprise that the Asianist-Atticist controversy should also have had its impact on developing rhetorical and compositional practice in Rome, with the result that the definition of *Latinitas* became increasingly bound up with a programme of promoting linguistic and cultural ideals through literary activity. Though the Romans had relatively little 'hallmarked' literature that could provide a grammatical model equivalent to that of ancient Attic, the belief in linguistic purism that the Atticist movement embodied chimed well with the idea that contemporary Latin was in need of 'cleansing', through the elimination of what the elite had come to regard as substandard or redundant, together with the promotion of 'correctness' and the establishment of a 'perfected' form of language commensurate with the established power of the Roman state (the new Athens) and the growing cultural ambition of its aristocracy.

The shift towards a less extravagant and more elevated form of expression initiated by the comic poet Terence (see 5.6) therefore gathered momentum in the first century BC, though ironically, the drive towards 'pure' Latinity, inspired in part by Greek ideas and ideals, was regularly in conflict with the overtly Grecizing tendencies of many writers as they sought to establish literary varieties of the language on the basis of Greek models. This confrontation with Greek is reflected not only in examples of pure imitation, as in the formation of linguistically alien compound adjectives (e.g. *altisonus* 'high-sounding', *ueliuolus* 'speeding under sail', etc.), but also in the extension of phenomena with a limited native presence, such as the use of adnominal *cum* 'with' + noun phrase as an alternative means of expressing such notions (e.g. *triplici cum corpore* 'with triple body' = 'triple-bodied', etc.), or the use of the accusative 'of respect' with passive participles, other passive verb forms, and adjectives (e.g. *perculsi pectora* 'struck (in) their hearts', etc.). There is therefore considerable evidence, from the beginning of literary activity down to the period of the early Empire, of periodic hostility to novel manifestations of such foreign influence and the snobbery which it engendered (the cautious position of Cato has already been noted, while Julius Caesar was perhaps the greatest exponent of purism in his generation). This finally subsided only when the Romans had become fully confident in the expressive and creative resources of Latin, and became more relaxed about the linguistic symbiosis which had been taking place, willy nilly and at all levels, as the Greco-Roman world slowly evolved into a more unified political and cultural entity. Attempts to reassert the primacy of Latin begin again only with the *de facto* decentralization of the Empire in later antiquity and the efforts of emperors to restore their universal authority.

A range of observations by different writers from different periods will help to give something of the flavour of Roman reactions to Greek over the ages. In his treatise *de Finibus* (I.3.8) Cicero quotes an anecdote (fragg. 87–93) from a poem of Lucilius (*c*.180–102 BC), in which a certain Albucius, a hyperenthusiastic hellenophile, has a joke played on him by the praetor Scaevola and his staff in Athens, who address him in Greek in accordance with his supposed desire to be a Greek rather than a Roman. Since Lucilius was a friend of Scipio Aemilianus, and undoubtedly broadly philhellene himself (cf. Horace's comment that he 'achieved great things by combining Greek with Latin words' (*Satires* 1.10.20)), this stands as a warning of the continuing need to maintain a 'balanced' perspective, a view endorsed by Cicero himself, who introduces the quotation by observing that only someone like Albucius, who wished to be called 'downright Greek' (*plane Graecum*), would not wish to read good material written in well-crafted Latin.

Such comments belong, of course, to an era in which the official use of Latin by Roman officials was still expected as a linguistic reminder of Roman domination, even when the language would not be well understood and translation was required. We may note here the explicit statement of the first-century AD historian Valerius Maximus (II.2.2−3), who contrasts the care taken by 'magistrates of old' to preserve the dignity of Rome in this respect, even if competent in Greek, with the state of affairs in his own time, when Greek harangues to the senate had become commonplace. Recall too that Cicero, in preparing his action against Verres for extortion while serving as governor of Sicily, had, as a non-magistrate, addressed the Syracusan senate in Greek, and was then accused, somewhat disingenuously, of having committed 'a shameful outrage' by his opponent Metellus (*in Verrem* II.4.147). And even though, in a slightly later period, Octavian (soon to become the first emperor with the title Augustus), unlike Aemilius Paullus after the battle of Pydna (168 BC: Livy 45.8, 45.29), had felt free, in the wake of his own victory over Antony and Cleopatra at Actium (31 BC), to make a speech in Greek at a venue outside Rome (Alexandria), his successor Tiberius (emperor AD 14–37), who also spoke Greek fluently and to whom Valerius Maximus had dedicated his *magnum opus*, was still strongly averse to the use of Greek by Romans in the Senate (Suetonius, *Tiberius* 71).

But the tide was already turning, and the emperor Claudius (ruled AD 41–54), who wrote histories of Etruria and Carthage in Greek, was apparently happy to regard Latin and Greek together as the two Roman languages, and even used Greek in the Senate to reply to Greek-speaking ambassadors (Suetonius, *Claudius* 42). Soon after, during the second century AD, a series of philhellenic emperors (Hadrian, Antoninus Pius and Marcus Aurelius) ushered in a period of economic resurgence in the East that led to increasing Greek membership of the equestrian and senatorial orders and a growing sense of the Empire as a Greco-Roman state in which the linguistic attitudes of Claudius were the norm. The first signs of a shift of policy towards more 'traditional' values come in the reign of Diocletian (emperor AD 284–305), who, after a period of great instability, sought to re-establish effective central government, restore economic order, and revive the traditional Roman religion. His largely unsuccessful efforts to beat rampant inflation by the issue of a price edict (AD 301) are instructive in that the introduction to the document is composed in Latin alone, while concessions are made to the Greek-speaking population of the Empire only in the practical details of commodity prices, which are given in both languages.

But attempts to re-establish the universal primacy of Latin as the official language of the Empire, which included the founding of Constantinople as a 'new Rome' and centre of Latinity in the East (AD 330), were doomed to failure once the Empire had been formally partitioned (after the death of Theodosius in AD 395) and the western territories started to fall away in the face of Germanic invasion, political instability, economic weakness and institutional fragmentation. Nonetheless, the growing acceptance of Greek in earlier periods largely coincided with the emergence of the view that Roman literary writers were not merely seeking to match the Greeks whose works they used as inspiration for their efforts, but rather were continuing, and even improving upon, a great tradition which was as much their possession as it was the Greeks', and which proudly demonstrated its evolving character in the overt blend of Greek and Roman elements that is so typical of Classical Latin literature.

6.2.2   Some specifics

We round off this section with some examples of the growing impact of Greek on Latin usage in the critical period of the fall of the Republic and the establishment of the Empire (see Coleman 1977 for a full survey).

Since we are dealing specifically with the standardization of Latin, the examples given are all characteristic of higher forms of the language in this period, reflecting the central role of Greek as a cultural language for the Roman elite. Greek influence on more popular varieties will be dealt with in later chapters: the process in this case was more typically 'bottom-up', providing testimony to a limited but important process of linguistic convergence conditioned by extensive, if only partially competent, bilingualism among the inhabitants of the Empire, and in particular by widespread exposure to the spoken Latin of speakers of Greek origin, the sheer prevalence of whose characteristic usage, increasingly settled after several generations, gradually came to affect that of even monolingual native speakers, albeit in a less self-conscious way than that with which we are principally concerned here.

We must, then, bear in mind that many Grecisms in literary Latin were simply the product of *imitatio*, and intended to be recognized as such. On the other hand it should not be forgotten that some of these Greek elements did become established, serving as 'markers' of specific genres, and much of Vergil's practice, for example, was routinely adopted by later writers of epic. In general, poets were naturally more tolerant (or perhaps more ambitious) in their adoption of Greek practice than prose writers, though historiography often employs a more 'poetic' style than other prose genres (see 6.5 below).

Phonology

Old Latin did not note aspirated plosives and Greek names and loan words containing them were at first assimilated to normal Latin phonology (cf. early loans such as *purpura/porphýrā* 'purple dye', *calx /khális* 'lime', etc.). As knowledge of Greek became more widespread, however, its aspirated consonants were increasingly noted (using CH, PH, TH) and pronounced as such, at least by educated speakers. Eventually this had some impact even on native vocabulary (most notably in words such as *pulcher* 'beautiful', *triumphus* 'triumph', etc.), cf. Cicero, *Orator* 160, who confirms that this change was still taking place during his lifetime. Some examples doubtless involved 'affected' pronunciations or hypercorrection, as satirized by Catullus (poem 84), but others almost certainly reflect an increasing awareness, thanks to Greek, of the native (though purely allophonic) aspiration of plosives in specific contexts.

The letters Z and Y were also introduced to represent Greek sounds more accurately (viz. initial /z-/ or medial /-zz-/ and /y/, respectively, earlier noted by S/SS and U), though problems of phonetic or orthographic interference with native Latin words do not arise in these cases until a later period, when further sound changes had occurred.

Morphology

By and large, Greek loans and names in preclassical Latin were assimilated to the corresponding declensional classes in Latin (i.e. *a*-stems to the 1st, *o*-stems to the 2nd, the remainder to the 3rd), and this remains the rule thereafter (thus Cicero chides himself for having used a Greek ending in a letter to his friend Atticus, *Epistulae ad Atticum* 7.3.1), though there are a few early experiments with Greek endings in Old Latin poetry, while elegiac and lyric verse of the Augustan age, in which the blending of Greek and Roman elements is of the essence, shows a particular liking for the Greek inflection of Greek names. Real interference, however, involving both inflectional and derivational suffixes, belongs to lower registers and the bulk of the evidence comes from a later period, as we shall see. For a later, settled, view, cf. Quintilian, *Institutio Oratoria* 1.5.58–64.

Syntax

The development of well-established but 'underexploited' resources
Particularly interesting under this heading is the radical development of participial syntax, which, under Greek influence, evolved to provide an important alternative to subordinate clauses containing finite verbs, with the participial expressions often retaining the relevant conjunctions (*ut, tamquam, etsi, nisi* etc.).

In Old Latin, and in popular Latin generally, there were only 'present' (i.e. imperfective) active and 'perfect' (often in fact perfective) passive participles, the so-called 'future' forms in *-urus* being almost exclusively restricted to periphrases with *esse* meaning 'to be about to X'. Though both the present active participle (rarely) and the perfect passive participle (more regularly) already had some clause-like functions alongside their adjectival ones (including the idiomatic use in agreement with a noun of the type *ab urbe condita*, lit. 'from the city (once) founded' = 'from the foundation of the city': cf. Plautus, *Bacchides* 424, *ante solem orientem* 'before the rising of the sun'; *Casina* 84, *post transactam fabulam* 'after the performance of the play'), the present active participle in particular was still thought of as primarily and essentially adjectival, often taking a genitive rather than an accusative object, and rarely taking any elaborate 'verbal' modification or complementation.

In Classical Latin, by contrast, though the present participle is still making up ground, both forms are regularly used as non-finite alternatives to conjoined or subordinate (adverbial) clauses containing finite verbs, thus promoting *inter alia* the much wider use of the present participle in absolute constructions, and both allow the more complex patterns of modification or complementation typical of finite verb forms (see Rosén 1999: 98–108). This development clearly owed much to the model provided by Greek, which had a full array of active and (medio-)passive participles formed to all aspect stems and to the future tense stem, and employed these routinely as one of its principal instruments of subordination. The development of a periodic style based directly on Greek practice therefore provided a natural context for the extension of participial functions in Latin, while the partial maturation of the future participle active and the still rare but increasing use of the active participle with a perfective-like function (e.g. Sallust, *Iugurtha* 113.1, *haec Maurus secum ipse diu uoluens tandem promisit* 'this the Moor, turning [i.e. having turned] it over in his mind for a long time, finally promised') and of the passive participle with an imperfective-like function (e.g. Livy 2.36.1, *seruum sub furca caesum medio egerat foro* 'he had driven a slave through the midst of the forum scourged [i.e. while being scourged] beneath a pillory') represent further steps towards replicating the full array of Greek options with the limited resources available to Latin, thereby introducing greater flexibility and symmetry into what was originally a highly defective 'system' with only two members of restricted functional range and only partial functional correspondence.

The revival of archaisms otherwise in serious decline   In other cases, however, the impact of Greek was to reinforce the use of inherited constructions that were otherwise in decline, and which therefore became particularly characteristic of those registers in which the desire to distance the language from contemporary norms was greatest. A good example has already been mentioned, namely the use of the accusative with various passive verb forms (the so-called *accusatiuus Graecus*). This had survived marginally in Latin with certain perfect passive participles originally of 'middle' meaning (though the semantic contrast between middle and passive had generally been lost in Latin), such as *indutus* 'having put on X' = 'clothed in X' (cf. Plautus *Menaechmi* 511–12, *indutum ... pallam* 'having put on a cloak'; Cicero already uses the ablative, however, implying a passive force (e.g. *de Oratore* 3.127)). The revival and extension of this usage in poetry (later copied by historians), and above all the further extension to finite verb forms, therefore strongly suggests the influence of the still highly functional Greek middle voice (cf. Vergil *Aeneid* 2.392–3, *galeam ... induitur* 'he dresses himself in/puts on the helmet').

A related revival was modelled on the well-known Greek construction involving body-parts, in which a second accusative is used in apposition to an individual ('strike X [on] the arm') and retained even with a passive verb ('get struck [on] the arm': cf. Vergil *Aeneid* 6.470, *nec ...*

uoltum sermone mouetur 'nor is she moved [in] her countenance by his appeal'; Sallust *Histories* 3.24, *terga ab hostibus caedebantur* 'they had their backs slashed by the enemy', the first and only example in Republican prose, though the construction later becomes quite common among the historians). This too seems to have survived marginally in Latin, but again only with passive participles (cf. the consistently simple, non-Hellenizing Latin of the *Bellum Africanum*, erroneously attributed to Caesar, in which we find *caput ictus* 'struck [on] the head' (78.10), and *bracchium . . . percussus* 'struck [on] the arm' (85.7), comparable to contemporary poetic attestations in overtly Grecizing contexts, e.g. Catullus 64.122 *deuinctam lumina somno* 'overcome [in] her eyes by sleep'). But the more adventurous uses with both active (e.g. Vergil *Aeneid* 10.698, *Latagum . . . occupat os* 'he smites Latagus [in] the mouth') and passive finite verb forms (cf. *Aeneid* 6.470 above) and even adjectives (e.g. Vergil *Aeneid* 5.97, *nigrantes terga iuuencos* 'bullocks dusky [on] their backs') look once again like cases of revival and extension under Greek influence, providing a set of marked, and metrically useful, alternatives to various native constructions, and overtly linking such self-consciously literary Latin to the Greek tradition.

Similar remarks apply to a range of other ancient inherited constructions with a diminished distribution in non-literary Latin of the period. We may include here: the growing appearance in poetry and historiography of an adnominal partitive or defining genitive dependent on neuter adjectives used as nouns (e.g. *prima uirorum* 'the first-rank of the men', Lucretius 1.86, for *primi uiri*, and *ad summum montis* 'to the top of the mountain', Sallust *Iugurtha* 93.2, for the usual *ad summum montem*); the extended use of a genitive 'of reference' in place of the normal ablative with adjectives not derived from the roots of transitive verbs, and with which the regular objective genitive of *pecuniae cupidus* 'desirous of money' would be impossible (e.g. *diues pecoris* 'rich in livestock', Vergil *Eclogues* 2.20; *aegram animi* 'sick at heart', Livy 1.58.9); and the extension in poetry of infinitival complements to a wider range of adjectives in place of consecutive relative clauses with subjunctive verbs (e.g. Vergil *Eclogues* 5.54, *cantari dignus* 'worthy to be sung (of)' for *dignus qui cantaretur*), as well as the use of an infinitive in place of a purpose clause or gerundive construction (e.g. Horace *Odes* 1.12.1–2, *quem . . . sumis celebrare* 'who do you take to celebrate?').

Note finally the generalized retention of pseudo-aspectual uses of present (= imperfective) and perfect (= perfective) infinitives in 'control' contexts in poetry and of present and perfect subjunctives in prohibitions more generally. As an example of the former consider Vergil *Georgics* 3.435–6, *ne mihi . . . carpere somnos neu . . . libeat iacuisse* 'may it not be my pleasure to snatch sleep [present infinitive] or lie down [perfect infinitive]' (recall here the formulaic legal phrase *ne . . . habuise uelet* 'that he should not wish to hold' [perfect infinitive] of the *Senatusconsultum de Bacchanalibus* ((3) in Chapter V), which provides good evidence for the native basis of the perfect construction). For the latter we may compare *ne hoc feceris* 'don't do this' [perfect subjunctive] with *ne hoc facias* 'don't do this' [present subjunctive] (and *noli hoc facere* 'be-unwilling to do this' [present infinitive]). In general, however, it is hard to see that any real semantic contrast is intended here, and the impact of the systematic Greek opposition of aspect is probably reflected only formally, in the continuing use in near-parallel function of these formerly contrasting exponents. On the basis of Cicero's practice one might argue that perfect subjunctives in prohibitions, like the *noli* + present infinitive construction, were more formal/literary than their counterparts with a present subjunctive, though metrical considerations are also relevant in poetry.

'Simple' imitatio   Many other Grecisms, however, represent what looks like pure imitation, in which the borrowed structures deviate significantly from any similar native usage and sometimes have no direct parallels at all. Even more than in the case of the preceding types, such 'alien' usages are almost entirely confined to the registers that first employed them, and sometimes to the specific contexts in which they were used for some special effect. As an example of the latter, we may mention here Horace's ironic extension, in the context of a conversation with a self-proclaimed hellenophile and connoisseur of Greek art, of the use of *audio* 'hear' to mean 'be called' in *Satires* 2.7.101. This is quite distinct from the native idiom *bene/male audio* 'to be in good/bad repute', and though replicating the ancient use of *clueo(r)*, is very clearly and deliberately modelled on one of the normal meanings of Greek *akoúō* 'hear'/'be called'.

The assignment of unusual cases to the complements of verbs normally used in other constructions provides another good illustration of the kind of phenomena that are relevant here. For example, the genitive after verbs of emotion, expressing the matter in respect of which the relevant feeling is aroused, was probably an inherited construction, but it had survived in Latin only with *misereor* 'I pity' and impersonal verbs such as *paenitet* 'there is regret', *pudet* 'there is shame' and *piget* 'there is disgust', the majority of such verbs instead taking accusatives or prepositional expressions (e.g. *de* + ablative). In principle, therefore, the occasional poetic use of the genitive with verbs such as *miror* 'wonder/admire' (e.g. Vergil *Aeneid* 11.126) and *inuideo* 'envy' (e.g. Horace *Satires* 2.6.83–4), in apparent imitation of the normal construction of their translation equivalents in Greek (cf. Priscian *Grammatica Latina* 3.316, and Quintilian *Institutio Oratoria* 9.3.17), might actually have been placed in the preceding section, but the failure of this option to become anything like a routine variant of the usual Latin constructions, even in the relevant 'high' poetic styles, suggests that the inspiration was provided in each case by a specific lexical equivalent in Greek, the pattern itself never becoming established.

Similar remarks apply to the poetic use of genitives after verbs of 'ceasing' (e.g. Horace *Odes* 2.9.17–18) and 'ruling' (e.g. Horace *Odes* 3.30.11–12), the use of the dative with *pugnare* 'fight' instead of *cum* + ablative (e.g. Propertius 1.10.21), and the characteristically historiographic construction first used by Sallust in *Iugurtha* 84.3, *neque plebi militia uolenti putabatur*, literally 'nor was military service thought [to be] for the plebs being willing' = 'nor were the plebs thought willing to undertake military service', for all of which it is extremely difficult to find any convincing native base. We may, however, contrast here the occasional poetic use of the dative rather than the accusative (± *ad*) to express goal with some inanimate nouns (e.g. Vergil *Aeneid* 5.451, *it clamor caelo* 'the shout goes [up] to heaven'), since even though Early Latin provides no evidence for such a use of the dative with inanimates, the attested examples all permit the possibility of personification and so of interpretation as extensions of the normal Latin option of using a dative with sentient beings (i.e. implying some advantage as well as a change of location) – albeit with some support from similar examples in Homer.

Finally, the syntax of infinitivals too shows some evidence of change under Greek influence. The *Koine*, as the language of technical and official discourse, made extensive use of nominalized infinitives headed by the definite article *tó* 'the'. This construction provided a simple device for turning even the most complex statement into a noun phrase that could then be used, like a gerund in English, both as a clausal subject or object and with prepositions. The structures concerned were frequently very complex, exhibiting elaborate complementation and modification, and as such proved particularly useful in legal and academic contexts, becoming a key marker of the relevant styles. By contrast, the use of infinitives (present only) as subjects and objects is very restricted in Early Latin. Furthermore, the attested examples typically lack any modification or complementation (e.g. Plautus *Captiui* 732, *non moriri certius* 'dying is not more certain', and *Bacchides* 158, *hic uereri perdidit* 'he has abandoned being ashamed'), while government by prepositions is simply unknown, the gerund being used instead. It therefore follows that, since even this very limited usage is systematically avoided by Caesar and Livy, and also by Cicero in his more literary output, the appearance of infinitives with the full range of nominal grammatical functions in Cicero's technical (i.e. rhetorical and philosophical) prose works, all based more or less directly on Greek sources, is almost certainly to be attributed to straightforward imitation of the *Koine*, particularly as limited modification and government by prepositions are both now tolerated, sometimes in combination with apparent efforts to replicate the effect of the Greek article through the use of a demonstrative or emphatic pronoun. Consider the following examples: *me . . . hoc ipsum nihil agere . . . delectat* 'this actual doing nothing pleases me' (*de Oratore* 2.24); *ipsum Latine loqui* 'actual speaking [correctly] in Latin' (*Brutus* 140); *beate uiuere uestrum* 'your living happily' (*de Finibus* 2.86); *inter optime ualere et grauissime aegrotare nihil . . . interesse* '[that] nothing intervenes between being maximally well and being most seriously ill' (*de Finibus* 2.43).

We should also note here the occasional use of a very un-Latin construction in overtly Hellenizing contexts, namely the so-called 'nominative and infinitive' with verbs of 'saying' and 'thinking' when the subject of the main verb and the subject of the infinitive are coreferential. More accurately, this construction actually involves the use of a 'bare' infinitive after a verb of 'saying' etc., the necessarily 'empty' subject position of which is syntactically and semantically controlled by the nominative subject of the main verb, so that any predicative adjective following a copular verb in the infinitival clause must also be nominative, cf. Catullus 4.1–2, *phaselus ille quem uidetis, hospites, ait fuisse nauium celerrimus* 'this pinnace that you see, my friends, says she was [claims to have been] the swiftest [nom.] of ships'; or Horace *Odes* 3.27.73, *uxor inuicti Iouis esse nescis* 'you do not realize you are the wife of invincible Jupiter', both occurring in contexts rich in Greek lexical and grammatical detail. With certain verbs and in the specified circumstances this is the normal construction in Greek, and it contrasts systematically with the use of the 'accusative and infinitive', involving an overt infinitival subject, in cases of non-coreferentiality between the two subjects. But normal Latin always uses the accusative and infinitive construction, employing an accusative reflexive pronoun to mark coreferentiality. The earliest examples of the nominative and infinitive construction in Latin come from Plautus, but *pace* Coleman (1977: 140), these are hardly evidence of an inherited native construction, once vibrant, but now in decline, since all are put in the mouths of Greeks (typically parasites or slaves) in plays with a Greek setting, e.g. *at censebam attigisse* (*Asinaria* 385, the slave Libanus), *si forte pure uelle habere dixerit* (*Asinaria* 806, a parasite). The construction is clearly a Grecism, used either for verisimilitude, as probably in Plautus, or later for the unmistakably Hellenizing colour that it provides in attributing words or thoughts to individuals (or boats!) with a Greek background in myth or history. The same applies to Vergil's use of the Greek 'nominative and participle' construction after factive verbs of knowing and perceiving, e.g. *Aeneid* 2.377, *sensit medios delapsus in hostis* 'he [i.e. the Greek Androgeos at the fall of Troy] realized he had fallen in the midst of enemies.'

But such syntactic Grecisms as have been noted, though unquestionably playing an important role in particular styles and genres, failed to have any significant impact on the evolution of Latin as a whole, since even those developments that made the most significant inroads into higher registers, such as the extended use of participial syntax, failed to pass down into more popular Latin or the Romance languages that continued it, returning only later, and then only in part, when the development and standardization of these languages as written media came in turn to be modelled on aspects of Classical Latin usage.

Lexicon

The lexicon is perhaps the area in which Greek influence was most pervasive and most lasting (cf. Coleman 1977: 105–6). Indeed, it would not be too much of an exaggeration to say that much of the technical and philosophical vocabulary of modern European languages is derived, directly or indirectly, from Latin words that owe their origins to the intense period of lexical borrowing and creativity that took place in the period of the late Republic and early Empire, with Cicero, as often, providing much of the relevant evidence.

While straightforward borrowing from Greek was common enough from the period of earliest contacts (which were often with West Greek speaking communities of southern Italy, cf. *poena* 'penalty' < *poínā*, *talentum* 'talent (money)' < *tálanton*, *gubernator* 'pilot' < *kubernā́tās*, etc.), and continued in popular spoken Latin as the influx of Greek speakers into Italy gathered pace (e.g. *colpus* 'blow', cf. French *coup*, < *kólaphos*, replacing *ictus*; *bracchium* 'arm', cf. French *bras*, < *brakhī́ōn*, replacing *lacertus*; *petra* 'stone', cf. French *pierre*, < *pétrā*, replacing *lapis*, etc.), such adoption and adaptation of Greek words was in fact comparatively rare in the higher registers of the language (*philosophia* 'philosophy' and *rhetorica/rhetorices* 'rhetoric' being obvious examples), where loan-shifts and calques are in fact much more common, perhaps as part of a conscious programme among the intelligentsia of playing down the debt to Greek and boosting the stock of native words. Among examples of the former we may note the extended use of *amo* 'love' in the sense of 'be in the habit of (doing)' on the model of *philṓ* (cf. Quintilian 9.3.17 on Sallust), of *casus* 'fall' in the sense of a grammatical 'case' on the model of *ptōsis*, or of *uirtus* 'manliness' in the sense of 'virtue' on the model of *aretḗ*, etc. Calquing, i.e. the novel compounding of elements of Latin to replicate the structure of Greek compounds, is, if anything, even more prevalent, and may be seen as the principal means by which a native vocabulary was created in the fields of philosophy, rhetoric and grammar among others. Obvious examples include *anti-cip-atio* and *prae-no-tio* 'pre-conception' modelled on *prólēpsis*, lit. 'pre-apprehend-ing' (cf. Cicero *de Natura Deorum* 1.44); *quali-tas* 'quality' modelled on *poiótēs*, lit. 'whatkindof-ness' (cf. Cicero *Academica* 1.6.24: subsequently *quanti-tas* 'quantity' followed the pattern of *qualitas* as well as the form and meaning of *posótēs*, lit. 'howmuch-ness'); *dis-tribu-tio* and *di-ui-sio* 'partition' modelled on *di(h)aíresis*, lit. 'apart-take-ing' (cf. Cicero *de Oratore* 3.203, *ad Herennium* 4.47); and *ad-iect-iuus* 'adjectival' or *sub-iect-iuus* 'of the subject', modelled respectively on the nominalized adjective *epítheton*, lit. 'upon-put-passive.adj', i.e. 'applied', and the nominalized participle *hypokeímenon*, lit. 'under-place-ed', i.e. 'supposed', etc.

6.3   Cicero

Against this background, and in anticipation of our discussion of some of the specific processes of selection and development that the final stages of standardization involved, some extracts from Cicero's rhetorical works will be instructive.

Many important observations come from the *Brutus*, which was composed in 46 BC in the form of a dialogue between Cicero and two of his friends, Marcus Junius Brutus, a leading Atticist and one of the future murderers of Caesar, and his closest confidant, the traditionalist antiquarian Titus Pomponius Atticus, with whom he corresponded regularly (16 books of letters survive from the period 68–44 BC). The content certainly reflects real issues of debate in such circles at the time, and we may fairly assume that the speakers are made to say more or less what their real-life counterparts actually believed.

Chapter 258, a speech given to Atticus, sets the scene by linking the notion of linguistic purity with the best of traditional Roman practice, while simultaneously asserting the present need for a 'nationalistic' purge of what the Roman elite saw as alien and substandard contemporary usage on the basis of a principled grammatical theory. (Recall that, for many generations now, Rome had had a large population of incomers from outside the city alongside the many thousands of Greek-speaking slaves, freedmen, traders, and teachers.) This demonstrates Atticus's legendary respect for *mos maiorum* 'ancestral custom', with change instinctively viewed as decay, though we may also note how Atticus validates his position by equating what he believes to be happening in Rome with similar developments in Athens, thereby contrasting a time when both Attic and Roman diction were supposedly in their prime with the allegedly chaotic present in both societies:

(1)   'You see', he continued, 'the ground at least and, as it were, the
foundation of the orator, namely faultless and pure-Latin diction.
Those possessed of praise for this hitherto have had it not for their
theory and expert knowledge but for their good usage, so to speak.
I pass over Gaius Laelius, Philus, or Scipio; the praise attached to
that generation was, as you said, for speaking good Latin as much
as for uprightness of character, though it was not shared by all,
since we see that their contemporaries Caecilius and Pacuvius spoke
poorly; still, practically everyone then spoke correctly, unless they
had lived outside this city or some alien trait of home environment
had corrupted them. But the passage of time has surely brought about
deterioration in this respect both at Rome and in Greece. For there
has been an influx into both Athens and this city of many tainted
speakers from different places. All the more reason, then, why the
language must be purged and theory, which cannot be changed,
applied like a touchstone, and why the thoroughly faulty principle
of contemporary usage must be avoided.'

Cicero, *Brutus* 258

A still more thoroughgoing policy of restoring standards by reference to
regular grammatical principles was advocated by Julius Caesar, who is said
by Atticus to 'correct corrupt and defective usage with pure and uncorrupted usage through the application of theory' (*Brutus* 261): we may
usefully compare here the surviving fragments of Caesar's own work on
'Analogy' (i.e. a principle of regularity based on proportional reasoning),
see Funaioli (1907: 147).

Cicero, however, shared with Atticus the view that precedent too
was significant, as is made clear in his discussion of the phrases *in
Piraea/in Piraeum* in a letter to Atticus (7.3.1: he was following the
practice of Terence – consistently recommended as a model – in using a
preposition, but acknowledges his mistake in using a Greek ending for
the noun) and in the extract below from the *de Oratore*. This dialogue
was composed in 55 BC but is set in 91: participants include the distinguished orator-statesmen Marcus Antonius, grandfather of the famous Mark Antony, Publius Sulpicius Rufus, Quintus Lutatius Catulus, and
Lucius Licinius Crassus, who is used as Cicero's mouthpiece and is the
speaker of the passage below. It is important to note, however, that
Crassus/Cicero also insists here that *consuetudo* 'contemporary usage', i.e.
that of the educated hellenophile elite, whom he saw as inheritors of the
tradition of the 'Scipionic circle' and its leading literary lights such as
Terence, should take priority in the event of conflict, even if knowledge
of precedent can help to identify what is best in current practice (this use
of *consuetudo*, incidentally, is a loan-shift based on a well-established

use of Greek *synḗtheia* 'custom', reflecting the phrase *eiōthuîa diálektos* 'customary manner-of-speech' as already used in Aristotle's *Rhetoric*, cf. Law (2003)):

(2)   But all forms of elegance in speaking, though refined by a formal knowledge of letters, are nonetheless increased by reading the orators and poets; for the old masters, who were not yet able to embellish what they said, almost all spoke with a beautiful clarity, and those who have familiarized themselves with their language will be unable to speak anything but pure Latin even if they want to. However, those words shall not be employed which our contemporary usage [*consuetudo nostra*] does not employ, except sparingly, for embellishment, as I shall show; but one who has diligently and thoroughly immersed himself in the ancient writings will be able to employ current usage in such a way as to employ only the choicest elements.
Cicero, *de Oratore* 3.39

Furthermore, in the *Orator*, the last of his rhetorical works, written at the end of 46 BC in the form of a letter to Brutus, Cicero also takes strong exception to what he sees as excessive reliance on purely theoretical considerations, which might, for example, lead to the spelling *medidies* for *meridies* 'midday' in accordance with the etymology, cf. *medius* 'middle' (*Orator* 158). Once again he is largely content to allow contemporary educated usage, which he often equates with what is aesthetically pleasing, to take precedence, sometimes even when changes such as the appearance of aspirated plosives in native Latin words had no theoretical justification (*Orator* 160). The following extracts deal (a) with variant forms of the genitive plural of the 2nd declension (*-um* and *-orum*), (b) with short and long forms of the perfect and pluperfect active (e.g. perfect infinitive *amasse* vs. *amauisse* 'to have loved'), and (c) with the irregularities resulting from vowel weakening and compensatory lengthening:

(3)   (a)   And even ancient precedent is now being corrected, late in the day, by some people who find fault with these irregularities. So instead of **deum** atque hominum fidem they say *deorum*. Even so, I believe former generations were unaware of the latter: or contemporary usage was perhaps just starting to grant this licence. Thus the same poet (i.e. Ennius) who had used the now rather unusual short forms:
   patris mei **meum factum** *pudet*
in place of *meorum factorum*, and:
   texitur, **exitium** *examen rapit*

in place of *exitiorum*, does not say *liberum*, as many of us do when
we say *cupidos liberum* and *in liberum loco*, but speaks as those
regularizers of yours would like:

> *neque tu meum unquam in gremium extollas **liberorum***
> *ex te genus*

and again:

> *namque Aesculapi **liberorum***

But that other well-known poet (i.e. Pacuvius) in his *Chryses* says
not only:

> *ciues, antiqui amici maiorum **meum***

which was normal then, but also, more problematically for us:

> ***consilium** socii, **augurium** atque **extum** interpretes*

and then continues:

> *postquam **prodigium horriferum**, **portentum** pauos*

forms which are certainly not now normal in all neuter nouns. For
I would never say ***armum** iudicium* (though it is found in the same
author: *nihilne ad te iudicio **armum** accidit?*) as freely as I venture
to say *centuria **fabrum** et **procum***, as the census records have it:
and I absolutely never say ***duorum-uirorum** iudicium* or ***trium-
uirorum** capitalium* or *decem-**uirorum** stlitibus iudicandis*. And
yet Accius has said:

> *uideo sepulcra dua **duorum** corporum*

alongside:

> *mulier una **duom uirum**.*

I know what is etymologically correct, but sometimes I speak in
accordance with established licence (just as I cite this either in support of *deum* or in support of *deorum*), sometimes as is necessary,
when I say *trium-uirum* not *uirorum*, and *sestertium **nummum*** not
*sestertiorum **nummorum***, because in these cases there is no variation
in usage.

(b)   Moreover, they (i.e the regularizers) forbid us to say *nosse* and
iudicasse, and tell us to say *nouisse* and *iudicauisse*. As if we were
unaware, in the case of this type of word, both that the use of the
full form is correct and that that of the reduced form is customary.
Terence therefore has both:

> *eho tu, cognatum tuom non **noras**?*

and later:

> *Stilponem, inquam, **noueras**.*

. . .

On the one hand I would not find fault with ***scripsere** alii rem*
and on the other I feel that *scripserunt* is etymologically more
correct, but I gladly follow customary usage, which accedes to the

demands of the ears. [NB this is not his normal written practice, however, even in the more colloquial letters.]

(c)   Then in the case of compound words, how nice to have *insipientem* not *insapientem*, *iniquum* not *inaequuum*, *tricipitem* not *tricapitem*, *concisum* not *concaesum*. As a result, some also want to have *pertisum* (i.e. for *pertaesum*), which once again customary usage has not approved. And what could be neater than the following, which is the product not of nature but of custom: we say *indoctus* with a short first letter, *insanus* with a long one, *inhumanus* with a short one, *infelix* with a long one, and to be brief, in words with the same first letters as in *sapiens* and *felix*, *in-* is pronounced long, in all others short; likewise *composuit* but *consueuit*, *concrepuit* but *confecit*. Consider the etymology, it will find fault: consult the ears, they will approve: ask why this is so, they will say that it is pleasing: speech must indulge the pleasure of the ears . . . But if usage, untutored, makes so much sweetness, what, after all, do we think is to be demanded of actual theory and learning?

Cicero, *Orator* 155–6; 157; 159 and 161

Since, therefore, the available criteria of *Latinitas* were potentially in conflict, it is not at all surprising that there should have been disagreements about priorities, though in later generations it is clear that Cicero's approach, based on the primacy of educated usage refined by awareness of traditional practice, had largely predominated, cf. Quintilian's remarks:

(4)   Language is based on theory (*ratio*), antiquity (*antiquitas*), authority (*auctoritas*) and usage (*consuetudo*) . . . Usage, however [which is later defined as 'the agreed practice of educated men', 1.6.45], is the surest guide in speaking . . . Though all require the application of critical judgement.

Quintilian, *Institutio Oratoria* 1.6.1–3

By then, it seems, *ratio* was typically invoked as a way of resolving an existing indeterminacy rather than as a principle for the restoration of supposed purity (or even the invention of new forms to replace irregular established ones): it is argued, for example, in 1.1.5–6 that *funis* 'rope', which is treated as both masculine and feminine in earlier writers, must in fact be masculine on the grounds that the formally parallel *panis* 'bread' is masculine (even though there are probably as many nouns ending in *-is* that are feminine as masculine, and indeterminacy remained for a number of nouns with this ending).

In addition to the discussion of such formal criteria, however, there is also growing reference in Cicero's work to the need for good Latin to be characterized by *urbanitas*, a notion which, in the linguistic context, clearly owes something to the stylistic standards and achievements of the great Attic orators of the past, if not always to the specific ambitions of contemporary proponents of the Atticist movement (the speaker in (5) is the dramatic Cicero):

(5)   There was a Roman knight of around this same period, Gaius Titius, who in my opinion seems to have progressed about as far as any Latin orator could without Greek letters and a great deal of experience. His speeches have such verbal wit, such a wealth of supporting precedent, such urbanity, that they seem almost to have been written with an Attic pen.

Cicero, *Brutus* 167

Cicero leaves us in no doubt, however, that this *urbanitas*, in accordance with its etymology, is the inalienable property of the city of Rome, and specifically of its established elite (the only group to practice oratory in the Senate and the courts):

(6)   Then Brutus inquired: 'What characteristic do you assign to these orators you mention, who are, as it were, foreigners?' 'What do you think?' I said. 'Nothing distinct from that I ascribe to the city orators, with one exception, that their oratory is not, so to speak, coloured with a certain urbanity.' Brutus replied: 'What exactly is this urban colour?' 'I don't know', I replied, 'only I do know that there is such a thing. You will understand presently, Brutus, when you arrive in Gaul; then you will hear words not current in Rome, though these can be changed and unlearned; it is much more important that there is some essentially urban quality that rings and resounds in the voices of our orators. And this is apparent not only in orators but also in others. I remember Titus Tinca of Placentia, a very amusing chap, being engaged in a battle of wits with my friend Quintus Granius the public crier . . . But even though he made just as many ridiculous interventions, Granius kept overwhelming him with some indefinable native-Roman flavour.'

Cicero, *Brutus* 170–2

But the key factor behind Cicero's growing insistence on *urbanitas* was almost certainly the massive influx of rural poor into Rome at the beginning of the first century BC, which had quickly re-energized the determination of the elite to distinguish maximally its own usage and practice from those of the newcomers (cf. (1) above). Subsequently, populist aristocrats seeking to challenge the authority of the Senate (*Populares*) might seek to demonstrate their solidarity with the masses by adopting key 'rustic' forms now also characteristic of the speech of the urban poor: to this end Cicero's enemy P. Clodius even changed his name from Claudius. It should be no surprise, then, that the notion of urbanity soon came to be contrasted overtly with 'rusticity', producing a sharp polar opposition: and despite its inherently old-fashioned quality, any trace of linguistic rusticity in his own class was seen by Cicero as a serious fault, as the following passage from the *de Oratore*, dealing specifically with pronunciation, makes abundantly clear (Crassus is again the speaker):

(7) But there is one fault that some deliberately affect: a rustic and countrified pronunciation (*rustica uox et agrestis*) appeals to certain people, so that their speech, if it has this sound, may seem all the more to retain the virtue of antiquity: just as your friend Lucius Cotta, Catulus, seems to me to take pleasure in heaviness of speech (*grauitate linguae*) and a countrified tone of voice (*sonoque uocis agresti*), and thinks that what he says will seem old-fashioned if it has a thoroughly rural quality (*plane . . . rusticanum*). But what appeals to me is *your* tone and delicacy (*tuus sonus et subtilitas ista*); I do not mean of language (*uerborum*) – though this is critical, yet it is the product of method (*ratio*), taught by letters (*litterae*) and reinforced by the custom of both reading and speaking (*consuetudo et legendi et loquendi*) – but this sweetness that comes from your lips: just as among the Greeks this is the peculiar property of the inhabitants of Attica, so in Latin speech it is above all the property of this city . . . Our citizens study letters less than the Latins, yet there is not one of the city folk of your acquaintance, among whom there is a minimum of letters, who does not easily beat Quintus Valerius Soranus, the most learned of all who wear the toga, in smoothness of voice (*lenitate uocis*) and in actual control of the lips and tone (*ipso oris pressu et sono*).

Cicero, *de Oratore* 3.42–3

Thus respect for precedent turns out, unsurprisingly, to be a *desideratum* only when it can plausibly be equated with a traditionally *urban* purity of diction (Crassus once again is the speaker):

(8) Consequently, since there is a distinct way of speaking peculiar to the race and city of Rome, in which nothing can be found fault with, nothing can displease, nothing can be censured, nothing sound or

smell of foreign parts, let us follow this, and learn to avoid not only rustic roughness but also outlandish foreign ways. For my part, when I hear my wife's mother Laelia – it is certainly easier for women to preserve the old ways uncorrupted, because they lack experience of conversation with large numbers and always retain what they have first learned – yet the way I hear her, I seem to be listening to Plautus or Naevius: she has a voice the very sound of which is so direct and straightforward that it seems to bring no trace of ostentation or mimicry. I therefore take the view that her father, her ancestors, spoke like this, not harshly like the man I mentioned, not broadly, not rustically, not with gaps, but firmly and evenly and smoothly.

Cicero, de Oratore 3.44–5

Accordingly, whenever archaisms had a rustic ring to them, Cicero had no hesitation in prioritizing the requirements of *urbanitas* by once again following the contemporary *consuetudo* of the city's ruling class. Some of the relevant forms and variants had once been typical of Roman Latin too, as we have seen in Chapters IV and V, but even when Cicero's generation was conscious of this, such considerations could never have been allowed to outweigh the contemporary Roman perception of the features in question as outlandish and substandard. Some examples of stigmatized rusticity are given in the following extracts:

(9)   (a)   Consequently, our friend Cotta, whose broad pronunciation [cf. (7) above], Sulpicius, you sometimes imitate by deleting the letter I and saying a very full E [i.e. by pronouncing the letters *-ei-* as [e:] rather than [i:], by now an exclusively rustic trait], seems to me to imitate not the orators of old but farmhands.

Cicero, de Oratore 3.46

(b)   What's more, they used to drop the last letter of those words whose last two letters were the same as in *optimus*, unless a vowel followed, something which now seems quite rustic but was once rather refined. So at that time this was not the stumbling block in poetry that the 'new' poets now avoid. For we used to say:
  *qui est **omnibu'** princeps*   [Ennius]
not *omnibus princeps*, and:
  *uita illa **dignu'** locoque*   [Lucilius]
not *dignus*.

Cicero, Orator 161

(c)   . . . so that now there is doubt whether certain words should be pronounced with *i* or with *u*, like *optumus* and *maxumus*, in respect of which we should take note that it was the ancient language which had the fuller sound [i.e. [u]] and, as Cicero says, a countrified quality, and that in general those generations preferred to pronounce and write such words with *u*.

[The change in orthography to -*i*- is said by Varro, as cited in Cassiodorus (see Keil 1857–80: VII.150), to have been due to Julius Caesar.]

Velius Longus (second-century AD grammarian,
see Keil 1857–80: VII.49), quoting Cicero

Before turning in the next section to a more detailed examination of what was happening in this critical period, we may sum up the discussion so far by observing that even in Cicero's time there was clearly the beginning of a consensus about the set of criteria for determining *Latinitas*. In this regard we may compare the list given by Cicero's contemporary Varro (preserved in Diomedes's *Ars Grammatica*, see Keil 1857–80: I.439), comprising *natura* 'nature', *analogia* 'proportional regularity' (an important element, along with etymology, of *ratio*), *consuetudo* '(educated) usage', and *auctoritas* 'authority', with Quintilian's 'definitive' list given above. Furthermore, despite obvious disagreements, there seems already to have been a body of opinion, with Cicero among its proponents, in favour of a variety which, as a priority, should embody the usage of the educated urban elite (i.e. a *consuetudo* characterized by *urbanitas*), but which must also take due note of the best practice of the past (thus acknowledging both *uetustas* 'antiquity' and *auctoritas*), albeit with a final outcome subject to minor correction and regularization according to grammatical principle (*ratio*).

In the end, of course, theoretical debate in such matters, necessarily based on a range of personal prejudices and preferences often inconsistently applied, proved to be rather less important than the slowly evolving convergence of practice 'on the ground', as various options became increasingly accepted or gradually fell from favour. Cicero was instinctively wise in grasping this crucial point in an era when other theorists were advocating a more radical approach to regularization and, on occasion, an artificiality at odds with contemporary intuitions of acceptability.

6.4   Development and Selection

6.4.1   Introduction

As already noted, one of the most striking consequences of the encounter with the Greek world was to promote not only a range of new syntactic and stylistic developments in the higher varieties of Latin, but also to instigate the borrowing, innovation and adaptation of vocabulary on a massive scale and in many different fields (see Palmer 1954: ch. 5 for a traditional account). For the earliest periods it is often impossible to know, given the very limited nature of the available sources, whether a word attested in a single literary fragment bears testimony to the inventiveness of an individual or rather reflects the Latinity of its times more generally, having simply fallen out of favour in later times.

But things are much clearer once the history of words can be better followed through. In the domain of technical vocabulary, for example, a careful examination of contexts of use can often show that words which once belonged to very specific domains had acquired more extended meanings over time, whether directly under the influence of Greek parallels in the ongoing effort to expand the expressive range of the language, or independently, by internal processes of semantic and metaphorical evolution. Obvious examples of the latter include *puto* ('trim/prune' > 'assess' > 'take a view, think (that)'), *opportunus* ('at the port' > 'convenient, suitable'), *secundus/aduersus* ('following/facing' (of winds etc.) > 'favourable/hostile'). Indeed, throughout the history of the language, the meanings of words originating in different professional or technical spheres were regularly adapted for wider use, including new specialized uses in more abstract domains of discourse. This process typically involved a period of experimentation and debate, and not all attempts to establish an extended use found ready acceptance. Rosén (1999: 43) gives the example of *inhibere*, already used in Augustan poetry with a general meaning of holding back movement, but criticized by Cicero (*Epistulae ad Atticum* 13.21.3) as a translation of *epékhein* in the philosophical sense of 'suspend judgement' on the grounds that this was in conflict with its primary nautical sense of 'row backwards', which clearly involves a reversal rather than a suspension of movement.

We may also note that words whose meaning had evolved in this way could then displace existing 'core' vocabulary items with which they had come into competition, sometimes pushing them into the colloquial register (as with *bellus*, under pressure from *pulcher*, which had shifted its meaning from 'perfect/fine' > 'beautiful'), sometimes into the literary domain (with the consequence that many then began to seem archaic, as with *reor* 'think', under pressure from *puto*, cf. Cicero *de Oratore* 3.153), and sometimes even replacing them altogether.

Thus even though rampant lexical creativity and experimentation were inevitable concomitants of the development of literary and technical genres, there was from the beginning a powerful countervailing force at work, operating just as much in the lexicon and in matters of word formation as in inflectional morphology and syntax, namely the model of the Greek *Koine* and the associated belief in the need for a linguistic 'norm'. These factors consistently militated against apparent redundancy or unmotivated variation, and the consequence was a continual review of resources and a constant weeding out of 'unnecessary' or 'unacceptable' options across the board. Since a great deal of information about morphological variation in the inflectional paradigms of Old Latin compared with those of Classical Latin has already been provided in previous chapters, we shall focus here on examples taken from the fields of word formation and syntax.

6.4.2 Word formation

While for all the reasons already stated the inventory of lexical items shows a significant increase in the period under review, there is nevertheless an overall reduction in the productivity of many types of word formation, often associated with a redistribution of their once core functions (see Rosén 1999: Part II, ch. 1). A particular case in point is the class of relational adjectives derived from nouns, which express meanings overlapping with those of the adnominal genitive. Cato's *de Agri Cultura*, for example, is full of such formations, many of them attested there for the first time. Typical examples from the corpus of Early Latin include *folia laurea* 'laurel leaves' (Cato *de Agri Cultura* 70.1), *amorem puerilem* 'a boy's love' (CIL I² 1216, first century BC), and *facinus muliebre* 'a woman's crime' (Plautus *Truculentus* 809). By the time of Caesar and Cicero, however, the productivity of adjectival formations of this type had declined dramatically, with the use of the genitive of corresponding nouns steadily gaining ground. Thus novel formations involving characteristically relational suffixes such as *-acus*, *-icus*, or *-ticus* become quite rare, while adjectives with independently 'meaningful' suffixes, such as *-osus* 'full of', *-atus* 'endowed with', and *-eus* 'made of' continue to gain ground. In Livy, for example, there are twelve new adjectives in *-atus* (of the type *linteatus* 'dressed in linen'), eight in *-osus* (e.g. *niuosus* 'snowy' and *siluosus* 'wooded'), and one in *-eus* (viz. *gramineus* 'grassy').

Similar observations apply to deverbal nouns, which originally functioned as simple gerunds and as such retained a verbal construction, cf. *quid tibi hanc tactio est* (Plautus *Poenulus* 1308), 'what business do you have touching her?', where the deverbal noun *tactio* 'touching' takes an accusative object (*hanc*) like the corresponding verb *tango* 'touch'. In this case the nouns in question lost ground both to the infinitive and to the gerund and gerundive, typically acquiring in the process more concrete, as well as more idiosyncratic meanings, while simultaneously losing the ability to take objects when 'transitive', cf. *exercitus* 'exercising' > 'army', *tactio* 'touching' > 'sense of touch', etc.

A concomitant of this development was a radical pruning of the sets of derivatives associated with a given verbal root, many of which had remained in competition for as long as the nouns in question retained their original function. Thus pairs such as *aditio* and *aditus* 'approaching', or *abitio* and *abitus* 'leaving' ceased to exist side by side, and only *aditus* 'arrival' and *abitus* 'departure' survive into Classical Latin, the choice here correlated with the fact that *-tus* was more productive in the classical language than *-tio/-sio*, the latter becoming increasingly restricted to derivations from frequentative and compound verb forms (e.g. *hortatio* 'encouragement', *consensio* 'agreement'). Similar remarks apply also to denominal and de-adjectival nominalizations of the type *amicitia* or *iuuentus*, where once again the variety of permissible formations was significantly reduced (with variants such as *amatio* or *iuuentas/iuuenta* also disappearing).

When doublets, or more rarely triplets, survived, there was in general an established difference in meaning (e.g. *ambitus* 'a circuit, illegal canvassing' vs. *ambitio* 'proper canvassing') or a tendency to try to distinguish them in meaning, sometimes by assigning them to different styles/registers (e.g. *pulcher* vs. *bellus* 'beautiful'). In other cases we might argue that differences in formation *per se* led to an intuitive semantic differentiation whereby more complex derivational patterns came to be associated with more general/abstract meanings, as in *inuidia* 'envy' vs. *inuidentia* 'envying', *ira* 'anger' vs. *iracundia* 'irascibility', *uitium* 'fault/vice' vs. *uitiositas* 'faultiness/viciousness', etc. This is not to say that genuine synonyms did not persist at any given time, like *sonus* and *sonitus* 'sound', or, in the domain of neologisms, *infinitio* (Cicero *de Finibus* 1.6.21) and *infinitas* (Cicero *de Natura Deorum* 1.26.73) 'boundlessness', but there can be no doubt that such a state of affairs ran counter to the currently influential view that redundancy was inherently undesirable, cf. *reprehendunt cum ab eadem uoce plura sunt uocabula declinata*, 'they [i.e. the analogists, who sought regularity] find fault when several nouns are derived from the same expression' (Varro, *de Lingua Latina* 9.90). In the event, Cicero's experiment with *infinitio* proved to be short-lived (this is the only attested example), and *infinitas* duly became the established term.

Finally, we may consider the case of de-adjectival adverbs, for which in Classical Latin the truly productive patterns were effectively reduced to *-e* for adverbs derived from adjectives of the 2nd/1st declensions, and *-(t)er* for adverbs derived from adjectives of the 3rd declension. Early Latin by contrast shows much richer and far less systematic patterns of adverb formation, with highly productive use of several other endings such as *-(i)tus*, *-(a)tim*, etc. (Later Latin, interestingly, provides evidence for a revival of the latter, especially in technical contexts, as well as for the spread of *-(t)er* beyond its classical domain.) The obvious result was considerable duplication of formation, with sets such as *large, largiter, largitus* 'plentifully' and *publice, publiciter, publicitus* 'publically/at public expense', much in evidence in the Old Latin corpus. Though there is still some wavering in Cicero in specific cases (e.g. *diuinitus* and *diuine, turbulenter* and *turbulente*, etc.), and while authors sometimes disagree (e.g. Caesar uses *largiter* while Cicero prefers *large*), the overall trend in the late Republic is already clear, namely a steady reduction of the options in the direction of the 'norm' as stated above. Unsurprisingly, where pairs survive, some effort is made once again to use them with different meanings, as with *antiquitus* = 'of old' vs. *antique* = 'in the old way', etc.

6.4.3 Syntax

We have noted on several occasions in earlier chapters that it is a characteristic of Old Latin to offer a variety of constructions from which Classical Latin made a selection (see also Rosén 1999: Part II, ch. 2), and this is clearly true of expressions of obligation. Thus alongside the modal verbs and periphrases taking infinitival complements, like *debeo* 'I ought', *oportet* 'it is binding', and *necesse est* 'it is necessary', the classical language also makes extensive use of the gerundive with *esse* in this function (e.g. *praeponenda [est] diuitiis gloria*, Cicero *Topica* 22.84, 'glory is to be preferred to riches', etc.). But other options previously available in Old Latin were either eliminated or at least severely restricted. Thus the quite widespread use of abstract nouns in *-tio/-sio + esse* to express general requirements (e.g. *oleae et ficorum insitio est per uer*, Cato *de Agri Cultura* 41.2, 'the grafting of olives and figs is (to be) done in spring') had very largely disappeared by Cicero's time in favour of gerundival constructions. Similarly, both *opus* 'need' and *usus* 'use' were used *inter alia* with the ablative to specify what was required (*usus* almost entirely preclassical in this sense), and the neuter of the perfect passive participle was not infrequently employed in this role as an abstract noun, as in *quod parato opus est para* (Terence *Andria* 523), 'prepare what needs to be prepared' (lit. 'that for which there is need of preparation'). In Cicero, by contrast, there is just one strictly parallel example, namely *cur properato opus esset* (*pro Milone* 49), 'why there should be need of haste'. The only other example, *opus fuit Hirtio conuento* (*ad Atticum* 10.4.11), 'there was a need for a meeting with Hirtius', is also of a type paralleled in Old Latin, but is more complex. The literal meaning is 'there was a need for [Hirtius having-been-met]', where the whole noun + participle expression complements *opus* as a noun phrase of the type *[Hannibal uictus] Romanos metu liberauit*, 'the defeat of Hannibal [lit. "Hannibal defeated"] freed the Romans from fear.' Both these uses are clearly residual at best, and even though the simple construction resurfaces in Livy (e.g. *maturato opus est*, 'there is need of haste', 8.13), the few examples have a distinctly formulaic look. In general, the use of *opus* with participial complements fell out of favour in the higher registers of classical prose, while in more colloquial styles they were replaced by infinitives and/or accusative + infinitive constructions (e.g. *nunc opus est [te animo ualere]*, Cicero *ad Familiares* 16.4.2, 'now there is a need for you to be strong in mind').

Similarly, the old use of the 2nd person of the present subjunctive, whether positively to express a command or with *ne* to express a prohibition, came to be restricted in Classical Latin to express only general precepts (e.g. *cum absit, ne requiras*, 'when it [i.e. that blessing] is absent, do not yearn for it', Cicero *de Senectute* 33), while the earlier use of *ne* with an imperative survived only in colloquial styles and in poetry (e.g. *ne fugite hospitium*, 'do not shun our hospitality', Vergil *Aeneid* 7. 202). Otherwise direct commands are expressed in Classical Latin by the imperative, and prohibitions by *noli/nolite* 'be unwilling' + the present infinitive (avoided in poetry, in part for metrical reasons, but also apparently felt to be 'prosaic') or *ne* + the perfect, i.e. perfective, subjunctive. These two options are employed on more or less equal terms by Cicero, but the latter was comparatively rare in Old Latin, and is also less popular than its rival in imperial literature, though later writers seem to have had personal preferences, and it is perhaps no surprise that more archaizing genres like history tend to show a higher incidence of *ne* + perfect subjunctive, as in Tacitus.

As a final example of elimination, we may briefly note here the general abandonment in Classical Latin of the independent use of the future perfect as a perfective future in main clauses. Examples without any suggestion of the anteriority of one future event over another are common enough in Old Latin, though it is perhaps significant that most involve 1st-person verb forms, in which the semantic component of personal intent particularly favours a perfective reading of the future action: e.g. *deus sum, commutauero* (Plautus *Amphitryo* 53), 'I am a god, I'll change it [the play]'; *cras habuero, uxor, ego tamen conuiuium* (Plautus *Casina* 786), 'tomorrow, my good wife, I shall have the party.' It may well be, therefore, that this usage represents the final residue of a once more widespread aspectual distinction. There are, however, contexts in which some other event is implied as a reference point, as in *quaere: ego hinc apscessero aps te huc interim* (Plautus *Miles Gloriosus* 200), 'conduct your search: in the meantime [i.e. before you have completed it] I shall have gone hence from you to here', and it was presumably from this kind of usage that the notion of temporal anteriority first developed. By the time of Classical Latin, however, this component of meaning had virtually been grammaticalized, with the only regular use of the future perfect being to mark the anteriority of a future event denoted by a subordinate clause over that of a future event denoted by the main clause, as in *qui prior strinxerit ferrum, eius uictoria erit* (Livy 24.38.5), 'whoever first draws [lit. will have drawn] his sword, his shall be the victory.' When the future perfect is used in both subordinate and main clauses in Classical Latin the meaning is one of simultaneous occurrence in the future, i.e. in contexts where a perfective meaning in the main clause is again required, as in *qui Antonium oppresserit, is bellum confecerit* (Cicero *ad Familiares* 10.19.2), 'he who crushes [lit. will have crushed] Antony will (also) have finished the war.' In general, however, the continued use of the future perfect in main clauses is rather colloquial, and in such contexts we sometimes still find apparently aspectual uses of 1st-person verb forms reminiscent of those of Roman comedy: e.g. *nusquam facilius hanc miserrimam uitam uel sustentabo uel abiecero* (Cicero *ad Atticum* 3.19.1), 'nowhere else will I tolerate [future – imperfective force] this utterly wretched life more easily, or more easily discard it [future perfect – perfective force].'

Alongside selection and elimination, however, there were also novel developments, and the important case of participial constructions has already been dealt with under the heading of Greek influence (see 6.2.2 above). We may simply add here that, though the present participle underwent rapid evolution as a verbal form in parallel with the perfect passive participle, particularly in free-standing predicative functions (i.e. = an adverbial clause), the future participle remained the poor relation throughout, with its principal use still the construction of a periphrasis with *esse*, and extended predicative, as well as attributive, uses remaining very rare (up to Cicero's time, for example, the only future participle used adjectivally with any frequency is *futurus* 'future/to-come'). The expansion of the range of the present participle, however, especially in the ablative absolute construction (e.g. *iubente Vercingetorige*, lit. 'with Vercingetorix ordering' (Caesar *de Bello Gallico* 7.26.1)), brought pressure to bear on the ancient circumstantial use of the ablative of verbal nouns in *-tus/-sus* + genitive (of the type *Caesaris concessu*, *de Bello Gallico* 7.20.2, 'with Caesar's permission'), and Rosén (1999: 108) puts forward the still to be fully explored hypothesis that the latter survived primarily not as a free variant of the ablative absolute, with its wide range of circumstantial meanings, but rather when the required meaning was in the general range of instrumentality.

A number of other developments and refinements in the verbal system may also be briefly mentioned here. The generalization of the subjunctive to all finite subordinate clauses expressing an indirect report, i.e. as a mechanical marker of what is not vouched for by the writer, has already been discussed in 5.5. A further difference between the modal usage of the Old Latin verb system and that of the classical language is the shift in the meaning of the present and imperfect subjunctives as used in wishes and conditional sentences. Thus there are still examples in Old Latin of wishes in which the present subjunctive is used to refer not only to the future, as standardly in Classical Latin, but also counterfactually to the present, for which the classical language normally uses the imperfect subjunctive (the present is occasionally retained as an archaism in poetry): e.g. *utinam nunc stimulus in manu mihi sit!* (Plautus *Asinaria* 418), 'I wish I had a goad in my hand now!' Similarly, the imperfect subjunctive was still regularly used in counterfactual wishes to refer to the past (e.g. *utinam te di prius perderent quam periisti e patria tua*, Plautus *Captiui* 537, 'I wish the gods had done away with you before you were lost to your country'), even though it was also starting to be used to refer counterfactually to the present, in the classical way. Correspondingly, the present subjunctive could still be used in conditional sentences in Old Latin to refer counterfactually to the present as well as to denote future possibilities, while the imperfect was still widely used to refer counter-factually to the past, even though it was also starting to be used to refer to the present, an uncertainty that had already created a situation in which the pluperfect subjunctive could optionally be employed in place of the imperfect to make it clear that past time reference was intended. Unsurprisingly, therefore, literary Latin removed these 'unfortunate' ambiguities, in large part by the time of Terence, by using the present subjunctive to refer to the future, and the imperfect subjunctive and pluperfect subjunctive respectively to refer to the present and the past. It should be noted, however, that at least until the time of Livy the imper-fect subjunctive continued to be used to refer to the past in certain special circumstances, i.e. with the distinctive sense of 'it was likely/going to be the case that X': e.g. *quas si occupauissent, mare totum in sua potestate haberent* (Caesar *de Bello Ciuili* 3.111.4), meaning 'if they had seized these (ships) [pluperfect], they were likely/destined to have the whole sea in their power [imperfect]', rather than simply 'would have had'.

As a final example of development in the verb system we may note the case of the passive voice (on which see especially Rosén 1999: 124–37). While much still remains uncertain, there appears to have been a pro-gressive evolution of the passive voice into a fully-fledged paradigmatic alternative to the active that could then be freely exploited in a range of discourse functions, particularly the maintenance of topical cohesion and/or the introduction of focal contrasts in a piece of extended narrative or exposition. This development entailed greater use of agentive expres-sions introduced by *a(b)* 'by', at least in so far as clauses with passive verbs were now being exploited as semantically, if not pragmatically, equivalent variants of active sentences in which the agent was specified of necessity. Thus the choice of a passive verb might, according to context, either background the subject in order to maintain an established discourse topic or foreground it in order to introduce a new one: a concomitant effect of the former, therefore, would be at least implicitly to focalize the expressed agent as new/contrastive information, and of the latter to background it as a piece of old information.

In Old Latin, by contrast, the passive voice was usually employed precisely to avoid specification of the agent, whether because it was unknown, unmentionable, or simply immaterial to the argument. The presence of agent-phrases was therefore typically motivated by specific grammatical circumstances, such as a desire to disambiguate accusative and infinitive constructions, when both agent and patient were animate, through selection of a passive infinitive with an agentive *a(b)*-phrase (in the active equivalent both the subject and the object would be in the accusative case), or the need to specify an agent with perfect participles, most of which were inherently passive and so allowed no other option.

The new developments did not, however, undermine the more traditional uses of the passive, and in many cases we can see both factors at work, as in the following extract from Cicero's *pro Milone: nam si umquam de bonis et fortibus uiris, si umquam de bene meritis ciuibus potestas uobis iudicandi fuit, si denique umquam locus amplissimorum ordinum delectis uiris **datus est**, ut sua studia erga fortis et bonos ciuis . . . declararent . . .* (2.4), 'for if the power of judgement over good and brave men has ever lain in your hands, or over meritorious citizens, if in fact the opportunity has ever been given to chosen men of the most distinguished ranks to declare their support for brave and good citizens . . .'. Here the agent of the gift of the opportunity is suppressed as non-specific and essentially irrelevant, but this independently motivated selection of the passive voice also allows the two principal conditional clauses to take the same grammatical form, so that both 'the power of judgement' and 'the opportunity to act' function in parallel as the subjects of intransitive verbs, thereby first establishing and then continuing a common theme (viz. the placing of men of good will in situations in which they can and should benefit their fellow citizens) in a formally consistent way.

The impersonal use of the passive, however, stands apart from these developments, and throughout the history of the language had the primary function of foregrounding the action over those participating in it. Agents are therefore normally suppressed (there can be no patient arguments present by definition), and on the rare occasions when an agent phrase is present, it is almost always of very low thematic salience, as in *pugnatum est ab utrisque acriter* (*Caesar de Bello Gallico* 4.26.1), 'the fighting was bitter on both sides', where the *ab*-phrase is in fact hardly agentive in force at all. The main exception to this principle is the idiomatic use of *factum (est) a me* 'it was done by me' as an anaphoric pro-verb with a near-compulsory focalized adverb, as often in comedy: e.g. *ne a me memores malitiose de hac re factum* (Plautus *Casina* 394), lit. 'so that you do not suggest that it was done **treacherously** by me [i.e. that I acted treacherously] in this matter', where the verb is simply a device for referring back in a non-specific way to an earlier event and some fur-ther specification of the manner in which it took place is clearly required.

Enough examples have now been given of the processes of selection and development that came to shape the overall form of Classical Latin, and it will be useful at this point to step back from the specifics and to look at the developed form of the standard language in more general terms, dealing first with the language of literary prose, and then with the language of poetry.

6.5   A General Overview of Classical Literary Latin

6.5.1   *The language of Classical Latin prose*

The major prose genres of oratory, history, philosophy, letters and, at a slightly later date, fiction, display a range of styles which nevertheless share one crucial attribute: they are all works of conscious art and artifice, and the Latin employed in them, despite being the most familiar variety of the language to modern readers, is anything but 'natural', even in the case of epistolography, the genre which appears to approximate most closely to the colloquial speaking style of the educated elite (cf. Russell 1990: Introduction).

As with poetry, prose writing began as part of the literary awakening inspired by the culture of the Hellenistic world, and we have already seen that the rhetorical works of Cato and others show the direct influence of Greek rhetoric from the outset alongside the exploitation of traditional native devices for raising the stylistic level. By the early first century BC there was a solid body of rhetorical teaching available in Latin, using Latin examples (e.g. the *Rhetorica ad Herennium*, wrongly attributed by tra-dition to Cicero), and it is not difficult to trace its influence in the dif-ferent styles adopted in subsequent work of all periods. But Cicero, as we have seen, played a unique and pivotal role in the development of Latin prose style, and all subsequent writers, even those who deliberately reacted against his particular manner, could not but acknowledge his unique position in the history of Latin letters, and his exceptional powers of inven-tion and controlled use of rhetorical figures eventually made his speeches 'classic' texts for classroom study. But great though Cicero's impact was in the field of rhetoric, it was his development of a varied discursive style for philosophical and other technical exposition that eventually proved to be most influential, providing a model for written intellectual discourse throughout antiquity and into the middle ages and beyond, not only in Latin, but also in the vernacular European languages when these at last began to be used for such purposes.

It is important to appreciate, however, that his overall influence was neither immediate nor overwhelming, and in this regard we should bear in mind that Cicero never attempted to write history. It is therefore no accident that the rhythmical, periodic character of Ciceronian prose was, quite consciously, avoided in the historical tradition represented by writers such as Sallust (86–34 BC) and Tacitus (c.AD 56–c.120), in which other forms of ornamentation had quickly become established as a long-term basis for the genre-conditioning of prose style: in particular, the linguistic archaism and sharply antithetical rhetorical style of the Greek historian Thucydides (c.455–400 BC) provided an important precedent for Roman successors in the field. Thus historians of the school of Sallust and Pollio (76 BC–AD 5) offered a powerful rival model to Ciceronian style, as did the adoption of a more pointed epigrammatic style in the early imperial period associated with the current fashion for declamation. The philosophical works of the younger Seneca (c.4 BC–AD 65) are a prime example of the latter, and many Renaissance writers still saw this as a valid alternative to Ciceronian practice. But even Seneca was a dedicated reader of Cicero, and his choice of the epistolary form surely owes something to the publication of Cicero's letters to Atticus. Significantly, Quintilian (c.AD 33–100) was already critical of Seneca's style (10.1.125–31), and himself taught and practised a developed form of Ciceronian prose writing, while Tacitus, who carefully avoids Ciceronian traits in his historical writing, also followed a generally Ciceronian approach in his *Dialogus de Oratoribus*.

Only in later imperial times, in the overtly philhellenic era of Hadrian (AD 76–138) and Antoninus Pius (AD 86–161), was there a truly marked reaction to Cicero, when a fashion for learned archaism and Old Latin writers like Cato, undoubtedly associated with the then thriving Atticist movement of the so-called Second Sophistic, came into vogue (see especially the work of the orator and epistolographer Fronto, c.AD 100–170). In some cases this antiquarianism was also linked to a reversion to the rhetorical techniques of Gorgias (c.483–375 BC: e.g. the emotive accumulation of vocabulary and use of rapid successions of short antithetical clauses, with emphasis on metaphor, word-play, poetic vocabulary and special rhythmic effects), which had previously been revived in the Greek-speaking world as part of the so-called Asianist reaction to the earliest Atticizing trends, and had resurfaced in the period of the Second Sophistic as Atticism once again gathered pace. This is particularly apparent in the work of the novelist Apuleius (born *c*.AD 125), who marks the beginning of a period in which literary pretentiousness and erudition of an increasingly elaborated kind came to characterize much belletristic prose writing.

Despite such differences and developments in matters of style, however, there is much that remains constant in Latin prose writing, especially as regards standards of grammatical correctness, which provided the backbone of the drive for formality and elevation from the everyday norm. Thus with the exception of deliberate deviations from the established rules of grammar, whether occasionally for special effect in letter writing and other lighter forms of composition such as Seneca's satirical *Apocolocyntosis*, or in a more sustained fashion, as in Petronius's imitation of the language of freedmen in the *Cena Trimalchionis*, the impression of Latin as a language subject to the strictest morphological and syntactic regulation is consistently maintained in elevated prose.

By contrast, some forms of technical writing, like the architectural treatise of Vitruvius (first century BC) and subliterary historical commentaries like the *de Bello Hispaniensi* (almost certainly composed by one of Caesar's officers), show more regular 'lapses' from classical norms, in part due to simple lack of control of the artificial rules and conventions on the part of the authors concerned, who clearly struggle at times to 'raise their game' on the basis of a limited literary and rhetorical education. In the latter work, for example, we find a number of colloquial characteristics used with some frequency, such as *bene* = 'very' with adjectives (used by Cicero only in his letters), *ipse* = non-emphatic anaphoric 'he' (a probable weakening and extension of the emphatic use where the expected demonstrative may be omitted, = 'that very one just mentioned'), the use of indicatives in circumstantial *cum*-clauses (*cum ad eum locum uenerunt*, ch. 3) and subjunctives in factual relative clauses (*nostri, qui fuissent equites Romani et senatores*, 'our men, who were Roman knights and senators', ch. 22), or of verbs of 'saying' followed by *quod*-clauses (*renuntiauerunt quod Pompeium in potestatem haberent*, 'they announced that they had Pompey in their power', ch. 36, which also reveals a poor grasp of the accusative/ablative contrast in prepositional phrases as well as the expected use of the subjunctive to mark reported content). Many of these features are simply 'normal' for non-literary Latin of the period: some continue earlier popular usage as seen in authors such as Plautus, later resurfacing more routinely in imperial vulgar Latin, some represent colloquial innovations of later times. Others, however, such as the sporadic use of unmotivated subjunctives in relative clauses, simply reflect the author's uncertainty about good usage. Lack of variation in vocabulary, poor organization of material, and repetitive forms of connection, especially involving the use of connecting relatives, also bear testimony to this writer's limited resources.

Vocabulary, no less than grammar, was another sure marker of intended stylistic level. Greek words, for example, normally indicate a familiar and colloquial tone (as in Cicero's letters to intimates who shared his generally hellenophile outlook (cf. Adams 2003: 297–347)) or mark a technical field in which the Greeks had already paved the way, and as such were regularly avoided in literary composition. Furthermore, ordinary Latin vocabulary for everyday things was also strongly disfavoured, most particularly in history, and writers often resort to periphrasis rather than risk 'lowering the tone': for example, Tacitus's *amissa magna ex parte per quae egeritur humus aut exciditur caespes* (*Annals* 1.65), 'most of the tools by which soil is shifted or turf cut out were lost', provides the original motivation for the expression 'to call a spade a spade'.

Correspondingly, higher level historical writing also allows both grammatical forms and lexical items which belonged outside the range of normal usage of their time, in many cases imparting an archaic or even poetic quality. We may note here, for example, Tacitus's liking for the old 3rd person plural perfect ending *-ere*, and his bold adoption of much apparently Vergilian vocabulary, such as *breuia* 'shoals', negative adjectives like *incustoditus* 'unguarded', *indefessus* 'unwearied', *intemeratus* 'undefiled', *inuiolabilis* 'invulnerable', and verbs such as *celerare* 'to hasten', *densere* 'to thicken', *notescere* 'to become known', *secundare* 'to favour', *ualescere* 'to grow strong'. History, however, despite this verbal proximity to poetry and its consistently high tone, tended very carefully to avoid the additional formality of established rhetorical rhythms (see below on clausulae).

Prose writing in general also made much use of elaborated 'periods', though, as noted, not all writers followed the Ciceronian model, and many deliberately reacted to it. A period may be defined as a complete syntactical unit made up of several clauses (including here participial expressions), in which the various aspects of a given situation or the various points of a given argument are brought together into a single complex structure in which the overall force of the whole can only be appreciated at the point at which all of its component parts have been heard or read. But where Cicero preferred structures composed of main clauses controlling a range of balanced subordinate clauses (that could be subordinated to one another as well as to a main clause), a property known as *concinnitas* 'elegant joining', the historians and others seeking to avoid a Ciceronian style tended instead to adopt a looser form of period in which a range of participial and other phrasal adjuncts was attached to a main clause in a less integrated way, so that the subordinated material is organized not as a set of parallel clauses but with an eye to variety and asymmetrical contrast (*inconcinnitas*). The former type therefore aims to convey an effect of logically coherent argument (good for forensic oratory and philosophy), while the latter seeks to provide a more striking form of expression that remains chronologically sequential while underplaying logical connection (good for dramatic historical narrative).

The following brief extracts from Cicero and Tacitus should help to make this contrast clearer. The first is taken from the beginning of the revised version of Cicero's speech in defence of Titus Annius Milo following the death of his political rival Clodius in a street fight in 52 BC. (The original was an unmitigated failure, as Cicero's nerve failed in the context of the military presence in the forum necessitated by the prevailing tension and violence in Rome; following his conviction, Milo later wrote from exile in Marseille that it was a good job things had worked out as they did, as delivery of the published version might well have prevented him from enjoying the fine local mullet.)

(10)   Cicero, *pro Milone* 1

etsi   uereor, iudices,   ne turpe   sit   pro fortissimo uiro   dicere
though fear-1sg, judges-VOC, lest base-NOM be-3sg.SUBJ for   bravest-ABL man-ABL speak-INF

incipientem timere minimeque deceat,   cum T. Annius   ipse   magis
beginning-ACC fear-INF least-and   be-proper-3sg.SUBJ, since T. Annius-NOM self-NOM more

de   rei-publicae salute   quam de   sua   perturbetur,   me ad eius
about republic-GEN safety-ABL than   about his-own-ABL disturb.3sg.SUBJ.PASS, me-ACC to his

causam parem   animi   magnitudinem adferre non posse,   tamen haec
case-ACC equal-ACC spirit-GEN greatness-ACC   bring-INF not be-able-INF, yet   this-NOM

noui   iudicii noua   forma   terret   oculos, qui   quocumque
new-GEN trial-GEN new-NOM form-NOM frighten-3sg eyes-ACC, which-NOM wherever

inciderunt, consuetudinem fori   et pristinum morem iudiciorum requirunt.
fall-3pl.PF,   habit-ACC   forum-GEN and former-ACC custom-ACC courts-GEN seek-3pl.

'Though I fear, gentlemen of the jury, that it is unseemly for one to be afraid when beginning a speech on behalf of the bravest of men, and that, since Titus Annius himself is more anxious for the safety of the republic than for his own, it is in the last degree unbecoming that I should be unable to bring to his case an equal greatness of spirit, yet the unprecedented aspect of this unprecedented trial alarms my eyes, which, wherever they have fallen, look in vain for the familar trappings of the court and the ancient procedure of judicial inquiry.'

Here we see at once that the sentence is logically organized around the two connected clauses *etsi* 'though . . .', *tamen* 'yet . . .' But the first of these incorporates a pair of conjoined subordinate clauses following *uereor* 'I am afraid', namely *ne turpe sit* . . . 'lest it be base . . .' and *minimeque deceat* . . . 'and (lest) it be least fitting . . .', the first of which includes an additional subordinated element (viz. the accusative and infinitive construction *pro fortissimo uiro incipientem dicere timere* 'that one beginning to speak on behalf of the bravest of men should be afraid'), while the second contains not only a parallel accusative and infinitive construction (*me . . . non posse* 'that I am unable . . .') but also an adverbial clause of reason (*cum . . . perturbetur* 'since he is anxious . . .'). Correspondingly, the 'yet' clause, which is the main clause of the sentence, contains a subordinated relative clause (*qui . . . requirunt* 'which look in vain for. . . .'), which in turn contains an additional subordinated clause introduced by *quocumque* 'wherever . . .'. These multiple levels of subordination contribute to a layered structure of some complexity, and accessing its meaning requires a complete and careful reading of the whole, as expected. The overall effect is one of logical progression, with each step in the argument spelled out, but with the full network of connections left incomplete until the very end.

The contrast with the following sentence, taken from Tacitus's *Annals* and describing Nero's behaviour just prior to the murder of his mother Agrippina in AD 59, is therefore quite stark:

(11)   Tacitus *Annals* 14.4

iam pluribus sermonibus, modo   familiaritate iuuenili   Nero   et rursus
now more-ABL talks-ABL,   at-one-time familiarity-ABL youthful-ABL Nero-NOM and again

adductus, quasi seria   consociaret,   tracto   in longum conuictu,
serious-NOM, as-if weighty-things-ACC share-3sg.IMPF.SUBJ, protracted-ABL in long-ACC feast-ABL,

prosequitur abeuntem, artius   oculis et pectori   haerens,   siue
follow-3sg.PRES leaving-ACC, more-closely eyes-DAT and breast-DAT clinging-NOM, whether

explendae   simulationi, seu periturae   matris   supremus aspectus quamuis
completing-DAT hypocrisy-DAT, or doomed-GEN mother-GEN last-NOM look-NOM though

ferum   animum retinebat.
brutal-ACC spirit-ACC check-3sg.IMPF.

'Now with conversation in full flow, Nero, at one moment displaying youthful familiarity and then in turn becoming serious as if sharing matters of consequence, escorted her on her way – for the banquet had been long protracted – fixing himself rather closely upon her eyes and breast, whether to add the final touch to his hypocrisy or (because) this last look upon his doomed mother checked his spirit, brutal though it was.'

In comparison with the extract in (10), the main clause, namely *prosequitur abeuntem* 'accompanied her as she left', is extremely short, with its subject, Nero, 'displaced' into an earlier position in the sentence so as to introduce the main topic in a timely way. Many of the remaining elements are then very loosely attached, whether as descriptive ablatival phrases (as at the beginning, *iam pluribus sermonibus* 'now with plentiful conversation', *modo familiaritate iuuenili* 'at one time with youthful familiarity') or as participial expressions, one of which is an 'absolute' phrase (*tracto in longum conuictu* 'the feast having been long protracted'), the others agreeing with Nero (*et rursus adductus* 'and again serious', *artius oculis et pectori haerens* 'clinging more closely to her eyes and breast'); note in particular that the first of this latter pair, though functioning in parallel with the ablatival expression *modo familiaritate iuuenili* as a descriptor of the emperor, is deliberately contrasted with it in terms of form (just as *et rursus* 'and again' conflicts with the expected repetition of *modo* = 'at another time'). In a similar way, the two limbs of the final 'whether . . . or . . .' appendage place a predicative dative of purpose and a complete finite clause side by side, a context in which the latter can be introduced without any overt conjunction to mark the fact that it too provides a possible reason for the emperor's behaviour (*because* has been added in the translation for clarity). This material is all still grammatically subordinated to the main clause, though very little of it takes the form of finite clauses introduced by explicit conjunctions (here we have only the *quasi*-clause dependent on *adductus*, and the final *seu*-clause). Nonetheless, in terms of its contribution to the depiction of the scene as a whole, it is cumulatively much more important than the brief and relatively colourless 'main' clause. Taking the sentence as a whole, therefore, both the artistry and the unity of its construction are again immediately apparent, but the manner of its composition is totally unlike that of the Ciceronian period, with brevity, counterpoint and vividness deliberately prioritized over a more 'regular' form of presentation dependent on subordinating conjunctions as the key markers of the progression of thought.

A final characteristic of Classical Latin prose writing that must be mentioned here is the use of deliberate rhythms based on particular patterns of light ($\breve{\ }$) and heavy ($\bar{\ }$) syllables (final syllables, marked x, may be light or heavy), most obviously at the close of sentences or cola, hence the name *clausulae*. Among the more familiar clausulae, derived as so much else from the practice of Hellenistic schools of rhetoric, are:

1   ¯ ˘ ¯ ¯ x   (cretic and spondee)
2   ¯ ˘ ¯ ¯ ˘ x   (double cretic)
3   ¯ ˘ ¯ x   (double trochee, widely viewed as 'Asianic')
4   ¯ ¯ ¯ x   (double spondee)
5   ¯ ¯ ˘ ˘ x
6   ¯ ˘ ¯ ˘ x   (hypodochmius)
7   ¯ ˘ ˘ ¯ ˘ x
8   ˘ ¯ ¯ ˘ x   (dochmius)

All of these permit some variation, especially through the 'resolution' of certain heavy syllables into two light ones, and it is noteworthy that both (4) in the list above and its dactylic equivalent, namely ¯ ˘ ˘ ¯ x, are in fact quite common in the historians, despite their otherwise generally restrained use of such devices. Indeed, this hexametric pattern associated with epic and didactic poetry is sometimes even extended, contrary to the generally accepted view that literary prose should be rhythmical but never metrical, beyond the end of a sentence or colon to cover a whole string of words, even though the usual poetic coincidence of word stress and verse ictus in both of the last two feet is not always followed. Extreme examples, which serve to emphasize once more the links between history and poetry, are provided by Tacitus:

(12)   (a)   . . . litore | terra|rum uelut | in cune|um tenu|atu
                    ¯ ˘ ˘ | ¯ ¯ | ¯ ˘ ˘ | ¯ ˘ ˘ | ¯ ˘ ˘ | ¯ x   (*Agricola* 10)

       (b)   urbem | Rom(am) a | principi|o re|ges habu|ere
             ¯ ¯ | ¯ ¯ | ¯ ˘ ˘ | ¯ ¯ | ¯ ˘ ˘ | ¯ x   (*Annals* 1.1)

In general, however, the clausulae most typical of oratory, i.e. (1) and (2) in the list above, are avoided in historical writing. On the other hand, use of this whole set of rhythmical endings dominates the work of writers such as Cicero, Seneca, Pliny and even Petronius, for whom they had clearly become second nature (it is therefore a moot point whether the freedmen in the *Cena Trimalchionis* are made to talk like this as a joke, or whether Petronius simply could not help himself). Nothing could be more indicative of the artificial character of Latin *belles lettres*, and deliberate failure to follow the expected rhythmic conventions of a given genre is in fact as rare as deliberate deviation from grammatical rule or the deliberate choice of stylistically inappropriate vocabulary.

6.5.2   The language of Classical Latin poetry

Though the generic range of classical poetry is again very wide, embracing epic, didactic, elegiac and lyric forms as well as drama and satire, there is a number of distinctive properties that may be identified as characteristic of at least the higher forms of poetic diction (see the collection of papers in Adams and Mayer 1999 for some recent scholarship on this subject, and especially the article by Coleman 1999).

One obvious trait is a liking for certain vocabulary items which, from the point of view of 'normal' Latin, were not only poetic but also archaic (cf. Quintilian 1.6.39: *uerba a uetustate repetita non solum magnos assertores habent sed etiam adferunt orationi maiestatem aliquam non sine delectatione*, 'words revived from ancient sources not only enjoy the patronage of great writers but also bring a certain majesty to the discourse, as well as some pleasure'). This practice was validated both by the archaizing character of Greek precedents, and by the fact that Roman poets had attempted in even the earliest Latin poetry to exploit native archaisms in a parallel way. Familiar lexical examples include *aequor* 'sea' for *mare*, *amnis* 'river' for *flumen*, *ensis* 'sword' for *gladius*, *letum* 'death' for *mors*, etc., as well as the use of simplex forms of many adjectives and verbs that had otherwise been replaced by compounds, such as *fessus* 'weary' for *defessus*, *linquo* 'leave' for *relinquo*, *temno* 'despise' for *contemno*, *suesco* 'be accustomed' for *consuesco*, etc. It should be emphasized, however, that 'affected' archaism, involving attempts to revive obscure or regional words, was until very much later regarded as a serious lapse of taste and judgement: the most favoured archaisms were those that were current in poetic discourse, precisely because they reflected the common usage of a tradition going back to Ennius and others, as subsequently developed and refined by poets such as Lucretius and Catullus in the course of forging a suitably stylized language for poetic discourse.

But despite the increasing formalization of literary prose and the emergence of a standard against which poets could react and experiment, there are in fact rather few such 'clearly' poetic lexical items, a situation which must reflect the fact that not only was there much overlap in subject matter (as between history and epic, for example, or didactic poetry and prose treatises on technical subjects), but that prose writers and poets enjoyed the same rhetorical education, with exposure to exactly the same corpora of texts and precepts. Nonetheless, there are some conspicuous lexical characteristics that serve to distinguish verse from prose, including the relatively high number of Greek words, incorporating their Greek sounds and sometimes even their Greek morphology. This is especially true of Greek proper names, which brought an allusive richness to contexts in which poets sought to link their own work to a distinguished Greek tradition.

Much more important, however, is the widespread use of ordinary words with meanings extended *inter alia* by means of classical tropes such as metaphor and metonymy to create striking images quite alien to other than the most self-consciously artistic forms of prose (especially history). Classic examples from Vergil's *Aeneid* of ordinary words used in what must on first hearing have seemed bold and difficult combinations include: *rumpit uocem* (*Aeneid* 2.129, 3.246) 'bursts forth a voice' (i.e. with causative sense, not simply = 'burst': corresponds to Greek *rhēgnýnai phōnēn*, as in Herodotus 1.85); *luce aena* (*Aeneid* 2.470) 'with brazen light' (borrowed from Homer *Iliad* 13.341); *eripe fugam* (*Aeneid* 2.619) 'snatch flight' (i.e. 'get away quickly'); *corpore tela . . . exit* (*Aeneid* 5.438) 'he passes the missiles by with his body' (i.e. 'avoids', a usage anticipated in Lucretius 5.1330: the usual meaning is 'go away', or sometimes in poetry 'go past'); *frontem rugis arat* (*Aeneid* 7.417) 'furrows [lit. ploughs] his forehead with wrinkles'; *recentem caede locum* (*Aeneid* 9.455) 'a place fresh with slaughter' (a phrase later adopted by Tacitus at *Histories* 3.19); and *caeso . . . sanguine* (*Aeneid* 11.82) 'with slaughtered blood' (i.e. 'of the slaughtered').

Overall, however, the contrast with prose writing is perhaps rather more apparent in matters of morphology and syntax. We may note first the various morphological archaisms that retain their place in poetry for traditional as well as metrical reasons. While literary prose in general maintained rather closer contact with contemporary educated speech, it seems that inflectional archaism in poetry was instinctively accepted as a signal of allegiance to both Greek and Roman predecessors in whose work the use of obsolete forms and words was deeply embedded. Examples include 1st-declension genitive singulars in disyllabic *-ai* [-aːiː], non-standard 2nd-declension genitive plurals in *-um*, 3rd person plural perfects in *-ere* [-eːre], 4th-conjugation imperfects in *-ibam* rather than *-iebam*, and present passive infinitives in *-ier*. Less immediately apparent is the artificial revival of formerly long vowels in final syllables, again for metrical reasons; this is especially common in 3rd person singular verb forms such as *aberat* ['aberaːt], *esset* [esseːt], *ponebat* [poːˈneːbaːt], *uidet* ['wideːt], *fuit* ['fuiːt], etc., a practice which sometimes led to purely analogical/metrical lengthenings of vowels that had always been short, as in *Aeneid* 12.883: *te sine, frater, erit? o quae satis ima dehiscat*, where *erit* must have a long vowel in the final syllable, i.e. be read as ['eriːt].

In syntax too we may note a number of features, which, though encountered in literary prose, occur with significantly greater frequency in verse and may fairly be regarded as among the key markers of poetic discourse. One of these is a marked tendency among the poets to assign transitive uses to some basically intransitive verbs, as in the following Vergilian examples: *ardebat Alexin* 'was burning (for) Alexis' (*Eclogues* 2.1), *arma uirumque cano* 'I sing (of) arms and the man' (*Aeneid* 1.1), *Tyrrhenum nauigat aequor* 'he sails (over) the Tyrrhenian sea' (*Aeneid* 1.67), *nec uox hominem sonat* 'nor does your voice sound (of) a man' (*Aeneid* 1.328), etc. This may perhaps be seen as a rather free extension of the well-established transitive use of certain normally intransitive verbs, such as those of emotion (e.g. *doleo* 'grieve (for)', *despero* 'depair (of)', *horreo* 'shudder (at)', *miror* 'wonder (at)', *rideo* 'laugh (at)', etc.) or, when compounded, of movement (e.g. *obeo* 'encounter', *percurro* 'traverse quickly', *subterfugio* 'evade', etc.).

It is also well known that Old Latin shows a considerable number of verbs that may be active or deponent (e.g. *arbitro(r)* 'think', *auguro(r)* 'take the auspices', *contemplo(r)* 'survey', *munero(r)* 'bestow', *populo(r)* 'ravage', etc., or among the semi-deponents with active presents, perfect *ausi* for *ausus sum* 'dared', *solui* for *solitus sum* 'was accustomed', etc.), suggesting that the language was beginning to eliminate a once developed class of middle verbs (i.e. passive in form, but typically with active-type meanings involving the subject as experiencer or beneficiary) in favour of more 'regular' active forms as the distinctive semantic properties of the middle became increasingly opaque. This tendency was particularly characteristic of popular spoken Latin, where the active tends to encroach on the deponent even when there was in principle a difference of meaning (e.g. *lauat* rather than *lauatur* = 'she is having a wash', Plautus *Miles Gloriosus* 252), and is again apparent in imperial vulgar Latin (e.g. *lauor* and *lauo* are used side by side = 'have a wash' by one of Petronius's freedmen (*Satyricon* 42)), but the classical written language generally opted for the deponent or semi-deponent variant as the more 'correct' form, even if variation between active and passive forms of certain verbs was also sometimes tolerated (e.g. *reuerto* and *reuertor* = 'turn (oneself) around').

As already noted, however, verbs of 'putting on/covering' or 'taking off' and, more rarely, other verbs involving an affected subject show optional retention of a middle use from the earliest times, as in Ennius's *succincti corda machaeris* (*Annales* 519 Sk) 'having girded their hearts with swords'. With the passage of time this usage was extended from examples with the perfect participle used as a middle (cf. *scissa comam*, Vergil *Aeneid* 9.478, 'tearing her hair'; *percussae pectora* 'beating their breasts', Vergil *Aeneid* 11.877) to finite verb forms, as in Vergil's *inutile ferrum cingitur* (*Aeneid* 2.510–511) 'girds on (himself) the useless weapon'. Ovid's *suffunditur ora rubore* (*Metamorphoses* 1.484) 'felt her face suffuse with shame' extends such usage still further. But a properly passive use remained the norm with most transitive verbs, and we may contrast the example from *Aeneid* 11.877 with Lucretius's *percussi membra timore* (5.1223) 'struck (in) their hearts with fear', where the context forces a passive meaning and the participle is in construction not with a direct object but with an accusative of the affected domain. This use of the so-called accusative of 'respect' with perfect passive participles was similarly extended to finite verbs forms, as in Lucretius's *tremit artus* (3.489) 'trembles (in) his limbs'. The revival and development of this construction, as of the preceding one, was doubtless influenced by comparable Greek usage, as already noted (see 6.2.2, 'The revival of archaisms otherwise in serious decline').

A further characteristic of poetic discourse is the retention of certain archaic uses of the infinitive, e.g. to complement adjectives in place of the normal construction with a gerund or gerundive: cf. *auidi committere pugnam* 'eager to join battle' (Ovid *Metamorphoses* 5.75) beside Sallust's *auidus . . . belli gerendi* (*Iugurtha* 3.5.3) lit. 'eagerly desirous of war being-waged'. Though originally nouns allowed only a gerund/gerundive as a dependent (cf. *love of doing X*, etc.), the infinitive had already emerged as a rival in this context in Old Latin, and the possibility was then retained in classical poetry: cf. *tantus amor casus cognoscere nostros* (Vergil *Aeneid* 2.10) 'so great a desire to know our downfall' beside Ovid's *amor sceleratus habendi*, lit. 'evil love of gaining' (*Metamorphoses* 1.131). Greek influence may again be relevant here, as noted above, though this was certainly involved in the re-establishment of the perfective use of the perfect infinitive after modal and control verbs, which was not current in Classical Latin outside poetry, where the extra syllable and trochaic ending of the perfect infinitive ($^-$ $^{\smile}$) were metrically useful: cf. Propertius's *ergo uelocem potuit domuisse puellam* (1.1.15) 'so he was able to tame the swift-footed girl'.

Finally, we may note a marked reduction in the use of prepositions in poetry compared with prose. In many cases the relevant construction may be seen as an archaism, in which a bare case form marks a spatial relation which in prose would require prepositional support (even though related figurative uses are normally prepositionless across the board). Typical examples include the accusative or, more rarely, the dative of goal (e.g. *Italiam . . . Lauiniaque uenit/litora*, Vergil *Aeneid* 1.2–3, 'he came (to) Italy-ACC and the Lavinian shores-ACC'; *Panthoiden iterum Orco/ demissum*, Horace *Odes* 1.28.10–11, 'the-son-of-Panthous sent-down once-again (to) Orcus/the underworld-DAT', where the dative implies subjective involvement on the part of the personified underworld), and the ablative of source (e.g. *nec uaga muscosis flumina fusa iugis*, Propertius 2.19.30, 'nor the wandering streams pouring forth (from) mossy ridges-ABL'), location (e.g. *et arce locari*, Vergil *Aeneid* 2.33, 'and [that it] be-placed (in) the citadel-ABL'), or path (e.g. *ibam forte Via Sacra*, Horace *Satires* 1.9.1, 'I was going by chance (along) the Via Sacra-ABL').

But perhaps the most striking aspect of Classical Latin poetry is the routine disruption of normal word order, which is only partly metrically motivated, and often contributes emphasis or contrast through the displacement of key words to focal positions or the juxtaposition of words that are grammatically unrelated but whose meanings are thereby made to interact. This is particularly apparent in the often wide separation of adjectives from the nouns they modify, a characteristic that can be exemplified in almost any selection of lines from any poet. The following extract from Ovid's *Metamorphoses* is typical:

(13)   Ovid *Metamorphoses* 1.177–180
ergo ubi   *marmoreo* superi   sedere   *recessu,*
so   when marble-ABL gods-NOM sit-3pl.PF retreat-ABL

celsior   ipse   loco   *sceptro*que   innixus   *eburno*
higher-NOM self-NOM place-ABL sceptre-ABL-and resting-on-NOM ivory-ABL

terrificam   capitis   concussit terque   quaterque
awe-inspiring-ACC head-GEN shake-3sg.PF three-times-and four-times-and

caesariem, cum qua   terram,   mare,   sidera   mouit.
locks-ACC,   with which-ABL land-ACC, sea-ACC, stars-ACC move-3sg.PF

'So, when the gods had sat down in their marble retreat, the king himself, higher than the rest in his place and leaning on his ivory sceptre, shook thrice and again the awe-inspiring locks of his head, with which he moved the land and sea and stars.'

6.6   Conclusion

Having dealt at some length with the refinements of language and style that characterized the formation of Classical Latin, as well as with the evolution of its more characteristic generic markers, it is important to recall that, discounting the comings and goings of stylistic fashion, the higher forms of written Latin, once standardized, changed very little in terms of grammar and lexicon throughout the remainder of antiquity. Even in the middle ages efforts to write the language 'correctly' continued unbroken, and were affected only by periods of decline in the educational system, which were in any case counterbalanced by classical revivals when circumstances permitted. But the language remained fully 'alive' in its more popular spoken forms, and at this level was subject to normal processes of change in a population largely unaffected by exposure to the standardized written language. These processes eventually saw spoken Latin evolve, on a regional basis, into the modern Romance languages, as the Roman state declined and finally collapsed, and the centralized political, military and educational institutions capable of imposing a stabilizing, or at least retarding, norm from above disappeared. In the chapters that follow the beginnings of this process of evolution will be addressed in detail.

References

Adams, J. N. (2003) *Bilingualism and the Latin Language*. Cambridge: Cambridge University Press.

Adams, J. N. and R. G. Mayer (eds.) (1999) *Aspects of the Language of Latin Poetry*. Oxford: Oxford University Press (for the British Academy).

Coleman, R. G. G. (1977) 'Greek influence on Latin syntax'. *Transactions of the Philological Society* 1975, 101–56.

Coleman, R. G. G. (1999) 'Poetic diction and the poetic register', in J. N. Adams and R. G. Mayer (eds.), *Aspects of the Language of Latin Poetry*. Oxford: Oxford University Press (for the British Academy), 21–93.

Funaioli, H. (ed.) (1907) *Grammaticae Romanae Fragmenta*. Leipzig: Teubner.

Horrocks, G. (2010) *Greek: A History of the Language and its Speakers* (2nd edn.). Wiley-Blackwell, Malden Mass. and Oxford.

Keil, H. (ed.) (1857–80) *Grammatici Latini*. Leipzig: Teubner.

Law, V. (2003) *The History of Linguistics in Europe*. Cambridge: Cambridge University Press.

Matthews, P. H. (1994) 'Greek and Latin Linguistics', in G. Lepschy (ed.) *History of Linguistics, Vol. II: Classical and Medieval Linguistics*. London/New York: Longman (Pearson), 1–133.

Palmer, L. R. (1954) *The Latin Language*. London: Faber and Faber.

Rosén, H. (1999) *Latine Loqui: Trends and Directions in the Crystallization of Classical Latin*. Munich: Wilhelm Fink Verlag.

Russell, D. A. (1990) *An Anthology of Latin Prose*. Oxford: Clarendon Press.

Chapter VII

Sub-Elite Latin in the Empire

7.1   Introduction: The spread of Latin

nec ignoro ingrati ac segnis animi existimari posse merito, si obiter atque in transcursu ad hunc modum dicatur terra omnium terrarum alumna eadem et parens; numine deum electa, quae caelum ipsum clarius faceret, sparsa congregaret imperia ritusque molliret et tot populorum discordes ferasque linguas sermonis commercio contraheret ad conloquia et humanitatem homini daret breuiterque una cunctarum gentium in toto orbe patria fieret.

Pliny Natural History 3.39

'And I am not unaware, that this work could rightly be thought to issue from an ungrateful and lazy mind, if it only mentioned obliquely and in passing (as done above) the land [i.e. Italy] that is at once daughter and parent of all lands. This land which is chosen by the will of the gods to make even the sky clearer, to gather the scattered powers and pacify the customs and bring together the discordant and wild idioms of so many peoples by the shared use of a language for communication, and to give civilization to mankind, and, in short, to bring about a single nation from all the peoples in the whole world.'

The above quotation, taken from the vast literary cabinet of curiosities of the ancient world that is Pliny's *Natural History*, is well known, since it represents one of the few passages anywhere in surviving classical literature where there is anything close to a mission statement of the Roman Empire. It is significant that, here in the middle of a passage which glorifies Italy, Pliny lists the unifying and beneficent effect of the Latin language alongside the gift of *humanitas*, 'civilization', to the conquered peoples of the Empire. Pliny represents Rome as having performed the story of the Tower of Babel in reverse. Where there was formerly a host of mutually incomprehensible languages, the Empire has substituted a single tongue, and enabled formerly warring tribes to communicate with each other. Furthermore, Pliny's picture of the linguistic situation within the Roman Empire seems not to be empty rhetoric, but is actually borne out by the facts. As we already saw in Chapter III, Latin replaced nearly all of the numerous languages spoken in the West before the Roman conquest, as the modern descendents of Latin, Portuguese, Spanish, French and Italian and the other minor Romance languages attest.

Pliny's statement gives the impression that when he was writing, in the middle of the first century AD (he died aged 55 in 79 AD, while watching the eruption of Vesuvius), Latin had already entered use as the language of the Empire. And to judge from the bulk of the epigraphic and documentary record, one might be inclined to accept his statement. In Gaul, for example, in the centuries preceding the Christian era, there is written evidence for the non-IE Iberian language, and the IE varieties Celtiberian and Gallo-Gaulish (i.e. Gaulish written in the Greek script). But from the first century BC on, these languages are no longer attested. At the same time the first Latin inscriptions appear in Gaul, and this is the predominant language of inscriptions under the Empire. A few Gaulish texts also appear after this date, but they are all written in the Latin alphabet, and the majority are found on domestic objects, with fewer than 20 monumental inscriptions on stone. In first-century Gaul, Latin had become the public written language (see further Woolf 1998). In Roman Britain, where there was no tradition of writing before the Conquest, the only possible written evidence for the native language is found in a handful of religious texts, called curse tablets, which may be written in British Celtic, although the large majority of texts of this type is written in Latin. In the letters written on wooden tablets found in Vindolanda and elsewhere on Hadrian's Wall, dating to the beginning of the second century AD, Latin is used by everyone, from the commanding officer's wife through the centurions down to the local military horse doctor.

Latin was certainly the language of the government of the provinces, and it was also being adopted by the local elites across the Roman Empire by the time Pliny was writing. We have the explicit testimony of Tacitus that in Britain and in France there were local schools giving a Latin education (*liberalibus artibus/studiis*) to the children of the native chieftains (Tacitus *Agricola* 21.2 and *Annals* 3.43). We can assume that this teaching was in the vein of the standard Roman education, and included reading and studying Vergil and Cicero. Tacitus accords Agricola the honour of instituting this practice in Britain, but it does not seem to have been a general policy for the Romans to make formal requirements of their subjects to adopt Latin, or to provide mechanisms to help them acquire the language. In general, the advantages in terms of access to power that Latin could give to a provincial was a sufficient incentive to learn it. In the words of Brunt (1976: 162), 'provincials Romanised themselves.' A member of the local elite with Latin could rise right to the top. Indeed, in the later Empire, it was possible for men such as Septimius Severus and Philip the Arab to become emperor, despite their origins in the provinces. The Latin of these men (and they were all men) would have been indistinguishable from the Latin of the educated elite at Rome: we are unable to detect whether Tacitus, for example, originally comes from, say, Gaul from his language, and Seneca and Martial do not betray their roots in Spain through any linguistic quirks. The language of their sisters and wives, who had not undergone the same intensive education, may have been more marked. We have the testimony of the *Historia Augusta* (*Septimius Seuerus* 15.7) that Septimius Severus had to send his sister back to Africa when she embarrassed him with her inability to master the standard language in Rome (*uix Latine loquens* 'scarcely speaking in (Classical) Latin').

But what was happening to the language of those who were not members of the Roman elite? What did they speak? Previous answers to these questions have covered a wide range of possibilities. According to some, the peasants in the Roman provinces would have continued to speak in the old native vernacular languages of the region, separated from the elite culture by language as much as by wealth and social standing. The eventual switch to Latin as a spoken language may have only taken place with the introduction of Christianity, and the preaching of universal salvation in Latin. Another model, now discredited among linguists but still tenacious among non-specialists, holds that the lower classes in the Roman Empire spoke 'vulgar Latin', a debased form of Classical Latin which was to evolve into the Romance languages. Neither of these models can be correct, and it is becoming clearer that the actual picture is a good deal more complicated than either of them. Indeed, it may be over-simplistic to talk of the linguistic situation of the Roman Empire in a unified sense. The situation was very different between the East and West of the Empire, different in Roman Britain and the provinces of North Africa, different even in the towns of Italy from Rome. In every modern language investigated by sociolinguists, groups with tight social networks and shared occupations and concerns share distinct speech varieties, and it is realistic to suppose that the same was true in the ancient world. Ancient sailors spoke differently from hill-farmers, and domestic slaves spoke differently from slaves on a *latifundium*. We know that the language of one religious/ethnic community, the Jews who lived in Venusia in southern Italy, was distinctive in its mix of Greek and Latin from their surviving funerary inscriptions (Leiwo 2003), and we have no reason to believe that this is a special case.

7.2 Bilingualism

We should therefore consider that the linguistic situation in the Roman Empire was marked, more than anything else, by huge diversity. In one area, Latin may have become spoken by the majority of the population early on, while in another, there may have been substantial pockets of speakers of vernacular languages (some of which were to remain in use beyond the Empire). In other cases there were almost certainly long periods of bilingualism or multilingualism. Bilingualism between Latin and vernacular languages other than Greek is frequently passed over in the surviving historical and geographical texts written by the Romans. From the perspective of Rome, Latin and Greek were the only two languages which mattered. Yet there is evidence from documentary and epigraphical texts of considerable bilingualism in the Roman Empire. To return to the case of Gaul, for example, we have already seen that, on public monuments, there was a discernible switch from Gaulish written in the Greek script to Latin from the beginning of the first century AD. But Gaulish continued to be spoken alongside Latin, and we have good evidence from two different sources for the presence of bilingual speakers, switching between the two languages. The first source is a large collection of incised pottery fragments, associated with the pottery manufacturing complex of La Graufesenque in southern France. In the middle of the first century AD vast numbers of pots were made at La Graufesenque, and the potters followed a practice of record-keeping, by detailing the numbers of different types of pots which were sent to the kiln on one pot included in the batch. They also used texts incised on pots as letters to merchants and others. We have nearly two hundred texts of this sort, but most are fragmentary, and even complete texts hardly appear as real 'texts' to the uninitiated. Most of the texts lack verbs, and just contain lists of potters' names, types of pots and numbers. The texts are mainly in Gaulish, written in Latin script, and using a Latin framework in their layout and Latin sigla and signs for numbers. Some texts are, however, written in Latin, and there is evidence for interference both ways, from Latin to the Gaulish and vice versa. Moreover, there seems to be a clear distinction between the texts written for internal consumption in the pottery and those which were written on pots intended for commercial sale. Potters sometimes leave their own names on pots for export, and when they do they tend to use the Latinate form of their name, with nominative singular -*us*, as for example, *Vindulus*, while on the Celtic texts written for use inside the pottery they use the Gaulish form of the name *Vindulos*. These texts record a community of workers who were happy to switch between Latin and Gaulish. Study of the onomastic evidence suggests that most of the potters were originally Gaulish, although there also appear to have been a few workers from Italy among the earliest potters (see Genin, Hoffmann and Vernhet 2002: 66f.), lending support to Adams's view that under Roman administration Italians at La Graufesenque instructed native potters in record-keeping and literacy, although they were happy for them to use the local language in their record-keeping (Adams 2003a).

The second source of information on bilingualism is a small group of very short texts, showing Gaulish and Latin used side by side in the second and third century AD. These texts are written on spindle whorls, decorated weights used to weigh down wool as it is spun. Twenty-one inscribed spindle-whorls are now known from finds in central and eastern France. Nine are written in Latin, two of which are reproduced below:

(1)   RIG II.2 p. 318 b and c
(a)   aue uale   bella   tu
      hello goodbye pretty-NOM.FEM you

      'Hello and goodbye, you pretty thing.'

(b)   aue domina   sitiio
      hello woman-VOC I-thirst

      'Hello mistress, I'm thirsty.'

The texts are addressed to women, presumably the spinners of the wool, and the language suggests that the speaker is male. It is therefore likely that the spindle whorls were gifts from men to their girlfriends. The 12 texts which are not written in Latin are written in Gaulish, or sometimes in a mixture of Latin and Gaulish, as in the following two examples:

(2)   RIG II.2 122 and 112
(a)   aue   uimpi
      hello (**Latin**) pretty-NOM/VOC.FEM (**Gaulish**)

      'Hello, you pretty thing'

(b)   nata   uimpi   curmi
      girl (**Latin**, possibly **Gaulish**) pretty-NOM/VOC.FEM (**Gaulish**) beer-ACC (**Gaulish**)
      da
      give (**Latin**, possibly **Gaulish**

      'Pretty girl, give me some beer!'

The use of the word *nata* is worth commenting on in this text. The word occurs in several of the Gaulish or Gaulish/Latin spindle whorls, and seems to reflect the convergence of a Latin term, *natus/nata* 'child' with a Gaulish one. Elsewhere in texts from Gaul *nata* occurs as a preferred term for 'girl' and this seems to reflect Gaulish influence on the Latin language of Gaul (Adams 2003a). The language of these texts may be close to the spoken language of one particular domain, informal and amorous speech between men and women, in this area of France at the time. It is possible that women retained the use of the vernacular language since they either had no access or only limited exposure to the male spheres in which Latin was used: education, the army, law, administration and public life.

The evidence of the pots from La Graufesenque and the spindle whorls of eastern Gaul under the Empire reveal some glimpses of the complexity in the use of languages in the Roman Empire. Even in these two cases we have only a very incomplete understanding of what was going on in actual speech, and we only know this much since these texts are of such a 'low' level, never intended for consumption outside tiny groups of people, that they have escaped the normative pressure to use Classical Latin for all writing. Evidence from elsewhere in the Empire suggests that similar circumstances prevailed in provinces other than Roman Gaul, with different vernacular languages continuing in use alongside Latin, their presence only revealed by chance intrusions into the documentary evidence. It is impossible to imagine that the existence of so much bilingualism did not entail great diversity in the Latin that was spoken around the Empire. We have already noted the story of how the emperor Septimius Severus was so embarrassed by his sister's speech that he sent her back home to North Africa from Rome, and that there is a possibility that Gaulish influence brought about lexical changes in the Latin of Gaul.

7.3   The Homogeneity of Spoken Latin

In the early Empire, Latin was spoken alongside many other linguistic varieties over a vast geographical area. But amongst this vast array of linguistic diversity, there is also a surprising amount of agreement. In all but the most remote areas of the Western Empire, the net result of centuries of bilingualism was the same: Latin rather than the native language won out as the language of the local population, leading to the eventual disappearance of nearly all of the vernacular languages. We have no evidence of any spoken Gaulish by the fifth century. And in the non-literary Latin texts which have survived from the Empire, there is a considerable amount of homogeneity. From our present state of knowledge, it is only rarely possible to locate a text written in a variety of Latin which deviates from the standard to a particular region of the Empire. This is partly the result of the fact that there were a number of standard formulae to express most of the messages the texts were intended to convey, even texts written in non-standard Latin. Formulae for the gravestone, formulae for the curse written down and then sent to the underworld, either dropped in a well or buried in a graveyard, formulae for the letters of administration which we have surviving from ancient military camps, even formulae for writing abusive graffiti – these formulae, and the conservative practices learned with the art of writing, and seen in the practice of professional scribes and individual writers alike, present a unified picture of a written culture which is striving to be as close to the standard of Vergil and Cicero as possible.

However, the apparent homogeneity of Latin in inscriptional and documentary sources cannot just be put down to the result of formulaic language and conservative scribes. Where there are deviations from the classical standard, the same deviation may be found over and over again, repeated countless times in inscriptions and other sources. Although there are many non-classical forms which are peculiar to the author of an individual text, and several which can be associated with a particular social grouping, in the majority of cases it is possible to see evidence for the same underlying linguistic change in documents from all over the Empire. We shall discuss below in detail some of the developments in question, but first we need to account for the similarity of the trends in the spoken language all over the Empire, despite the fact that the language was spoken over such a wide area in an age when there were no mass media, and when it could take a traveller months to get from Rome to outposts of the Empire. Part of the explanation for the apparent homogeneity of spoken Latin must lie in the mobility of large parts of the population. Readers of the letters of Cicero or Pliny are used to the idea that the Roman elite moved around the Empire on administrative or military tours of duty, but may not be so aware that the rest of the population was equally mobile. Service in the army, trade and slavery are three obvious causes for people to move far from their homes, but the rest of the population were probably less fixed than is sometimes thought. Peasant farmers and pastoralists (by no means two mutually exclusive groups) around the Mediterranean were habituated to migration, sometimes on an annual basis between winter and summer pastures, or between farm and fishing ground, or between a trade in a nearby town and the country. At other times environmental pressures, such as drought or blight, might force movement from one region to another. Finally, and perhaps most importantly, state-sponsored mobility, that is to say, colonies of free Romans planted in Italy and in the Empire, accounts for a massive movement of population around the Empire. It has recently

Map 7.1 Places where texts discussed in Chapter VII were found

been estimated that at the time of Augustus at least 40 per cent of Roman *seniores* did not live in the same community where they were born (Scheidel 2004: 21). Coupled with this huge movement of population in space, we must also take account of the permeability of Roman society in the late Republic and early Empire. It was possible for local elites to join the Roman elite, and it was possible for freed slaves to become owners of thousands of slaves themselves. In this world where there was so much geographical and social mobility, local differences in speech tended to become levelled, and long-term divisions in the language were kept to a minimum.

7.4 Four Individuals Speaking and Writing Latin in the Early Empire

We can see something of the linguistic situation in spoken Latin in the early Empire through the close examination of four sample texts, one a loan agreement written on a wax tablet, two letters from opposite ends of the Empire, and an inscription. Each of these texts can be associated closely with the speech of a specific individual at a specific date, and from them we can get a flavour of the similarities and the differences in spoken Latin in the first and second centuries BC. We also gain an insight into some of the careers of some of the speakers of Latin at this date. It is not irrelevant to the earlier discussion of the multilingual and mobile population of this period to note that certainly one, and probably three, of our authors spoke Latin as well as other languages. Three of our texts were written by those serving in, or attached to the army, and the fourth by a grain merchant. All four of our texts were written by men, as indeed are the vast majority of texts which survive from the ancient world. As we have seen, this gender bias in the texts may correlate with a dichotomy in the learning of Latin among the peoples of the Empire. Women were mostly excluded from the public spheres where a knowledge of Latin was required, and in consequence they may have retained the use of native languages for longer, as is suggested by the evidence of the spindle whorls from Gaul and the anecdote of the emperor's sister whose standard of Latin caused red faces in Rome.

We have deliberately not included in our selection texts from two of the best-known sources of sub-elite Latin at this date, the graffiti from Pompeii (for which see Väänänen 1959) and the representations of the speech of the freedmen in Petronius's *Satyricon* (for which see Boyce 1991 with Adams 2003b), which have been the normal staple of handbooks of vulgar Latin. In the one case the texts are usually too short or too formulaic to know for certain that they correspond to speech, and in the other, we cannot be certain how much weight to accord to the views of a member of the elite about the speech of the lower classes in a satirical novel, especially when those views are transmitted through a fragile manuscript tradition. In the absence of other evidence, Petronius was for a long time seen as a mine of information about the spoken language of his time. But now documentary evidence has been found which gives access to Latin written by the speakers of sub-elite varieties themselves. However, we shall not completely ignore the evidence of Petronius and Pompeiian inscriptions, and we shall include it where relevant to the discussion of a particular text.

As will be clear in our discussion of these texts, we are indebted to one scholar in particular for the work of identifying and elucidating their language: J. N. Adams (see Adams 1977, 1990, 1994, 1995, 1999 and 2003a). It is not overstating the case to say that his work on these, and many other Latin texts, over the last 40 years has led to a complete reassessment of what we know about spoken Latin; he has single-handedly made a greater contribution to our understanding of the language than any other member of the scholarly community.

7.4.1   *Gaius Nouius Eunus and changes in the phonology of Latin*

Our first text comes from Italy at the beginning of the Empire and can be precisely dated to 15 September 39 AD. It is a wax tablet recording the extension of a loan to a freedman and grain merchant Gaius Nouius Eunus, which survives among a larger archive of such tablets in Murecine near Pompeii where they were preserved following the eruption of Vesuvius (edited in Camodeca 1999, text number 68). The language of this loan agreement is largely formulaic, and it tells us little about the syntax of Latin spoken at this date (see Calboli 1999 for the syntax in other tablets in this archive, and Flobert 1994 more generally on their language). However, it is of considerable interest for the phonology of spoken Latin, since it is written twice, once in the hand of Gaius Nouius Eunus, on the sealed inside of the tablet, and then again by a professional scribe on the outside. Gaius can form his letters with a practised hand, but he tends to spell words as he pronounces them, and he does not follow the orthographical conventions of the time. His deviations from the classical norms in this text (and in the three others surviving in his hand) give a good idea of how one individual represented his own Latin at this date. In the presentation of the text that follows, the line beneath the text of Eunus is the text written on the outside of the tablet by the professional scribe, who, as can be seen, uses an orthography which is largely the same as that given in modern editions of classical texts. (The abbreviation given at the start of the text is the reference according to the standardized system in Oates et al. 2005, for citation of papyri, tablets and ostraca.)

(3)   T.Sulpicii 68

Cn(aeo)	Domitio	Afro		A(ulo)	Didio	Gal[l]o	co(n)s(ulibus)
Cn(aeo)	Domitio	Áfro		A(ulo)	Dìdio	Gallo	co(n)s(ulibus)
Gnaeus-ABL	Domitius-ABL	Afrus-ABL	(and) Aulus-ABL	Didius-ABL	Gallus-ABL	consuls-ABL.pl

XVII		k(alendas)	Oct[o]beres
XVII		k(alendas)	Octobres
(on the) 17(th day before) kalends-ACC.pl October-ACC.pl			

C(aius)	Nouius	Eunus	scripssi	me	debere	Hesuco	C(aii)	Cessaris
C(aius)	Nouius	Eunus	scripsi	me	debere	Hesycho	C(aii)	Caesaris
Gaius	Nouius	Eunus	I-wrote	me-ACC	owe-INFIN	Hesychus-DAT	Gaius-GEN	Caesar-GEN

Augustì	Germanic(i)	ser(uo)	Eueniano	stertertios	mile	ducentos
Augustì	Germanici	ser(uo)	Eueniano	sestertios	mille	ducentos
Augustus-GEN	Germanicus-GEN	slave-DAT	Euenianus-DAT	sestertii-ACC.pl	thousand	200-ACC.pl

quiquaginta nummos reliquos ratione omini putata,
quinquaginta nummos reliquos ratione omni putata,
fifty cash-ACC.pl left-ACC.pl reckoning-ABL every-ABL considered-ABL

quos ab eo mutos accepi, quem suma iuratus promissi
quos ab eo mutuos accepi, quam summam iuratus promìsì
which-ACC.pl from him in-loan-ACC.pl I-receive, which-ACC total-ACC on-oath I-promised

me aut ipssi Hesuco aut C(aio) Sulpicio Fausto
me aut ipsì Hesycho aut C(aio) Sulpicio Fausto
me-ACC either himself-DAT Hesychus-DAT or Gaius-DAT Sulpicius-DAT Faustus-DAT

redturm k(alendis) Noembrib[u]s primis
redditurum k(alendis) Nouembribus primis
will-return-ACC Kalends-ABL November-ABL first-ABL

per Iobe Optumm Maxumu et nume dibi Augustì
per Ìovem Optumum Max(umum) et numen dìuì Aug(usti)
by Jupiter-ACC best-ACC greatest-ACC and godhead-ACC divine-GEN Augustus-GEN

et Genium C(aii) Cessaris Augustì;
et Genium C(aii) Caesaris Augusti;
and genius-ACC Gaius-GEN Caesar-GEN Augustus-GEN

quot si ea die non soluero, me nont solum peìurio teneri
quod si ea die non soluero, me non solum peiurio teneri
but if that-ABL day-ABL not I-shall-have-paid, me-ACC not only breach-of-oath-ABL be-held-INFIN

set etiam peone nomine in de sigulos sestertios uigienos
sed etiam poenae nomine in dies sing(ulos) HS XX
but also penalty-GEN name-ABL in days-ACC.pl successive-ACC.pl sestertii-ACC.pl 20-ACC.pl

nummo obligatum iri et eos HS I CCL, q(ui) s(upra) s(cripta) s(unt),
nummos obligatum ìrì et eos HS ∝ CCL, q(ui) s(upra) s(cripta) s(unt),
cash-ACC.pl be-liable-INFIN and those sestertii 1250, which above written are,

probos recte dari stipulatus et Hessucus C(aii) Cessaris
p(robos) r(ecte) d(ari) stipulatus est Hesychus C(aii) Caesaris
good-ACC.pl properly be-given-INFIN he-exacted Hesychus-NOM Gaius-GEN Caesar-GEN

Augustì ser(uus) spepodi C(aius) Nouius Eunus.
ser(uus) spopondi C(aius) Nouius Eunuus.
Augustus-GEN slave-NOM I-promised Gaius Nouius Eunus.

Actum in colonia Iulia Augusta Putolis
Act(um) Puteolis
done in colony-ABL Iulia-ABL Augusta-ABL Puteoli-LOC

'In the consulship of Gnaeus Domitius Afrus and Aulus Didius Gallus (39 AD), on the 15th September, I Gaius Nouius Eunus, wrote that I owe Hesychus Euenianus, the slave of Gaius Caesar Augustus Germanicus, twelve hundred and fifty sestertii cash outstanding, by every considered reckoning, which I received from him as a loan, and which total I promised I would repay either to Hesychus himself or to Gaius Sulpicius Faustus on the First of November, by Jupiter Optimus Maximus and the godhead of Divine Augustus and the Genius of Gaius Caesar Augustus. But if I shall not have repaid on that day, I shall be held not only by my breach of oath, but also by way of a penalty, I shall be liable to 20 sestertii on each successive day, as well as the 1250 sestertii, which are mentioned above. Hesychus has exacted the pledge that good coin is properly given and I, Gaius Nouius Eunus, have sworn to it. Done in the colony of Iulia Augusta, at Pozzuoli.'

Many features of Eunus's spelling are in accord with the picture of spoken Latin which is revealed in the roughly contemporary Pompeian graffiti, and some are in line with phenomena which we have already observed in varieties of Republican Latin. Thus Eunus is prone to omit nasals, both at word end (*nume* for *numen*, *Iobe* for *Iouem*) and internally before a following stop, as *quiquaginta* for *quinquaginta*, and *sigulos* for *singulos*. We know that what was written in the normal orthography as vowel followed by *-m* at the end of a word represented a nasalized vowel, even in the recitation of high style poetry, so Eunus's omission of the letter in words such as *Iobe* for *Iouem* and *summa* for *summam* is no surprise, and may indicate that the pronunciation of nasal-ized vowels in these environments was optional for him. Indeed, on two occasions, he writes *-m* at the end of a word, with no vowel: *redturm* for *rediturum* and *Optumm* for *Optimum*. It could be that these writings are an alternative strategy to represent a nasal vowel for which there is no single letter equivalent in the alphabet.

Eunus is also absolutely consistent in writing the diphthong *-ae* as *-e*, for example *Cessaris* for *Caesaris* and *peone* for *poenae*. In no text that he writes himself does he use the diphthong *ae* where it would be written in Classical Latin. In some varieties of Republican Latin this diphthong was monophthongized to [ɛ] (with some fluctuations and hypercorrec-tions present in the classical language, as *scaena*, ultimately a loanword from Greek *skēnē*, and the alternative spellings of the word for 'hedge', notably a word relating to the rustic landscape, *saepes* and *sepes*). Eunus's consistent spelling of the name *Cessaris* rather than *Caesaris* is especially noteworthy. Eunus does show some indications in this document that he is deliberately trying to 'upgrade' his language in the formal situation of the oath that he is making. For example, when referring to Juppiter by his title *Optimus Maximus* he uses the forms with the medial vowel *-u-* rather than *-i-*, *Optumm* and *Maxumu*, which are certainly archaic by this date, and likely only to be retained in this religious formula. But in this, his most formal speech register, he spells the name of the emperor as *Cessar* throughout, which indicates that he does not have access to the diphthong in his speech at all. It is likely that for most speakers at this date and in later periods the diphthong *ae* no longer existed, and knowing when to write *ae* and when to write *e* was entirely a learnt rule. Likewise, Eunus does not have access to the Greek sounds of the rounded front vowel [y] and the aspirated *ch*, both present in the name of the slave who acts as lender of the money, Hesychus, whose name he spells as *Hessucus*.

However, some features which are observed in non-standard registers of earlier periods are not present in Eunus's speech:

1   The omission of final *-s* after a rounded back vowel is frequently found in early Republican inscriptions and in the text of Plautus and other Early Latin poets before Catullus, as discussed in Chapter IV. But final *-s* is only omitted in two words in this text, *de* for *dies* and *nummo* for *nummos*, and in the first of these the omission may be facilitated by the following *s* at the beginning of *singulos*. Eunus seems to have pronounced nominative singulars in *-us* with a final *-s*, as did most of those who left graffiti on the walls in Pompeii. Cicero (*Orator* 161) explicitly comments that the dropping of final *-s*, in words such as *omnibu'* for *omnibus* 'all' (dative-ablative plural) and *dignu'* for *dignus* 'worthy', once was acceptable in refined Latin, but now appears *subrusticus* 'rural' (text (9b) at 6.3).

2   The dropping of the aspirate *h-* from the beginning of words, and the corresponding overcompensation of inserting *h-* at the beginning of words where no *h* was present in Classical Latin was associated with the speech of the lower classes and rustics in the Republican period, as we know from Catullus's epigram (84), which pokes fun at a certain *Arrius* for locutions such as *hinsidias* ('hambushes') for *insidias*, and from some words such as *arena* 'sand' for which the hypercorrect spelling *harena* is also found. In this, and the three other texts which he writes, Eunus always uses *h-* in the 'correct' position. In graffiti from Pompeii, *h-* is sometimes left off words such as *habere* 'to have', but hypercorrect *h-* is rare.

3   The monophthongization of *au* to *o* was likewise found in some Early Latin inscriptions from outside Rome, and is a feature of the speech of some of the urban poor within Rome in the first century BC and onwards. Alongside inscriptional evidence for the change of *au* to *o*, there are examples of monophthongized forms in the informal language of the elite; thus Cicero uses the diminutive *oriculum* of *auris* 'ear' in a letter to his brother, and we can also find hypercorrections that have become standard in Classical Latin, such as *plaudere* 'applaud', from original *plodere*, retained in the semantically distant

compound *explodere* 'drive off, reject'. There is also an anecdote preserved in Suetonius's *Life* about the emperor Vespasian that explicitly states that educated Romans noticed that forms with the diphthong *au* were more socially prestigious than those with the monophthong [o], since a senator Florus is reported to have corrected the emperor when he used the term *plostrum* 'wagon' rather than the 'correct' *plaustrum*. Vespasian, who may have deliberately been using a form closer to the language of the urban plebs, responds by greeting Florus the next day as Flaurus, the joke being that the upgraded version of his name was homophonous with the Greek word *phlaurós* 'worthless'. But Gaius Nouius Eunus conserves *au* wherever it occurs: *Faustus, Augusti, aut*, and in Pompeian graffiti the words written with *o* for *au* are restricted to certain lexical bases, including *plostrum*.

It seems significant here that for each of these developments we have surviving metalinguistic comments from members of the Roman elite. It appears that these developments were particularly stigmatized as markers of the speech of the underclass, and consequently were recognized and avoided by many speakers in the early Empire, in a way that other developments, such as the monophthongization of *ae* and the dropping of final *-m* were perhaps not. In the case of the monophthongization of *au* to *o*, the pressure from the standard language was sufficient to check the development altogether, and the monophthongized diphthong never became a general feature of spoken Latin.

Eunus's text provides us with one of the earliest examples of the confusion of *b* and the consonantal *u* attested in Latin, in his writing *Iobe* for *Iouem* and *dibi* for *diui*, where the written *b* probably represents a bilabial fricative [β]. The confusion between *b* and consonantal *u* is a feature of many sub-elite documents after this date, and there is always a preference for writing *b* rather than *u*, since the latter can represent a vowel as well as a consonant. Eunus always represents a Classical Latin *b* with the letter *b*, so we need not think that in his dialect the consonant has also developed to a fricative, nor is there evidence from Pompeii to suggest that this change had taken place there.

Eunus's spelling also reveals much about his suprasegmental phonology. Particularly noteworthy are the effects of the accent on his pronunciation of words. In languages with a strong stress accent, unstressed syllables carry less phonological weight and are less diagnostic for the hearer's perception of a word. The insertion and the loss of vowels in unstressed syllables is consequently tolerated, and Eunus shows both processes. He always writes forms of *omnis* with an anaptyctic *i*, for example *omini*, and he consistently renders the combination *-br-* as *-ber-* in *Octoberes*

'October' and in another document *Septeberes* for *Septembres* 'September'. He drops medial vowels in *redturm* for *redditurum*, and probably also in the word for the monetary unit sestertius, which he writes at one place as *stertertios*, which may show a correction for his spoken **stertios*. High vowels in hiatus with other vowels are particularly prone to omission in Eunus's orthography. Thus he always writes the place name *Puteoli* as *Potolis*, *de* for *dies* and *mutos* for *mutuos*. It is possible that he even uses the same spelling in his cognomen, which he always writes as *Eunus* but the scribe once represents as *Eunuus*. There are other examples of such spellings in his other autograph documents, where he writes *tra* for *tria* 'three', *quator* for *quattuor* 'four' and *mila* for *milia* '1,000'. These spellings probably represent a pronunciation with a glide (such a stage must lie behind the modern name for *Puteoli*, Italian *Pozzuoli*, where the medial *zz* is the outcome of a sequence **-ty-*). It is noteworthy that this development also takes place when the high vowel was itself accented, as in *dies* and *tria*, indicating that there was a concomitant shift of accent to the more open vowel of the two (and there are examples of this process having taken place in Romance, for example Italian *lenzuolo* 'sheet' derived from **lintjólum*, Classical Latin *linteolum* 'linen strip').

Eunus also shows confusion over the writing of geminate consonants. The sibilant *s* is generally doubled in the middle of a word, even after *p*, as in *scripssi* and *ipssi*, and continuants are frequently, and stops occasionally, written single in place of double, as *suma* for *summam*, *mile* for *mille* and, in other texts, *faris* for *farris* 'spelt' and *quator* for *quattuor* 'four'. There is little evidence from the Pompeian graffiti for a comparable simplification of geminate consonants at this date, and these spellings need to be interpreted carefully. It is possible that they reflect imperfect learning on Eunus's part – note the forms *milia* 'thousands', *far* (nominative singular) and *quartus* 'fourth'. In the case of *s*, the doubling may be no more than the generalization of a spelling rule that *s* was written double after long vowels and diphthongs which we find referred to in the rhetorician Quintilian. However, in the case of the other geminates, nearly all of the writings with a single consonant occur after an accented syllable. Eunus may have heard the length of the consonant following an accented syllable as part of the cumulative effect of the stress, and not have indicated the geminate in his writing. The automatic co-occurrence of vowel length with the position of the accent perhaps already evident in Eunus's speech was to lead to a reformulation of the entire vowel system in spoken Latin, as we shall see later. Apart from the monophthongization of *ae*, Eunus still appears to have the vowel phonemes of Classical Latin, although we can see the weak points in the system.

7.4.2   *Chrauttius: a non-native speaker?*

Our second text is a letter found at Vindolanda, a Roman station on Hadrian's wall in the most northerly province of the Empire, Britannia (published in Bowman and Thomas 1994, and now available, with all the Vindolanda texts, at Vindolanda Tablets Online http://vindolanda. csad.ox.ac.uk/). The letter can be dated to shortly after 100 AD. Excavations at Vindolanda have revealed a considerable number of wooden tablets which were used to record documents relevant to the military administration as well as personal correspondence. The author of this letter, Chrauttius, is a soldier or veteran, and his name is taken to indicate that he has a Germanic origin. The letter is addressed to an old military acquaintance, who is styled Veldedeius in the address of the letter, but referred to as Veldeius in the text. Vel(de)deius appears to be a Celtic name, so it is likely that neither the author nor the recipient is a native Latin speaker, although both are probably conscripts in the army from the area that is now Belgium and Holland, rather than native Britains. The family relationships of the individuals mentioned in the texts are obscure: Chrauttius addresses Veldedeius as *frater* 'brother' and refers to *parentibus nostris* 'our parents', but the onomastics suggest that they were not related. It is, in fact, not uncommon in Roman epistolary style to use *frater* as an intimate term of address and *parens* can also mean 'elders' not 'parents'. Note that Chrauttius also refers to a certain Thuttena as their sister. Both she, and the Virilis and Velbuteius who are mentioned in the letter, are thought to have been Celts on onomastic grounds. There are also complications surrounding the presence of the letter at Vindolanda, since it seems to have been addressed to London.

(4)   T.Vindol. 310

Chrauttius   Veldeio   suó   fratri
Chrauttius-NOM Veldeius-DAT his-DAT brother-DAT

contubernali antiquo plurimam salutem
mess-mate-DAT old-DAT most-ACC greeting-ACC

et rogo te   Veldei   frater   miror
and I-ask you-ACC Veldeius-VOC brother-VOC I-wonder

quod mihi   tot   tempus nihil
that me-DAT so-many time-ACC nothing

rescripsti   a   parentibus   nostris
you-have-written from parents-ABL.pl our-ABL.pl

si quid   audieris   aut
if anything you-have-heard or

Quotum in quo numero
Quotus-ACC in what-ABL number-ABL

sit et illum a me salutabis
he-is-SUBJ and him.ACC from me-ABL you-will-greet

uerbis meis et Virilem
words-ABL.pl my-ABL.pl and Virilis-ACC

ueterinarium rogabis
vet-ACC you-will-ask

illum ut forficem
him.ACC that castrating-shears-ACC

quam mihi promissit pretio
which.ACC me-DAT he-promised price-ABL

mittas per aliquem de nostris
you-send through certain-ACC of our-ABL.pl

et rogo te frater Virilis
and I-ask you-ACC brother-VOC Virilis-NOM

salutes a me Thuttenam
you-will-greet from me-ABL Thuttena-ACC

sororem Velbuteium
sister-ACC Velbuteius-ACC

rescribas nobis cum
write-back-SUBJ us-DAT how(?)

se habeat
himself-ACC he-holds-SUBJ

opto sis felicissimus
I-wish you-are-SUBJ very-fortunate.NOM

uale
Farewell

Londini
London-LOC

Veldedeio
Veldedeius-DAT

equisioni cos(ulari)
groom-DAT of-governor-DAT

a Chrauttio
from Chrauttius-ABL

fratre
brother-ABL

'Chrauttius sends his best greetings to his brother and old mess-mate Veldeius. And I ask you, brother Veldeius, I am surprised that you have written nothing to me for so long, whether you have heard anything from our parents or about Quotus, in what division he is and will you greet him from me in my own name, and will you ask the vet Virilis to send me the castrating shears which he promised to sell to me through one of our acquaintances. And I ask you, brother Virilis, greet sister Thuttena from me (and as for) Velbuteius, write back to us how he is. I hope that you are in the best of fortune. Farewell.

Address: London, For Veldedeius the groom of the governor, from his brother Chrauttius.'

Unlike the letter of Gaius Nouius Eunus, considered above, this letter has been dictated and written by a professional scribe, apart from the final greeting, which may be in Chrauttius's own hand. The scribes at Vindolanda were well trained in the standard language; we know that some had read the classical 'canon' since in one tablet a line of Vergil is written out. In general in the Vindolanda tablets, the spelling reflects the Latin educational norms. There are generally only sporadic examples of the phonological developments that we saw in Gaius Nouius Eunus's autograph. For example, the diphthong -*ae* and final -*m* are almost always written where we would expect to find them, and there is no evidence for the confusion of *b* and *u*. In this text the scribe shows that he knew his job by the avoidance of such spellings, and he even uses an apex to mark the long final vowel in *suo*. Hardly any of the spellings here would be out of place in a modern edition of a classical text.

However, the orthographic competence conceals some curiosities of idiom and syntactic construction, which appear to have slipped past the scribal censor. Indeed, internal evidence from the text itself suggests that the text was taken down from dictation, rather than re-composed by the scribe. This emerges from the apparent greeting in the middle of the letter, intended for Veldedeius, to Virilis. Chrauttius asks Veldedeius to get in touch with Virilis, but then he addresses Virilis directly, to whom his thoughts are now directed (this is a more likely explanation than that Virilis in this line is to be construed as a genitive with *sororem* 'sister', two lines later). It is unlikely that a professional scribe would have used a direct address to a third party in a letter of this type, and we can surmise that the scribe was sticking fairly close to Chrauttius's words, even if he was spelling them in the classical style.

Although this letter appears to have been taken down as dictation, Chrauttius still relies on a number of formulaic expressions of the epistolary genre. For example, the opening phrase *et rogo te Veldei frater* 'and I ask you brother Veldeius', is a commonplace among surviving Roman letters; similarly, variants of the closing sign-off, *opto sis felicissimus,* turn up elsewhere in surviving texts. The presence of a number of these formulaic phrases in the text give, at first sight, the impression that Chrauttius is adept in Latin. Phrases such as *si quid audieris,* and *miror quod nihil rescripsti* and *ut forficem quam mihi promissit pretio mittas* appear to show a command of Latin subordination processes. However, on closer inspection it becomes clear that fitting these phrases together is more difficult for Chrauttius. It is possible that he is not a native speaker and, like many learners of a new language, he has learnt set phrases with which he can get by in conversation, but when he needs to construct a longer passage of discourse he comes unstuck. It will be helpful here to set out the structure of the central portion of the letter again with numbers added to the different sense units to aid the discussion below:

1.	*et rogo te*	and I ask you
2.	*miror quod nihil rescripsti*	I am amazed you have not written back
3.	*a parentibus nostris si quid audieris*	from our parents, if you have heard anything
4.	*aut Quotum in quo numero sit*	or Quotus in what unit he is
5.	*et illum a me salutabis*	and him you will salute from me
6.	*et Virilem rogabis*	and Virilis you will ask
7.	*illum ut forficem mittas*	him that you send the shears
8.	*et rogo te*	and I ask you
9.	*salutes a me Thuttenam*	greet Thuttena from me
10.	*Velbuteium rescribas*	Velbuteius write back
11.	*cum habeat*	how(?) he is

When set out like this it becomes clear that Chrauttius has very few syntactic devices to unite the longer clauses into a larger hypotactic structure. For classicists used to reading the periodic sentences of Cicero, it may be tempting to give Chrauttius the benefit of the doubt, and to take *si quid audieris* of clause 3 to be dependent on *rogo* of clause 1, with a parenthetic insertion of clause 2. But this may be over-generous to the author, since the dependency on the initial *rogo* clearly breaks down in clauses 5 and 6, and we further see a repetition of the *rogo te* formula in clause 8 followed by a subjunctive. Mostly, Chrauttius joins different clauses with a simple conjunction, four times *et* and once *aut,* and the last clause (10) is juxtaposed with no connection. When the text is set out as above, it also becomes clear that Chrauttius is over-reliant on fronting the topic of a dependent clause outside the clause, and assigning it to the accusative case: **Quotum** *in quo numero sit,* **illum** *ut forficem* *mittas,* **Velbuteium** *rescribas cum habeat.* In none of these clauses is there any rationale for putting the fronted item in the accusative, and Chrauttius seems to use this as a default case for fronted topics, or perhaps the scribe has tidied up the Latin by putting forms which were uninflected by the speaker into the accusative. If sentences formed in this way do not reflect some syntactic rule of Chrauttius's first language, the fronting of the topics can be best explained as a learner's over-generalization of a syntactic pattern which allows him to make maximum usage of the phrases he has learnt.

There are indications also that Chrauttius became confused by the more complicated subordinating procedures. The most intricate sentence he constructs involves the request to ask the vet Virilis to send him the shears: *et Virilem ueterinarium rogabis illum ut forficem quam mihi promissit pretio mittas per aliquem de nostris.* Literally, this translates 'and Virilis the vet, you will ask him that the shears which he promised to me at a price you will send through one of our people.' But how can Veldedeius ask Virilis that Veldedeius send the shears? Surely Virilis must send them, in which case Chrauttius has used the wrong person in the verb, second person *mittas,* rather than third person *mittat.* In the next clause he moves to address Virilis directly, and it may be that he has already made the switch in this clause in anticipation. Alternatively, Chrauttius does still want Veldedeius to send him the shears, but he has conflated two sentences into one, a request to ask Virilis for the shears, and a request for Veldedeius to send them himself.

Apart from the jumbled syntax, an idiom of the text also reveals the possibility that Latin may not be Chrauttius's first language. The expression *tot tempus,* literally 'so many time' occurs in place of expected *tamdiu* or *tantum tempus.* The phrase *tot tempus* is unparalleled anywhere else in surviving Latin. Normally, *tot* is only used with count nouns, and *tantus* would be used with non-count nouns. But Chrauttius has either confused a phrase such as *tot dies* with the noun *tempus,* or perhaps he has generalized one word to mean 'so many' or 'so much', and has chosen the form which does not decline rather than the inflected form *tantus.*

If we accept that Chrauttius is a non-native speaker of Latin, we still must ascertain whether he uses the language in written communication and formal situations only, or whether there is anything to suggest that he was communicating with native Latin speakers and learning the language by ear. Many of the spoken features which we would expect to be present in his language may have been disguised by the practice of the scribe. However, there are indications that Chrauttius's Latin did share features of the spoken language. For example, Chrauttius uses the pronoun *illum* twice as an anaphoric or resumptive, to refer back to a topic put at the beginning of the sentence. We find in other texts (including the next one to be studied), a similar preference for the pronoun *ille* at the expense of classical *is*, which eventually disappears altogether from the spoken variety, and a preference for fronting topics and referring to them later in the sentence through resumptive pronouns.

In summary, this text shows how we can begin to see beneath some of the cracks in the standardized Latin produced by a professional scribe, and glimpse the language of the speaker himself. Unfortunately we have only this one letter of Chrauttius, and cannot build up a picture of him as a language user. In the next text, we are more fortunate.

7.4.3   *Claudius Terentianus, bilingualism and developments in syntax and morphology*

The third text we shall discuss comes from roughly the same time as the Vindolanda letter of Chrauttius. This letter was written on papyrus and belongs to a larger archive of letters associated with a Roman soldier Claudius Tiberianus and his family found in Karanis in central Egypt (most recently re-edited in Cugusi 1992–2002). Among this archive there are a number of letters written by Claudius Tiberianus's son, Claudius Terentianus. The son writes to his father both in Latin and in Greek – there are five letters in each language surviving. Claudius Tiberianus and his family were bilingual, no doubt like many other families in the Empire. Many scholars have asked what factors prompted Terentianus to write at one time to his father in Greek, and at another time in Latin. There is no clear temporal distinction between the Latin and the Greek letters, and some of the Greek letters cover similar topics to the Latin letters, such as requests for items to be sent, and domestic concerns. However, it is possible that the Latin letters are more closely connected with family affairs than the Greek ones, and it is in the Latin letters that Terentianus seems most at ease, and Latin may have been the language spoken at home. It is possible that in at least one case he deliberately writes about a personal matter in Greek as a distancing device, attempting to make his request sound more formal and using the most widely used official language of Roman Egypt at the time.

Terentianus generally follows the common practice of using scribes to write his letters, but the scribes in the Greek-speaking East of the Empire did not seem to have received such a stringent training in Latin as the scribes in the West, since in his letters we find many more examples of the phonological changes that have taken place in the language which are generally absent from the documents at Vindolanda. In the letter we have chosen, where Terentianus makes a particularly urgent appeal to his father on behalf of his mother, it is possible that Terentianus himself was also the writer of the letter. Unfortunately this letter is less well preserved than some of the other ones he writes, and we shall accordingly use material from them also in our discussion which follows.

(5) P.Mich. 469

Claudius   Terentianus   Claudio   Tiberiano
Claudius-NOM Terentianus-NOM Claudius-DAT Tiberianus-DAT

patri   suo   plurimam salutem.
father-DAT his-DAT most-ACC   greeting-ACC.

salutat te   mater   mea   et or[at] te   si potes
she-greets you-ACC mother-NOM my-NOM and she-begs you-ACC if it-is-possible

fieri   ut emas ille[i aliqua   comm]ercia. uidit
become-INF that you-buy her-DAT certain-ACC.pl goods-ACC.pl she-saw

Germani   libertam   a[dd]ente[m] alia   lineo
Germanus-GEN freedwoman-ACC applying   other-ACC.pl linen-DAT

et qumqupibit illuc   bal[teum]. uide   si potes
and she-wanted   that-ACC.NEUT belt-ACC.NEUT see-IMPER if you-can

imbenire minore   pr[etium], merca.   mater
find-INF   lower-ACC price-ACC   buy-IMPER. mother-NOM

mea   minore bolt.   cu[lcit]as   quas illei
my-NOM lower-ACC she-wants cushions-ACC.pl which her-DAT

[a]ttuli non [placent] il[lei   ]magne,
I-brought not   are-pleasing her-DAT . . . greatly   (??)

. . . [fa]c erg[o si p]otes m[erca]re et mihi
do-IMPER. therefore if you-can buy-INF   and me-DAT

[tu] rescreibae.   [s]e   eni circumcupiscere
you   write-back-IMPER. she-ACC for   desire-INF

[i]llum diceba[t] se   eni sitlas   et fur[ca]
it-ACC   she-said   she-ACC for   buckets-ACC and fork-ACC

[hab]ere se   et ut mittas illei   di[.....].
have-INF. she-ACC and that you-send her-DAT. ?

-]nes dico illei   et ego nolim   [pe]tere
?   I-say her-DAT and I   I-do-not want fetch-INF

illas   sed posso tibi   epistula scribere
them-ACC.pl but I-can   you-DAT letter-ACC write-INF

et mittet   tibi   si imuenerit. ergo
and he-will-send you-DAT if he-will-find. Therefore

[m]erca minore   pretium rogo ut
buy-IMPER lower-ACC price-ACC I-ask   that

satisfacias   ille[i]   et   illec   enim
you-will-satisfy her-DAT and she-NOM for

[. . .] im meo   a   domu . . .   caru
. . .   in   my-ABL from home-ABL . . . dear-ACC

en enim habemus sequndu deum
  for   we-hold   following god-ACC

te   et tu   nos   saluta   qui   nos   amant
you-ACC and you-NOM us-ACC greet-IMPERAT who-NOM.pl us-ACC they-love

ual(e)
farewell

Κλαυδίω   Τιβεριανώ   σπεκουλ(άτορι)
Claudius-DAT Tiberianus-DAT *Speculator*-DAT

'Claudius Terentianus sends his best greetings to his father Claudius Tiberianus. My mother greets you and she asks if it could be arranged that you buy her certain goods. She saw the freedwoman of Germanus applying different (decorations) to her linen, and she wanted that belt. See if you can find these things at a relatively low price, (and) buy them. My mother wants them at a relatively low price. The cushions which I brought for her she does not like very much, so do make an effort to buy (them) if you can and write back to me. For she said that she wants them, and that she already has buckets and a fork, and that you should send her (*lost*). . . . I say to her "and I do not want to fetch them, but I can write a letter for you, and he will send them to you if he finds anything." So please, buy at a cheaper price, so that you keep her happy for she . . . at home. For we hold you dear, following god, and you hold us dear. Greet those who love us. Farewell.
Address: (in Greek) To Claudius Tiberianus, the *speculator*.'

Phonology

Terentianus's spelling is in some respects archaic in comparison with the Latin orthography normally employed in modern printed texts. Terentianus still writes *ei* for the long *i* (*rescreibae* for *rescribe*) and he sometimes writes *q* to represent a velar before a back vowel (*qumqupibit* for *cumcupiuit*). This serves as a reminder that, in the absence of printed schoolbooks or dictionaries, there was no standardized orthography of Latin, and certain spelling conventions may have been retained long after they disappear from official inscriptions. These old-fashioned conventions apart, Terentianus's spelling shows that his language has undergone many of the same phonological changes that we saw already in the document written by Gaius Nouius Eunus. Final *-m* is omitted as often as it is written in, for example, *eni* for *enim*, *minore pretium* for *minorem pretium* etc., and *b* is often written for classical *u* as *bolt* for *uult* and *imbenire* for *inuenire*. Although Terentianus writes out the diphthong -*ae* in some words, there can be little doubt that he pronounced it as a monophthong, as is shown by his spelling of *rescreibae* 'write!' for classical *rescribe*. This example is doubly telling, since Terentianus uses the diphthong *ae* to represent what would be a short final -*e* in Classical Latin, indicating that in final position the original diphthong is now pronounced as a short vowel. Final syllables are usually unstressed in Latin, and in this position there is a consequent tendency to shorten long vowels at the end of the word. Already in preclassical Latin vowels in final syllables were shortened in disyllabic words when the first syllable was light (so called 'iambic shortening'), giving classical *ego* 'I' from original **egō* (compare Greek *egṓ*). And even in the classical language there are examples of shortening of final -*ō*, first sporadically in the elegiac poets: *findŏ* 'I split' in Propertius, *ergŏ* 'therefore' in Ovid, and then more frequently in later verse. In the less elevated language of Terentianus, there may have been a general loss of the length distinction in final unaccented syllables.

The loss of distinctive vowel length in final syllables may also help to explain some other spellings in the Terentianus archive, which are in accord with those found in the Pompeian graffiti. In the letters there are three instances where the verb-ending -*it* is written -*et*, such as *dicet* 'he/she says' for *dicit*. We find similar spellings in the graffiti of Pompeii, for example *bibet* for *bibit* 'he/she drinks'. These spellings may reflect the merger of long *ē* with short *i* which took place when distinctive vowel quantity was lost (see 8.3.1). In the 2nd conjugation, verbs of the type *habeo*, the stem vowel of the paradigm is *ē* as in *habēs*, *habēmus*, *habētis*; in the third conjugation short *i* is found in the same positions: *scribis*, *scribimus*, *scribitis*, leading to an overlap in the paradigms when the vowels merged. Writers would have had to have learnt which verbs were spelt with *i* and which verbs were spelt with *e*, and the spellings *dicet* and *bibet* reflect hyper-corrections with *e* for *i*, even though, in the 3rd person singular the 2nd-conjugation verbs have a short *e*, *habet*.

If this interpretation of these spellings is correct, then we can build up a picture of the vowel system of Terentianus's Latin. We have seen evidence for the loss of length distinctions, the merger of short *i* and long *ē*, and the merger of the outcome of the diphthong *ae* and short *e* in final unstressed syllables. Terentianus consequently had, in final and perhaps other unaccented syllables, a distinction between three different front vowels:

1   /i/ the outcome of Classical Latin *ī*,
2   /e/ the outcome of Classical Latin *i* and *ē*,
3   /ɛ/ the outcome of Classical Latin *e* and *ae*.

As we shall see in the next chapter, the same developments of the vowel system, even in accented syllables, were to affect spoken Latin in later centuries.

Morphology and syntax

More so than any of the other texts we consider in this chapter, Terentianus's letters allow an insight into how the spoken language was undergoing morphological and syntactic change. Most readers will be familiar with the fundamental grammatical changes from Latin to the Romance languages: a general drift away from synthetic verb forms (especially in the future, the passive, and eventually in the preterite, as in French), nominals inflected for case, and variable word order, and towards analytic nominal and verbal constructions and head-first word order. In the most simplistic terms, these changes can be seen as the erosion of morphology with compensatory gains for syntax. Terentianus is still using a language with the same number of cases as Classical Latin and the full array of Latin verb forms – with a few simplifications, such as *posso* 'I can' for the irregular classical *possum*. However, it is possible to see in his Latin changes which show the beginning of the Romance developments. Terentianus's lexical choices also show the emerging pattern of Romance; for example, the pronoun *ille* (sometimes reinforced with final -*c*, as *illuc* in place of classical *illud* or *illum*) serves as the default 3rd person anaphoric pronoun, as it will do in the Romance languages (French *il* and Italian *egli*) in place of the monosyllabic classical *is*. Note also that the dative *illei* is used here (and four other times in the letters) with reference to a female, and never to a man, which suggests that the innovation of a specifically feminine dative **illaei* (here with monophthongization of *ae*), the ancestor of Italian *lei*, has already taken place.

In Terentianus's Latin, the core grammatical uses, nominative as subject, accusative as object, dative as indirect object and genitive as the case of adnominal dependency are preserved as in the classical languages. But the peripheral uses of the cases, and in particular the construction with prepositions, show signs of confusion. In Classical Latin both the accusative and the ablative occur after prepositions, but only four prepositions are construed with both cases, *in* 'in', *sub* 'under', *subter* 'under' and *super* 'over', all of which have a directional sense with the accusative and a locative sense with the ablative. However, when local expressions are collocated with verbs of rest or of motion, the context guarantees whether a directional or locative meaning should be inferred, and in Latin, as in many other languages, there was at all periods some overlap between the two. In one of Terentianus's other letters, an example of this confusion can be found, where he writes *apud te* 'at your house' with the motion verb *uenio* 'come':

spero me   celerius   apud   te   uenturum
I-hope me-ACC more-quickly at-the-house-of you-ACC come-FUT.INF
'I hope to come to your house soon.'

The distinction between the ablative and accusative with the prepositions *in* and *sub* was consequently small. With all other prepositions, the choice between the two cases was entirely determined lexically. Moreover, in two of the three major declension classes, the feminine *a*-stems (1st declension) and the consonant-stems (3rd declension), the combination of loss of final -*m* and the erosion of length distinctions in final syllables meant that the two cases came to sound the same as well. It is no surprise, therefore, to find that Terentianus has generalized the accusative as the default case for prepositions. We find the preposition *cum* (which Terentianus usually spells *con*) used with the accusative rather than the classical ablative on a number of occasions in his letters, for example, *con tirones* (with recruits-ACC.pl) 'with the recruits', where there can be no question that an accusative rather than an ablative is used. The Pompeian graffiti show that some speakers there had made the same generalizaton of the accusative as the default case after prepositions; note for example *cum discentes suos* (with learner-ACC.pl his-ACC.pl) 'with his pupils' (CIL IV 698).

The ablative and the accusative overlapped not just in their occurrence after prepositions, but also in other adverbial functions. In our letter of Terentianus the phrase *merca minore pretium* 'buy it at a lower price' occurs twice. Here *minore* is written for *minorem*, with the normal loss of final -*m*, and *pretium* must be a masculine accusative, with a switch in gender from the classical neuter *pretium* (note that Terentianus does not exhibit orthographic confusions between the ablative and the accusative in this declension class). We therefore have an example of an accusative in place of an ablative, the usual case used to signify the price of something. As Adams suggests, this use of the accusative is an extension of existing functions of the accusative, which can signify the dimension or degree of something, in its range of meanings relating to spatial and temporal extent (compare the range of meanings of English *for*: 'it stretched *for* five miles', 'it sold *for* five million'). But this semantic overlap is also bolstered by the trend to use the accusative in place of the ablative after prepositions, and it shows that the ablative is a moribund case-form. Learners of the language, and speakers such as Terentianus who also knew Greek (which does not have an ablative case), may have tended to avoid the case, replacing it either with the accusative, or by expressions with prepositions rather than the bare case-form. In support of this contention we should note that Terentianus completely avoids the use of the ablative absolute, one of the most frequent Classical Latin constructions with the ablative.

The most important syntactic development of Terentianus's Latin is in word order. We have already remarked in earlier chapters that a feature of the classical language is a default position of the verb at the end of the clause, from where it could be moved for emphasis or effect. In Terentianus's letters, sentence-final position is clearly not the default for the verb. Indeed, in his letters as a whole the order subject-verb-object predominates (although often the subject is not actually expressed), for example *emas aliqua commercia* 'you buy her certain goods', *uidit Germani libertam* 'she saw Germanus's freedwoman', *ego nolim petere illas* 'I do not want to fetch them.' Divergences from this order are usually either formulaic (as in the phrase *salutat te mater mea*, which occurs in two other letters), or else they involve pronouns. There seems to have been a general tendency to place unaccented pronouns next to the verb, either following it or in front, as in the final phrase, *saluta qui nos amant* 'greet those who love us' (which may well be formulaic).

Some of the exceptions to the subject-verb-object order are found in the accusative and infinitive construction to represent indirect statements. Terentianus uses this construction, both in formulaic expressions, such as *opto te bene ualere* (I-hope you-ACC well be-well-INF) 'I hope that you are well', which occurs in other Latin letters, and occasionally in non-formulaic contexts, such as in the sentence *se eni(m) circumcupiscere illum dicebat se eni(m) sitlas et furca(m) habere se* 'she said that she wants it, and she said that she has buckets and a fork' (the second half of the sentence presumably referring to the sort of utilitarian, but unwanted, items which Terentianus's mother is used to receiving from her menfolk). The continued life of the accusative and infinitive in Terentianus is perhaps unexpected. Petronius represents the freedmen in the *Satyricon* as using clauses introduced by *quod* and *quia* in place of the Classical Latin accusative and infinitive, as, for example, *dixi quia mustela comedit* (I-said that weasel-NOM.sg ate-3sg) 'I said that the weasel ate them' (46.4), and this construction eventually wins out in the Romance languages. Terentianus however always uses the accusative and infinitive or slips into direct speech, despite the fact that as a Greek speaker he has access to, and uses in his Greek letters, complement structures exactly parallel to Latin *quod* and *quia* clauses. Indeed, many accounts of the Romance developments argue that Greek-Latin bilinguals were partly responsible for introducing and propagating complement structures of this type. It is, of course, possible that Terentianus has been taught to avoid *quod* and *quia* to introduce reported speech, and it may be that the classical appearance of the word order of *dicebat se sitlas et furca(m) habere*, is evidence that this is a learned construction. However, Terentianus also shows subject-verb-object word order in an accusative and infinitive construction in the same sentence, *se circumcupiscere illum*. Moreover, closer inspection reveals *dicebat se sitlas et furca(m) habere* is not so 'classical' after all, since a second *se* is written following the infinitive *dicebat se sitlas et furca(m) habere se*. Terentianus has repeated the pronoun which functions as the subject of the infinitive in order to have it next to its verb. If the accusative and infinitive were entirely learned, such a repetition would have been unlikely.

7.4.4   Iasucthan and the language of verse

Our final example of Latin in the Empire is around a century later than the letters of Chrauttius and Claudius Terentianus. Unlike the other texts we have looked at, this text was inscribed in stone and set up as a deliberate record of the achievements of an individual, Marcus Porcius Iasucthan. The text comes from the Roman military outpost at Gholaia, now known as Bu Njem or Bu Djem, in the Libyan desert 200 km from the sea. The military camp there was founded at the beginning of the second century AD and excavations have unearthed a number of ostraca with short Latin documentary texts on them as well as the more extensive inscriptions in stone. The ostraca, which date to the middle of the third century, are mostly formulaic in nature, and include short letters and daily duty reports relevant to the activities and administration of the camp (published in Marichal 1992). The writers of the ostraca have received some formal training in Latin literacy, they generally exhibit confident and well-formed handwriting, and they are aware of Latin spelling conventions. However, despite the formulaic and repetitive nature of these short texts, there is clear evidence that many of the authors were not competent speakers of Latin. There is confusion between nominative and other cases and uses of syntactic constructions which are not paralleled in other non-standard Latin documents, but which can be explained as interference from local vernacular languages. One extreme example, a fragmentary ostracon written by a man who refers to himself as Flaniminus (a metathesis of the cognomen Flamininus), will suffice to give an idea of the linguistic competence of some of the soldiers serving in the camp.

(6)   O.BuDjem 101
Catulo   ag(enti)   Emili[us]   Flaniminus   bice   piciparis
Catulus-DAT *agens*-DAT Aemilius-NOM Flamininus-NOM in-place-of principal-GEN

scias   domine   benise   a   meos
you-know-SUBJ master-VOC came-INF to (*ad*) my-men-ACC.pl

refuga   Aban   barbarus   tertium   idibus   Febrarias
deserter-NOM? Aban-NOM? barbarian-NOM third-ACC.sg ides-ABL.pl February-ACC.pl

transmisi a te   per   . . .
I-have-sent to you-ACC through . . .

'To Catulus the *agens*, Aemilius Flamininus, *uice principalis* (sends greetings). May you know, my lord, that there came to my men a deserter, the barbarian Aban on 11th February. I have sent to you . . .'

This document shows many of the phonetic changes we have already seen in the documents written by Gaius Nouius Eunus and Claudius Terentianus: monophthongization of *ae* (*Emilius* for *Aemilius*), *b-* written in place of classical *u-* (*bice* for *uice*, *benise* for *uenisse*), confusion of geminate and simple consonants (*benise* for *uenisse*), and loss of high vowels in hiatus (*Febrarias* for *Februarias*). Note that there is no evidence in this text, nor from the other ostraca from this site, for the merger of long *ē* and short *i* that we discerned in Terentianus. Yet this short text also contains Latin forms which seem to represent fundamental difficulties with the language. The writing *piciparis* for *principalis* shows not just a change of *l* to *r*, but also the omission of the first *r* (the omission of *n* before stops is found in other documents, for example those of Gaius Nouius Eunus). The phrase *a meos* in place of expected *ad meos* is also unparalleled at this date, and may show the influence of the local Punic language, in which final *d* is prone to loss. More striking than these phonological features is, however, the lack of command over Latin syntax. Following the formulaic introduction *scias domine*, 'you should know, my lord', we expect an accusative and infinitive construction; *benise* corresponds to Classical Latin *uenisse*, the expected infinitive, but is followed by a nominative (*refuga . . . barbarus*), not an accusative. Other ostraca from Bu Njem also show the nominative in place of the accusative after the preposition *per*. Confusion between nominative and accusative is very strange for Latin of this date. It is true that for many 1st-declension nouns the loss of final *-m* leads to an apparent equivalence in the two cases in the singular, but this overlap is not paralleled in the other declensions, and, as we saw above, there is evidence that speakers such as Claudius Terentianus were eroding the distinction between the accusative and ablative, but keeping the category of nominative apart. Flaniminus shows further evidence of a more general confusion of case syntax in the dating formula, *tertium idibus Febrarias*, where he construes the ablative *idibus* with the accusative *Febrarias*. Flaniminus cannot be the only learner of Latin who had difficulty with the dating system, and here he has confused the ablative, used if referring to the actual days of the kalends, nones and ides, with the accusative which occurs when referring to days which precede them.

Texts such as the ostracon cited above therefore show that at Bu Njem Latin was used as a language of administration. The non-standard features of a text such as this also show that Latin was a spoken language, not just used for written documents, and that it was spoken by soldiers amongst themselves. However, not all soldiers were fluent in Latin, as the text cited shows, and they may also have used local languages to communicate.

It is in this linguistic milieu that we shall consider the poem set up by the centurion Marcus Porcius Iasucthan at Bu Njem. The text (reproduced here from Adams 1999) is 33 lines long, and in general it shows Classical Latin orthography, without the confusion of, for example, the diphthong *ae* and vowel *e* found in other texts, reflecting the fact that, much as was the case with Chrauttius's text, it had passed, at some stage in its composition, through a scribe who knew the Latin spelling conventions. However, the language reveals that it certainly was not the original composition of a professional scribe. We shall only reproduce half of the text here, omitting the initial five lines honouring the name of the emperor Marcus Aurelius and the local governor.

(7)   Adams 1999

Portam uetustate conlabsam lapidi   quadrato arco   curuato   restituit
gate-ACC age-ABL   collapsed-ACC stone-ABL squared-ABL arch-ABL curved-ABL he-restored

Omnes   prateriti   cuius   labore   uitabant
all-NOM.pl predecessors-NOM.pl of-which labor-ACC they-avoided

Rigido uigore   iuuenum   tertia augustani   fecerunt
firm-ABL vigour-ABL young-men-GEN.pl third-? Augustans-NOM.pl they-did

Creto   consilio hortante   parato   magistro
fixed-ABL design-ABL encouraging-ABL prepared-ABL magistrate-ABL

Iuncta   uirtus   militum   paucorum uelocitas   ingens
joined-FEM.NOM virtue-FEM.NOM soldiers-GEN.pl few-GEN.pl   speed-FEM.NOM huge-NOM

Usui   compendio lapides   de   longe adtractos   chamulco
use DAT case-ABL   stones-ACC.pl from afar   dragged-ACC.pl traction-engine-ABL

Sub arcata   militum   uirtus   funib(us) cannabinis   strictis
under arches-ACC.pl soldiers-GEN.pl virtue-NOM ropes-ABL.pl hempen-ABL.pl drawn-ABL.pl

Iam nunc contendunt fieri   cito   milites   omnes
now   now   they-strive   to-be-done quickly soldiers-NOM all-NOM.pl

Arta uirtute sua opera aeternale fecerunt
close-ABL virtue-ABL their-ABL work-ACC eternal-ACC they-did

Subsequentes stipendiis antecessorum onestia bona sumebant
following-NOM.pl services-DAT.pl predecessors-GEN.pl honourable-ACC.pl goods-ACC.pl they-were-taking

Urguente tempore hiemis necumqua cessauerunt
pressing-ABL season-ABL winter-GEN never they-stopped

Celerius excelsae turres quater diuisae cum uoce militum a terra uenerunt
more-quickly high-NOM towers-NOM fourfold divided-NOM with voice-ABL soldiers-GEN from ground-ABL they-came

Torrens uirtus leg(ionis) III Aug(ustae) p(iae) u(ictricis)
rushing-NOM virtue-NOM legion-GEN III Augusta *pia* *uictrix*

Haec ut fierent milites omnes sibi zelum tradebant
these-NOM.pl in-order-that they-be-done soldiers-NOM all-NOM.pl themselves-DAT zeal-ACC they-were-handing

Animaduertentes quod priores sibi uestigia fecissent
noticing-NOM what earlier-NOM.pl themselves-DAT footsteps-ACC they-had-made

Nunc et ipsi titulis suis uirtutis deuotionis ornauerunt
now and same-NOM.pl marks-ABL their-own-ABL.pl virtue-GEN devotion-GEN they-adorned

'He restored the gate, which had collapsed through age, by a squared stone in a curved arch. The work of which all our predecessors had avoided, the third Augustans did with firm vigour of young men, by a fixed plan, and with the magistrate prepared and encouraging them [*or* 'the magistrate Paratus . . .']. The valour of a few soldiers (and) huge speed linked for use – stones, dragged from afar by a traction engine for ease, under the arches – the valour of the soldiers with hempen ropes drawn tight. Now all the soldiers strive for it to be done quickly. By close valour they did their eternal work, following the services of their predecessors they took up honourable good works. With winter pressing on they never ceased. The high towers came quickly from the earth, divided in four (stages?), with the voices of the soldiers. The rushing valour of the Legion III Augusta *pia uictrix*. In order that this should be done all the soldiers handed zeal to one another, noticing that their predecessors had made tracks for them, now they themselves adorned them with their own marks of virtue and devotion.'

The translation of this extraordinary text largely follows that given by Adams, but owing to Iasucthan's limited competence it must remain questionable whether we have really correctly interpreted what he meant to say. Iasucthan largely avoids subordinating and embedding structures, and in general fails to link sentences or make explicit the sequence of thought, so that we cannot be sure even where sentences begin and end.

The obscurity is probably a result of Iasucthan's attempt to write in verse. Although this text does not scan in any recognized classical metre, we can be certain that it is an attempt at verse partly because of the acrostic spelling of his name and title with the initial letters of the lines (highlighted here in bold) – for Iasucthan this was probably the most important feature. Acrostic patterns of this type are never found in Latin prose texts written at this date. There is also a parallel acrostic verse inscription written by another centurion which does scan from the same site.

Although Iasucthan's poem does not scan as conventional Latin poetry, there is a discernible stress rhythm at the end of each line. Every line-ending of the text cited here can be fitted into a hexameter rhythm, with a stressed syllable followed by two unstressed syllables, then a stressed and unstressed syllable: ´ x x ´ x. (The two difficult cases, *necumqua cessauerunt* and *III Aug. p. u.* can be made to scan in this way if we take *cessauerunt* to be written for spoken *cessarunt*, and *III Aug. p.u.* to be written for spoken *tert(i)ae Augustae*). The line-endings will not scan according to the Latin rules of quantity, however, and the first parts of the lines cannot, for the most part, be fitted into the hexameter at all, even if scanned only with a stress accent. It appears that Iasucthan understood the hexameter only from having heard it, and what was distinctive to him was the coincidence of accentual stress and verse beat at the end of each line. Indeed, for most speakers of modern English, it is only at the end of the Latin hexameter line that the rhythm is heard when Latin poetry is read out loud. If Iasucthan was a non-native speaker of Latin, we cannot be sure whether his failure to hear Latin long and short vowels was a result of his imperfect command of Latin phonology, or whether it actually reflects a more general breakdown in the vowel quantity system in the spoken Latin of Africa at this date. In support of the latter explanation we have later statements in grammarians and other sources (such as Augustine of Hippo, *de Doctrina Christiana* 4.10.24) that may suggest that vowel length was less distinctive in Latin spoken in Africa than elsewhere (see now Adams, forthcoming: chs 4 and 8 for discussion of the African pronunciation of Latin). It is possible that length had become an automatic concomitant of accent placement: stressed vowels were long, unstressed vowels were short.

Although he may have been a non-native speaker of Latin, Iasucthan must have had considerable exposure to the language in his service in the army (at least for 15 years if he had been promoted from the ranks), and a sufficient command of it to be able to function as an effective centurion. Since he was able to identify, albeit to a limited extent, the rhythm of Classical Latin verse, he must have heard some hexameter poetry during his career in the army, even though he had clearly never had any serious training in the mechanics of verse. His attempt at poetry therefore reveals some of the other features which may have seemed to him characteristic of the genre, and in his use, or over-use, of poetic features we can begin to see some of the gaps between the everyday Latin that a speaker such as Iasucthan would have used, and the elevated language of classical verse. Note for example, Iasucthan's placement of verbs. Every main verb in the cited passage except one comes at the end of a line and at the end of its sense unit (as far as these can be discerned). Iasucthan seems to have over-generalized one rule of classical high style, that verbs come at the end of their clauses. It is worth noting that in the other verse inscription from Bu Njem, the centurion Quintus Avidius Quintianus, who can write hexameters that actually scan, ends only 2 of his 18 lines with a verb, in contrast to Iasucthan who does this 10 times in the 16 lines cited here.

Iasucthan's use of the ablative may also show an attempt to elevate his language to a higher register. As we have already remarked in our discussion of Terentianus's language, the ablative case, particularly when used without a preposition, seems to have been in retreat in the spoken language. Iasucthan has a fondness for expressions with an abstract noun joined with a concrete adjective in the ablative, such as *rigido uigore* 'with firm vigour', *creto consilio* 'with a fixed plan', *arta uirtute* 'with close valour'. Whereas the expressions with the nouns *uigor* and *uirtus* do follow Classical Latin norms, with an ablative representing the attendant circumstances of the action, the ablative of *consilium* cannot be so used in Latin, and it appears that Iasucthan has generalized the pattern from the other phrases. These expressions are clearly not taken from Iasucthan's normal speech, as is shown by the bizarre lexical choice of adjectives, which presumably reflects a desire to imitate transferred epithets of Classical Latin verse (compare also other phrases of this type such as *uelocitas ingens* 'huge speed' and *torrens uirtus* 'rushing virtue').

Iasucthan also includes ablative absolute constructions in his poem: *hortante parato magistro*, *funib(us) cannabinis strictis* and *urguente tempore hiemis*. The phrase *hortante parato magistro* requires some further explanation: the first and last word clearly mean 'with the magistrate urging them on', but what about *parato*? This could be the name of the magistrate, *Paratus*, as previous commentators have taken it, but this individual is not mentioned again, and elsewhere in the inscription all the glory is allocated to Iasucthan himself. So it is perhaps better to see this as another participle, from the verb *paro* 'I prepare' but this time with the passive used incorrectly when Iasucthan intends an active meaning. The whole clause could therefore be translated 'with their master having prepared them and urging them on.' Another indication that Iasucthan may not be altogether happy in using absolute constructions is the curious construction *lapides de longe adtractos*. Syntactically, the accusative here makes no sense, since there is no verb after which it can be construed, and it seems best to take this as an absolute construction parallel to the *funib(us) cannabinis strictis* in the next line. The use of the accusative, rather than the ablative, is therefore in line with the accusative and ablative overlap we have already identified from the letters of Terentianus.

We have already noticed some peculiarities of Iasucthan's vocabulary, and we can add further examples to the list of otherwise unparalleled expressions: *subsequentes stipendiis antecessorum* 'following the service of the predecessors' (the use of *subsequor* with the dative is unparalleled, but it could be analogical to the dative after *succedo*); *onestia bona sumebant* 'they took up honourable good works' (the meaning of the phrase is unclear, *onestia* here is taken to derive from an *i*-stem adjective **honestis*, standing in place of *honestus*, although the phrase *(h)onestia bona* is unmatched in this sense elsewhere; it is possible that *onestia* is an ablative from an otherwise unparalleled noun **honestia*, wrongly created from *honestus* on the analogy of pairs such as *peritia* 'experience' beside *peritus* 'experienced', or simplified from **honestitia*); *turres a terra uenerunt* 'the towers came [for *rose*] from the earth'; *milites omnes sibi zelum tradebant* 'the soldiers handed zeal to themselves.' These lexical oddities may be a further sign that Iasucthan was not at home in Latin idiom, but they also show that to him, Classical Latin verse was a register in which it was possible to extend the normal meanings of words greatly, and full of constructions which were never heard in speech. Iasucthan's inscription therefore tells us perhaps more about what spoken Latin was not rather than what it was, and in it we can see how far removed the language of Vergil was from the language of the military camp. Indeed, the gap was so great that a centurion, who was presumably able to converse with his superiors and to issue commands and carry out administrative tasks in Latin without any difficulty in making himself understood, is barely comprehensible when he attempts the high style of Classical Latin poetry. Already by the beginning of the third century, Classical Latin is virtually a foreign language to speakers such as Iasucthan.

The four speakers of Latin whose language we have examined in this chapter have taken us progressively further away from the classical standard of the elite. These texts represent only a tiny fraction of the surviving Latin of this period, and even among non-literary texts they are unusual in their departure from the classical norm. They presumably are representative of a much wider spectrum of non-standard Latin in the spoken language of their day, which is hidden behind the façade of the uniform written idiom which we find in most texts. We shall see in the next chapter that the façade was to remain in place even after the collapse of the Roman Empire.

References

Adams, J. N. (1977) *The Vulgar Latin of the Letters of Claudius Terentianus* (P. Mich. VIII, 467–72). Manchester: Manchester University Press.

Adams, J. N. (1990) 'The Latinity of C. Novius Eunus'. *Zeitschrift für Papyrologie und Epigraphik* 82, 227–247.

Adams, J. N. (1994) 'Latin and Punic in contact? The case of the Bu Njem ostraca'. *Journal of Roman Studies* 84, 87–112.

Adams, J. N. (1995) 'The language of the Vindolanda writing tablets: An interim report'. *Journal of Roman Studies* 85, 86–134.

Adams, J. N. (1999) 'The poets of Bu Njem: Language, culture and the centurionate'. *Journal of Roman Studies* 89, 109–34.

Adams, J. N. (2003a) *Bilingualism and the Latin Language*. Cambridge: Cambridge University Press.

Adams, J. N. (2003b) 'Petronius and new non-literary Latin'. in J. Herman and H. Rosén (eds.), *Petroniana: Gedenkschrift für Hubert Petersmann*. Heidelberg: Winter, 11–23.

Adams, J. N. (forthcoming) *Regional Diversity in Latin*. Cambridge: Cambridge University Press.

Bowman, A. and D. Thomas (1994) *The Vindolanda Writing Tablets (Tabulae Vindolandenses II)*. London: British Museum Press.

Boyce, B. (1991) *The Language of the Freedmen in Petronius' Cena Trimalchionis*. Leiden: Brill.

Brunt, P. A. (1976) 'The Romanization of the local ruling classes in the Roman Empire', in D. M. Pippidi (ed.), *Assimilation et résistance à la culture gréco-romaine dans le monde ancien: travaux du VIe Congrès international d'études classiques (Madrid, septembre 1974)*. Paris: 'Les Belles lettres', 161–73.

Calboli, G. (1999) 'Zur Syntax der neuen vulgärlateinischen Urkunden aus Murecine', in H. Petersman and R. Kettemann (eds.), *Latin vulgaire – latin tardif V: Actes du Ve Colloque international sur le latin vulgaire et tardif, Heidelberg, 5–8 septembre 1997*. Heidelberg: Winter, 331–44.

Camodeca, G. (1999) *Tabulae Pompeianae Sulpiciorum (TPSulp.). Edizione critica dell'archivio puteolano dei Sulpicii*. Rome: Quasar.

Cugusi, P. (1992–2002) *Corpus Epistolarum Latinarum, papyris tabulis ostracis servatarum*, 3 vols. Florence: Gonnelli.

Flobert, P. (1995) 'Le latin des tablettes de Murécine (Pompéi)'. *Revue des études latines* 73, 138–50.

Genin, M., B. Hoffmann and A. Vernhet (2002) 'Les productions anciennes de la Graufesenque', in M. Genin and A. Vernhet (eds.), *Céramiques de la Graufesenque et autres productions d'époque romaine. Nouvelles recherches: hommages à Bettina Hoffmann* (Archéologie et Histoire Romaine 7), Montagnac: M. Mergoil, 45–104.

Leiwo, M. (2003) 'Greek or Latin, or something in between? The Jews of Venusia and their language', in H. Solin, M. Leiwo and H. Halla-aho (eds.), *Latin vulgaire – latin tardif VI: Actes du VIe Colloque international sur le latin vulgaire et tardif, Helsinki, 29 août –2 septembre 2000*. Hildesheim/New York: Olms-Weidmann, 253–64.

Marichal, R. (1992) *Les Ostraca de Bu Djem*. Libya Antiqua, Supplement VII. Tripoli: Directorate-General of Antiquities, Museums, and Archives.

Oates, J. F., R. S. Bagnall, S. J. Clackson, A. A. O'Brien, J. D. Sosin, T. G. Wilfong, and K. A. Worp (2005) *Checklist of Greek, Latin, Demotic and Coptic Papyri, Ostraca and Tablets*. Online edition. http://scriptorium.lib.duke.edu/papyrus/texts/clist.html, accessed December, 2005.

Scheidel, W. (2004) 'Human mobility in Roman Italy, 1: The free population'. *Journal of Roman Studies* 94, 1–26.

Väänänen, V. (1959) *Le latin vulgaire des inscriptions pompéiennes*. Berlin: Akademie.

Woolf, G. (1998) *Becoming Roman: The Origins of Provincial Civilization in Gaul*. Cambridge: Cambridge University Press.

Chapter VIII

Latin in Late Antiquity and Beyond

8.1 Introduction

This chapter covers a far greater time-span than any of the previous chapters in this book, roughly from the third century AD to the end of the first millennium. Assigning an end-point to the history of the Latin language is no easier than giving a date to the end of antiquity. One conventional position, codified in the first edition of the *Cambridge Ancient History* of 1924–39, places the end of ancient history in 324 AD when the Christian emperor Constantine became sole ruler of the Roman Empire. But this makes little sense as an end-point historically, and even less linguistically, since there is no change in Latin datable to 324 AD. Nor does a terminus such as the fall of Rome or 'the barbarian invasions' have much to recommend it. The barbarian invasions are no longer seen as the devastating end of ancient culture that they once were (indeed they seem largely to have been presented as such only three or four hundred years later, during the Carolingian period). The reasons for continuing the more detailed history of Latin as late as 1000 AD will become apparent in the text that follows. However, although the history of Latin does not stop at any of these points, it does slow down. The continued presence of a prestigious standard makes the linguistic changes 'go underground'. Texts are no longer written reflecting the way people spoke, but the way they were taught to write. As Latin moves further away from speech, the linguistic changes and peculiarities become increasingly artificial, and of less interest to the linguist. The history of Latin becomes the history of education, of book-learning and the story of a cultural artefact, a history we feel unqualified to write.

8.2   Latin, Romance and Proto-Romance

Pope Gregory V, sometimes called the 'first German Pope', died in Rome on 18 February 999. The Latin epitaph on his tomb survives, and is written in 16 lines of elegiac couplets:

(1)   MGH PLMA V.2 110

Hic quem   claudit humus   oculis   uultuque   decorum
this   whom-ACC conceals earth-NOM eyes-ABL face-ABL=and handsome-ACC

    Papa   fuit quintus   nomine   Gregorius
    Pope-NOM was   fifth-NOM name-ABL Gregory-NOM

Ante tamen Bruno   Francorum regia   proles
before however Bruno-NOM Franks-GEN   royal-NOM offspring-NOM

    Filius   Ottonis de   genitrice   Iudith
    son-NOM Otto-GEN from mother-ABL Judith

Lingua   Teutonicus, Vuangia   doctus   in urbe   5
language-ABL German-NOM, Worms-ABL educated-NOM in   city-ABL

    Sed iuuenis   cathedram sedit apostolicam
    but   young-man-NOM seat-ACC   he-sat apostolic-ACC

Ad binos   annos   et menses   circiter octo
to   two-ACC.pl years-ACC.pl and months-ACC.pl around   eight

    Ter senos   Februo   connumerante dies
    thrice six-ACC.pl February-ABL counting-ABL   days-ACC.pl

Pauperibus diues   per   singula sabbata   uestes
poor-DAT.pl rich-NOM through each-ABL Sabbath-ABL clothes-ACC.pl

    Diuisit   numero   cautus   apostolico   10
    he-distributed number-DAT prudent-NOM apostolic-DAT

Usus   Francisca, uulgari   et   uoce   Latina
Used-NOM Frankish-ABL vulgar-ABL and speech-ABL Latin-ABL

    Instituit populos   eloquio   triplici.
    he-taught people-ACC.pl eloquence-ABL triple-ABL

Tertius   Otto   sibi   Petri   commisit ouile
Third-NOM Otto-NOM him-DAT Peter-GEN entrusted   sheepfold-ACC

    Cognatis   manibus   unctus   in imperium
    related-ABL.pl hands-ABL.pl anointed-NOM in   rule-ACC

Exuit   et postquam terrenae   uincula   carnis   15
he-stripped and after   earthly-GEN.sg bonds-ACC flesh-GEN.sg

Aequiuoci   dextro   substituit lateri
same-named-GEN right-DAT he-placed   side-DAT

'This man whom the earth conceals, handsome in eye and countenance was Pope, Gregory V in name, but earlier called Bruno, royal offspring of the Franks. He was son of Otto and of his mother Judith. A
German in speech, he was educated in Worms, but while still young sat
on the apostolic throne for around two years and eighteen months, ending
on the 18th February. Generous to the poor, he distributed clothes every
Sabbath to 12 paupers, careful to limit himself to the same number as
the apostles. He spoke Frankish, the vulgar tongue and Latin, and taught
the people with a triple eloquence. Otto III entrusted the sheepfold of
St Peter to him and was anointed emperor by the hands of his son.
He sloughed off the chains of earthly flesh and took his place at the right
side of the Pope of the same name (Gregory the Great, whose tomb was
nearby).'

As the Pope had died young after a short rule, the writer of these lines
has some trouble in finding enough to say. Fortunately for the historian
of the Latin language, Gregory's linguistic accomplishments are therefore
singled out for praise. However, there is dispute as to exactly which three
languages he is credited with speaking at Rome. The word *francisca*
'Frankish' can be taken to mean German, the language of the Frankish
rulers of France, but in an earlier line Gregory had already been
described as *lingua teutonicus* 'a German by language', and many
scholars have instead taken 'Frankish' to mean French, the language of
the inhabitants of Frankish lands (so, for example, Wright 2002: 205–6).
If *francisca* means 'French', then the other languages Gregory spoke at
Rome must be Italian and Latin; if it means 'Frankish' then *uulgari* could
just mean the spoken Romance idiom as opposed to Classical Latin.

It may come as a surprise to modern readers that this papal epitaph is
the earliest extant text which can be interpreted to imply a distinction between
the language spoken by the populace of Rome and Latin. If *francisca*
does refer to French and not German (and this is uncertain), it is also
the first occurrence of the notion that French and Italian are separate
languages, and the first time a name is given to the French language.
We might have expected the separate Romance idioms to have been
delineated much earlier than 999 AD, a date exactly midway between the
Augustan era and the current day. However, authors writing after the fall
of the Western Roman Empire who discuss language before this time are
aware of the distinction between spoken and written varieties, but they

do not have any problem in envisaging all of these varieties as part of the same language. It is true that sometimes writers represent themselves treading a difficult path between a correct and Classical Latin and a more easily understood but less polished variety, but in doing so it is clear that there is a middle ground between the two extremes, not a chasm dividing them.

The continuum between the spoken and the written languages seems to have lasted longer in Italy than in France. One hundred and fifty years before Gregory V's epitaph we already see the gap between speech and written Latin in northern France being almost too wide to bridge. Handbooks of the French language often begin with the 'Strasbourg oaths' in 842, the first conscious attempt to write down a spoken register distinct from Latin (see (5) in 8.5). The oaths occur in the account of a sworn allegiance between the Frankish rulers Louis and his brother Charles at Strasbourg, where they are represented as switching between *lingua romana* 'the Roman language' and *lingua teudisca* 'the German language'. However, it should be emphasized that the *lingua romana* also encompasses Latin as well as what we think of as early French. In Nithard's account of the Strasbourg allegiance, he explicitly describes as *lingua romana* both the speech in Latin made by the brothers before their pledge and the short text of the oaths sworn by the kings and their armies.

Pope Gregory V's epitaph is therefore one of the very first texts which definitely announces the birth of new languages out of Latin. This does not mean that it is the death certificate of Latin, however. We are also told that Gregory used Latin as a spoken as well as a written language. The audience whom he addressed in Latin presumably included not just educated members of the elite for whom knowledge of the classical language was a mark of prestige, but also visitors to Rome such as clergy from Germany or the British Isles, bilingual in Latin and German or Irish or English, or from different parts of the Romance speech area, such as the Iberian peninsula, for whom the Roman vernacular may have been more difficult to follow.

The Latin Gregory spoke cannot have been far different from the Latin of his epitaph, and it is immediately striking how 'classical' this Latin is, despite the presence of non-classical forms and constructions. A modern student who has studied Vergil and Ovid at school or university should have little trouble in understanding it, nor, perhaps, would an educated Roman of 100 AD, although the latter would be more puzzled by the Christian idioms and imagery, such as the reference to death as a 'sloughing of the chains of earthly flesh'. The epitaph is written in elegiac couplets which mostly follow classical scansion, albeit with a few oddities. The inscription shows none of the 'mistakes' of orthography or morphology which we saw in the texts discussed in the previous chapter.

The vocabulary is largely consistent with that of Latin used during the Roman Empire. Only two words, other than proper names, occur in it which are not found in the *Oxford Latin Dictionary*, which covers authors and texts up to 300 AD, *apostolicus* 'apostolic' (line 6) and *aequiuo-cus* 'of the same name' (line 16); both of these are already found in texts from before 400 AD. Other words have changed their meaning or form slightly, such as *ad* used in line 6 to express duration of time, whereas in the earlier language it can only mean 'until' or 'after', or the short-ened form *Februo* for *Februario* in line 8, which seems to be an attempt to create an archaic form, based on the analogy of pairs of words with and without the *-arius* suffix, such as *arena* 'sand, arena' and *arenaria* 'sand-pit, sand'. Syntactic uses also show some deviations from the classical standard. For example, the ablative participle *connumerante* in line 8, here meaning 'counting in' is best taken as an impersonal 'if one counts in the 18 days in February'; the classical language might have used here a passive participle in an absolute phrase *diebus connumeratis* 'with the days counted in'.

Latin at the end of the first millennium AD can be best described as a 'living fossil'. Whereas other languages are continually evolving and changing, Latin seems to have been preserved in its broadly classical form, and it was to remain fixed for the next thousand years. Despite an abund-ance of surviving material all the way from the later Roman Empire to the Middle Ages and beyond, we have very few surviving documents which even attempt to reproduce anything other than the highest, most formal registers (despite the humble protestations of writers who claim to be writing for the peasants as much as for the learned). Other registers must have existed beneath this, and these are the varieties which developed into the Romance languages: Italian, French, Spanish etc. We saw in the last chapter that, already in the high Roman Empire, the norms of the written language obscured much of the variation which must have been present in spoken Latin, and this problem remains for the rest of the period. As the spoken varieties moved apart further from the classical norm over time, the link between what was said and what was written progressively weakened, and this meant that learning to write also involved learning not just letters and spelling rules, but also classical morphology, syntax and vocabulary. The prestige of the written word, reinforced by the perception that Latin was a 'sacred language' of the Christian religion, led to a conscious rejection of innovation or experimentation in the standard.

This is not to say that the standard was a monolithic entity. As we have seen in Gregory's epitaph, some vocabulary items have shifted in meaning, and neologisms were added to the lexicon. Syntactic construc-tions have been extended from a particular context to a wider scope and moribund verbal forms have been re-utilized. We shall see some of the changes in the standard in more detail later in this chapter, but first we need to clarify how these developments reflect what is happening in the spoken language. Finding out what developments take place in the spoken varieties of Latin is not straightforward. The method usually employed to do this is to reconstruct the spoken language by working back from changes which have taken place in French, Italian, Spanish and the other Romance varieties, and attempting to locate these developments in time using the evidence from texts which show non-classical features. We shall present a synopsis of these developments below as a guide for issues in the rest of the chapter. But first it worth clarifying some of the methodological issues involved in using the evidence from Romance.

When they reconstruct 'back' from the Romance languages, linguists use the techniques of comparative reconstruction (sometimes labelled 'the comparative method'). We saw in Chapter I that Proto-Indo-European, the parent language of the Indo-European family, is a hypothetical entity arrived at by comparison of its 'linguistic daughters'. The comparison of the Romance languages correspondingly can be used to produce 'Proto-Romance'. It is important to remember that Proto-Romance is a hypothetical construct, and differs from a 'real' language' in a number of particulars, just as we saw that Proto-Indo-European differs from a real language. Proto-Romance is reconstructed as a unity, with limited variation across time and space. The comparative method works on the assumption that if any innovation has taken place in one part of the speech area, this is necessarily the end of the period of linguistic unity. Moreover, after the end of the parent language, it is assumed that speakers of different linguistic varieties have no contact with each other or indeed with the parent. In short, the comparative method is predicated on the model of a linguistic 'family tree'. To illustrate, figure 8.1 gives an example of a possible family tree for the Romance languages (omitting Romanian and the smaller languages). In this family tree French, Italian, Spanish and the other Romance languages are represented as the branches on the tree, and the point where they all join represents Proto-Romance. Once the languages have separated, they are considered as independent, and hence all the changes which they undergo jointly are reconstructed for Proto-Romance. It follows that the early developments of French took place separately from those that took place in Italian and Spanish, and that all must derive from a parent language which shows divergence from the standardized Classical Latin.

But we know enough about the linguistic situation in the first millennium to know that it was very different from this model. Firstly, throughout the whole period speakers within the Romance area were able to communicate with each other. In 953 we know that John, later Abbot

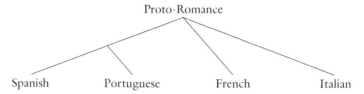

Figure 8.1   One possible family tree for the Romance languages

of Gorze (near Metz in northeastern France), acted as envoy for the German King Otto I to the court of Abd al-Rahman III, caliph of Cordoba in southern Spain. The life of John records that he had no difficulty in conversing with the Christians from Cordoba, and was immediately able to talk about any subject with them (Smith 2005: 24). This is less than 50 years before Gregory's epitaph, and 100 years after the Strasbourg oaths, both of which have been taken to signify the end of the Latin language! This story becomes plausible if we assume that speakers, particularly those with some education, were able to modify any regional differences in order to communicate. Secondly, the Latin standard continued to be known and to influence the spoken language. As we have already seen, until the ninth and tenth centuries no one writing in Latin had any conception that the spoken language might be anything other than Latin. There was a wide array of registers from the highest and most formal language of the written documents down to the spoken vernacular, and only after the Carolingian period do we see any awareness of an unbridgeable gulf between the two.

In summary, where the family tree model presents Proto-Romance as a linguistic unity, idealized at one point in time and space, we should instead envisage a linguistic continuum, spread over what was once the Western Roman Empire and lasting for many centuries. Comparison with similar situations shows that in such a linguistic situation, it is possible to have clearly differentiated dialects, but innovations which spread through all of them. In Modern British English dialects, for example, features of the dialect of London and surrounding areas (so-called 'Estuary English'), such as the replacement of intervocalic *t* with a glottal stop, have spread to the spoken dialects of Manchester and Glasgow, although these still retain their own peculiar features. The example of Greek shows the same thing happening in the ancient world. We know that Greek was already divided into dialects by the time of the earliest documents, written in Mycenaean Greek from around 1300 BC, but all the dialects have shared in common certain developments after Mycenaean Greek, such as the palatalization of labio-velars and the innovation of certain morphological items and syntactic constructions, even though some of the dialect divisions already present in Mycenaean Greek have been retained. We must therefore accept that Proto-Romance cannot have existed in the way that the linguistic models imply, but that Latin was a continuum across both space and society, varying from the spoken varieties to the written standard.

8.3   From Latin to Romance

In this section we present a synopsis of the developments which we assume took place in the spoken language from the evidence of the Romance languages (some of these developments have already been discussed in Chapter VII, but it will be useful to group them all here). Where possible we have tried to link these developments with evidence from inscriptions and textual sources. However, it should be noted that the features presented here do not describe a single linguistic variety, to be placed in opposition to the written standard (the 'Vulgar Latin' of some handbooks). Rather they collect together developments which took place to a greater or lesser degree across the whole speech area in the period under consideration. As we shall see, the starting points of some of these innovations can be found in texts from the early Roman Empire, but the innovatory and the original variants in many cases co-existed for centuries. For more details on these changes the reader is advised to consult either Väänänen (1981) or Herman (2000).

8.3.1   Phonology

Vowels

Classical Latin vowels were distinguished through the feature of length; long and short vowels could occur at any position in the word. The Classical Latin prosodic accent was one of stress. The combination of distinctive vowel length and a stress accent is not typologically common across the world's languages, and prone to replacement. Stress is a cumulative effect of pitch, loudness and length of the stressed syllable, and non-native speakers of a language with vowel length and stress tend to hear either long vowels as stressed or stressed vowels as long. In spoken Latin the frequent conflict between vowel length and prosodic stress led to the eventual loss of length as a distinctive feature, as in the modern Romance languages. The locus of the accent in Classical Latin was retained in Romance, but all accented vowels came to be pronounced long, all unaccented vowels short. It is difficult to date when this change became generalized across the whole of the Romance speech area with accuracy. Already in Latin of the Republic, in some environments long vowels were shortened when not under the accent: this is the process known as 'iambic shortening' whereby long vowels following an accented short vowel in disyllabic words became short vowels. For example, Latin *ego* 'I' and *duo* 'two' have short final vowels which are unexpected in comparison with Greek *egó* 'I' and *dúo* 'two' but which can be explained by the iambic shortening rule.

In these early cases of vowel shortening, the long vowel merges with the short vowel of the same quality, so, for example, *ō* in *egō merges with the inherited short *o*. But when short vowels are lengthened under the accent and unaccented long vowels are shortened in the imperial period and later, a different set of mergers takes place, some of which we have already noted in the last chapter. In general (excluding individual developments in peripheral areas such as Sardinia, Sicily and in the East), long *ē* merges with short *i* and long *ō* merges with short *u*, neither long *ī* and long *ū* merges with any other vowel; the low vowels long *ā* and short *a* merge with each other. This seems to reflect a qualitative difference between the long and short mid-vowels which is noted by some ancient writers on language: the long mid-vowels were pronounced more close than their short 'counterparts'. Figure 8.2 summarizes the changes that took place in the vowel systems as long and short vowels were merged. Note that the net effect of these changes is the establishment of a vowel system with distinctive mid-close and mid-open vowels in place of one with length distinctions but only three distinctive vowel heights.

We can judge from analysis of the inscriptions at Pompeii, and from the texts discussed in the last chapter, that the feature of length was not yet lost in documents from the first century. In accented syllables short and long vowels are generally distinguished. However, in unaccented, and particularly final syllables, an expected long *e* is spelt with *i* and an expected short *i* is spelt with an *e* not infrequently, suggesting that here the short and long vowels are falling together. Particularly telling are the confusions of the diphthong *ae*, which became a simple vowel, with short *e* (the new vowel [ɛ]) in unaccented syllables, which confirms length is no longer distinctive in this environment. The diphthong *au* was maintained in most of the Romance area until the latter half of the first millennium.

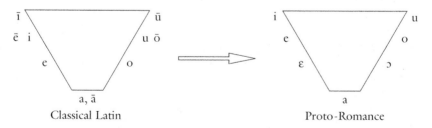

Figure 8.2 Classical Latin to Proto-Romance vowel systems

By the end of the fourth century, there is also evidence for the loss of the length distinction in accented syllables, and we find a number of writers commenting on the tendency to ignore vowel length in speech.

Other changes affecting the vowel system are:

1   vowels /i/ and /e/ merge as /j/ before /o/ /u/ /a/, hence *-ia* written for *-ea*, *-iolus* for *-eolus* etc.;
2   combinations of like vowels prone to contraction: *tuus > tus* 'your' etc.;
3   sporadic lowering of vowels before following /-r/, sometimes motivated by a low vowel earlier in the word: *ansar* for *anser* 'goose', *passar* for *passer* 'sparrow' etc.;
4   syncope of short vowels in syllables immediately before or after the accented syllable: for example *caldus* for *calidus* 'hot', **frigdus* for *frigidus* 'cold' etc. This process has also affected some words in the classical language, for example, syncopated *ualde* 'greatly' alongside *ualidus* 'strong'.

Consonants

The phonological developments of the consonants are most easily dealt with under separate headings.

Palatalization   All Romance languages have undergone palatalization of dental and velar consonants before /j/, and all but the Sardinian dialect palatalize velar consonants before front vowels. Palatalization before /j/ (which itself often arises from earlier /i/ or /e/ before a back vowel) becomes general by the fifth century AD, and is revealed through inscriptional and manuscript spellings showing confusion between *-tiV-* and *-ciV-* (e.g. *tercium* for *tertium* 'third' and *conditio* for *condicio* 'contract'), which imply that the sequences /tj/ and /kj/ have merged as [tʃ]. Orthographic confusions between *-diV-*, *-giV-* and *-zV-* (e.g. *oze* for *hodie*) imply a parallel merger of clusters with voiced consonants to [dʒ], which we know took place in most of Western Romance. The use of the letter <z> to represent the outcome [dʒ] may have reflected the influence of the learned pronunciation of <z> in Greek words as [dz]. The cluster /kwj/ is simplified to /k/ leading to spellings such as *reqescit* for *requiescat*. At a later stage, we also find examples of mergers of /k/ and /g/ before /i/ and /e/ with the outcome of the earlier clusters with /j/, for example *septuazinta* written for *septuaginta* 'seventy', implying a palatalized pronunciation [tʃ/dʒ] for these cases as well.

Lenition and loss of occlusion of intervocalic stops Western Romance languages show voiced stops (or derivatives of them) for unvoiced stops in positions between two voiced elements, e.g. Spanish *pueblo* < *populus* 'people' and *fuego* < *focus* 'fire'. This is well attested in inscriptions from the fifth century on, and sporadically much earlier in Latin papyri from Egypt. These, as well as Classical Latin voiced stops, may develop to fricatives in intervocalic position. The majority of examples before the fifth century involve the labial stop *b* which shows frequent interchange in writing with consonantal *u*, often in initial as well as medial position. This suggests that the two sounds partially merged as a bilabial fricative [β].

Weakening and loss of consonants in coda position This heading covers both the loss of consonants at the end of a word and the reduction of consonant clusters. In the Romance languages final consonants are generally lost, except for final *-s* which is retained in Iberian Romance and in Gaul. As we saw in 4.2.1, the loss of final *-s* in Italy may go back as far as the third century BC. In non-homorganic clusters the consonant in the syllable coda is assimilated to the following consonant: for example /ks/ becomes /ss/ or /s/, as in the forms *uisit* for *uixit* 'he lived' and *ussor* for *uxor* 'wife', both of which are taken from memorial inscriptions. Some clusters themselves derive from otherwise unattested syncopated forms, thus French *froid* and Italian *freddo* derive from an unattested (except as Italian!) [freddo], which in turn is the outcome of classical *frigidum* 'cold' following syncope and assimilation of the cluster *-gd-* to *-dd-*. Geminate consonants are also simplified in most parts of the Romance speech area.

Loss of /h/ The loss of the aspirate is general in Romance, and is already well attested in inscriptions from Pompeii, although it is likely to have been a feature of formal speech throughout most of the period, owing to the influence of education. Indeed in the second half of the first millennium we find spellings of classical *mihi* 'to me' as *mici* or *michi*, showing that writers have been taught to pronounce a form with a medial sound foreign to their phonology. The aspirated consonants *ph th ch*, which were a feature of the educated pronunciation of Greek loanwords, were also lost from speech. Where there was still contact with Greek speakers, the spoken language adopted the change of *ph*, etc. to fricatives, which had taken place in spoken Greek at the beginning of the Christian era.

8.3.2   Morphology and Syntax

Many of the developments from Latin to the Romance languages can be viewed as part of a general long-term drift away from the *synthetic* to the *analytic*. For example, in the marking of comparative adjectives, the language moves from a synthetic form with suffix (as Latin *grandior* 'greater' alongside *grandis* 'great') to an analytic formation, generalizing the combination of *magis* or *plus* 'more' with the simple form of the adjective, already found with some adjectives and adverbs in the classical language. The end result of this change is found in Spanish and French comparatives of the type *mas grande* and *plus grand* 'greater'. The change from synthetic morphology to analytical structures frequently also involves a shift from marking at the end of the word or phrase (as in *grandior*) to marking the beginning (as **mas grande**), and corresponds to the shift from basically head-final to basically head-first order in nominal and verbal phrases. It may not be too fanciful to relate the change to analyticity to the spread of Latin as a second language. Given a choice between a synthetic construction with complex (and often irregular) morphology and an analytic construction which can be generalized across the board, language learners tend to prefer the latter option (Thomason and Kaufman 1988: 55).

Nominal case morphology

The only modern Romance language to preserve case distinctions is Romanian, which maintains (in feminine nouns) two separate cases: nominative/accusative and genitive/dative. Romanian is presumed to be derived from Latin varieties spoken in Pannonia (roughly modern Bosnia and Serbia) and Moesia (roughly modern Bulgaria), which were separated from the majority of other Romance speakers for much of the period after the fall of the Western Roman Empire. The language shows signs of heavy influence from the surrounding Slavonic varieties. An early merger of the nominative and accusative into a single case may have been a regional peculiarity, since there is some evidence of confusion between the two cases in Latin inscriptions from the third century, especially from Pannonia. (Note, however, that the majority of these inscriptional confusions involve the writing of -*as* for the feminine nominative plural, which can also be explained through the levelling of nominative -*ae* and accusative -*as* on the analogy of 3rd-declension nominative -*es* and accusative -*es*). In the rest of the Romance area case distinctions were only maintained in Old French and Old Provençal, which marked a subject case (the old nominative) against an oblique case.

Loss of the Latin case distinctions happened over a number of successive stages, and interacted with other developments, such as the merger
of some case forms in some declensions from phonological changes, and
the rise of more rigid word orders to encode subject and object roles.
Figure 8.3 (after Banniard 1992; 518) attempts to represent the successive stages by which the cases merged in the development from Classical
Latin to Romance varieties spoken in France. This interpretation of the
data needs to be viewed with caution, since our written texts may retain
classical usages much longer than they were present in the spoken
language. For example, Banniard reckons that stage III is only reached
in the mid-eighth century, but it is likely that many speakers had lost a
functional command of the ablative case much earlier than this. We already
saw in the analysis of the language of Claudius Terentianus in Chapter VII
that there was considerable overlap between ablative and accusative for
some speakers already in the high Empire, particularly after prepositions,
and prepositional constructions came to replace nearly all the original
uses of the ablative. However, Banniard argues that the ablative eventually syncretized with the genitive and dative, rather than earlier with
the accusative, owing to the persistence of some ablative forms used
with an instrumental function in late post-classical texts. The merger of
the genitive and dative is placed before this, since we first have
widespread evidence for a confusion between the two cases in the fifth
and sixth centuries, at which time we also see the rise of prepositional
phrases using *de* or *ad* to replace genitive and dative case functions.
Both *de* and *ad* are used with possessive meaning, while *de* also replaces
the partitive function of the genitive and *ad* is used to mark dative
complements of verbs.

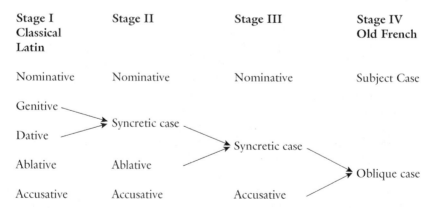

Figure 8.3 Banniard's model of the loss of separate Latin cases in four stages

Changes in the nominal gender system

Latin has three genders but the Romance languages have only two, masculine and feminine. Various different factors contributed to the loss of the neuter gender, and the concomitant reassignment of neuter nouns to other genders. In the classical language, nominal gender is not dependent on either natural sex or on inflectional class, although there is a broad correlation between the 1st declension, female sex and feminine gender, and the 2nd declension, male sex and masculine gender. In the Romance languages these broad correlations have been extended, with the eventual identification of the three categories in each case. Nearly all Romance nouns originally ending in -*a* are feminine in gender and do not refer to males, nearly all nouns that originally ended in -*us* (Romance -*o*) are masculine in gender and do not refer to females. Thus the many Latin tree names which ended in -*us* but were of feminine gender, such as *pirus* (f.) 'pear-tree', *ulmus* (f.) 'elm-tree' have been shifted into the masculine in Romance: Italian *pero* (m.) 'pear-tree', *olmo* (m.) 'elm-tree'. A few exceptions remain with retention of the Classical Latin gender, as Italian and Spanish *la mano* 'hand' from Latin *manus*. Nouns of the 3rd declension are either masculine or feminine, grammatical gender correlating with natural sex where it is a feature of the noun. The 4th and 5th declensions are lost; 4th-declension nouns are transferred to the 2nd declension, with which they share nominative and accusative endings -*us* and -*um*; polysyllabic 5th-declension nouns, which are all feminine, are transferred to the 1st declension. The assignment of all nouns in the 2nd declension to the masculine gender exclusively, at the expense of the neuter, already seems to have started in the speech of some individuals in the high Empire. One character in Petronius's novel *Satyricon* (the freedman Dama) uses masculines *uinus* and *balneus* for the classical neuters *uinum* 'wine' and *balneum* 'bath', and Claudius Terentianus has *pretius* (masculine) in place of *pretium* 'price' as we saw at 7.4.3.

Pronouns

The Latin pronominal system undergoes extensive restructuring in Romance. Table 8.1 summarizes the main developments. In the written records we have of late imperial and post-imperial Latin, the moribund forms *is*, *hic* and *idem* are used in a wide variety of different uses, as indeed is also *ipse*.

The verb

The principal change in the finite forms of the verbal system involves the replacement of the Classical Latin synthetic future and synthetic passive

Table 8.1 The fate of Latin pronouns in Romance

	is	*hic*	*iste*	*ille*	*ipse*	*idem*
Original function	weak anaphor	1st person orientated deictic	2nd person orientated deictic	remote deictic	emphatic/ contrastive 'self'	identity 'the same'
Fate	lost	only survives in fixed syntagms	becomes 1st person deictic (sometimes reinforced by *ecce*, e.g. Italian *questo*)	1 reinforced by *ecce* as remote deictic (e.g. Italian *quello*) 2 develops to article 3 develops to third person pronoun	1 becomes pronoun of identity 2 develops as deictic in some areas	lost

with analytic formations. The synthetic future in *-bo* or *-am, -es, -et* existed alongside an alternative expression of futurity already in the language of Plautus, a periphrasis of the type *daturus sum* 'I shall give', and in sub-literary texts from the Empire and later this periphrasis continues alongside other means of referring to future events. The future formation which won out in most Western Romance languages is still relatively easy to identify: futures such as French (*il/elle*) *écrira*, and Italian *scriverà* 's/he will write' are univerbations of *scribere habet* to-write s/he-has 's/he has to write' (*habere* being used as a modal to mark obligation in postclassical Latin, Adams 1991). Fulfilment of obligation must come into effect at a future point in time, and hence there is a natural slide from markers of obligation to markers of futurity. The construction with *habere* must have become grammaticalized as a future in the spoken language by the seventh century, the date of the historical compilation of Fredegarius which contains a pun involving the city name *Daras* and a spoken form *daras* meaning 'you will give', (contracted from *dare habes*, see Herman 2000: 74). In the period before the seventh century we find a number of competing ways of representing futures in texts. In outlying areas of the Romance speech community other periphrases become grammaticalized as future: infinitive with *debeo* 'I have to . . .' in Sardinian and infinitive with *uolo* 'I want to . . .' in Romanian.

The Classical Latin passive system combines both synthetic forms (in the present, future and imperfect) and analytic forms (in the perfect, future perfect and pluperfect). In Romance languages the analytic forms have spread at the expense of the synthetic, with apparent shift in the time reference of the earlier perfect passive, as the following table shows (the Proto-Romance forms are represented in Classical Latin orthography for ease of exposition):

	Present	Past
Latin	*clauditur* 'it is shut'	*clausum est* 'it was shut'
Proto-Romance	*clausum est* 'it is shut'	*clausum fuit* 'it was shut'

The shift can be explained by the fact that formations of the type *clausum fuerat*, *clausum fuerit* and, more rarely, *clausum fuit* existed in the earlier language alongside the pluperfect *clausum erat*, future perfect *clausum erit* and the perfect *clausum est*. For many speakers there was a natural slippage between reference to actions and resulting states when the passive was used, which, combined with the analogy to the past reference of simple *fuit* 'was', led to the adoption of *clausum fuit* as the sole marker of the passive past. By analogy to this the periphrasis *clausum est* was felt to be 'present', and in turn ousted *clauditur*. The decline of synthetic passive morphology also contributed eventually to the loss of a separate category of deponent verbs.

Other aspects of verbal morphology were restructured, and we shall merely mention some of these changes here. Phonological developments, particularly the merger of *i* and *e* vowels in final syllables, had knock-on effects on the inflectional morphology of some finite forms. There was some confusion between different conjugations, particularly the 2nd and 3rd, as we have already seen in the letters of Claudius Terentianus discussed at 7.4.3, where we find *dicet* rather than *dicit*. Verbs were also transferred from the 3rd to the 4th conjugation, as the example of Italian *fuggire*, French *fuir* from Latin *fugere* shows. Latin authors of a later date show tendencies to confuse the imperfect and perfect subjunctives as well; after the changes affecting vowels in final syllables, a contracted perfect subjunctive form, such as *amarim*, was not distinguished from the imperfect subjunctive *amarem*, and uncertainties over 'sequence of tenses' rules led to a merger of the two moods. Eventually the imperfect subjunctive and the perfect subjunctive were lost altogether in most Romance varieties. In the non-finite forms of the verb, even more categories disappear. The Latin supine, perfect infinitive, gerundive and participle all fall out of use in Romance, and the undeclined gerund takes over many of the functions of the participle.

Word order

In modern Romance languages the head of a phrase standardly precedes its modifiers, hence verbs stand before nominal objects, nouns before adjectives or genitive complements, adverbs stand after verbs and infinitives after modals. Many scholars have attempted to view the development from Latin to Romance as representing a shift from a 'head-final' order (also termed OV or object-verb) to 'head-first' (or VO, verb-object). We have already seen earlier in this work that the head-final word order associated with Classical Latin may have been less prevalent in spoken Latin than in more heightened and formal registers. Moreover, in literary texts word order was further complicated by stylistic factors such as rhythm and metre, antithesis and saliency. Although there is a tendency to prefer head-first structures at a later stage of the language, it is not possible to make hard and fast rules. The formation of the future from a periphrasis of infinitive and *habere* meaning 'have to' sheds some light on the interplay between word order and other factors, as well as the chronology of word order changes. We know that the grammarian Pompeius, who worked in the fifth or early sixth century, composed his grammatical works largely by dictation, so his word placement may be particularly close to formal speech. He uses *habere* as a modal with infinitive both preceding and following, the former denoting possibility, the latter obligation. The order with *habere* after the infinitive seems to originate as a stronger, emphatic form, as other modal verbs in Pompeius tend generally to occur before the infinitive (Adams 1991). In this author, therefore, the future use has not yet been grammaticalized, and the head-final order is not yet blocked by any word order rule. It seems then that despite a trend towards head-first structures, different word order patterns are still possible in the middle of the first millennium. We shall discuss word order in Late Latin and Romance patterns in more detail below in section 8.4.

Complementation and other subordinating procedures

Romance languages show the extension of some Latin complement clause structures with overt complementizers. Thus the accusative and infinitive construction for complements of verbs denoting speech and mental activities is replaced either by clauses introduced by *quod* or *quia* (or, after the sixth century, *que*). This construction does occur in the highest style Classical Latin, but was generally limited to complements of factive verbs expressing emotion, for example *gaudeo quod* 'I am happy that'. We have, however, already met the use of *quod* after verbs of speaking followed typically by a verb in the subjunctive in the sub-literary Latin of the *de Bello Hispaniensi* at 6.5.1. The only survival of the accusative and infinitive construction is for verbs denoting perception. The reason for its maintenance here, and a motivation for its loss elsewhere, is that the subject of the complement clause can also be interpreted as the object of a perception verb, but not for other types of verb. Compare the following Latin sentences:

1 *uideo puellam ambulare* 'I see that the girl is walking.'
2 *uideo puellam* 'I see the girl.'
3 *dico puellam ambulare* 'I say that the girl is walking.'
4 **dico puellam 'I say the girl.'

The accusative subject/object in sentence (1) can also be understood without the infinitive, as in sentence (2). But there is no parallel support for sentence (3). Speakers thus appear to have opted for complement structures which more clearly demarcated the clause boundaries. The complementizer *quod* or *quia* also replaces *ut* (or its negative counterpart *ne*) which in Classical Latin introduces inherently future-referring complement clauses after verbs such as *impero* 'I order', *rogo* 'I request', *moneo* 'I warn' etc. (the 'indirect command' clauses of traditional Latin grammar).

In Latin, many verbs can take a simple infinitive as complement if the subject of the complement clause is coreferential to the main verb, for example Latin *uolo bibere* 'I want to drink.' In Romance, this complement type is continued, although for all verbs except modals or similar, such as *uolo* 'I want', *possum* 'I can', *debeo* 'I should', there is here too a drive to have overt complementizers. The prepositions *ad* or *de* are grammaticalized as complementizers standing before the infinitive of the verb (this is the origin of structures such as French *j'ai commencé à travailler* 'I began to work' and *j'ai décidé de travailler* 'I decided to work').

In Classical Latin, the use of the subjunctive is obligatory in both complement clauses introduced by *ut* and those which were dependent on verbs of asking and questioning (i.e. the 'indirect command' and the 'indirect question' of traditional grammar). This is no longer the case in Romance; clauses which reproduce the substance of a question may be in the indicative, as indeed are clauses introduced by *quod/quia/que*. The subjunctive may occur, but under the same conditions governing its appearance in main clauses. In effect, the situation is now very similar to what we saw in preclassical Latin texts discussed above at 5.5. The subjunctive reverts to being a modal marker pure and simple, rather than conveying information about the status of the clause it is in.

We have already seen that *ut* is lost as a marker of complement clauses, but it also drops out of the language in its function of introducing adverbial clauses of purpose and result. The subordinator *cum* is also lost. Instead, we find new markers involving the same element *quod/quia/que* which served to introduce complement clauses (often combined with other particles or adverbs, e.g. Italian *benchè*, French *bien que* 'although' from *bene que* 'although').

8.3.3 Vocabulary

In many ways the easiest changes to track between Latin and Romance are the changes in vocabulary. Many Latin texts from the late Empire and beyond reveal their status as postclassical from the presence of neologisms, or the avoidance of classical vocabulary or the shifted meanings of earlier words, as we have already seen in the discussion of the epitaph of Gregory V. Some general trends in the development of vocabulary can be noted here.

Replacement of Classical Latin forms

Many Classical Latin words do not survive into Romance; it is no accident that often these are monosyllabic, or with an irregular declension: for example *edo* (3rd person singular *est*) 'eat' which is replaced by *comedere* (Spanish *comer*) and *manducare* (originally 'chew') (Italian *mangiare*, French *manger*); *eo* (3rd person singular *it*) 'go' is replaced in most inflected forms by either *uadere* (Italian and Spanish *vado*, French *je vais*), *ambitare* (Spanish *andar*, Italian *andare*) or *ambulare* (French *aller*); *os* (genitive *oris*) 'mouth' is replaced by *bucca* 'cheek, gob' (Italian and Spanish *bocca*, French *bouche*). These replacements also are found in written texts, yet their distribution does not always correspond to the single term that survives in the modern languages. For example, the Greek doctor Anthimus, who lived in Italy and France at the end of the fifth and beginning of the sixth century, never uses the classical form *edere* in his diet book *de Obseruatione Ciborum*. But he replaces *edere* not just with the term *manducare*, which survives in French and Italian, but also with *comedere* (used 23 times compared to 37 instances of *manducare* (Löfstedt 1959: 40, with corrected figures)) with no discernible difference in meaning. Other short forms are replaced by diminutives, for example *oricula* replaces *auris* 'ear' (Italian *orecchio*, French *oreille*) and **auicellus* replaces *auis* 'bird' (Italian *uccello*).

Borrowings

A number of basic vocabulary items are borrowed from Greek, many imported through the medium of Christianity (for which see the next section), for example *col(a)pus*, borrowed from Greek *kólaphos* 'blow' replaces Latin *ictus* 'blow' and becomes standard in Romance (Italian *colpo*, French *coup*); *gamba* (with unexplained voicing of the initial consonant) from Greek *kampḗ* 'bend, knee-joint (of a horse)' replaces *crus* as the word for 'leg' (Italian *gamba*, French *jambe*). The common Romance word for 'word' *parabola* (Italian *parola*, French *parole*) derives from a Greek word *parabolē* 'comparison' which is used in the Greek translation of the Old Testament of the Bible to render a Hebrew term with a semantic range from 'comparison' to 'speech'; the Latin Bible translators adopted it in turn, and from there it spread to the spoken varieties (Löfstedt 1959: 81f.).

Semantic shifts and extensions

Notable in this category are the promotion of formerly low-level terms to replace the classical equivalents, for example *casa* 'hut' replaces *domus/aedes* 'house' (Italian *casa*, French *chez*); *caballus* 'workhorse' replaces *equus* 'horse' (Italian *cavallo*, French *cheval*) and *bisaccium* 'saddlebag' replaces *pera* 'satchel' (Italian *bisaccia*, French *besace*). These changes appear to suggest that the spoken language of the lower levels of society won out over the Latin of the elite, but we should be careful about extending this as a general rule. It was once thought that the replacement of Latin *caput* 'head' by *testa* (French *tête*, Italian and Spanish *testa*), which in Classical Latin means 'pot' or 'crock', was another example of a popular word winning out over an elite term. However, Benveniste (1954) showed that in Late Latin *testa* could be used as a medical term for the skull (compare English *brainpan*), and that the medical use is a more likely origin than the slang term.

8.4   Latin and Christianity in the Late Roman Empire

The central event in the first millennium AD is the adoption of Christianity as the religion of the Roman Empire. Eventually, Christianity was to change everything, and it is Christianity that separates the ancient world from the modern. The spread of the new religion after it gained the emperor's support is scarcely believable. Estimates vary as to the number of the Christians in the Empire when Constantine became emperor, but most scholars agree that they constituted less than 20 per cent of the population as a whole. By the end of the fourth century it was the pagans who were a beleaguered minority. Pagan temples were attacked and closed down, while churches arose in their place. Pagan oracles ceased to function as did gladiatorial games. The Bible was to replace classical mythology as the principal source of stories and exempla, and as the basic means of teaching literacy. But what effect was Christianity to have on Latin?

In order to answer this question we must first answer the question of whether there is an identifiable 'Christian Latin'? The first Christian texts we have in Latin are the writings of the Christian apologists Tertullian and Minucius Felix from *c.*200 AD, roughly contemporary accounts of the life and death of Christian martyrs, such as the *Acts of Perpetua and Felicitas,* and the Early Latin translations of the Bible (called the *Old Latin* versions) whose exact date we do not know but which preceded the translation by Jerome (known as the Vulgate) made at the end of the fourth century. These are a diverse set of texts, written in widely varying styles, from the condensed and intricate Latin of Tertullian to the Old Latin Bible versions whose translators attempt a close rendering of the Greek text of the gospels, occasionally without completely understanding what they were translating. However, ever since antiquity there has been a notion that the Christians had their own particular linguistic register; St Augustine writing in the fourth century talks of the *ecclesiastica loquendi consuetudo* 'church manner of speaking' in the *City of God* (10.21). The attempt to classify and describe 'Christian Latin' was taken up enthusiastically in the twentieth century by the Dutch scholar Jos Schrijnen and his pupils, most notably Christine Mohrmann. They argued that the Christians were marked out by particular shifts in the meanings of words, and new lexical creations. They based their analyses on the totality of Christian Latin, including the voluminous fourth-century writings of authors such as Augustine and others. They claimed that the Christian vocabulary was not limited solely to terms relating to Christian narrative, belief or ritual (such as the Greek loans *apostolus* 'apostle', *angelus* 'angel' and *baptizare* 'baptize'), but also included words such as *ueraciter* 'truly', *subsequenter* 'subsequently' and *conuertibilis* 'changeable' (Schrijnen 1935). Christian authors were also supposed to have exhibited syntactic and morphological peculiarities of language, such as a predilection for the 'hanging nominative' construction (where a nominal form in the nominative has no syntactic function in a sentence), and a fondness for forming factitive verbal compounds with the second element *-ficare.*

Christian writers in the period of the Roman Empire presented the Christian faith as the religion of the poor, the powerless and the underprivileged, united in faith against continual persecution. For example, Lactantius (*Divine Institutions* 5.1.15–16, written at the beginning of the fourth century) claims that the Christian scriptures are scorned by the *sapientes et doctos et principes* 'the wise, the learned and the leaders' because they are written in a common and simple language, as if they were addressing the people. Taking such texts at face value meant that scholars such as Schrijnen could support their identification of a particular social dialect with the faithful. However, a better understanding of the history of the early Church now makes clear that Christians were integrated into different levels of society, and that it is mistaken to think of them as a coherent and unified group, such as would develop their own register. Christians were found in all walks of life, distributed throughout the Empire. In the third century, there are many examples of men and women of property and influence who are attached to the Christian faith, including Marcia, the concubine of the emperor Commodus, and members of the local elites from Asia Minor to southern Spain (Brown 2003: 63f.). In the words of one historian, the 'lasting impression left by the early church membership is one of social diversity' (Lane-Fox 1986: 336). The image of the early Christians as united through persecution and divine favour, and their protestations of humility are better seen as rhetorical stances, which can be explained as part of their theological message. Christians presented their humility as a mark of their strength: in the words of St Paul 'God hath chosen the foolish things of the world to confound the wise' (*I Corinthians* 1.26).

We should consequently be wary of assuming that the language of Christian authors is necessarily any closer to the spoken idioms of the underclass than that of other writers or that it is significantly different from other varieties of colloquial/non-literary Latin. The language of the Christian authors Tertullian, Lactantius and Augustine is no further from the classical standard than that of the pagan Ammianus (*c.*330–95). All of these authors are aware of and steeped in classical precedents to their writings, and sought the prestige which accompanied 'correct' use of language. It is certainly true that there is a number of new lexical items which are associated with the Christian faith (although these are not necessarily limited to Christian authors), and that the reliance on the Bible led to a new model for the standard, at least in genres such as sermons, chronicles, saints' lives and pious travelogues. But the forms which Schrijnen gives as specifically Christian which are not related to aspects of Christian belief and practice are actually few in number, and they are mainly lexical creations of the fourth century and later which happen not to occur in the dwindling number of pagan authors at the time. For this reason many scholars never supported the notion of a special register of Christian Latin, and most have now abandoned it (see, for example, Löfstedt 1959: 68–70 and Coleman 1987).

In order to illustrate the effects Christianity had on Latin, we shall not use any of these high-style writers. Instead we shall take a text written in a much less elevated register, which also serves to illustrate more clearly the growing gap between the higher literary styles and the colloquial register of the educated. The work we have chosen, the *Itinerarium Egeriae* (known in older scholarship as the *Perigrinatio Aetheriae*), also happens to be the earliest surviving Latin prose work of any length written by a woman. The *Itinerarium* contains 50 chapters of a larger work describing Egeria's journey from the south of France on a pilgrimage to the holy land, and some of the places which she visited. Since its first publication at the end of the nineteenth century there has been considerable debate over the identity of the author, and her date and provenance. The consensus is now that she wrote at the end of the fourth century (Väänänen 1987: 8). Egeria was probably not a nun, as she is described in earlier literature, but a woman of some wealth and status. In contrast to the literary works of her contemporary Augustine, Egeria does not show signs of a deep acquaintance with non-Christian authors. Rather, her frame of linguistic reference is the Latin Bible translation, and in this she stands with the majority of Christian writers after the fourth century, who look back to the Bible as their measure of correct Latin, rather than to Cicero. Furthermore, Egeria would have used the Old Latin versions of the Bible, which preceded the Vulgate, and which were less stylized and classicizing.

To exemplify Egeria's Latin, we take a section from near the end of the work, where she describes some of the pilgrims' activities on Whitsunday (50 days after Easter in the Christian Calendar), including a visit to the site where the Biblical story of the apostles speaking in tongues is set.

(2) *Itinerariun Egeriae* 43, 2–4

Cum autem mane factum fuerit, procedit omnis populus
when however in-the-morning done-ACC.sg has-been, goes all-NOM people-NOM

in ecclesia maiore, id est ad Martyrium, aguntur etiam
in church-ABL greater-ABL, that is to Martyrium-ACC are-done now

omnia, quae consuetudinaria sunt agi; praedicant
all-NOM.pl, which-NOM.pl customary-NOM.pl are to-be-done; preach

presbyteri, postmodum episcopus, aguntur omnia legitima,
priests-NOM.pl afterwards bishop-NOM are-done all-NOM.pl correct-NOM.pl,

id est, offertur iuxta consuetudinem, qua dominica
that is, is-offered following custom-ACC, which-ABL.sg lord's-ABL.sg

die consueuit fieri; sed eadem adceleratur missa in
day-ABL.sg was-custom to-be-done; but same-NOM is-hastened mass-NOM in

Martyrium, ut ante hora tertia fiat. Quemadmodum enim
Martyrium-ACC, that before hour-ABL third-ABL is-made. As for

missa facta fuerit ad Martyrium, omnis populus
mass-NOM made-NOM has-been at Martyrium-ACC, all-NOM.sg people-NOM.sg

usque ad unum cum ymnis ducent episcopum in Syon, sed
each to one-ACC with hymns-ABL they-lead bishop-ACC in Syon, but

hora tertia plena in Syon sint.
hour-ABL third-ABL full-ABL in Syon they-may-be

3. Ubi cum uentum fuerit,   legitur ille   locus   de actus
when when come   has-been, it-is-said that-NOM place-NOM from acts-ACC.pl

apostolorum, ubi   descendit spiritus,   ut   omnes   linguae
apostles-GEN, where descended spirit-NOM, so-that all-NOM.pl tongues-NOM.pl

intellegerent, quae   dicebantur; postmodum fit   ordine
might-understand, which-NOM.pl they-were-said; after   becomes order-ABL

suo   missa.   Nam presbyteri de   hoc   ipsud,   quod
its-ABL mass-NOM.sg for   priests-NOM.pl about this-ACC self-ACC, which-NOM

lectum   est, quia ipse   est locus in Syon, alia   modo
read-NOM is, because same-NOM is place in Syon other-NOM now

ecclesia   est, ubi quondam post passionem Domini collecta
church-NOM is, where once   after passion-ACC Lord-GEN gathered-NOM.sg

erat multitudo   cum apostolis,   qua hoc   factum   est, ut
was crowd-NOM.sg with apostles-ABL.pl, where this-NOM done-NOM was as

superius diximus, legunt ibi de   actibus   apostolorum. Postmodum
above   we-said, they-read there from acts-ABL.pl apostles-GEN afterwards

fit   ordine   suo   missa,   offertur et ibi, et iam ut
becomes order-ABL its-ABL mass-NOM.sg, is-offered and there, and now that,

dimittatur populus, mittit uocem   archidiaconus et dicet: 'Hodie
are-dismissed people, he-sends voice-ACC archdeacon-NOM and he-says: 'Today,

statim   post sexta   omnes   in Eleona parati   simus   [in]
immediately after sixth-ABL all-NOM.pl in Eleona prepared-NOM.pl let-us-be in

Inbomon'. Reuertitur ergo   omnis   populus   unusquisque
Inbomon.' he-returns   therefore all-NOM.sg people-NOM.sg each-NOM.sg

in domum   suam   resumere se,   et statim   post
in home-ACC their-own-ACC to-take-up themselves, and immediately after

prandium ascenditur mons   Oliueti,   id est in Eleona,
lunch-ACC is-climbed   Mount-NOM of-Olives-GEN, that is in Eleona,

unusquisque quomodo potest, ita ut nullus   christianorum remaneat
each-NOM.sg how   is-able, so that no-NOM Christian-GEN.pl remains

in ciuitate, qui   non omnes   uadent.
in city-ABL who-NOM.pl not all-NOM.pl they-come.

'But when morning has come, all the people proceed to the greater church,
i.e. to the Martyrium, and all the things are done there which are cus-
tomarily done; the priests preach and then the bishop, and everything is
done by the book, i.e. an offering is made following custom, as is customary on the Lord's Day. But on that day the mass in the Martyrium
is speeded up, so that it happens before the third hour. And when the

mass has been done at the Martyrium, all the people, down to the last one, lead the bishop with hymns to Sion, [so that] they may be in Sion when it is fully the third hour.

3. And when they have come, the passage from the Acts of the Apostles is read where the Holy Spirit descended so that all tongues understood the things that were being spoken, and the mass takes place afterwards in its proper order. For the priests read about this very thing there from the Acts of the Apostles, because this is the same place in Sion – now the church is different – where once, after the passion of Christ, the crowd was gathered with the Apostles, and where this was done, as we said above. Afterwards the mass takes place in its proper order, and an offering is made there. And now, so that the people may be dismissed, the archdeacon lifts up his voice, and says: 'Today, let us all be ready in Eleona, in the Imbomon, immediately after the sixth hour.'

So all the people return, each to their own house, to rest themselves, and immediately after lunch they climb the Mount of Olives, i.e. to Eleona, each as best they are able, so that none of the Christians stays in the city who do not go.'

The presence of a Christian influence in vocabulary in this text is clear. Greek loans, now completely nativized, are used to refer to people and things connected with the Christian church: *ecclesia* 'church', *presbyterus* 'priest', *episcopus* 'bishop', *archidiaconus* 'archdeacon', *(h)ymnus* 'hymn'. Native Latin terms have changed their meaning as they are used in a Christian context: *passio*, used in Varro and Apuleius to mean 'emotion' or 'effect' now refers uniquely to the suffering and death of Christ or the martyrs; *praedico* 'proclaim' takes on a specific meaning of preaching in a Christian service. New Latin terms also arise: *missa* here is taken to mean 'mass' (the Christian ritual meal), although it can also mean '(ritual) dismissal' in the *Itinerarium*. There are various explanations of how *missa* came into use, it may be a calque of Greek *pompē* 'procession' or a misanalysis of the phrase *ite missa est* 'go, it is over' said at the end of the liturgy.

However, we can use Egeria's texts for more than unearthing Christian vocabulary. The style of the text is obviously colloquial, with considerable pleonasm and repetition, and no attempt to build up periodic sentences in the classical manner. Instead, clauses are normally placed alongside each other with banal connectives, and sometimes we find parataxis in place of hypotactic constructions. For example, at the end of section 2, what appears to be an adverbial purpose clause 'they lead the bishop *so that* they may be in Sion when it is fully the third hour' is introduced with a marker of parataxis *sed* 'but'. Egeria's style is her own, but it is hard not to think that she has been at least encouraged in her narrative techniques by the Old Latin Bible translations which in turn followed the Hebrew and Greek versions in their relatively straight-forward, pleonastic and paratactic style.

Egeria's Christian faith led her to feel she could dispense with the normal classical models of Latinity, if she ever had any exposure to such things, and this freedom means that her text is a treasure trove of devi-ations from the standard, giving us the best picture of the developments in the direction of the Romance languages in the fourth century. However, the work only survives in one manuscript, which was copied in the Italian monastery at Monte Cassino in the eleventh century, and this means that we cannot be sure always that the orthography is Egeria's own, and not that of a later copyist. Accordingly we shall pass over phonological features in this work and only note two morphological peculiarities. Two 3rd person plural forms of verbs in the 3rd conjuga-tion have *-ent* in place of *-unt* (*ducent* and *uadent*), and in section 3 we find *dicet* for *dicit*. The latter writing may just be a reflection of the confusion between *i* and *e* in final syllables (see 7.4.3 and 8.3.1), or could derive from a later error of transcription, but taken together the two phenomena suggest a confusion between the verbs in the 2nd and 3rd conjugation, arising through their partial merger in some parts of the paradigm (e.g. 2nd person singular *-ēs/-is*). In Spanish and French the 3rd person plural of old 3rd-conjugation verbs derives from *-ent* (Spanish *viven*, French *vivent* beside Latin *uiuunt* 'they live').

In the realm of syntax, there is much more to be said. We find many features that are in concordance with the proto-Romance features dis-cussed above (8.3), including the following (not all of the following points can be illustrated from the text sample given, but some are known from other passages in the *Itinerarium*):

1   Prepositions are used indiscriminately with the accusative and ablative, e.g. *procedit . . . in ecclesia maiore*; *ante hora tertia* (both ablative for accusative), *de hoc ipsud*; *de actus Apostolorum* (accusative for ablative). The preposition *de* takes over many of the functions of the pure ablative and genitive, both partitive and possessive and also takes over from *ex* and *ab* as marking source or origin, e.g. *legitur ille locus de actus Apostolorum*.

2   The pronouns *ille* and *ipse* are widely used, sometimes with a sense close to that of a definite article, or with little of their original force. In the phrase *de hoc ipsud*, *ipse* is also apparently used pleonastically to strengthen *hoc*.

3   The synthetic passive is still widely used, but there is some evidence to suggest that a periphrasis with the past tense of *esse* is gaining ground to mark past tense passives, e.g. *ubi cum uentum fuerit* which

links to a main verb in the present. If the text of the section *linguae intellegerent, quae dicebantur* is correct, it should presumably be taken to mean 'so that tongues *were* understood, what they were saying', and *intellegerent* is written for *intellegerentur*, perhaps showing a failure to master the synthetic passive form.

4   The subordinating particle *ut* is used in a number of places, but there is confusion between its construction with the indicative and with the subjunctive, and it is not used where expected at the end of section 2. The subordinator *quemadmodum* has temporal force as well as modal 'how', perhaps calqued on the Greek conjunction *hōs* 'how, when'. The subordinator *cum* is used pleonastically after its equivalent *ubi*; combinations of equivalent conjunctions and particles of this sort are frequent in Later Latin, (Löfstedt 1956: II 219–32) and may reflect attempts to bolster up moribund classical forms. In the final sentence of section 3, Egeria shows some confusion when attempting to combine shorter clauses into a complex structure: *ut nullus Christianorum remaneat in ciuitate qui non omnes uadent*, seems to be a conflation of *nemo remaneat qui non uadit* 'no one stays who does not go' and *omnes uadunt* 'all go'.

Egeria thus confirms some of the phenomena affecting the spoken language which we already know from the Romance evidence. In one area, however, this text substantially increases our knowledge of what is going on 'beneath the standard' and that is the order of the major sentence constituents. As is clear from reading even a short passage of the text, the word order is not classical. The verb is only situated at the end of its clause in short subordinate clauses in the above extract; it is never situated at the end of a main clause. What is particularly striking is the frequency with which the verb is placed in initial position in its clause, or immediately after the subordinating element: *procedit omnis populus* 'all the people go', *aguntur etiam omnia* 'everything is done', *legitur ille locus* 'that passage is read out' etc. Most of these examples involve intransitive or passive verbs, but there are also examples of transitive verbs in initial position, as *mittit uocem archidiaconus* 'the archdeacon makes a speech' (which is a formula found elsewhere in the *Itinerarium*). Where the verb does not stand in the first position, often the element that precedes it is emphatic or contrasted with something else. Note for example that subjects involving scope-bearing adjectives, such as *omnes linguae* 'all languages', *nullus christianorum* 'no Christian', may also stand before the verb. Time expressions involving *statim* occupy the slot before the verb, as *statim post prandium* 'immediately after lunch', and so do some expressions involving important religious events such as *dominica die* 'on the Lord's day' and *post passionem Domini* 'after the passion of Christ'.

There are therefore some grounds for seeing an underlying order with the verb occupying the first position in the sentence, with an optional focus slot before it, which may be filled by a verbal argument (subject as the default) or an adverbial phrase. In diagrammatic form:

(Focus) Verb Subject Object

Exactly analogous constituent structures are found in the early stages of Italian and other Romance languages (cf. Renzi and Andreose 2003: 220f.). The verb stands first in its clause, although any constituent can be fronted for focus before it. Some sentences in the passage above appear at first sight not to be so amenable to this analysis. Take, for example, the following sentence:

omnis populus usque ad unum cum ymnis ducent episcopum in Syon
'all the people, down to the last one, lead the bishop into Syon with hymns'

Here there are two different constituents, the subject of the verb (*omnis populus usque ad unum*) and the adverbial phrase *cum ymnis*, placed in front of the verb. On closer inspection, however, the first fronted clause can be seen to be standing outside the sentence proper (in other words it is 'left-detached') and just reiterates the narrative theme. An English equivalent would be 'So as for the whole crowd, they go . . .'. In support of this interpretation note that the verb is not in concord with the subject. Elsewhere in the passage *omnis populus* is construed with a 3rd person singular verb, but here the verb in the sentence is 3rd person plural. The sentence can be therefore analysed as follows:

omnis populus usque ad unum   cum ymnis ducent episcopum in Syon
Left-detached element   Focus   Verb   Object. . . .

Left-detached structures of this type (topics) are also common in the Romance languages.

8.5   Latin after the Collapse of the Roman Empire

In 476 the last Roman emperor in the West, appropriately named Romulus Augustulus, abdicated. Unlike other last emperors, such as Atahuallpa of the Incas or the Chinese Puyi, Romulus Augustulus was neither executed nor re-educated. Instead he enjoyed a long retirement in his villa on the Bay of Naples. The fate of the Western Empire, separated now from the Greek East, was hardly any worse in the short to medium term. In Rome, the Senate continued to meet and govern, and it even minted its own coins, stamped with the legend *Roma Inuicta* 'unconquered Rome' in the early sixth century (Brown 2003: 193). Many former Roman lands were now barbarian kingdoms: parts of North Africa had been ceded to the Vandals as early as 435, and the Visigoths had been in Spain for as long. But, contrary to their depiction in popular culture, the barbarians had other interests than rape and pillage. They were Christians, and the local elites were often able to retain their properties and possessions. Many of the administrative structures of the Roman Empire were maintained after 476, even though there was now a fragmented rule. Roman Law remained the dominant legal code in the lands around the Mediterranean. The Roman land tax continued, and in many areas local landowners continued to collect tax on behalf of the state, and gathered their own militias to enforce their power (Smith 2005: 161f). The church adopted and continued administrative models and techniques from the Roman imperial bureaucracy (Noble 1990).

As Roman bureaucracy survived into the sixth century, so did Latin. Its maintenance as the language of law and administration is shown by the existence of two different groups of documentary texts from the period after the end of the Western Empire. From North Africa, 45 wooden tablets, known as the *Tablettes Albertini*, record private legal contracts written in Latin at the end of the fifth century (Courtois et al. 1952) and attest to the maintenance of Latin under the Vandals. And over 150 slate tablets from north central Spain, dating to the sixth and seventh centuries, show Latin used for a wide range of purposes in the Visigothic kingdom: accounts, letters, spells and writing exercises (Velázquez Soriano 1989 and 2000). We shall give an example of one of these slate tablets, since it shows Latin used in an everyday, non-literary context. The following short text is dated to the seventh century, and is better preserved than most of the slates, although the endings of the first two lines are missing. It is one of a number of the slates to preserve an administrative order, all of which start with the heading *notitia* 'notice'.

(3)   Slate text no. 54 (Velázquez Soriano 1989: 241, 2000: 73)

notitia   i(n) qua   ordenatu   est quos   . . .
notice-NOM in   which-ABL ordered-NOM.NEUT is   which-ACC.pl

consignemus Simplicio,   id est VI sesq . . .
we-require   Simplicius-DAT, that, is, 6   six

cum agnus   suus   det   scroua una,   uacca   una
with lambs-ACC.pl his-ACC.pl let-him-give sow-ACC one-ACC, cow-ACC one-ACC

hospitio,   Matratium   qum pariat   in corte
hospitium-DAT, Matratius-ACC when gives-birth in stable-ABL

domni   sui   Valentini,   uitulas   duas
master-GEN.sg his-GEN.sg Valentinus-GEN.sg, calves-ACC.pl two-ACC.pl

tri(ti)cu   mod(ios)   XXV
wheat-ACC.sg measures-ACC.pl 25

'Notice in which it is ordered which . . .
we require of Simplicius, that is 6 six . . .
together with his lambs let him give one sow, one cow to the hospitium.
Matratius, (let him give) two calves, when (his cow) gives birth in the
stable of his master Valentinus (and) 25 measures of wheat.'

Since we have the original text itself, we can use it to get a better idea
of the phonological developments which have taken place than we can
in most manuscript material. In this, and the other slates, we see evidence
for the confusion of the original long *e* and short *i*, and long *o* and short
u characteristic of the emergence of the Romance vowel system: *ordenatu* (l. 1) for *ordinatum* 'ordered', *agnus suus* (l. 3) for *agnos suos* 'his
lambs'. Unaccented medial vowels in open syllables may be syncopated,
as in *domni* for *domini* 'of his master'. And the hiatus vowel in Classical
Latin *pareat* 'may it give birth' is written with *i* in *pariat*. Among the
developments in consonants final *m* is frequently omitted, as *scroua* for
classical *scrofam* 'sow' and *uacca* for *uaccam* 'cow'. The writing *scroua*
with medial *u* suggests that the writer may have pronounced the word
[scroβa], voicing the fricative in medial position; such writings are however rare on these slates, and only involve confusion between *u* and *f*.
In *corte* for classical *cohorte* 'stable' we see the loss of the aspirate. Despite
these departures from Classical Latin orthography, we should be under
no illusions that the writer of this text is not well versed in classical spelling
rules. The word *hospitio*, for example, shows neither the loss of the aspirate nor the confusion of *-tio* and *-cio* which we assume are general in
speech at this date (and which are evidenced in other tablets). The writer
differentiates between the preposition spelled *cum* and the conjunction
which is spelt *qum*, presumably for *quum*, and thus shows the survival of
an orthographic distinction between the two words which dates back to
the middle of the Republic; the two words had become homophonous
already by the second century BC!

The morphology and syntax also show a mixture of classical and
contemporary forms. The preposition *cum* is found with the accusative,
and there seems to be some confusion over the case of the personal
argument of *consignemus*, which here means 'we require' as in other slate

documents. The interpretation given here assumes that the accusative *Matratium* (l. 4) is a second object after *consignemus,* parallel to the dative *Simplicio* (l. 2) (for discussion see Velázquez Soriano 1989: 241). However, elsewhere in this document we find the genitive and dative distinguished, and unsupported by prepositions. The Classical Latin temporal conjunction *cum,* probably absent from the spoken language by this date, is used here with a present subjunctive verb. Finally, it is worth noting that the passive *ordenatu est* may be an example of the periphrastic passive with present tense reference, replacing the synthetic form.

The *Tablettes Albertini* and the documents on slate from Spain show the continuing aspiration to write standardized Latin in a range of private contexts. However, the main vehicle for the continuation of Latin was the Church. After the collapse of the Roman power structures and during the fragmentation of the Empire into separate kingdoms in the fifth century, Latin was retained as the language of both written and oral communication in the Church through the use of Bible readings, commentaries, sermons, songs and prayers in Church services. The authority and the prestige of the scriptures and the writings of the church fathers meant that there was respect for and adherence to their original texts. The unchanging and universal nature of the Latin language mirrored the perception that the Church held the unchanging and universal truth.

For the highest ranking clergy and nobles Latin remained the language of literary, philosophical and historical works. In the sixth century, for example, Gildas wrote the history *On the Ruin of Britain,* Boethius wrote the *Consolation of Philosophy* (showing an acquaintance with Greek learning), Gregory of Tours wrote the *History of the Franks* and Venantius Fortunatus, an Italian living in northern France, wrote poems in classical metres on Christian themes and in praise of his aristocratic patroness Radegund. Authors such as Gregory of Tours might deplore their own standard of Latinity, and excuse themselves on the grounds that *philosophantem retorem intellegunt pauci, loquentem rusticum multi* 'few understand an orator when he philosophizes, many understand a peasant who speaks' (Preface to the *History of the Franks*). But this is part of a wider aesthetic of humility in Gregory, as in other Christian writers, which extends to presenting his own age as in a much worse state than it actually was. We should not be misled into thinking that his history was intended for a wider audience than the learned elite (Banniard 1992: 50f.), although the style and grammar has moved considerably from the classical norm of the late Republic and early Empire.

Alongside these literary creations of the elite, we also find texts written in a less elevated Latin for a much wider public. The monastic Rule of St Benedict, composed at around 530 AD, was intended to be read (or heard), understood and probably also partly learnt by all the monks in a monastery. The Rule survives in many manuscript copies, the earliest dating from around 700, from all over Europe, and the diversity of manuscript readings makes it particularly problematic for textual editors (see Coleman 1999). We give an example from it here, to illustrate a register of language which is more formal than that of Egeria's travelogue, but without literary pretence. The following excerpt is taken from the description of the monks' daily offices, a section which shows a higher proportion of non-classical forms than the bulk of the rule, and follows the text of de Vogüé and Neufville (1972).

(4)   Rule of St Benedict 9.5f.
Quibus   dictis,   dicto   uersu,   benedicat abbas   et,
which-ABL.pl said-ABL.pl, said-ABL.sg verse-ABL.sg let-him-bless abbot-NOM and,

sedentibus omnibus in scamnis,   legantur uicissi a fratribus
sitting-ABL.pl all-ABL.pl in benches-ABL.pl, let-be-read, in-turn by brothers-ABL.pl

in codice   super analogium tres   lectiones, inter quas   et
in book-ABL on   lectern-ACC three-NOM.pl lessons-NOM, among which-ACC.pl and

tria   responsoria   cantentur: [6] duo   responsoria   sine
three-NOM.pl responses-NOM.pl let-be-sung. Two-NOM.pl responses-NOM.pl without

gloria dicantur; post tertiam   uero lectionem, qui   cantat dicat
glory-ABL let-be-said. after third-ACC.sg but   lesson-ACC.sg, who-NOM he-sings let-him-say

gloriam. [7] Quam dum   incipit cantor   dicere, mox
glory-ACC. Which-ACC.sg as-soon-as he-begins singer-NOM to-speak, soon

omnes   de sedilia   sua   surgant, ob   honorem et
all-NOM.pl from seats-ACC.pl their-ACC.pl let-them-rise because-of honour-ACC and

reuerentiam sanctae Trinitatis. [8] Codices autem legantur in uigiliis
reverence-ACC holy-GEN Trinity-GEN. Books-NOM.pl however let-be-read in vigils-ABL.pl

diuinae auctoritatis, tam   ueteris testamenti quam noui,   sed et
divine-GEN authorship-GEN, as-much old-GEN testament-GEN as   new-GEN, but also

expositiones   earum,   quae   a nominatis   et
explanations-NOM.pl them-GEN.pl, which-NOM.pl by well-known-ABL.pl and

orthodoxis catholicis patribus   factae   sunt. [9] Post has
orthodox-ABL.pl Catholic-ABL.pl fathers-ABL.pl made-NOM.pl are.   After these-ACC.pl

uero tres   lectiones   cum responsoria sua,   sequantur
indeed three-ACC.pl lessons-ACC.pl with responses-ACC.pl their-ACC.pl, let-follow

reliqui   sex psalmi,   cum alleluia canendi. [10] Post hos,
remaining-NOM.pl six psalms-NOM.pl with alleluia-ABL to-be-sung.   After these-ACC.pl

lectio   apostoli sequatur, ex corde recitanda,   et uersus, et
lesson-NOM apostle-GEN let-follow,   from heart-ABL to-be-recited-NOM and verse-NOM and

supplicatio litaniae, id est quirie eleison. [11] Et sic finiantur uigiliae
petition-NOM litany-GEN that is   *Kyrie*   *eleison*   and thus let-be-ended vigils-NOM.pl.

nocturnae.
night-NOM.pl.

'When these things have been said, and when the verse has been said, let
the Abbot give a blessing; then, with everyone seated on benches, let three
lessons be read from the book on the lectern by the brothers in turn,
and between the lessons let three responses be sung. Two of the
responses are to be said without a "Gloria" but after the third lesson let
the one who sings say the "Gloria". As soon as he begins, let everyone
get up from their seats out of honour and reverence for the Holy Trinity.
Let there be read books in the Night Office of divine authorship, both
the Old and the New Testament, but also the explanations of them which
have been made by well-known and orthodox Catholic fathers. After these
three lessons with their responses let the remaining six Psalms follow, to
be sung with "Alleluia". After these, let there follow the lesson from the
Apostle, to be recited by heart, and the verse and the petition of the litany,
that is the *Kyrie eleison*. And so let the Night Office be finished.'

The style of the rule is similar to earlier Latin technical works on subjects such as agriculture (for example Cato) or medicine (for example
Celsus), particularly with those written in a 'compact' style (borrowing
the terminology of Langslow 2000: 379). There is frequent use of the
passive in order to suppress the subject; nominalizations vary with relative clauses (*cantor* 'singer'/*qui cantat* 'who sings'); short explanations
follow technical terms (*supplicatio litaniae, id est quirie eleison* 'the petition of the litany – i.e. the *Kyrie eleison*'); short sentences with directives
expressed in the subjunctive follow on from one another in staccato form.
Benedict's Latin can therefore be seen as part of a longer tradition of
plain Latin style specific to technical manuals.

A comparison with the Latin of the *Itinerarium* and even with the slate
tablet from Spain, also shows that the language retains many classical
features which we presume had been lost in most spoken registers by this
time, and which we list below:

1 ablative absolute: *quibus dictis* 'with these things said'; *sedentibus omnibus*
   'with everyone sitting down';
2 synthetic passives: *tria responsaria cantentur* 'three responses are to
   be sung';
3 gerundives: *psalmi, cum alleluia canendi* 'psalms to be sung with
   alleluia'; *lectio . . . ex corde recitanda* 'lesson to be recited by heart';
4 present participles: *sedentibus* 'sitting';

5   pronouns *hic* (*post hos* 'after these' etc.) and *is* (*expositiones earum* 'explanations of them') are retained.

Despite these classical features, the Rule also shares linguistic features with the other late texts which we have discussed. Note, for example, the use of accusatives after the prepositions *cum* and *de*: *cum responsoria sua* 'with their responses'; *de sedilia sua* 'from their seats (the classical language would have used *ex* or *a* rather than *de* here). The vocabulary shows not just Christian and ecclesiastical terms and extensions, such as *uersus* '(biblical) verse', *benedico* 'bless', *psalmus* 'psalm', *analogium* 'lectern', *lectio* 'lesson' etc., but also semantic and formal changes in other vocabulary. For example, for the verb meaning 'sing' Benedict prefers the form *canto*, to *cano*, selecting the form which is to survive into Romance (Italian *cantare*, French *chanter*), except when he forms a classicizing gerund *canendi* when *cano* is preferred.

Latin texts such as the Rule of St Benedict were instrumental in spreading the language throughout a Christian community which stretched beyond the boundaries of the Western Roman Empire and the speech area of the Romance languages. Peoples who had never been under Roman rule, such as the Irish and the Germans, or where the Roman occupation had never taken deep roots, such as in the north of England, engaged with the Christian faith through Latin texts and the Latin Bible. The use of Latin beyond the boundaries of the Roman Empire is not new. Even before the spread of Christianity, Latin's status as a written language had led to its use in official documents outside Roman juris-diction, as in a (recently re-read) loan-note on a wax tablet found at Tolsum in northern Holland (Vollgraff 1917). However, nothing in earlier times had come close to matching the extent of the use of Latin in Ireland, Britain and Germany after their conversion to Christianity. Latin was part of the package with Christianity in the West, and as such it was to have considerable influence on the development of the vernacular languages, Irish, Anglo-Saxon, and the Old German and Dutch varieties spoken on the continent. As Christianity took root, the monasteries of Ireland and northern Britain became the new centres of learning and repositories of Latin texts. Indeed, the earliest existing manuscript text of the Rule of St Benedict, now in the Bodleian Library in Oxford, was written in Britain in around 700, only a little more than a hundred years after Pope Gregory I sent a mission to convert the Anglo-Saxons.

While the seventh and eighth centuries saw a growth in literacy and use of Latin in the British Isles, in France and Italy learning fell into decline, while southern Spain and North Africa came under Muslim rule. In this period in the former Roman Empire old administrative structures such as the land tax were gradually abandoned, with a consequent decline in the wealth and prestige of local elite landowners, who saw military power as a quicker route to advancement than learning and culture (Heather 1994: 195f.). We no longer find courtly poetry in the seventh and eighth centuries in the style of Venantius Fortunatus. Many pagan Latin authors ceased to be read, cited and copied. The schools, which had been in decline since the end of the fourth century, now disappear from the record along with the grammarians who taught in them (Kaster 1988: 463ff.).

When churchmen educated in Latin in the British Isles came into contact with the Latin of the continent in the eighth century, it was a shock. Boniface, born in Devon and educated in southern England, spent most of his life as a missionary in Germany. He was deeply versed in Latin, and himself wrote a Latin grammar as well as corresponding with popes and church leaders across Europe. When he came across priests in Bavaria in around 746 who used the formula *baptizo te in nomine patria et filia et spiritus sancti* 'I baptize you in the name of the father and son and Holy Spirit' (rather than the correct Latin *in nomine patris et filii*) he ordered a rebaptism. The letter from Pope Zacharias to Boniface, gently rebuking him for his officiousness, still survives (number 68 in Tangl 1916). However, the linguistic purity and prescriptivism of Boniface was soon to win out over the permissiveness of the Pope. Charlemagne, crowned king of the Franks from 768 and emperor in Rome in 800, sponsored a linguistic 'back to basics' campaign. One of Charlemagne's earliest edicts was that priests who make mistakes in or who do not know God's law should be removed from office (Banniard 1992: 349f.). Charlemagne found a steadfast ally and executive of his language reforms in the English priest Alcuin, born in York a generation after Boniface. Like Boniface, Alcuin also wrote on grammar, and he used his writings and his position as abbot at the great monastery of Tours to promote reforms in the teaching and orthogaphy of Latin. We can see the effects of these reforms in the manuscripts of the Rule of St Benedict. In 787 Charlemagne requested a copy of the Rule from Benedict's own monastery, Monte Cassino in Italy. Charlemagne and his circle wished to get back as close as possible to the authentic text, and purge the errors that had already crept into the manuscript tradition. The reforms of Alcuin meant more than going back to basics however. Manuscripts take on a new look in the Carolingian age, with the first punctuation marks and the use of capital letters to guide the reader.

It may be no accident that it is soon after the reforms that we see the first signs of real strain and difficulty of comprehension between the written form of Latin and the spoken language. We find the earliest textual reference to *rustica romana lingua* 'the unpolished Roman language' in Canon 17 of the Council of Tours in 813:

ut easdem omelias quisque aperte transferre studeat in rusticam romanam linguam aut thiotiscam, quo facilius cuncti possint intellegere quae dicuntur

'let each be keen to transfer these same homilies into the unpolished Roman language or the German language, so that everyone may be able more easily to understand what is said.' (see Wright 2002: 142f. on the translation of *transferre* as 'transfer' rather than 'translate').

It is tempting to link the attempt to get back to an earlier standard of language with the realization that the continuum with the spoken language was no longer applicable. In trying to peg back written language by a couple of hundred years or more, Alcuin and his followers had taken it away from the competence of the majority of speakers, at least in France (we should remember that in Italy at least, the first consciousness of the separation of spoken and written language is much later as we saw in 8.2 above).

A generation after the Council of Tours, we find the first representations of what the *rustica romana lingua* might have sounded like. We have already mentioned the Strasbourg oaths sworn in 842 and it is appropriate to reproduce the longer oath here. We include with the word-by-word gloss a 'translation' of the text into the Classical Latin equivalent (based on Ewert 1935: 22f. with some changes and additions).

(5) Nithard 3.5

Pro deo amur et pro christian poblo et nostro commun saluament,
Ad dei amorem et ad christiani populi et nostrum commune saluamentum,
For god love and for christian people and our common salvation,

d'ist di in auant in quant deus sauir et podir me
de isto die in antea, in quantum deus scire et posse mihi
from this day in advance in so-far-as god to-know and to-have-power me

dunat, si saluarai eo cist meon fradre Karlo et in ajudha et in
donauerit, sic saluabo ( ) istem meum fratrem Karolum, et in *adiutatem et in
gives, thus I-will-save I this my brother Charles and in aid and in

cadhuna cosa, si cum om per dreit son fradra saluar dift, in o
omne, ( ) sicut homo per directum suo fratri saluare debet, in hoc
every thing, thus so man through right his brother to-save ought in this

quid il mi altresi fazet, et ab Ludher nul plaid nunquam
ut ille mihi similem faciat, et ab Lodhario nullum placitum nunquam
which he to-me likewise he-does, and from Louis no agreement never

prindrai, qui,   meon   uol,   cist meon fradre Karle in
inibo,   quod, per meam uoluntatem, isti meo   fratri   Karolo in
I-will-enter, which, my   will,   this my   brother Charles in

damno sit
damno   sit
harm   let-it-be.

'For the love of God and for the salvation of the Christian people and
for our common salvation, from this day forward, in as much as God has
allowed me to have knowledge and power, so shall I support this my brother
Charles, both in aid and in everything, as a man should by right support
his brother, provided that he does likewise to me. And I shall never enter
into any pledge with Louis, which, with my consent, may be of harm to
this my brother Charles.'

Comparison of the oath with the Latin version shows the divergence
between the spoken vernacular and written Latin in France in the ninth
and tenth centuries (the only known surviving manuscript of Nithard's
chronicle dates to around 1000 AD, so some uncertainty remains about
whether all the features of the oath can be projected back to 842). We
shall give a brief synopsis of some of the developments in the language
below, but it should be obvious to the reader that full discussion of this
text belongs in a history of French, rather than a history of Latin.

Many of the sound changes which we associate with the genesis of
Romance, and in particular French have taken place already in the text
of the Strasbourg oath, note the following:

1   merger of short *i* and long *ē*, short *u* and long *ō* in *sauir* for *sapēre*,
    podir from *potere*, *amur* for *amōrem*, *dunat* for *dōn-*;
2   monophthongization of *au* in *cosa* for *causa*;
3   development of [ə] in final syllables from the merger of short *e* and
    o, revealed by the vacillation between writing *e*, *a* and *o*: *fradra/
    fradre*; *Karle/Karlo*;
4   palatalization in *fazet* for *faciat*;
5   loss of medial consonants in *plaid* for *placitum*, *eo* for *ego*, *ajudha*,
    a noun formed from Latin *adiutare*;
6   lenition of medial consonants in *sauir* for *sapēre*, *podir* from *potere*,
    fradre for *fratrem* etc.;
7   frequent loss of final syllables, e.g. *amur* for *amōrem*, *il* for *ille*, etc.

The case system has almost completely broken down. Although the
nominative is still distinct from the 'oblique' case in the pair *deus* and

deo, there is no distinction in the marking of dative, genitive, ablative or accusative. In verbal morphology, we find that the new future is fully grammaticalized in *saluarai* and *prindrai*. The vocabulary shows new creations and extensions, such as *cadhuna* (French *chacune*) 'every' from a collocation **cata una* involving the preposition *cata* borrowed from Greek, or *cist* 'this' from a collocation *ecce iste*. In syntax we can see new procedures for subordination in place, such as *in o qui* to introduce an adverbial clause, and the replacement of the relative *quod* by *qui(d)* in the final line.

The text of the Strasbourg oath reveals that by the closing centuries of the first millennium, written Latin ceases to reflect the undercurrent of living speech. The Latin of Gregory V's epitaph, given in 8.2, is entirely an artificial creation in a learned language, striving to follow rules that have been learned in school or in the study of earlier models, rather than reflecting the grammar of a native speaker. Latin is now a cultural artefact, as it was to remain until the present day. Through its use in scholarship, medicine, science, law, and as the language of the Catholic Church it long retained a status as a world language unmatched by any other variety no longer spoken. And despite some obvious recent decline, especially in the period after the Second World War, a Finnish radio station still broadcasts the news in Latin, Oxford and Cambridge (and other) Universities still employ orators to write and deliver Latin speeches on special occasions, children's books are still regularly translated into Latin and in 2007 the online encyclopaedia *Wikipedia* had more articles in its Latin version than in Welsh. But this is a language learned wholly from books, not from the mouths of speakers; its grammar is purely prescriptive and fixed in perpetuity. The story of Latin in the last thousand years is not therefore the story of a conventional language, but that of a cultural sign, symbolizing privilege, and granting access to knowledge and power (Waquet 2001, Farrell 2001), a role which it has only very recently relinquished in the face of technological and social revolution and the associated shifts in cultural and economic priorities. This is an interesting story, but not one for linguistic historians to try and tell.

References

Adams, J. N. (1991) 'Some neglected evidence for Latin *habeo* with infinitive: The order of the constituents'. *Transactions of the Philological Society* 89.2, 131–96.

Banniard, M. (1992) *Viva voce: Communication écrite et communication orale du IVe au IXe siècle en Occident latin.* Paris: Institut des Études Augustiniennes.

Benveniste, E. (1954) 'Problèmes sémantiques de la reconstruction'. *Word* 10, 251–64.

Brown, P. (2003) *The Rise of Western Christendom* (2nd edn.). Oxford:Blackwell.

Coleman, R. G. G. (1987) 'Vulgar Latin and the diversity of Christian Latin' in J. Herman (ed.), *Latin Vulgaire – latin tardif: Actes du Ier Colloque international sur le latin vulgaire et tardif, Pécs, 2–5 septembre 1985*. Tübingen: Niemeyer, 37–52.

Coleman, R. G. G. (1999) 'Vulgarism and normalization in the text of the *Regula Sancti Benedicti*' in H. Petersman and R. Kettemann (eds.), *Latin vulgaire – latin tardif V: Actes du Ve Colloque international sur le latin vulgaire et tardif. Heidelberg, 5–8 septembre 1997*. Heidelberg: Winter, 345–56.

Courtois, C., L. Leschi, C. Perrat and C. Saumagne (eds.) (1952) *Tablettes Albertini, Actes privés de l'époque Vandale*. Paris: Arts et métiers graphiques.

Ewert, A. (1935) 'The Strasburg Oaths'. *Transactions of the Philological Society*, 16–35.

Farrell, J. (2001) *Latin Language and Latin Culture: From Ancient to Modern Times*. Cambridge: Cambridge University Press.

Heather, P. (1994) 'Literacy and power in the Migration period' in A. K. Bowman and G. Woolf (eds.), *Literacy and Power in the Ancient World*. Cambridge: Cambridge University Press, 126–148.

Herman, J. (2000) *Vulgar Latin*, (translated by R. Wright). University Park, PA: Pennsylvania State University Press.

Kaster, R. A. (1988) *Guardians of Language: The Grammarian and Society in Late Antiquity*. Berkeley/London: University of California Press.

Lane-Fox, R. (1986) *Pagans and Christians*. Harmondsworth/New York: Viking.

Langslow, D. (2000) *Medical Latin in the Roman Empire*. Oxford: Oxford University Press.

Löfstedt, E. (1956) *Syntactica: Studien und Beiträge zur historischen Syntax des Lateins* (2 vols.). Lund: Gleerup.

Löfstedt, E. (1959) *Late Latin*. Oslo: Instituttet for Sammenlignende Kulturfoskning.

Noble, T. F. X. (1990) 'Literacy and the papal government in late antiquity and the early middle ages' in R. McKitterick (ed.), *The Uses of Literacy in Early Medieval Europe*. Cambridge: Cambridge University Press, 82–108.

Renzi, L. and A. Andreose (2003) *Manuale di linguistica e filologia romanza*. Bologna: Mulino.

Schrijnen, J. (1935) 'Le latin chrétien devenu langue commun'. *Revue des études latines* 12, 96–116.

Smith, J. M. H. (2005) *Europe after Rome*. Oxford: Oxford University Press.

Soriano, I. Velázquez (1989) *Las Pizzarras Visigodoas: Edición crítica y estudio* (Antigüedad y Cristianismo VI). Murcia: Universidad de Murcia.

Soriano, I. Velázquez (2000) *Documentos de época visigoda escritos en pizzarra (siglos VI–VIII)*, Monumenta Palaeographica Medii Aevii, series hispanica 2 vols. Turnhout: Brepols.

Tangl, M. (1916) *Die Briefe des heiligen Bonifatius und Lullus*, Monumenta Germaniae historica, Epistolae selectae 1. Berlin: Weidmann.

Thomason, S. G. and T. Kaufman (1988) *Language Contact, Creolization and Genetic Linguistics*. Berkeley and Los Angeles: University of California Press.

Väänänen, V. (1981) *Introduction au latin vulgaire* (3rd edn.). Paris: Klincksieck.

Väänänen, V. (1987) *Le Journal-épitre d'Égérie (Itinerarium Egeriae): Étude Linguistique*. Helsinki: Suomalainen Tiedeakatemia.

de Voguë, A. and J. Neufville (1972) *La Règle de Saint Benoît*, (2 vols). Paris: Cerf.

Vollgraff, C. W. (1917) 'De tabella emptionis aetatis Traiani nuper in Frisia reperta'. *Mnemosyne* 45, 341–52.

Waquet, F. (2001) *Latin: or the Empire of a Sign: From the Sixteenth to the Twentieth Centuries*, translated by J. Howe. London: Verso.

Wright, R. (2002) *A Sociophilological Study of Late Latin*. Turnhout: Brepols.

Glossary

ablative The case used to mark separation, literally and metaphorically, but with a wide range of other functions (including in Latin the marking of a location with prepositions).

ablaut System of vowel alternations marking inflectional and derivational categories.

accusative The case of the direct object of a verb, but with a range of other functions (mostly adverbial).

affricate A consonant produced by uttering a plosive immediately followed by a fricative (i.e. with delayed release). In German, *z* represents an affricate [ts], and in English *ch* in the word *chop* represents an affricate [tʃ].

allomorphy The use of different grammatical exponents (morphs) to express the same morpheme. For example, in English, /-s/ and /-en/ are allomorphs of PLURAL in *cats* and *oxen*.

allophone One of the different sounds that constitute a phoneme. For example, in English aspirated [tʰ] (as in the word *top*), and unaspirated [t], (as in the word *stop*) are allophones of the *t* phoneme.

alveolar Term describing consonants which are produced through restricting or blocking the flow of air through the mouth in the region of the alveolar ridge, situated behind the upper teeth. In British English *t* and *d* represent alveolar consonants.

aorist Term taken from Ancient Greek grammar to describe a verbal stem with perfective aspect. Corresponding forms in Sanskrit and PIE are also labelled aorist, although they need not have the same aspectual meaning.

apodosis Term for the clause in a conditional sentence which sets out the consequence of a hypothetical state of affairs. In English and Latin the apodosis normally follows the protasis.

argument The term verbal argument is used to denote any of the necessary elements which a given verb requires to form a grammatical sentence. For example, in English the verb *put* requires three arguments, a subject, an object, and a phrase or adverb denoting location.

aspect A category of the verb found in many languages which distinguishes actions and events according to how they are viewed in time, rather than when they occur in time. In English *I ran* and *I was running* both refer to actions in the past, but differ in aspect. See **perfective**, **imperfective**.

aspiration Aspirated plosives are produced with a delay in the onset of voicing following the release of the consonant; this is heard as an audible puff of breath following the consonant. In spoken British English aspiration is a concomitant feature of voiceless plosives in word-initial position.

asyndeton, asyndetic Two or more words or phrases which are understood to belong together but which do not have any overt conjunction, such as 'and', are said to be in asyndeton or asyndetically joined. For example, in the English sentence 'Has car, will travel' the phrases 'has car' and 'will travel' are in asyndeton.

athematic Verbal and nominal paradigms which do not include the thematic vowel are called athematic paradigms, and their inflectional endings are termed athematic endings.

augment Term taken from Greek grammar for a prefix or stem-modification used to mark indicative verb forms that refer to past events. More widely used for corresponding phenomena in other IE languages and reconstructed PIE.

back vowel A vowel, such as [u] or [o], produced with the tongue moved to the back of the mouth, usually with concomitant lip rounding.

bilabial fricative A consonant produced by restricting the flow of air between the lips enough to produce audible friction. In Spanish *b*, when in the middle of a word, represents a bilabial fricative [β].

bimoraic Having two moras (see **mora**); in other words, consisting of two short vowels, or one long vowel, or a diphthong.

clitic A lexical or grammatical element that has the semantic status of a full word, but which cannot stand on its own, having the phonological status of a suffix or prefix. In Latin the connective *-que* is a clitic; it has the meaning 'and', but it is always attached to the preceding word and cannot begin a sentence or clause.

close vowel See **high vowel**.

CM Abbreviation for the **comparative method**.

cognate Genetically related. If two words, sounds or features are cognate, it is hypothesized that they both continue a single word, sound or feature of the parent language.

colon Term taken from ancient grammar to describe a group of words shorter than a sentence which belong together as a syntactic and metrical unit.

comment See **topic**.

comparative method (CM) The techniques used to reconstruct the parent language of a linguistic family, involving the establishment of regular and systematic correspondences between related languages.

compensatory lengthening Phonological change involving the lengthening of a vowel following the loss of one or more of a group of following consonants.

complement Any element which somehow completes the construction of a verb (or of any other part of speech). The complement of a verb may therefore be a simple object, or it may be a dependent clause, such as 'that he was coming' in the sentence 'He said that he was coming.'

control A 'control context' is one involving a verb such as 'promise', 'decide', 'ask', 'forbid' or 'seem', which automatically supplies one of the arguments of a dependent verb. For example, in the English sentences 'He promised to go' and 'He decided to go', the subject of the infinitive is the same as the subject of the main verb, but in 'He asked Mary to go' and 'He forbade Mary from going', the object of the main verb is supplied as the subject of the dependent verb.

correspondence set A set of cognate items in related languages which share the same feature.

counterfactual A hypothetical clause in conditional sentences which assumes a state of affairs which is contradictory to the actual past or present state of affairs.

dative The case used to mark the indirect object of a verb, but with certain other functions in addition.

daughter language Language which is genetically descended from an earlier language (the parent). French, Italian and Spanish are daughter languages of Latin.

de-adjectival Derived from an adjective.

denominal Derived from a noun.

dental Term describing consonants which are produced through restricting or blocking the flow of air through the mouth in the region of the teeth. In modern French and Italian, *t* and *d* usually represent dental consonants.

deponent verb A verb in Latin which has a passive form, but an active (or middle) type of meaning. Semi-deponent verbs combine active and passive forms in the same paradigm.

deverbal Derived from a verb.

diachronic Occurring over a passage of time. In linguistics, diachronic variation, i.e. variation over time, is often opposed to synchronic variation, variation between different speakers at a single moment in time.

elision Term describing the loss of a vowel before a following vowel.

enclitic A clitic which attaches to the preceding word. In Latin *-que*, *-ne* and *-ue* are enclitics.

family A group of languages which are held to derive from a single language (which is called the parent language of the family).

family tree A mapping of a language family showing the relations between the different languages and sub-groups.

figura etymologica A traditional stylistic term to describe a construction where the object of a verb shares the same lexical root as the verb. An English example would be 'to give gifts.'

flap Term describing consonants which are produced through restricting the flow of air through the mouth with a very rapid movement of the tongue across another part of the mouth. In American English *t* in the middle of a word such as *writer* often represents an alveolar flap.

focus A word or phrase which is emphasized, or contrasted through its position at or near the beginning of the sentence.

fricative A consonant produced through restricting the flow of air through the mouth to the point where audible friction is produced. In English *th* and *f* are fricative consonants.

front vowel A vowel, such as [i] or [e], produced with the tongue moved to the front of the mouth, usually with concomitant lip spreading.

fronting The process of moving one element within a sentence to the beginning of the sentence proper. In the English sentence 'What are you doing?' the interrogative *What* is fronted.

genitive The case used to mark an adnominal dependent (e.g. the man's house), but with a range of other functions.

grammaticalization The historical process whereby an element with an original lexical meaning becomes reinterpreted as having a grammatical meaning. For example in Late Latin the word *habeo* in the phrase *scribere habeo* means 'I have to' or 'I must'. This is subsequently reinterpreted as a grammatical marker of the future tense, as in Italian *scriverò* 'I shall write.'

high vowel A vowel, such as [i] or [u], produced with the tongue high in the mouth. Also called a *close vowel*.

hypercorrection Term describing a sociolinguistic process of language change. Speakers produce hypercorrections when they attempt to adjust their language to a different, normally more prestigious variety, and overcompensate. For example, speakers of English dialects, or non-native speakers of English without the sound [h] in their own variety, may produce hypercorrect forms such as *hoffice* rather than *office* when using standard English.

hypotaxis The process of combining syntactic units through explicit processes of subordination, making some clauses dependent on other ones, opposed to parataxis. In English a sentence such as 'Spare the rod and spoil the child' employs parataxis, and could be rewritten with hypotaxis as 'If you spare the rod, you will spoil the child.'

IE See **Indo-European**.

imperfective One member of the aspectual opposition perfective/imperfective: verb forms built to an imperfective stem denote an action viewed by the speaker as having an internal contour of continuation, progression or iteration, but without external bounds.

Indo European (IE) The name of the language family that comprises Latin and many other languages originally spoken across Europe, the Near East and northern India. Other members of the family include Greek, Sanskrit, the Celtic languages (Irish, Welsh and others) and the Germanic languages (Gothic, Old Norse, German, English and many others).

infectum The name given to the verbal stem from which the Latin present, imperfect and future tenses are formed. The infectum stem of the verb *amo* is *am(a)-*, the infectum stem of *ueho* is *ueh(e)-*.

injunctive Term for a particular verbal paradigm in the Indo-Iranian languages, formed with the endings of a past tense verb but without the augment, usually present in past tense verbs. The injunctive was employed in specific contexts, including some prohibitions. By extension the label injunctive is also used for analogous formations in Ancient Greek and other languages.

innovation Any linguistic development which replaces an earlier feature. Innovations may take place in any area of the language: sound, vocabulary, morphology or syntax. Typically innovations take place only in some languages in a family, and separate branches will have undergone different innovations.

instrumental Case typically used to designate the instrument or means by which an action is performed.

labial Term describing consonants which are produced through restricting or blocking the flow of air through the mouth in the region of the lips. In English *p* and *b* represent labial consonants.

labio-velar Term describing consonants consisting of velar stops with concomitant rounding of the lips (represented by the notation k^w, g^w and g^{wh}).

laryngeal Name for any of three consonants reconstructed for PIE, in this work represented by the notation $*h_1$, $*h_2$ and $*h_3$. The reconstruction of these consonants explains aberrant patterns of vowel alternation in many IE languages, and is termed 'the laryngeal theory'.

locative   Case typically used to designate placement at a certain point in space or time.

low vowel   A vowel, such as [a], produced with the tongue low in the mouth. Also called an *open vowel*.

matrix clause   A clause which is superordinate to another clause may be called its matrix clause. For example, in the English sentence 'He said that he was coming', the clause 'He said' can be called a matrix clause.

medio-passive   Term to describe a voice opposed to the active in many IE languages which combines the functions of the middle and the passive.

mid vowel   Vowels such as [e] and [o], which are neither high nor low: such vowels may be further distinguished as close/high-mid [e, o] or open/low-mid [ɛ, ɔ].

middle   Term taken from Ancient Greek grammar to refer to a set of verbal forms which are opposed both to the active and the passive in some paradigms, and more widely used to cover equivalent structures in other IE languages including Latin (including many deponent verbs). Typically the subject of a verb conjugated in the middle has some involvement in the verbal action (e.g. as experiencer or patient) beyond, or distinct from, that of a verb conjugated in the active. For example, 'Mary got washed' might involve Mary doing the washing to herself, or conceivably someone else doing the washing to/for Mary. The passive voice involves a grammatical limitation to the second of these options. Accordingly, the term middle is also more loosely used to mean medio-passive.

modal formation   A verbal formation which is marked in some way for the category of mood.

modification   Term describing any syntactic structure which involves the addition of elements to expand and extend the meaning of the basic sentence, but which are not required in order to make the sentence grammatically complete.

monophthongization   The process through which an original diphthong is changed to a simple (usually long) vowel.

mood   A category of the verb in most IE languages relating to the type of utterance in which the verb appears, and the speaker's attitude to the truth of the utterance. Typically, the indicative mood is used in factual statements, the imperative mood in commands, the subjunctive mood in possibilities and the optative (in some languages) in wishes.

mora (plural **moras**, adjective **moraic**)   Term for prosodic units into which syllables can be divided. In this work it is assumed that a short vowel counts as one mora, a long vowel or diphthong counts as two moras.

morph   A segment of a word realizing one or more morphemes.

morpheme An abstract unit of grammatical analysis representing a value for some grammatical category, and realized by one or more morphs. For example, the morpheme PLURAL (a value of the category number) is realized by the morph /-s/ in *cats*.

Mycenaean Greek Earliest attested form of Greek, comprising mainly short administrative texts written in the Linear B syllabary on clay tablets.

nasal Term describing consonants which are produced through blocking the flow of air through the mouth while allowing air to flow through the nasal cavity. In English *n* and *m* represent nasal consonants.

nominative The case of the subject of a sentence, or of a subject complement after a copular verb.

open vowel See **low vowel**.

optative Form of the verb in Ancient Greek and the ancient Indo-Iranian languages which would typically be employed in wishes (but has many other functions). The optative is a mood marked in opposition to the indicative.

palatalization The process whereby, before high front vowels and semivowels, dental/alveolar consonants are affricated and velar consonants come to be articulated further forward in the mouth, eventually leading to a complete change in pronunciation. Some of the different outcomes of palatalization can be seen in the development of the Latin sequence *ce* (in the word *centum* 'hundred') in the Romance languages, compare French *cent*, with initial [s], Italian *cento* with initial [ʧ], and Spanish *ciento*, with initial [θ].

paradigm All the inflected forms of a given lexeme, arranged systematically according to the categories expressed by the endings, as an example of how to decline nouns or conjugate verbs of the general inflectional class to which the illustrative lexeme belongs.

parataxis The process of combining syntactic units through placing them alongside each other, without signifying any hierarchical order between them, opposed to hypotaxis. In English a sentence such as 'Spare the rod and spoil the child' employs parataxis, and could be rewritten with hypotaxis as 'If you spare the rod, you will spoil the child.'

parent Language from which another language (the daughter language) is genetically descended. Latin is the parent language of French, Italian and Spanish.

passive A set of forms within the paradigm of all transitive verbs, the subject of which denotes the patient. A sentence with a passive verb is often called a passive sentence.

perfect The name given to various tenses in the IE language family which involve reference to the present relevance of a past event (e.g. 'Have you seen the file?' where the act of seeing was in the past, but the question relates to the hearer's experiential state at the present moment).

The perfect in Greek and in the early Indo-Iranian languages correspond closely, and are the basis of the reconstructed perfect in PIE. The perfect in Latin (and Romance) partly corresponds to this, but also contains elements from a distinct PIE past tense (corresponding to the Greek aorist), leading to a dual function.

perfective   One member of the aspectual opposition perfective/imperfective: verb forms built to a perfective stem denote an action viewed by the speaker as constituting a single complete whole.

perfectum   The name given to the verbal stem from which the Latin perfect, pluperfect and future perfect are formed. The perfectum stem of the verb *amo* is *amau-*, the perfectum stem of *ueho* is *uex-*.

phoneme   Term used to describe a set of similar sounds which are grouped by speakers of a language as a single functional unit. For example, in English the /t/ phoneme is realised in different contexts as either aspirated [tʰ], as in the word *top*, or unaspirated [t], as in the word *stop*. Although these two *t* sounds are phonetically distinct, native speakers hear them as the same 'sound'.

PIE   See **Proto-Indo-European**.

plosive   A consonant produced through the complete blockage, and subsequent release, of the flow of air through the mouth. In standard English *p*, *b*, *t*, *d*, *k*, and *g* all represent plosives.

primary endings   Some early IE languages have two closely related sets of verbal endings, one of which (primary endings) typically refer to events which take place in the present, and the other (secondary endings) which typically refer to events in the past (or in a hypothetical domain).

proclitic   A clitic which attaches to the following word. In Latin the preposition *in* and the connective *et* are both proclitic, even though they are written as separate words in modern texts.

prolepsis (adjective **proleptic**)   Term used to describe the movement of any element out of the clause where it logically belongs to an earlier superordinate clause.

protasis   Term for the clause in a conditional sentence that sets out the hypothetical state of affairs from which consequences may follow if it is/should be realized. In English the protasis is usually introduced by the word *if*, in Latin by the word *si*.

Proto-Indo-European (PIE)   The name given to the hypothetical ancestor of the Indo-European language family. Proto-Indo-European is not directly attested, but elements of it can be reconstructed through comparison of the known Indo-European languages.

proto-language   A language which is hypothesized to be an earlier stage of an attested language or a group of attested languages, but is not itself attested. It is often possible to use techniques such as the comparative method to reconstruct proto-languages. The prefix *proto-* can be attached to the name of any language or language family, to give the name of the proto-language for that language or family. For example, Proto-Semitic is the name of the proto-language of the Semitic language family. Proto-Indo-European (PIE) is the reconstructed proto-language of the Indo-European (IE) language family.

qualitative ablaut A type of ablaut which involves alternation between different vowels, typically in IE languages between the vowels *e* and o.

quantitative ablaut A type of ablaut which involves alternation between a long vowel and a short vowel of the same quality and absence of such a vowel.

reduplication Morphological device used in IE inflection and derivation whereby the initial consonant, or in some cases the initial consonant cluster, of a lexical item is repeated with a following vowel. For example, in Latin the verb *cano* 'I sing' has a perfect stem *cecin-* 'sang' formed by reduplication.

resonant Name for any of the reconstructed PIE sounds *r, *l, *m, *n, *i or *u. These sounds form a distinct class within PIE, since they may function both as the nucleus of a syllable, i.e. as a vowel, and at its margins, i.e. as a consonant.

Romance IE sub-group comprising the languages which are derived from Latin, including French, Italian, Spanish, Portuguese and Romanian.

root Term applied to the basic units of the lexicon. Roots can themselves combine with inflectional endings to make full words, or they can combine with affixes to form a number of different lexical stems. Most roots have meanings which relate to verbal actions.

Sabellian IE sub-group comprising languages spoken in Central and Southern Italy in the first millennium BC, and known chiefly from inscriptional remains. Sabellian languages include Oscan, Umbrian and South Picene.

Sanskrit Name for the ancient language of India, used in this work to cover both the language of the Vedic hymns and the later stages of the language (sometimes called Classical Sanskrit).

secondary endings Some early IE languages have two closely related sets of verbal endings, one of which (primary endings) typically refer to events which take place in the present, and the other (secondary endings) which typically refer to events in the past (or to hypothetical situations).

sibilant Sibilants are a class of fricatives which are typically produced by bringing the front of the tongue into close proximity with the roof of the mouth, resulting in audible turbulence. Sibilants comprise the *s* sounds, including those represented by English *s, z, sh*.

SOV Abbreviation for Subject-Object-Verb, referring to a word-order pattern in which the verb follows the object.

stem   A lexical base which needs only the addition of inflectional endings to be a full word. In IE linguistics a stem is normally understood to consist of a root morpheme and one or more affixes.

stop   Another term for *plosive*.

sub-group   A group of languages within a language family which are taken to be closely related to each other.

subjunctive   Form of the verb in many languages which would typically be employed to mark possibilities (but has many other functions). The subjunctive is a mood marked in opposition to the indicative (and the optative).

SVO   Abbreviation for Subject-Verb-Object, referring to a word order pattern in which the verb precedes the object.

synchronic   Occurring at a single point in time.

syncope   Process in the history of languages in which a short vowel drops out in the middle of a word. In Latin *caldus* is a syncopated form of *calidus* 'hot'.

syncretism   General term for the collapse of two originally distinct categories into a single category. Case syncretism refers to the merger of two or more nominal cases into a single case. For example, in Latin, the original ablative, locative and instrumental cases have syncretized to give the case labelled the ablative in traditional Latin grammar.

synizesis   Term describing the merger of two vowels constituting two syllables into a single articulatory unit forming one syllable.

thematic noun paradigm   The noun paradigm reconstructed for PIE with the thematic vowel before the endings (and inherited as the second declension in Latin). The inflectional endings are partly unique to this paradigm and therefore sometimes termed 'thematic endings'.

thematic verbal paradigm   The verbal paradigm reconstructed for PIE with the thematic vowel before the endings. The inflectional endings are partly unique to this paradigm and therefore sometimes termed 'thematic endings.'

thematic vowel   Some PIE paradigms are reconstructed with a vowel throughout the paradigm occurring before the inflectional endings. The vowel is realized either as *e or *o. The term *thematic* is taken from the word for 'stem' in other European languages (e.g. French *thème*).

topic   Syntactic term to describe a word or phrase which stands at the front of a sentence and which denotes what the sentence is about. For example, in the English sentence, 'Love, his affections do not that way tend' (*Hamlet*), 'Love' is the topic, and the rest of the sentence can be described as the 'comment'.

univerbation   The process whereby two separate words are so closely associated that speakers begin to understand them as a single word. In Latin *respublica* is a univerbation of the words *res* and *publica*.

velar   Term describing consonants which are produced through restricting or blocking the flow of air through the mouth in the region of the soft palate or velum (situated at the back of the mouth). In English *k* represents a velar consonant.

verbal argument   See **argument**.

vocative   The case of address.

voice   A category of the verb. In many IE languages verbs show separate paradigms which relate the subject to the verbal action in different ways. For example in Latin the present paradigm of the active voice, *amo, amas, amat*, means 'I love', 'you love', 'he loves', but the present paradigm of the passive voice, *amor, amaris, amatur*, means 'I am loved', 'you are loved', 'he is loved'.

voiced   Consonants are said to be voiced when they are uttered with simultaneous vibration of the vocal cords. In English, *b*, *d*, and *g* represent voiced sounds.

voiced aspirates   Term used to describe a series of consonants reconstructed for PIE which were both voiced and aspirated. Similar consonants can be heard in some modern Indian languages.

voiceless   Consonants are said to be voiceless when they are uttered without simultaneous vibration of the vocal cords. In English *p*, *t*, and *k* represent voiceless sounds.

The International Phonetic Alphabet
(revised to 2005)

CONSONANTS (PULMONIC)

	Bilabial	Labiodental	Dental	Alveolar	Postalveolar	Retroflex	Palatal	Velar	Uvular	Pharyngeal	Glottal
Plosive	p b			t d		ʈ ɖ	c ɟ	k g	q ɢ		ʔ
Nasal	m	ɱ		n		ɳ	ɲ	ŋ	N		
Trill	ʙ			r					ʀ		
Tap or Flap		ⱱ		ɾ		ɽ					
Fricative	ɸ β	f v	θ ð	s z	ʃ ʒ	ʂ ʐ	ç ʝ	x ɣ	χ ʁ	ħ ʕ	h ɦ
Lateral fricative				ɬ ɮ							
Approximant		ʋ		ɹ		ɻ	j	ɰ			
Lateral approximant				l		ɭ	ʎ	L			

Where symbols appear in pairs, the one to the right represents a voiced consonant. Shaded areas denote articulations judged impossible.

CONSONANTS (NON-PULMONIC)

Clicks	Voiced implosives	Ejectives
ʘ Bilabial	ɓ Bilabial	ʼ Examples:
ǀ Dental	ɗ Dental/alveolar	pʼ Bilabial
ǃ (Post)alveolar	ʄ Palatal	tʼ Dental/alveolar
ǂ Palatoalveolar	ɠ Velar	kʼ Velar
ǁ Alveolar lateral	ʛ Uvular	sʼ Alveolar fricative

OTHER SYMBOLS

ʍ Voiceless labial-velar fricative

w Voiced labial-velar approximant

ɥ Voiced labial-palatal approximant

ʜ Voiceless epiglottal fricative

ʢ Voiced epiglottal fricative

ʡ Epiglottal plosive

ɕ ʑ Alveolo-palatal fricatives

ɺ Voiced alveolar lateral flap

ɧ Simultaneous ʃ and x

Affricates and double articulations can be represented by two symbols joined by a tie bar if necessary.

k͡p t͡s

VOWELS

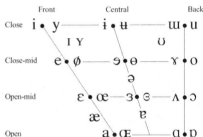

Where symbols appear in pairs, the one to the right represents a rounded vowel.

SUPRASEGMENTALS

ˈ	Primary stress	ˌfoʊnəˈtɪʃən
ˌ	Secondary stress	
ː	Long	eː
ˑ	Half-long	eˑ
˘	Extra-short	ĕ
ǀ	Minor (foot) group	
ǁ	Major (intonation) group	
.	Syllable break	ɹi.ækt
‿	Linking (absence of a break)	

TONES AND WORD ACCENTS

LEVEL		CONTOUR	
e̋ or ˥	Extra high	ě or ˩˥	Rising
é ˦	High	ê ˥˩	Falling
ē ˧	Mid	e̍ ˩˦	High rising
è ˨	Low	e̎ ˥˧	Low rising
ȅ ˩	Extra low	e̋̏ ˧˥˧	Rising-falling
↓	Downstep	↗	Global rise
↑	Upstep	↘	Global fall

DIACRITICS

Diacritics may be placed above a symbol with a descender, e.g. ŋ̊

̥ Voiceless	n̥ d̥	̤ Breathy voiced	b̤ a̤	̪ Dental	t̪ d̪
̬ Voiced	s̬ t̬	̰ Creaky voiced	b̰ a̰	̺ Apical	t̺ d̺
ʰ Aspirated	tʰ dʰ	̼ Linguolabial	t̼ d̼	̻ Laminal	t̻ d̻
̹ More rounded	ɔ̹	ʷ Labialized	tʷ dʷ	̃ Nasalized	ẽ
̜ Less rounded	ɔ̜	ʲ Palatalized	tʲ dʲ	ⁿ Nasal release	dⁿ
̟ Advanced	u̟	ˠ Velarized	tˠ dˠ	ˡ Lateral release	dˡ
̠ Retracted	e̠	ˤ Pharyngealized	tˤ dˤ	̚ No audible release	d̚
̈ Centralized	ë	̴ Velarized or pharyngealized	ɫ		
̽ Mid-centralized	e̽	̝ Raised	e̝	(ɹ̝ = voiced alveolar fricative)	
̩ Syllabic	n̩	̞ Lowered	e̞	(β̞ = voiced bilabial approximant)	
̯ Non-syllabic	e̯	̘ Advanced Tongue Root	e̘		
˞ Rhoticity	ɚ a˞	̙ Retracted Tongue Root	e̙		

© 2005 IPA www.arts.gla.ac.uk/IPA/fullchart.html

Bibliography of Reference and Other Works

CIL = *Corpus inscriptionum latinarum* (1862–), various editors. Leipzig and Berlin.

OLD = Glare, P. G. W. (ed.) (1968–82) *Oxford Latin Dictionary*. Oxford: Oxford University Press.

SEG = *Supplementum Epigraphicum Graecum* (1923–). Leiden.

Inscriptiones Graecae (1873–), various editors. Berlin: G. Reimer (later editions, De Gruyter).

Sylloge Inscriptionum Graecarum[3] (1915–24), edited by W. Dittenberger and F. Hiller von Gaertringen. Leipzig: S. Hirzel.

Thesaurus linguae Latinae (1900–), various editors. Leipzig: Teubner (from 2000 Saur-Verlag).

Adams, J. N. (2003) *Bilingualism and the Latin Language*. Cambridge: Cambridge University Press.

Adams, J. N. (forthcoming) *Regional Diversity in Latin*. Cambridge: Cambridge University Press.

Adams, J. N. and R. G. Mayer (eds.) (1999) *Aspects of the Language of Latin Poetry* (Proceedings of the British Academy 93). Oxford: Oxford University Press.

Allen, W. S. (1988) *Vox Latina: The Pronunciation of Classical Latin* (2nd edn.). Cambridge: Cambridge University Press.

Baldi, P. (2002) *The Foundations of Latin*. Berlin/New York: Mouton de Gruyter.

Devine, A. M. and L. D. Stephens (2006) *Latin Word Order: Structured Meaning and Information*. Oxford: Oxford University Press.

Ernout, M. and A. Meillet. (1959) *Dictionnaire étymologique de la langue latine: Histoire des mots*, revised by J. André (4th edn.). Paris: Klincksieck.

Herman, J. (2000) *Vulgar Latin*, translated by R. Wright. University Park, PA: Pennsylvania State University Press.

Hofmann, J. B. and M. Leumann (1965–79) *Lateinische Grammatik* (Handbuch der Altertumswissenschaft, II 2.1, 2.2, 2.3). Munich: Beck. (Vol. 1 *Lateinische Laut- und Formenlehre*, by M. Leumann, 1977. Vol. 2 *Lateinische Syntax und Stilistik*, by J. B. Hofmann, revised by A. Szantyr, 1965 (3rd edn.). Vol. 3 *Stellenregister und Verzeichnis der nichtlateinischen Wörter*, by F. S. Radt and A. G. Westerbrink, 1979.)

Kühner, R. and C. Stegmann (1912–76) *Ausführliche Grammatik der lateinischen Sprache*. Hannover: Hahn. (*Teil I. Elementar-, Formen- und Wortlehre*, by R. Kühner (2nd edn.), revised by Friedrich Holzweissig, 1912. *Teil II. Satzlehre*, by R. Kühner and C. Stegmann, 2 vols (5th edn.), revised by A. Thierfelder, 1976.)

Löfstedt, E. (1956) *Syntactica: Studien und Beiträge zur historischen Syntax des Lateins* (2 vols). Lund: Gleerup.

Meiser, G. (1998) *Historische Laut- und Formenlehre der lateinischen Sprache*. Darmstadt: Wissenschaftliche Buchgesellschaft.

Palmer, L. R. (1954) *The Latin Language*. London: Faber.

Reinhardt, T., M. Lapidge and J. N. Adams (eds.) (2005) *Aspects of the Language of Latin Prose* (Proceedings of the British Academy 129). Oxford: Oxford University Press.

Väänänen, V. (1981) *Introduction au latin vulgaire* (3rd edn.). Paris: Klincksieck.

Walde, A. (1938) *Lateinisches etymologisches Wörterbuch* (2 vols), revised by J. B. Hofmann (3rd edn.). Heidelberg: Winter.

Index

Printed in Great Britain
by Amazon

81651914R00190